JUST PAST?

JUST PAST?

The making of Israeli archaeology

RAZ KLETTER

LONDON   OAKVILLE

Published by
Equinox Publishing Ltd.
UK: Unit 6, The Village, 101 Amies St., London SW11 2JW
USA: DBBC, 28 Main Street, Oakville, CT 06779

www.equinoxpub.com

First published 2006

British Library Cataloguing-in-Publication Data
A catalogue record for this book is available from the British Library.

ISBN   1-84553-085-3   (hardback)

Library of Congress Cataloging-in-Publication Data
Kletter, Raz.
  Just past? : the making of Israeli archaeology / Raz Kletter.
    p. cm.
  Includes bibliographical references and index.
  ISBN 1-84553-085-3 (hb)
    1. Excavations (Archaeology)--Israel--Political aspects. 2. Israel--Antiquities--Political
aspects. 3. Israel. Rashut ha-'atiḳot--Officials and employees. 4. Israel--Politics and
government--20th century. 5. Archaeologists--Israel. I. Title.
  DS111.K57 2006
933'072'05694--dc22   2005008378

Typeset by Kate Williams, Swansea.
Printed and bound in Great Britain by Antony Rowe Ltd., Chippenham.

Study as if you were to live forever; live as if you were to die tomorrow.

Edmund of Abingdon, first known MA holder of
Oxford University, d. 1240 (quoted in Morris 1978: 8)

CONTENTS

LIST OF ILLUSTRATIONS

All photographs courtesy the Israel Antiquities Authority (IAA), except Figure 1 by the author and Figures 10, 13, 19, 22, 23 and 28, from Ginzach Leumi (GL) documents by the author.

1. Map of tours of archaeological officers, June–August 1948.
2. Second tour of officers. (a) Megiddo, 29 July 1948. Yeivin (left), B. Mazar (seated centre) and probably the military commander of Megiddo (right). (Photograph probably by Ben-Dor, IAA 2401) (b) Megiddo, 29 July 1948. A camouflaged evacuation post for wounded soldiers still occupies the constructed (misnamed "Aegean") tomb in Schumacher's trench. (Photograph probably by Ben-Dor, IAA 2402) (c) Nazareth [?]. Armoured vehicle accompanying the archaeologists. (Photograph by Ben-Dor, IAA 2408)
3. The "cave strongpoint", Beit Jubrin 1949. Ashlar wall exposed by military trenches. (Photograph by Ory, IAA 60)
4. Selbit (Sha'alabim) 1949. Abandoned Arab village, showing courtyard with antiquities. (IAA 320)
5. Jaffa, old city, c. 1950. The "Arab soap factory – [Hana] Damyani and Sons" building. Note the zone and house number registration, signifying that it was destined for preservation. The building is Mamluk or early Ottoman and it survived. The family was known in Jaffa, and had nineteenth-century ancestors who served several European countries. See Kark (1990: 256) for a very similar photograph from 1977.
6. Abandoned village of Khartiyeh, November 1948. Mud houses with tools. (Photograph by Ory, IAA 143)
7. Jaffa, old city, November 1948. Excavations by Guy. (IAA 15220)
8. Kh. Jalameh 1949. Some inhabitants are seen; the village was occupied.

Today it is unoccupied, near Kibbutz Lehavot Haviva. (Photograph by Ory, IAA 956).

9. Sindiyanna on a tour. New settlers draw water from the ancient Caesarea "upper aqueduct". (IAA 1511)

10. The interdepartmental committee at Suq el-Khan, Galilee, 3 May 1950. Yeivin is standing at the centre (wearing a tie). (GL44864/18)

11. The house of mosaics at Beit Jubrin, 1949. (IAA 56)

12. Copying mosaics at Beit Jubrin, 1954. Seated at the front is Leah Offer, who later funded the textile laboratory of the Israel Museum. The teacher (standing) is perhaps Teodoro Orselli. (IAA 10421)

13. The frozen funds. Letter from Harold Williams to the Israel-America Archaeological Foundation, 1 November 1957. (GL11-5451)

14. Ashkelon "museum", 1949. The sign says "Out of Bounds by Order". (Photograph by Ory, IAA 496)

15. Ashkelon, 1949. "The family of the antiquities guard" with Ory's daughter (behind). Note the basket of oranges on the left. The first IDAM guards started work in 1951. This, then, is the family of the former guard, Mohamad Ismail Radi (according to an undated Mandatory period list), who lived at the site at least until 1949. (Photograph by Ory, IAA 941)

16. Rishpon, 1951. Hired excavation workers, before the relief work system. (IAA 1302)

17. New immigrant from the Atlas Mountains working at Ozem in 1956 as a relief worker. (Photograph by Gophna, IAA 14866)

18. The permanent exhibition of the IDAM, Jerusalem 1951. Between 1948 and 1956 the museum had 36,000 visitors. (IAA 4502)

19. Part of a letter about the PAM from Illife to Ben-Dor, 2 September 1948, written on "Government of Palestine, Department of Antiquities" stationery (heading erased). (GL44874/16)

20. PAM, inner court with damage from the 1967 War. (Photograph by Burger, IAA 49239)

21. The Olivet–Zilberstein house, home of the IDAM 1949–65. (IAA 1264a)

22. English rendering of the original Hebrew temporary plan for the governmental museum and IDAM offices, 1952. (GL44873/10)

23. English rendering of the original Hebrew plan for a complex of museums by Hiram. This version is probably from 1955. The portrait gallery and some antiquities components are not shown here. (GL44873/10)

24. Judean Desert (Nahal Hever) survey, 1955. (Photograph by Aharoni, IAA 12,344)

25. Excavations at "Gat": installation for removal of debris, 1956. (Photograph by Porat, IAA 16252)

26. Visit to Caesarea excavations, 1955. Yeivin (left), President Ben-Zvi (second from left), Shalom Levi (right). (Photograph by Schulman, IAA 12,779)

TABLES

INTRODUCTION

Digressions, incontestably, are the sunshine; – they are the life, the soul of reading! – take them out of this book, for instance – you might as well take the book along with them; – one cold eternal winter would reign in every page of it; restore them to the writer; – he steps forth like a bridegroom ... but the author ... in this matter, is truly pitiable: For, if he begins a digression, – from that moment, I observe, his whole work stands stock still; – and if he goes on with his main work, – then there is an end to his digression.

Sterne (2004 [1760]: 63–4)

Frozen US Intelligence money; Tedi Kollek; a Palestinian absentee in Cyrenaica; David Ben-Gurion; growing watermelons on the Tell of Ashdod; General Moshe Dayan; a camouflaged evacuation post in the middle of the Megiddo excavations; Shemuel Yeivin; Masada; sacred *genizot* in the Galilee; the wonderful rock found by Reverend P. of Brighton; Binyamin Mazar; the Institute for Dietary Education of the Ministry of Supplies and Rationing; Yigael Yadin; a deceased representative on the Supreme Council of Archives; the Rockefeller Museum; cigars and Chivas Regal; resting one's head on Marlene Dietrich's legs ... All these things are part of *Just Past?*, for this book tells the story of the creation of Israeli archaeology in the 1950s and early 1960s. It is unlike any other book on the archaeology of the "Holy Land", since it isn't just a chronological parade of important excavations and interesting finds, but a history of intrigues, funding, failures and, above all, dreams. It is an archaeological graveyard, full of lost finds and lost causes beside the well-known excavated plots.

Just Past? is a book about the past, but there is hardly a page without some new fact or story, in the sense that it has never been published before. I have been an archaeologist for over twenty years now, but almost all of these stories were new even to me. These are the genesis stories, the stories of the birth of Israeli archaeology, from the first hour, day, year. Everything was new; and abandoned, and destroyed. It was a peculiar Garden of Eden, in which the two eternal gods of archaeology – creation and destruction – reigned supreme.

The book is based upon a unique treasure trove of thousands of official documents, never published before, from the State of Israel Archive, Ginzach Leumi (GL). Most of the documents come from the Israeli Department of Antiquities and Museums (IDAM), but some are also from the Ministry of Education and Culture and the Prime Minister's Office. I have also used many newspaper clippings, even from obscure periodicals in Hebrew that no longer exist. The Hebrew language has changed considerably since the 1950s and some of the charming "archaic" nuances are lost in translation. The original filing codes of the documents are meaningless to readers, so I refer to the current archive file number, usually followed by the number and/or date of the individual document.

The State of Israel Archive is by far the largest and most important source for the history of Israeli archaeology and also gives a wide scope, since the documents are not limited to one institution only. Most documents originate from the IDAM, so the views and facts relating to this body are well represented. In the 1950s there were only two other significant archaeological bodies in Israel. Unfortunately, documents from the Israel Exploration Society (IES) and from the Department of Archaeology of the Hebrew University were partially lost. *Just Past?* is the first publication to use primary archival materials about early Israeli archaeology.

The documents reveal a surprising picture. Much was written about archaeology in Palestine during the Ottoman and British Mandate periods (Mazar 1936; Sukenik 1952; Silberman 1982; Shavit 1989; Braun 1992; Reich 1992a; Ben-Arieh 1999a,b, 2000, 2001; Abu el-Haj 2002; on excavators see Drawer 1985, 2004; Blakely 1993; Momigliano 1995; on the Hebrew University see Katz & Heyd 1997). Very little has been published about Israeli archaeology after 1948 and archival documents have not been used. Biographies of Israeli archaeologists are rare and not very critical (Silberman 1993; Aharoni 1998); obituaries are short and, naturally, positive (Kochavi 1981; Avigad 1989; Ben-Tor 1989; Dever 1989). The regular products of archaeological writing – excavation and survey reports and the like – are not very helpful; nor are the textbooks (Albright 1949; Aharoni 1978, 1986; Stern 1993; the best are Mazar 1990 and Stern 2001). Criticisms are also rare, and are almost always limited to very narrow arenas: the political place within the Israeli–Palestinian conflict or the accusation about the "Biblical archaeology" bias (Shay 1989; Kempinski 1994; Abu el-Haj 2001). We read much about the "myth of Masada", for example (Ben-Yehuda 1995, 2002), but nothing about why, by whom and when the decision was made to start excavations at Masada, who provided the funding and how Yadin became the excavator. Anything not overtly political was neglected; while politics were often of more relevance to the authors than to their subjects. Also, archaeologists neglected their own history, leaving the field to scholars from other disciplines specializing in recent periods (e.g. Feige 1998; Shavit 1997). A community focused on the study of some distant human past must also acknowledge its own roots: its genesis. Without knowing the origins and history of Israeli archaeology, there can be no open-minded evaluation of it.

The title of the book, *Just Past?*, implies the obvious: our business here is the past, more specifically the recent past, from 1948 to 1967. Some of us lived through it, but now it is remote. Time makes for a formidable stratigraphy:

where is the spade to penetrate its layers, year by year? Already, it forms a puzzle from light and darkness, fame and oblivion. Scandals and scoundrels populate our pages, side by side with respectable professors. The scale is small, at times minute, but human drama is not measured by size alone.

The title is also supposed to indicate that there never is "just" a past. We create our own versions of the past. Written and rewritten, used and abused, the past is not a world in itself. Everything related to archaeology in Israel/Palestine is immediately used as cannon fodder in the context of the Israeli–Palestinian conflict. *Just Past?* focuses on Israel and on Israelis. It does not and cannot represent the other groups, but it does not ignore them. It has been written not to please any particular group, nor to judge the past, but to understand it better. It tries to cover all aspects of the past, even if some do not please us in the present. Integrity is the highest requirement for a study of the past; followed by scepticism. Because archaeology is woven into the fabric of so many aspects of society, anyone interested in Israel/Palestine, in the past or present, can find something in this book, even if he or she does not agree with my conclusions.

Just Past? is a private study that reflects my personal views and nothing else. I thank the Israel Antiquities Authority (IAA), my employer, for permission to use photographs from its archives. Otherwise, I used no IAA data that are not available to the general public. If I (seldom) refer to recent events about archaeology in Israel, it is to well-known events, and only to explain the relation to the older documents. To the best of my knowledge, all the GL files that I quote are available to the public. The documents are all well over 30 years old and they do not contain any military secrets. I was not permitted to see classified files, and none have been used. The GL documents that originated from the army or from the Ministry of Defence are few, and these were all cleared through a security check. The book was approved by the Censor at Tel Aviv (No. 120/2005). Those who seek nuclear secrets will not benefit from reading this book and, hopefully, I need not be kidnapped by a mysterious blonde. I saw no reason to change anything in the content of the documents. I have made slight grammatical or stylistic changes to make meanings clearer for modern readers, and translations have been edited. The translation of names of people and places in Hebrew is notoriously problematic. Whenever possible, I follow the spelling used in the period in question; otherwise I prefer simple or common forms (especially for place names). In some cases that involve private individuals I have replaced names with initials to guarantee privacy (following the Israeli law of Zin'at ha-Prat). Most of these cases are not offensive in any way.

Writing *Just Past?* also meant considering my own life over the past twenty years: a mixture of Meissen porcelain and Biblical parchment; breathing the damp Tel-Aviv air in August with cool English eccentricism; sandals dusted with Negev *leoss* mixed with fields of rye, and forests and elks. *Just Past?* is dedicated to my wife, Kristel.

ACKNOWLEDGEMENTS

This book would not have been possible without the help of many friends and colleagues to whom I am deeply indebted. They include: Uzi Ad, Anan Azab, Sarah Ben-Arieh, Michal Ben-Gal, Baruch Brandl, Yehuda Dagan, Alon de-Groot, Imanuel Eisenberg, Nurit Feig, Livnat Iechya, Hava Katz, Martin Peilschtöcker, Yosef Porath, Arieh Rochman, Yossi Stepansky and Edwin van den-Brink (IAA); Ram Gophna and Zeev Meshel (Tel Aviv University); Amos Kloner (Bar Ilan University); Irit Ziffer and Uza Zvulun (Eretz Israel Museum, Tel Aviv); Roni Reich (Haifa University); Emanuel Anati (Italy); John Bowman (Melbourne); Baruch (Benedict) Isserlin (Leeds); Keren Levi (Hukuk); Elisheva Belhorn (former manager of the Tiberias Museum); Zvika Shaham (Jaffa Museum); and Morag Kersel (Cambridge). I wish to thank the IAA for letting me reproduce photos from its archives, especially Yael Barschak and Nogah Ze'evi, as well as all the staff of the State of Israel Archive, Jerusalem, for their patience and efficiency. I am deeply grateful to Avner Pinchuk of the Association for Civil Rights in Israel, for his advice concerning this book and his encouragement to proceed with its publication.

A very small section of Chapter 7 was published formerly in the *Journal of Hebrew Scriptures* in 2003. I wish to thank the journal and its editor, Ehud Ben-Zvi, for permission to include it here. Finally, I owe a great debt to all the Equinox staff, and especially Kate Williams, for their patience and dedication in getting this book published.

ABBREVIATIONS

AICF	America–Israel Cultural Foundation
ASOR	American School of Oriental Research
BIES	*Bulletin of the Israel Exploration Society*
CAAR	Scientific Committee for the Advancement of Archaeological Research
CNRS	Centre nationale de la recherche scientifique
GL	Ginzach Leumi [State of Israel Archive]
GTC	Government Tourist Corporation
IAA	Israel Antiquities Authority (from 1990)
ICOM	International Council of Museums
IDAM	Israeli Department of Antiquities and Museums (1948–89)
IDF	Israel Defence Forces [Zahal]
IEJ	*Israel Exploration Journal*
IES	Israel Exploration Society
JNF	Jewish National Fund
LA	Law of Antiquities [Khoq ha-Atiqot]
LIAA	Law, Israel Antiquities Authority [Khoq Reshut ha-Atiqot]
OSS	Office of Strategic Services
PAM	Palestine Archaeological Museum ("Rockefeller Museum")
PJCA	Palestinian Jewish Colonization Association
QDAP	*Quarterly of the Department of Antiquities of Palestine*
UNCCP	UN Conciliation Commission for Palestine
USIS	US Information Service

1   ARCHAEOLOGY AND THE 1948 WAR

In the middle of the excavation area, a camouflaged evacuation post for the
wounded   (GL44875/9)

It is easy to be dead.   Charles Sorely (*c.*1917)

GROUND ZERO

On 16 December 1947, senior Hebrew archaeologists met to discuss the place
of archaeology in the future Hebrew state. They included professors at the
Hebrew University Leo Ari Mayer and Eliezer Lipa Sukenik; the Committee of the Israel Exploration Society (IES) Itzhak Ben-Zvi (later President of
Israel), Moshe Schwabe, Itzhak Ernst Nebenzahl (State Comptroller of Israel,
1961–81), Binyamin Mazar, Haim Zeev Hirschberg, Avraham Bergman and
Shemuel Yeivin (Yeivin was also chief translator of the Mandatory government: GL44869/1, letters dated 4.7.48, 22.9.48); and members of the Mandatory Department of Antiquities Immanuel Ben-Dor, Michael Avi-Yonah, Pinhas
Penuel Kahane and Ruth Kallner (later Amiran). Two other dignitaries, Moshe
Stekelis and Bruno Kirschner, could not attend the meeting. In this hectic
period (Pilowsky 1988), all the participants still believed that the Rockefeller
Museum must remain united, and most of them thought that the Hebrew state
should erect its own department of antiquities that would protect ancient places
(which were an "immeasurable national asset"), carry out and license excavations, supervise museums, make a general survey, develop large-scale research
and "enter the idea of saving ancient assets and their study into the hearts of the
people" (GL44868/7, report by Mayer 8.1.48). They recommended a department
with two sections: a central office headed by a director and deputy director and
a network of supervisors.
    Sukenik and Yeivin (later joined by Hirschberg and Stekelis) held the minority
view that the department of antiquities should remain united for the Hebrew
and Arab states (like the customs office or the postal service, following the then
current UN partition plan). Only supervision would be separated; the director

1

and deputy director would be one Jewish and the other Arab, perhaps changing positions occasionally (GL44868/7, 8.1.48). Yeivin explained this view:

> A separate department without a museum, library and archive is worthless. A united museum without a department of antiquities has no future and no right of existence. Mainly, we have to maintain some position regarding the antiquities of the Arab part, which includes most of our remains; otherwise everything there will be lost and ruined.
> (GL44868/7, minutes signed Kallner (Amiran): p. 1)

Sukenik was even more extreme. He wanted a united department because he believed that the heavy monetary burden of a department of antiquities should not fall on the shoulders of the young state. It would also help to save antiquities in the Arab part and sustain cooperation with Arabs, which he felt was one of the beautiful creations of the British administration. It was noted that Sukenik:

> Does not believe that the Jewish state will keep its antiquities, and we must keep the antiquities against the pressure of the developing state. We must place scientific sovereignty above political sovereignty. We are interested in the archaeology of the entire land, and the only way is by a united department.
> (GL44868/7, minutes signed Kallner (Amiran))

Suggestions for a budget were prepared next. The majority proposal was for a budget of 34,170 Palestine pounds (Lira) for the museum, library and archives, which were to remain united for both states. Each state would contribute 10,000 Lira, Jerusalem (which was to become an international area) 4,170 Lira and the Rockefeller fund a further 10,000 Lira. The separate Hebrew department of antiquities would include a manager, deputy manager, chief supervisor, scientific secretary, two supervisors, an architect, a surveyor, three clerks, a driver and a butler, at the cost of 23,450 Lira per year. In addition, a one-off special allowance of 16,000 Lira would be needed for the establishment of the department. According to the minority view, the united department for antiquities would need a budget of 72,200 Lira. Each state would contribute 30,000 Lira, Jerusalem 2,200 Lira and the Rockefeller fund 10,000 Lira. The minutes were received by the Situation Committee (Va'adat ha-mazav) of the Jewish Agency, and read by David Ben-Gurion (GL44868/7, 25.1.48).

On 27 April 1948 the same archaeologists reported to the Jewish Agency that the Hebrew officials had not been able to reach the Rockefeller Museum since the second half of December 1947. They continued work in the Schocken Library, which was named after Zalman Schocken (1877–1959), the owner of *Ha'aretz* newspaper from 1936 (his son, Gustav-Gershom Schocken, famously edited *Ha'aretz* from 1939 until 1990). Funding would be stopped in May, but the British intended to maintain the museum under one official and 15–20 guards. Until the situation was clarified, a minimal budget of 1,500 Lira was requested for the Hebrew archaeologists in Jerusalem, on the pretext that they were a "section of the museum" that would help to prevent the museum falling into Arab hands. Robert Hamilton (Director of the Department of Antiquities of Palestine, 1937–48) and John Iliffe (Keeper of the Palestine Archaeological Museum, 1931–48) promised a further 1,500 Lira (GL44868/7 no. 2, 27.4.48; GL44880/17, 31.8.48).

During the 1948 War, Jerusalem was besieged and the new state was fighting for survival, suffering a devastating death toll of 6,000, or 1 percent of its population of around 600,000 people (Sivan 1991: 17–26). Conditions until the later part of the war were chaotic and desperate, and issues surrounding antiquities were not a high priority. Archaeological activity was halted.

The Hebrew archaeologists continued a sort of research, using a card index (50,000 items) of objects, some 5,000 photographs, 200 books and three typewriters, taken (mostly) by consent from the Rockefeller Museum in early May with the help of British military vehicles (GL44868/7, handwritten questionnaire; GL44883/12, 22.6.48: p. 12; GL44864/14 no. 4). The archaeologists continued to work on material from excavations and prepared a catalogue of the available archaeological libraries in West Jerusalem. They also supervised and protected antiquities in areas occupied by Hebrew forces (Yeivin 1955b: 3). The nature of their work finds expression in a humorous description of Jerusalem under siege, written by a journalist during the first ceasefire:

> One more neighbour I have, a learned Jew, a Doctor of Philosophy, who while carrying the water home has the habit to spill half on the ground. Against this he has one merit, that he is the symbol of hope and faith in goodness. He draws all his hope on the power of the soul. Therefore (and since he has no other material at hand) he constructed a shelter of books in one of his rooms … The foundation is made from a platform of the volumes of the *Encyclopaedia Britannica*. That is a solid basis, which even British mortars [of the Arab legion] cannot penetrate … On them, a layer of ancient Greek and Roman authors are laid; and the uppermost cornice, which is a sort of a capital for the cultural layers, is composed of *Vilna Shas*. Protected in the confines of this fortress, no evil will find him, and he sits under the shade of a battery of wisdom and reads … a detective romance, for in days of bombardment and shelling (so he says) it is difficult for a man to concentrate on any idea or thought …
>
> (Ben-Horin in Naor 1988: 207)

On 27 June 1948 a letter was sent to the cultural unit of the army, signed "Kuniuk Handler", most probably from Moshe Kaniuk (a member of the IES committee in 1949/50 and father of the writer Yoram Kaniuk), and Shemuel

Handler, who belonged to the Tel Aviv branch of the IES and was a member of its council (*BIES* **15** (1949/50): 60). Moshe Kaniuk was Director of the Tel Aviv Museum of Art between 1932 and 1962, and a member of the first Archaeological Council of Israel. The spelling "Kuniuk" reappears in another letter from Yeivin (GL44865/7, 17.8.52). The letter was sent when the establishment of an antiquities unit had already been discussed, but the two did not know that because Jerusalem was cut off. Kaniuk and Handler opened by mentioning the national and scientific value of the country's antiquities. Formerly, the Mandatory Department of Antiquities had maintained – or tried to maintain – them. The state of Israel was created without a governmental institution able to supervise antiquities. In the meantime, battles in Arab areas caused neglect to old houses, collections, museums and shops. As a result they were:

> destroyed and sabotaged, even outside acts of battle. All kinds of "amateurs" or "men of action" laid their hands on the antiquities; the former for themselves and the latter to sell to collectors or to owners of antiquities shops. Among other examples we can mention that the local museum of Caesarea has been broken open and, with no guard, is being emptied fast. Tell Megiddo is in a similar situation … In Tel Aviv a rumour spread that the men of Ezel [Irgun Zeva'i Leumi, one of the underground pre-state organizations] robbed the famous shop of Afghani in Jaffa and are selling their loot.
>
> (GL1342/21)

Kaniuk and Handler pointed out that ancient remains were also found during fortification works, some of considerable importance, but were broken and thrown away. In their view, a few hours of work could expose and save such discoveries. Often, even a superficial examination of remains brought to the surface would suffice. A caring "householder" should be placed urgently to salvage such remains. Since all men of science who could and should head this act were in Jerusalem, the two offered their services on a voluntary basis, and proposed to take responsibility in the meantime. They would devote themselves to collecting neglected antiquities, registering and keeping them in a safe place such as the Tel Aviv Museum, until told to do otherwise by an authorized governmental body. They would also check and, if needed, expose remains discovered during acts of war:

> We apply to you because the matter concerns not [just] remains in areas of Hebrew settlement under jurisdiction of civilian-municipal authorities, but those found in conquered areas and under military supervision. Clearly an initiative is required by a military body that knows the importance of the matter and holds dear the value of past remains, in order to draw the attention of the supreme command and ensure that the steps to fix the situation in the future are taken …
>
> (GL1342/21)

The first step in handling the archaeology of Israel was the appointment of three archaeological army officers, Yeivin, Ben-Dor and Binyamin Mazar, during the first lull in the fighting in early June 1948. Ben-Dor and Mazar were also employed by the political department of the Jewish Agency (GL44868/7, 2.6.48). Yeivin became the first Director of the Antiquities Unit [Mahleket ha-'Atiqot], which in August 1955 became the Israel Department of Antiquities and Museums [Agaf ha 'Atiqot ve ha-Muzeonim], abbreviated to IDAM. Since there is no exact English translation for the Hebrew terms, and for the sake of simplicity, I shall refer to both the Antiquities Unit and its successor as the IDAM. Ben-Dor, who excavated at Nahariya and Achziv, became Yeivin's Deputy Director. Both worked formerly in the Mandatory Department of Antiquities and Mazar was teaching at the Hebrew University. The three were placed under army command at the Jerusalem front, as they lived in Jerusalem; no such appointments were made at other fronts.

Few documents remain from this period and those that do are mostly handwritten on scraps of paper or Mandatory period forms. Mazar, Yeivin and Ben-Dor, writing as civilians on behalf of a "committee of scientific institutions for matters of antiquities", applied to the secretary of the government in Tel Aviv on 25 June 1948, urging the government to establish a department of antiquities:

> During the continuation of acts of war and construction made now, quite many dear remains of our past in the land are found by chance and are destroyed and ruined not by malice, but from lack of knowledge and lack of a department and administration. Moreover, the state includes many ancient monuments, left without any supervision after the former government department of antiquities was dismantled ... Suffice it to mention Accho with all its historical buildings that nobody takes care of; Caesarea, which is being destroyed methodically and the Tells of Megiddo and Beth Shean that face a danger of ruin and complete destruction ... A third type of problem is private and public collections in occupied areas that are robbed (in Jerusalem, in Jaffa, in Caesarea).
>
> We believe that the antiquities unit, which will handle these matters and also arrange all works of excavation and antiquities, must have close relations with the Ministry of Labour and Construction ... We suggest adding the unit [*makhlaka*] of antiquities to this ministry ...
>
> (GL44868/7, 25.6.48)

In his letter of resignation as Director of the IDAM of 1959, sent to the head of the civil service (GL44880/13 no. 282), Yeivin said that he started work on 13 July 1948, and for the first two weeks prepared for the establishment of the IDAM. A handwritten document, probably by Yeivin, suggested that the department would need a team of 20 workers in wartime, and 52 in peacetime (GL44868/7).

Mazar, Yeivin and Ben-Dor asked for a budget of 23,180 Lira from the government, including 9,620 Lira for salaries for 14 workers, with Yeivin as Director and Ben-Dor as Deputy Director. Since the status of Jerusalem was not yet clear, they suggested first establishing a supervision unit in Tel Aviv (GL44868/7, 25.6.48). The IDAM was established along on these lines, but it took another full month.

In the meantime, on 29–30 June 1948, Yeivin, Ben-Dor and Mazar toured in the north as archaeological officers (GL44875/9 no. 1; Fig. 1). They sent a report of this tour and a letter to the government of Israel at Tel Aviv (GL44875/9 no. 2, 8.7.48). Both documents are signed only by Yeivin, who apparently typed them at home. The letter stated the urgent need to establish a department of antiquities, especially since many members of the former Mandatory Department of Antiquities continued work in Jerusalem after 15 May, "and these officials receive their salary from the treasury of the state". The three added that since the tour was made by the order of General Headquarters, they had sent a copy of the report to Yigael Yadin (formerly Sukenik), then Chief of Operations, as well as to the Minister of Construction and Public Works, to which the department of antiquities should be affiliated (GL44875/9):

> Report of the visit of Members Immanuel Ben-Dor, Shemuel Yeivin and Binyamin Maisler [i.e. Mazar] to various fronts of the country to identify the situation regarding the protection of ancient remains
>
> A. The visit of Immanuel Ben-Dor to central and northern Sharon (29.6.48–30.6.48)
>
> On 28 June I visited the ruins of Caesarea and [the nearby] Kibbutz Sedot-Yam. There were two collections at Caesarea: a major museum under the supervision of the [Mandatory] Department of Antiquities, and a small museum in the office of the Greek Patriarch.
>
> From the governmental museum all the objects have disappeared (more than a hundred fragments of inscriptions, parts of pillars and decorated stones; apart from a few fragments thrown on to the street outside the building). According to information from the commander there, the army took the objects out of the building after its requisition. After the objects were left in the street, without owners and supervision, a large number of them were collected at Hana Senesh House in Kibbutz Sedot-Yam. As far as we know some of these items reached the municipal museum of Haifa and some reached private antiquities dealers in Tel Aviv. If the major part was collected at Hana Senesh House, then this part was saved from extinction; but it must be stressed that it was done without the permission of any authority, and without any notification.
>
> The collection at the Greek Patriarch's office was destroyed. Some of the inscriptions were lying on the floors of the rooms among broken furniture,

but without a full list it is impossible to state how many remains were robbed. Between the fragments I have found one intact Greek inscription. Since the building is now open and without a guard, I placed that fragment in the house of (medical) Dr [Anith] Hamburger at Binyamina for safekeeping.

I also visited Sedot-Yam, but since the *mukhtar* [an official Mandatory title for head of village] of the place was missing, I could not really verify if some of the remains that were in Caesarea were transferred to Hana Senesh House. On the other hand I found that in recent times some buildings and a few trenches had been built in the settlement, in the antiquities area. Naturally, these works were done without any authorized supervision and perhaps important archaeological data were lost forever. During my visit I saw several finds discovered at the time of these works ... [details, including 40–50 gold coins and 30 Greek silver coins].

On 29 June I visited the Crusader fortress of Athlit. The place is completely deserted; it has no posts and no guard. The small museum there and the office of the Mandatory Department of Antiquities near it were completely destroyed. Files were torn and scattered, furniture and pottery vessels smashed with utter vandalism. This institution should be renewed, and made a regional museum and storage station for archaeologists who make exploration tours of the Sharon and the Carmel Mountains.

From talks with the people of Hadera and Binyamina, I found that many ancient remains are gradually being destroyed during the making of various works of fortification caused by the present times, for lack of supervision and an institution available for giving advice and guidance.

B. The visit of Shemuel Yeivin to the valley of Accho (29.6.48)

With the kind help of the officers of the headquarters of Zidoni [brigade], I could visit the valley of Accho on 29 June, that is, Accho city, which I toured for more than two hours, and the environs of Nahariya and Achziv.

In this conquered district I found that, generally, the situation is more or less satisfactory, since no robbery was performed in Accho, and the authorities managed to save the Accho houses and by this the Accho monuments. The mosque of Jissar Pasha is closed and locked, and an Arab official holds the keys. According to him, nothing was taken from the mosque and during my visit to the building all seemed in order. Only one of the Crusader buildings formerly used as wood stores by a rich Arab merchant still holds wood; immediate steps must be taken to clean and preserve this building. The guard of the former Department of Antiquities, Mahmud el-Lakham, remained in Accho, and needs to be relieved from the enforced labour duties required from time to time of the local population, and restored to protecting the ancient monuments, as he was before the liquidation of Mandatory rule. [El-Lakham was a guard in Accho in 1950/51 (GL1430/14;

GL44880/18 no. 5671). In September 1953 he applied for the position of guard at Athlit, with the help of Zeev Goldman (GL44869/4), but was not successful.]

I was told that the aqueduct of Suleiman Pasha was slightly damaged near the current front line, but could not visit it because of difficulties of transportation. Near the village of es-Sumeriya is a pit from which sand is taken for building, etc. Some Phoenician antiquities were found there – according to notification by Mr Otto Stiel of Nahariya – so the army authorities must be warned to cease use of that pit, or at least collect the antiquities and deliver them to the museum of the local municipality of Nahariya.

Surrounding Nahariya itself the works of fortification and air raid defences almost did not touch ancient remains, except in one place, where a Roman tomb was used as a shelter. Mr Stiel stands on guard in Nahariya and sees that no chance object will be lost by lack of attention or neglect. Near Achziv (ez-Zib) the Arabs probably managed before leaving the place to rob a few tombs in the Phoenician cemetery, but there are no large-scale damages.

I could not go further north and east owing to insufficient time at my disposal. It should be pointed out that here also no general order was given to the security forces about how to treat ancient remains or chance finds discovered during actions, and they were also not warned to pay attention to this.

C. The visit of Binyamin Maisler to the Jezreel valley and lower eastern Galilee (28.6.48–29.6.48)

On the morning of 28 June I visited Bet She'arim (Sheikh Ibreik). Visits to the ruins of the city and to the cave complexes ceased in the months of troubles, so there was no need for a special guard. Yet it is necessary to fix the fences and clean the area of weeds and wild plants. The Zeid building is completely deserted. The plan is to establish a small museum in this building, with objects from Bet She'arim and its vicinity …

In the afternoon I visited Megiddo. The building of the archaeological expedition of the [Oriental Institute of the] University of Chicago was not damaged during the battle for Megiddo. Some of the objects and library that belong to Chicago University were transferred in two trucks from this building to the museum at Haifa by Mr [Alexander] Rash [later head of the Haifa Municipal Museum], who received authority for this act from the American institution and from the authorities at Haifa. A large number of work tools and a few antiquities were left; some have disappeared and some are still kept in three rooms and in the storeroom. The headquarters there tries to protect the objects, but cannot take full responsibility for them. It will be the duty of the antiquities unit that will be established to keep and save them from ruin. I think all the objects should be removed to a place of safety at Haifa, and a detailed report be given to the Oriental Institute of the University of Chicago about all the materials available to it. Also, explicit orders should be given in higher places about the Tell and the expedition building at Megiddo.

On 29 June I visited various places in Tiberias and the vicinity together with the military governor of Tiberias and Mr [Pesah] Bar-Adon. The remains of the Kefar Nahum Synagogue and the nearby monastery were not at all damaged, and Reverend Peter keeps guard there. The military headquarters takes care of the site. In Et-Tabkha the property in the German Catholic buildings was stolen, and the monks were transferred to one of the Italian buildings on the mountain. The Byzantine mosaics were saved from destruction, but need treatment. The Italian Church on the Mountain (Monte delle Beatitudini) is intact and is not used as a military target. The women's monastery was badly hit, but no signs of robbery are evident in it.

In the evening I visited also Beth Yerakh [Kh. Kerak]. The fenced area of excavations was not at all damaged and has no fortifications, but is entirely covered by weeds and this demands immediate treatment.

In Tiberias itself there were many robberies, and they are especially evident in the Scottish house and in the home of Dr Hart, which also contained antiquities. Part of Dr Hart's library is held by the Tiberias police. The "Damascene room" was transferred to the Haifa Museum based on the recommendation of the Supervisor of Enemy Property [Mefake'akh al Rekhush Oyev]. Dr Goldman, who had certificates authorizing him to treat antiquities from the supervisor of enemy property in the district of Haifa and the Haifa Museum, acted here.

D. General notes

It must be stressed that all the military commanders we met showed understanding and willingness to help, but did not know what to do and whom to apply to; and they, as well as those who are interested in antiquities of our land, were happy to meet people authorized to explain to them how to act. No doubt the immediate need is to act to fix the situation. We allow ourselves to offer the following suggestions:

A. Hasten as much as you can the establishment of the antiquities department, which will have a proper organization for immediate action, and would be able to gather all the news and finds and keep them in its collections and archives so that they are not lost forever.

B. Give it complete authority to handle collections and remains, to prevent duplication of authorities so that one does not know what the other is doing, and each one treats problems that necessitate unified treatment and care in different places and manners. That indeed happened in Tiberias and Haifa, where the municipality and the Custodian for Enemy

9

Property [Apotropos al Rekhush Oyev] handle matters that should be handled by an organization of antiquities covering the entire country.

C. Issue immediately a general order to all army brigades along the following lines:

1. Where any kinds of remains, such as walls, foundations, mosaics, etc., are found, work must be stopped if possible ... at least to avoid damage.

2. Single finds, whether found during work or in houses or in collections, must remain in place and be guarded. If there is no possibility of guarding them, they must be sent to the nearest headquarters, and from there to one of the central places: Jerusalem, Tel Aviv, Haifa, Sturman House at Bet Yosef, Sarah House at Tel Adashim, or the Nahariya Museum, whichever is nearest. General Headquarters should be notified of such finds and their transfer.

One must stress that an order like this, given upon our advice in the district of Jerusalem, has already borne fruit. Questions and news about finding remains and small finds were received, and a few highly important archival collections were saved.

Yadin, Chief of Operations, replied in July that the "troubles of recent time prevented General Headquarters from effectively treating these problems and the damage was considerable". Yadin spoke with the Minister of Defence, and they agreed that the government must issue an antiquities law. As an immediate and practical act, he would issue orders to all military commanders following the lines suggested in the report of the tour. Yadin added: "due to the heavy burden of work I would thank you if you could send me a draft of such an order (although from a professional archaeological view I would have agreed to do it)". He asked that the orders include a short introduction on the value of antiquities; how to act when they were discovered (considering the necessity to continue some military acts) and a list of archaeological experts in the entire country to answer emergency calls. Yadin promised to add orders requiring commanders to notify him about army activities that impacted on antiquities, and said that he would try to deliver the notices to the archaeologists (GL44875/9 no. 3).

Various orders were issued by the army; one is found next to Kaniuk and Handler's letter (but undated and unsigned). In another example, General Headquarters informed the IDAM that the army was ready to issue an order for saving antiquities, but warned that it would be maintained only if IDAM employees could reach a damaged site within 48 hours from the time of notification:

Antiquities – safekeeping and treatment

A. If a soldier finds antiquities, or objects that look like antiquities, he must immediately inform his commander and hand him any ancient object found, which can be removed.

B. The commander of the unit will post guards at the site, immediately notify the district commander and hand him each removable object.
C. If the site of the find is outside the regularly guarded area of the unit, the district commander will post a guard of district troops and immediately notify the IDAM in the government, telephone 3495 Jerusalem.
D. The district commander will give any needed help to the representatives of the IDAM who come to visit the site. After their visit, the guard will be cancelled.

(GL44875/9 no. 1420, 9.11.49; Yeivin remarked that it was impossible to reach the Negev in two days, GL44875/9 no. 1470)

On 15 July 1948, Ben-Dor, Yeivin and Mazar wrote to David Remez at the Ministry of Labour and Construction. They asked him to "be interested in the fate of the antiquities department". No solution had been found following the discussions in April, and they wrote that "the neglect in this field is very large. In fact, there is no efficient supervision of the antiquities of our land and scientific collections." As archaeological army officers they tried to save from destruction whatever could be saved in Jerusalem, and toured the country during the ceasefire. They suggested affiliating the department of antiquities to Remez's ministry. Having failed to meet Remez in Tel Aviv, they applied to other government ministers and to Zeev Sheref, the Secretary of Government. They all showed goodwill, but nothing happened. They wrote that the matter was urgent, "especially as the area of rule of the government of Israel grows, with historical and archaeological places, collections and museums, left without scientific supervision". They asked Remez to promote the establishment of the department of antiquities (GL44868/7 no. 6).

On 27 July 1948 the Antiquities Unit was established, attached to the Ministry of Labour and Construction (GL44864/14 no. 4). Of the first 15 workers, ten came directly from the Mandatory Department of Antiquities, and Yeivin re-entered service after a short break. The first salaries were based on those of the Mandatory period (GL44883/8). One year later, on 26 September 1949, the government decided to transfer the unit to the Ministry of Education (GL44868/7 nos. 12620, 9691).

A list of "historical places" was prepared around June 1948, briefly defining their nature. The text explained that most of these sites were guarded formerly, but the dissolution of the Mandatory authority had endangered historical monuments. The "experience of the upheavals of 1936–39 shows that lack of authority encourages villagers to ruin monuments for use as building materials"; so close supervision must be maintained (GL44875/9). The list separated the Hebrew and Arab areas of the time. There were 16 Hebrew sites: six synagogues (Meiron, Korazin, Kefar-Nahum, Bet She'arim, Beth-Alpha and Hamat Gader); a Byzantine church (Tabkha); four Byzantine cities in the Negev (Shivta, Halusa, Avdat and Mamshit); two mainly Canaanite sites (Beth Yerakh and Beth Shean); two Crusader forts (Athlit and Arsuf); and Caesarea. The Arab area included 18 sites: synagogues (Gush Halav and Jericho); Jewish graves (Zippori); Roman-Byzantine remains (Zippori, Samaria, Ashkelon and 'Ujja el-Khafir); churches (Samaria, Mount Grizim and Beit Jubrin [Bet Govrin]); a Crusader fort (Monfort); one late fort (Shefar'am); Canaanite sites (Nahariya, Megiddo, Shechem and Lachish); "Israelite period" sites (Samaria and Shiloh) Islamic sites (Mafjar and Ramla); and Accho. Ramla and Lod were added in handwriting below, although Ramla was already on the list (the addition was probably made after their conquest in the middle of June). The continuing war soon made this list redundant.

Yeivin, Mazar and Ben-Dor carried out a second tour between 28 July and 2 August 1948 under the command of the Jerusalem front. It seems that the main mission was to check a case of plunder that happened at Megiddo, although this was not stated explicitly. The tour covered main sites in the north of Israel (Figs 1 and 2). The conditions were still chaotic: the three needed military "passes". One pass from 1 August 1948 allowed them to visit Accho, Nahariya and Shefar'am; another was for visiting the ancient Accho jail and underground halls. Most of the report from this tour (GL44875/9) is quoted here.

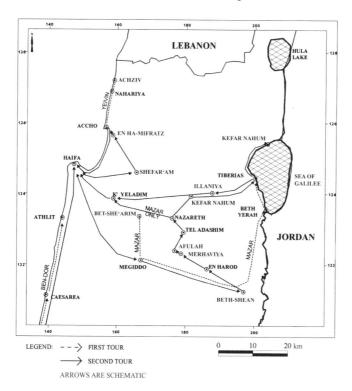

Figure 1. Map of tours of archaeological officers, June–August 1948.

On Wednesday, 28 July, we went out from Tel Aviv and arrived in Haifa. There we talked with Mr Rash about transferring his collection to the Haifa Museum and with Mr Yo'av Fogelson, an antiquities collector and nominee of the Friends of Antiquities [a civilian body of volunteers; cf. GL44864/8 no. 2], as well as with Mr [Ralph] Parker, a member of the archaeological team at Megiddo.

On Thursday 29 July we went out from Haifa to the northern front command and – with its help – to *the command of the Golani [Brigade]* ... [The army provided them with a light truck. The three talked with "member" Shemuel Savorai, manager of Sturman House in En-Harod and now cultural officer of the Golani Brigade, administration officer Eli Gavrieli, and welfare officer Nathan Shor about archaeological positions in the future.]

We visited *Megiddo* on Thursday afternoon. Deputy commander Ephraim Reiner toured the Tell with us [Fig. 2a] and permitted us to check the stores of the American Chicago expedition at Megiddo. Events have almost not touched the Tell itself. In the middle of the excavation area, a camouflaged evacuation post for wounded was arranged [it occupied the constructed "Aegean" tomb in Gotlieb Schumacher's excavations; Fig. 2b]; defensive trenches dug into the slope of the Tell did not do much damage there, and in that regard the damage is minimal and the situation is satisfactory. On the other hand, the situation in the stores of the expedition and in its equipment is very serious. When Dr Maisler visited the place a month ago, he instructed the commander not to allow any taking out of furniture or other objects from the place. The commander promised this, and partly stood up to his promise, but he could not disobey orders brought to him on behalf of various military authorities. And the authorities were generous. Orders to seize equipment were brought from the *Tuval* [or *Muval*?], from the Custodian for Enemy Property [Apotropos al Rekhush ha-Oyev], from the air force and from other authorities. Representatives of these authorities searched for objects and equipment which they needed, but were careless to look with caution. Files and papers were thrown down on the earth, torn, and ruined; closed cupboards were broken open, glasses shattered, objects piled into heaps upon each other without order and in general the offices look as if after a real "pogrom". We need not stress how great is the damage caused to the good name of the state. In this case the private property of a scientific team from a friendly country was molested and robbed in a vandalistic, irresponsible way like this. Mr Rash of Haifa, who according to his words received a nomination on behalf of the Chicago team to handle this property, has managed to take out of Megiddo the library and part of the collection of antiquities and equipment. These things are kept now in a collection that will serve as a nucleus of the municipal museum of Haifa. In our view, one must immediately demand that the

Figure 2. Second tour of officers. (a) Megiddo, 29 July 1948. Yeivin (left), B. Mazar (seated centre) and probably the military commander of Megiddo (right). (Photograph probably by Ben-Dor, IAA 2401) (b) Megiddo, 29 July 1948. A camouflaged evacuation post for wounded soldiers still occupies the constructed (misnamed "Aegean") tomb in Schumacher's trench. (Photograph probably by Ben-Dor, IAA 2402) (c) Nazareth [?]. Armoured vehicle accompanying the archaeologists. (Photograph by Ben-Dor, IAA 2408)

army authorities hand over a few trucks to Mr Rash in order to take out of Megiddo the rest of the antiquities and the scientific equipment for safekeeping in the Haifa Museum, rather than losing or ruining them as has already happened so far.

On the Tell we saw a "Proto-Greek" [=Proto Aeolian] capital of the Israelite period, and we suggest removing it, once a request has been approved by the Chicago team, to one of the museums where it can be exhibited.

After the long tour at Megiddo we drove to *Sturman House* in En Harod, for we were told that a few antiquities [from Megiddo] were located there for protection from extinction. We found that following the suggestion of the manager of Sturman House, and with the permit of the *Tuval* [*Muval?*], Mr [Nehemia] Zimbalist [later Zori] took 60 pottery vessels and 180 glass plates of photos. We took the plates with us to Haifa. Mr Zimbalist promised us that he would return the antiquities at any moment ... [details on Sturman House].

From En-Harod we travelled to *Beth Shean*. Due to mines it was impossible to visit the excavations area, but we visited the deserted town and found that a few columns and ancient capitals, formerly displayed in the municipal garden, are still there. One must warn the military authorities to avoid damaging or removing the objects. While touring the area we were told that the Crusader period tower at Zar'in [Jezreel] was ruined by the army after the conquest of the village. This is further evidence as to the importance of cooperation between the army authorities and the Antiquities Unit ...

We stayed overnight at *Merhavyah* and from talking to the members there it became clear that due to digging works, an early Canaanite tomb was discovered where a bronze sword was found, now kept by a teacher at the Kibbutz. We were also told about the discovery of a complex of underground rooms under the water pool, presently impossible to visit. Also a decorated sarcophagus of stone is found at Merhavyah. We exchanged words also with member Stefan to supply photos and to represent the Friends of Antiquities there, and with P. Bar-Adon to represent this body in the entire region.

Next morning, 30 July. We drove to *Tel Adashim*. There is a small museum there, a "field tent" arranged with love and knowledge ... Member Yariv Shapira handles the museum ... From him we learned that remains of antiquities at 'Afulah are being destroyed. From Tel Adashim we drove to the *Nazareth* police. The commander there, Mr Avraham Yaffe [later Director of the Parks Authority], willingly accepted all our requests and placed at our disposal the guard of an armoured car [Fig. 2c] in order to visit Kefar Kana and Zippori.

We first went out to *Kefar Kana* and visited the Franciscan Church of the Miracle of Wine, probably built upon the ruins of a Jewish synagogue of the

5th–6th centuries, for under the floor of the main hall of the church there is a section of a mosaic with an Aramaic inscription starting with the words "*Demir Letov …*", a very typical 5th–6th-century version of inscriptions in honour of donors for synagogues. We also visited the other ancient remains of architecture around the church and the small collection of antiquities … Since Dr Maisler felt sick, we stayed a while in the church until he rested and could continue on his way with us. We therefore returned to the Nazareth police only at dusk, and were forced to give up the visit to Nazareth itself and Zippori. In any case, we managed to find in Nazareth that the former Inspector of Antiquities, Na'im Ephendi Makhouli, left the city two months ago and went abroad. We left Dr Maisler at the central hospital near Kefar Yeladim [*sic*. the youth village near Kefar Khasidim?] and went to Tiberias.

At *Tiberias* we called the municipal engineer Mr Landau and with him toured the city's citadel. Apparently the citadel holds within it few ancient parts – perhaps from the Crusader period, but the date of construction is debated. Some think that it is from the 17th century and some date it to the days of Thahar el-Omar (mid-18th century). Anyway, if a certain sum of money could be invested in cleaning the building and removing debris, and in fixing and restoring the existing part, it would serve as a beautiful and glorious monument to the city, and would be a tourist attraction. Moreover, with a relatively small investment one may immediately prepare one of the rooms to serve as a municipal museum, for the time being a small one. Such an institution is already needed, to collect in it the antiquities found in some houses and institutions now evacuated, like fragments of inscriptions and carved building stones (capitals, etc.), found in the Mission hospital. Now nobody takes care of them and they are gradually disappearing. The alleged "Damascene" room was removed – for no reason and [without] authority – to Haifa, etc. [They located one room in the citadel for keeping the Tiberias antiquities and decided to allocate the budget to fix it.]

Afterwards we visited the Mission hospital, now occupied by Israel's defence forces. [This was the first hospital at Tiberias, built in 1894 by Dr David Torrance. It continued to serve as a maternity hospital after 1948 (Eliav 1978: 429; Sarid 1983).] We found several fragments of inscriptions that we knew should have been here – strewn in various corners – and some other stones. We talked with the administrative manager of the hospital, Dr Wilton. He was very kind and offered us a room near his office in which it was possible to gather and keep all these remains temporarily. Mr Landau took it upon himself to see that everything is gathered in this room; but clearly this arrangement is only temporary. The removal of debris from the room in the citadel must be hastened.

The ownership rights of the above-mentioned "Damascene" room in the home of the late Dr Hart, and of his library, which is, as far as it is known, kept in the Tiberias police building, requires investigation. Some say that the deceased left his property to the YMCA organization. [Indeed, the building near the Russian Church at Migdal (Magdala) became a YMCA hostel.]

There were more collections and objects in the city in houses of foreign residents, which were deserted during the "events" ... Furthermore, a few antique remains are embedded within various buildings (such as the famous lion relief), and now is the time to tear them out and gather them in a safe place.

After a two-hour visit we came back from Tiberias to the hospital at Kefar Yeladim through Lubia and Illaniya. We found the army tearing to pieces [mehozez] the houses of this village and others (near Mount Tabor). The attention of General Headquarters should be raised to the fact that before this kind of demolition, people who have knowledge of antiquities should visit, because in many villages ancient building stones are embedded, some of them carved and some carrying inscriptions (like the synagogue inscription at 'Iblin). Now is the time to save them and bring them to a safe place. From the hospital at Kefar Yeladim we returned, together with Dr Maisler, who now felt better, to Haifa.

Saturday afternoon we visited the Arab part, accompanied by the city engineer, Mr Rozhanski. There the army is now levelling a central street from Feisal Square to Hamra [Paris] Square. From the engineer we learnt that this had been planned a long time ago, but was only now being done. Yet it seems to us that some remarks must be made about this matter. With our own eyes we saw the ruins of half of a building used as a synagogue in the old Jews Street. Although it is not very old, it is still a Jewish synagogue once called Elijah the Prophet Synagogue. Jews living there, who were travelling between the ruins, told us that 2–3 other church-buildings were ruined. The Ḥammam al Basha, a very interesting building although not very ancient, was saved just by chance from ruin, since it is a few metres away from the zone of demolition. A school near a Greek Orthodox church was ruined and the church itself was somewhat damaged inside from the force of demolition and its doors were broken. It seems that with a little attention it would have been possible to avoid damaging these holy buildings. The attention of the army authorities must immediately be drawn to this issue so that in the future there will be no similar acts of destruction, even if they are in accordance with city planning, without consultation with the Antiquities Unit for avoiding damage to holy and historically interesting buildings. [For Haifa in the 1948 War see Karsh (2001).]

At dusk we visited Ẓidoni headquarters, to arrange our visit the next morning to the area conquered by it. There Officer Kutik greeted us in a friendly manner ...

On the next morning, 1 August 1948 we returned to the Zidoni command, and although Officers IR and Kutik made every possible effort, they could not supply us with army transport. Eventually, after a lot of sweat, they got us a taxi for Shefar'am. Here too we were kindly greeted by Officer Aharon … He also promised to follow all the rules of the Chief of Staff about finding and guarding antiquities. He put at our disposal one of the Christian village residents, Abdallah Abu Kirilos, and an armed soldier to guide us in our visit. First we went to the synagogue building which probably dates to the 17th century. It was cleaned before we came on the order of the army (formerly it was a stable and refuse dump for the Muslim village dwellers). It is almost whole and intact, but needs certain repairs and a good solid door, and the courtyard, full of debris and earth at present, needs cleaning. Here too Mr Pinkerfeld should visit soon to prepare an estimate for the cleaning and removal of debris. From there we went to visit the hill south of the village, where a few ancient graves are located (from Roman-Byzantine periods). Two citadels exist at Shefar'am, mainly from the days of Thahar el-Omar. One still stands and is used by the village governor; the other on a hill to the south is partially ruined. There is a nice place for a trial excavation on the Tell free of modern buildings. Such an excavation is the most pressing need, since it is still unknown when the place was first settled and for which periods.

From Shefar'am we went to En ha-Mifratz [near Accho], where the local teacher, Mr Zvi Sapir, is interested in the remains of the past and familiar with the antiquities of Accho. Unfortunately the man was not there at the time and we could not see him. From there we went to *Accho*. We visited the jail and wanted to visit the underground rooms found recently. Member Hirschfeld and the commander of the jail, Officer MR, showed a great deal of kindness and generosity, but owing to a lack of suitable lighting tools (the acetylene lamps were not functioning) it was impossible to visit these rooms.

We also visited the city itself for a short time and saw the chairman of the local committee Mr Ahmad Abdu, who at our request called on Mahmud el-Lakham, who was the keeper of antiquities on behalf of the Mandatory government … [references to letters concerning him]. The said Mr Ahmad Abdu asked us about the plan for the restoration of Accho prepared formerly during the days of the Mandatory government. Of course we could say nothing to him about this; it is not our business to say at this time whether the restoration is possible from any point of view. But as for preserving antiquities, we have to note that with a relatively small expenditure it will be possible to clean and restore the old buildings; and possibly to clean the underground room complex and open access to it and install electric lights, and so turn the city into a place that attracts tourists and becomes an important factor in the region's economy.

> From Accho we returned to Haifa ... [They talked with Dr [Walter] Moses about the planned museum for knowledge of the country (*yediat ha-aretz*) at Tel Aviv. On 2 August 1948 they visited David Hacohen of the Haifa municipality. They offered both of them places on the future archaeological advisory council. Then they visited the collection of Rash. At dusk they returned to Tel Aviv.]
> This tour proved once again the urgent need to solve the problems of antiquities in army works and other works performed at various places of the country in order to save the remains of the antiquity of the land.
> (GL44875/9)
> [The word "work" was used obsessively by that generation, and much more often than today.]

Yeivin made a list of urgent acts of preservation at Tiberias, Shefar'am, Beth-Alpha, Accho and several other sites, and started to organize a permanent body of supervision. With that aim in mind he wrote to the Minister of Public Works on 6 August 1948, asking to arrange certificates of passage from the army authorities for Philip Guy (who served as the first Director of the IDAM's Excavations and Survey Department), Jacob (Hebrew Ya'akov) Pinkerfeld, Ya'akov Ory and Michael Avi-Yonah. This would enable them to supervise the many sites under military rule (GL44875/9 no. 5). Yeivin attached a draft of such a certificate:

> Mr ... (+photo) is appointed by the government as supervisor for maintaining historical sites and their antiquities. He must be given all help in visits to areas occupied by the army. He should be helped as much as possible with means of transportation ...
> Signed _____ Chief of Intelligence   (GL44875/9 no. 4)

WAR DAMAGE

Like most wars, the 1948 War damaged sites and antiquities, especially since it was a prolonged war and many battles took place in and around settled areas. War damage to antiquities happened all over Palestine, and not just by Israelis, but this book only discusses Israel. Most of the information about the damage to antiquities comes from Israel, and we should be grateful to the first Israelis for documenting it, for without them we would know next to nothing about this issue (Fig. 3).

Throughout the war, there were no more than three supervisors of antiquities (GL44864/14, report 14.10.48): Pinkerfeld was the chief supervisor, with

Amiran in the north and Ory in the south. The guards' battalion (see Ch. 5) was active only after March 1950. Transport conditions and the tasks undertaken by the early supervisors were terrible (GL44875/9, 4.3.49), but they started to report cases of damage. Pinkerfeld wrote to the liaison officer of the Ministry of Defence on 24 September 1948:

A. In Tiberias the army started to blow up a wide zone of houses in the old city … In some of our representative's visits there we stressed in talks with all those responsible the special importance of the old stone with lion relief, which was built inside one of the walls. We were promised that this 3,000-year-old antiquity would be protected. But on my last visit I found that this stone had been blown to pieces.

B. In many blasting works around the country, archaeological/historical monuments are destroyed, without the IDAM receiving timely information about the beginning of the works. Thus our representative cannot visit in advance and mark the monuments for safekeeping as antiquities.

C. In the German monastery of El-Tabkha, books from the library were destroyed and dispersed. The collection of tools and ancient sherds suffered heavily. A real danger faces the ancient Christian church mosaic there. Somehow the building is deserted and open to trouble, without a guard and with no one taking responsibility for it. The commander of the "Jordan" battalion promised me that this church – one of the most important monuments in the eyes of world Christianity – would be locked up and he would keep the key; but I have received no news that this has been done.

D. Segments after segments were torn from an ancient mosaic at Selbit and taken as souvenirs by soldiers. [The two rectangular stones at the bottom left of Figure 4 carried faint inscriptions, and were probably part of the chancel of a Byzantine church. They were mentioned in the IDAM's first press communication (GL44864/14, 7.10.48).]

E. The ancient synagogue at Beth Alpha is used as storage for explosives … I ask you to see to the evacuation of these materials, which endanger the site. (GL44875/9 no. 6)

Later, Pinkerfeld reported that the fragments of the lion relief were collected and kept in Sha'ar Ha-Golan (GL44875/9, 15.11.48). Details of it were first published before 1948 but it was discussed again by Landau (1967: 172, pl. 8:1). Later it was restored and moved to a museum in Jerusalem (Keren Levi, pers. comm., Jan. 2005). On 21 November 1948, Pinkerfeld complained that regular work was prevented because of the need for urgent responses to new situations caused by the war and the lack of transport. The IDAM supervisers tried to reach

Figure 3. The "cave strongpoint", Beit Jubrin 1949. Ashlar wall exposed by military trenches. (Photograph by Ory, IAA 60)

Figure 4. Selbit (Sha'alabim) 1949. Abandoned Arab village, showing courtyard with antiquities. (IAA 320)

sites immediately after their conquest and secure help from commanders. They could not make any plans for a regular system of supervision of all historical sites. The IDAM had one car that was privately owned by a supervisor, compared to the eight cars that had been available to the Mandatory Department of Antiquities (GL44864/14 no. 6). Pinkerfeld asked for "minimal requirements": two assistants (architect and technician) and a chief labourer. In a fuller report from this period, Pinkerfeld described how the IDAM was "in continued written contact" with army authorities to prevent destruction, blasting or stealing, although their efforts were not always crowned with success. They maintained personal relationships with commanders and made special tours, preferably immediately after conquest, to sites such as Beit Jubrin, Majdal and Ashkelon. They placed signs: "Out of Bounds" or "Forbidden to Blast" (see Fig. 14, p. 118). Shefar'am was considered to be one success of this system:

> My visit and negotiation with the command post prevented the immediate blasting of the Al-burj castle near the castle of Shefar'am. I was promised that if there is a need to demolish this *khirbeh* (which is a military position!) in the future, I shall be given at least a chance to prepare its plan first. But with the change [for good] of the military situation, one may hope that the danger to this monument completely passed.
>
> (GL44875/9, report up to 15.11.48: p. 4)

In Jerusalem most direct war damage probably occurred before the establishment of the IDAM. Later the main problems were vandalism and robbery. The Dormition and the Notre Dam monasteries remained near the new border and were out of bounds to civilians. Keeping their contents safe caused considerable worries to the IDAM. At the end of 1948, Ben-Dor wrote that during the siege of Jerusalem:

> The IDAM also acted in placing in order [*hasdarah*] museums in the areas occupied [by Israel]. This act was performed at the request of the political department of the Jewish Agency and of the headquarters of the Jerusalem front and, as a result of it, the French archaeological museum of Notre Dam was secured and David's Tomb on Mount Zion was placed in order. The organization of the archaeological museum of Dormition on Mount Zion did not succeed, due to acts of war and plunder made later.
>
> (GL44864/14 no. 4; cf. GL44868/7, 22.6.48)

On 23 September 1948, Ben-Dor reported that Professor Moshe David Cassuto had received a letter from Monseigneur Gustavo Testa, the Vatican delegate in Jerusalem, complaining about the disappearance of 36 volumes of the *Encyclopaedia Italiana* from the Vatican embassy on Mount Zion, after it was conquered by Israel. Testa (1886–1969), who later served in Berne and was Cardinal in Munich, reminded Cassuto of "the relation of the Vatican to Jews during the Nazi government", and hoped that the books would be returned. The stolen books may have belonged to Testa, which explains his concern (Bialer 1985: 173, 176 n.34). (The Vatican was rather hostile to Israel at first and it was years before normal political relations were established; Ben-Horin 2002: 993–1032.) Ben-Dor asked for an inquiry to find the guilty soldiers. He testified that although he and Mazar had "placed in order" the offices of the Vatican embassy, they were told that soldiers had "removed" these volumes (GL1342/18 no. 1).

On 21 November 1948, Ben-Dor wrote to Captain Joshua Prawer (later a professor at the Hebrew University) and to Father Pascal of the Notre Dam monastery with copies of a list (not found) of the monastery's antiquities, which he and Mazar composed on 7 June 1948 (GL1342/18 nos. 1, 3). On the same day he wrote to the military commander of Notre Dam:

> I thank you for this morning's conversation, in which you agreed to leave the antiquities of the museum of Notre Dam in place. As you know, we placed the museum in order according to the suggestion of the Ezioni [Brigade] headquarters and notified the French Consul in Jerusalem about it.
>
> Any change in the situation now would have caused damage to antiquities and diplomatic complications with the French government authorities.
>
> (GL1342/18)

On 11 April 1949, Yeivin and Kahane met Major Yosef Nevo, Commander of the Sixth Brigade, together with Dr Meir Mendes of the Ministry of Religious Affairs. Various visits to the Dormition monastery and other places proved that the antiquities and valuable libraries were not safe. For "significant reasons" the removal of the valuables elsewhere was impossible, and satisfactory security was, for the time being, not feasible owing to "technical and financial problems". Nevo suggested that civilian guards might be placed, and was ready to issue orders to his forces to obey such guards. He promised to close the rooms where antiquities and books were found at the Dormition and Notre Dam monasteries, in the presence of representatives of the IDAM, and give "passes" to IDAM supervisors. The report of the meeting went on to say: "Sixteen books that were collected during the last visit from the Franciscan Cunaculum [building], in a very bad state, will be given to P. Kahane for safekeeping; according to a list he will make and give to the army authorities" (GL1342/22, 11.4.49). Another memorandum was prepared by Officer Mordechai Gicherman (later Professor Gichon of Tel Aviv University) on behalf of the Sixth Brigade:

1) The brigade commander ordered me to handle the problem of the antiquities and their safekeeping. That means the Dormition, Notre Dam

and other places. According to the conversation between you and the brigade commander, one must establish – in my view soon – civilian guarding in these places. To do this I wish to be given as soon as possible the list of names of these guards. They must be given the appropriate official certificates bearing the signature of the military authorities. A leader of these guards must be nominated to deal with all the problems concerning the guards and to keep in constant contact with us.

2) The battalion commanders will be supplied with a list of names of IDAM supervisors. I require this list to be given to me as soon as possible. The said supervisors will be issued with fixed visit permits to the military areas.

3) Dr Kahane can receive at this office, at any hour he wishes to, the permit to remove the books from Mount Zion, according to the list that he brings with him.

[signed] M. Gicherman, Operations Officer

(GL1342/22 no. 634, 15.4.49)

On 27 April 1949, Ben-Dor wrote to Gicherman explaining that the formation of a battalion of guards was still under discussion, so the IDAM was unable to appoint civilian guards at Mount Zion (GL1342/22 no. 10). He asked that to prevent further damage the correct orders be issued to commanders there, who changed from time to time. Ben-Dor asked that a former agreement to brick up the rooms containing antiquities at the Dormition be carried out. On 10 September 1951 Kahane reported to Yeivin:

The fathers of the Notre Dam complain bitterly about the attitude shown by the army to the antiquities collections in their monastery. Indeed, the large and important collection suffered badly during the war, but out of the list of antiquities made on 7 June 1948 (copy handed to the French General Consul) it is clear that at that time a large part of the collection still existed. As far as I know, the building did not change hands after this date, but a few antiquities were destroyed by the blast of an Arab shell. The rooms where the antiquities were gathered during the war, when the list was made, were sealed by wooden partitions; but since then and up to now a large number of antiquities have been stolen and destroyed. So at present only a very small part of the collection is kept, and even this part will disappear no doubt unless immediate steps for its safekeeping are taken.

The monks' claim is that the army has not so far paid attention to their demand that the collection be returned (the antiquities are kept in rooms occupied by the army), and as a result a large part of the collection was lost. The army is now ready (through the services of the IDAM) to return the remaining antiquities to the monks, but the army is not ready to pay the cost of transfer and also does not allow monks, who wish to perform the transfer with their own hands, to enter into the rooms where the antiquities are kept. As one intelligence officer reported, the authorities of the army have not yet decided whether they will let porters enter the site where the remains of the collection are found. Of course, the monks are not ready to pay for transferring the antiquities, which in their view are the responsibility of the government of Israel. In a talk a short while ago with the monks, they explained that the rude behaviour of the army and the insufficient guard brought them to such a state that they keep to themselves the right to act diplomatically (through the French General Consul). They even spoke about propaganda against the attitude shown on behalf of the government of Israel.

In order to prevent further conflicts we think it desirable that the government will pay for the transfer of antiquities, and that the army will let external porters do the transfer under supervision of the IDAM.

(GL44880/13 no. 6599; cf. Segev (1984: 84))

With the removal of the remaining antiquities the matter was solved. The Notre Dam monastery was sold in 1971 and later became home to the Hebrew University.

Several shops selling antiquities in Jerusalem were robbed or damaged. Olaf Matson's shop, "Art Ancient and Modern", near the King David Hotel, was robbed in June 1948. On 1 February 1949 some remaining finds were removed by Officers Gicherman and Hammer (later Dothan) for safekeeping. Some boxes of antiquities still remained in the shop, but the Custodian for Absentees' Property (Apotropos al Nichsei Nifkadim) refused to handle the case because Matson was a Swedish national. The army (under General Moshe Dayan) also refused to help. Finally, Yeivin and a policeman removed the remaining antiquities on 28 February 1949 (GL44864/14 no. 4; GL44880/10, letters February 1949). Early in 1951 Matson handed a lawsuit to the Division of Insurance and Suits of the Israel Defence Forces (IDF), headed by Yehiel Ross. The police tried to discover whether he had transferred the shop to an Arab before he left Jerusalem in 1948, which would make it absentee property (GL44880/10 no. 1128, 16.3.51). The robbery could not be blamed on Arabs because the area was conquered almost a year before it happened (GL44880/10, letters 6.6.51). Yeivin informed the Ministry of Defence that he could not give firsthand evidence because he had never visited Matson's shop before the war, but hearsay suggested that he had been trading in antiquities. He mentioned how Gichon (formerly Gicherman, and by then a lieutenant colonel) and Dothan had removed some antiquities from this shop and how it had been decided to take all the antiquities from the shop as a precaution. The IDAM estimated their value as approximately 40 Lira, and was willing to hand them back to their owner. Yeivin enclosed a "confidential dossier" with details and lists of antiquities:

Based on these documents, you will see that it is impossible to accept the claim of the police, that there were no antiquities at all in Mr Matson's shop. I even heard that there was quite a large collection of coins there, but these were already missing when I visited the place ...

On my meeting with one person in this affair I am not willing to submit a written report, but if a high official from your department happens to be in Jerusalem early next week I would love to talk with him about it.
(GL44880/13 no. 5561, 29.4.51)

Who the "one person" was we can only guess; Yeivin met the official, but did not reveal the name in writing. The Ministry of Defence accepted responsibility (GL44880/10 no. 2860, 24.6.51) and Yeivin sent the list of objects to the Ministry of Foreign Affairs and to the Swedish Consulate (GL44880/13 nos. 5015a; 6177). The objects, weighing 250 kg, were finally shipped to Matson in January 1956 (GL44880/13 no. 8868a).

Another shop robbed was that of Ohan (the spelling is uncertain). A report (GL44880/14) lists the antiquities moved to the IDAM on 24 December 1948 for safekeeping, including 541 oil lamps, 40 dipper juglets, 23 jugs, 54 flint tools, 7 inscribed metal bowls and 8 Arabic manuscripts. They were formerly stored in the office of the Custodian for Absentees' Property. And in a letter of 22 June 1948, Ben-Dor mentioned that he and Mazar took care of the antiquities collections of Dr Cana'an (probably Dr Tawfik Cana'an (1882–1964), scholar of Palestinian folklore, who was active in the Palestine Oriental Society; his collection of amulets remained with the family and was donated in 1995 to Bir Zeit University) and the Company for the Distribution of Holy Books (Mefizei Kitvey ha-Kodash), a missionary society (GL44868/7, 22.6.48).

Other collections were damaged in Accho. A collection of 17th–18th-century weapons was probably stolen from the Accho jail (GL44875/9 no. 6, 9.8.48). On 16 December 1949, Yeivin wrote to Ben-Dor:

As for Accho, we must take note of the sealed room in the offices of the Governor of Western Galilee, where there is a collection of Arab finds, mostly from the deserted villages. Most of them are new and are interesting as a folkloristic, not antiquities, collection. In any case, I do not think it would be fair or tactful to exhibit objects taken from Arab houses in the vicinity, from the aspect of relations with the remaining Arab community [yishuv]. A museum will be in Accho in due course, when there will be something to display in it, real antiquities, and when the question of ancient Accho in general will be resolved ...
(GL44880/13 no. 1903)

At Caesarea, only some of the Greek inscriptions robbed in the early days of war were later returned (GL44864/14 no. 713a: p. 2). At Jaffa, the Ustinov collection (see below) "disappeared". Pinkerfeld visited Jaffa on 5 September 1949 (GL44864/8 no. 21). He found a Roman period marble door of a tomb, thanks to information from Dr Muzner (Mosberg?) and Dr Koyfman (Kadman) (IDAM "R" no. 44; GL44864/8 no. 8, 28.7.49). Another part from the same door, inscribed tombstones and a relief of a woman were found and taken for safety (IAA negative 52; cf. Pinkerfield 1955: 28). On 15 September 1948 Ory was invited to visit the military police on Jaffa Road in connection with "interrogations about Mr Guy's tours near Herzeliya". On that occasion he saw remains of "the famous collection of Baron Ustinov nearby. The finds are strewn in courtyards outside the Baron's botanical garden; some fragments served as entrance steps to one house." In his assessment, some of these finds were important and should be taken to safety (GL44864/8 no. 7). Pinkerfeld took them on 28 September 1948 (IDAM "R" nos. 47–52; cf. GL44875/9, full report up to 15.11.48) (Fig. 5).

On 12 December 1948, Schwabe wrote to the IDAM. During the first cease-fire he had met the commander of the Jaffa forces and mentioned that he was interested in finding the collection of Baron Plato Von Ustinov (an ancestor of the actor Peter Ustinov), which included most of the inscriptions of the Jewish cemetery of Jaffa (cf. Pedersen 1928). The commander, who was an acquaint-

Figure 5. Jaffa, old city, *c*. 1950. The "Arab soap factory – [Ḥana] Damyani and Sons" building. Note the zone and house number registration, signifying that it was destined for preservation. The building is Mamluk or early Ottoman and it survived. The family was known in Jaffa, and had nineteenth-century ancestors who served several European countries. See Kark (1990: 256) for a very similar photograph from 1977.

ance of Schwabe and interested in archaeology, directed one of his men to make inquiries. In his letter to the IDAM, Schwabe asked for the letter he had received as a result of the inquiries to be placed in the archive and, if possible, the information it gave to be checked (GL44864/8, no. 106). The letter was handwritten on 9 July 1948, on a Mandatory period "cable wireless" telegram form:

> To the Commander of the Jaffa forces.
> Baron Ustinov is probably not alive. Fifty years ago he was in Ethiopia and there he married an Ethiopian wife. They had a daughter who married an Arab named Jamal. The daughter, who is *c.* 45 years old, deals in antiquities. Her husband Jamal has the same job. They live in Jerusalem. They have a villa in the Katamon neighbourhood. Their workshop is located in Jerusalem. They have there two large stores with antiquities of immense value. The stores are in St Julian St., a few houses from the YMCA on the corner of the street.
> [initialled] MKẒ   (GL44864/8 no. 13)

Yeivin (GL44864/8 no. 19) promised to try to locate the collection in Jerusalem, but feared that it was in no-man's-land. In fact, Baron Ustinov's daughter, Tabitha (Peter Ustinov's aunt), and her husband, Anis Jamal, had fled to Beirut, and their house in Jerusalem had become the property of the Custodian for Absentees' Property (Ustinov 1977: 326; for the Jaffa building see Kark 1990: 178). Yeivin thought that the larger part of the Ustinov collection had been sold and parts of it were probably dispersed in Jaffa. One newly found fragment fitted tombstone no. 7 from the Baron's collection (GL44864/8, Ben-Dor 25.7.49; cf. no. 3970 of 24.11.50). It is perplexing, for it is certain that the Baron left Israel in 1913 and took his collection to London. It reached Norway and is still there (Skupinska-Løvset 1976: 17–21). So all the antiquities mentioned in relation to the 1948 War were perhaps heavy items, "abandoned" by the Baron.

THE MEGIDDO AFFAIR

The worst case of war damage to antiquities in 1948 happened at Megiddo. It was the worst case not because of the scale of the damage, but because it was the result of actions by various authorities in the IDF, and not an act of damage through battle or vandalism by some low-level unit. The details are not available to the public (although *Herut* newspaper reported the case in a single sentence on 1 August 1950). What follows is the best account I can give, collected from scattered data in open files. In the 1920s–1930s, Megiddo was the largest, and one of the most important, excavations in Palestine, carried out on behalf of the Oriental Institute of the University of Chicago. The project was stopped by the Second World War, and the buildings housing finds, tools and the archive and library of the expedition, located on the Tell, were looted. Some archaeologists tried to prevent the damage, and various items were saved (described in the reports above).

The affair was mentioned in several other documents. Five or six vessels from Megiddo reached Mordechai Minkowski (later Megiddon), a private antiquities collector in Tel Aviv and for some time a Friend of Antiquities. Amiran noticed them on account of their registration numbers. The IDAM instructed Minkowski to return these vessels for reasonable compensation, which he duly did (GL44864/8 no. 163, 26.1.49 and no. 3337; GL44864/14 no. 713a). Yeivin mentioned the Megiddo affair in a letter of 27 December 1948 (GL1342/22), where he stated that he was involved in an investigation into it following a special request from the Ministry of Defence. His conclusions were that it was impossible to avoid the plunder of collections or damage to sites by individual soldiers or groups from the IDF by the means used so far: written orders, "private agreements" with commanders and police investigations after the act. The Director-General of the Ministry of Defence, Eliezer(?) Peri, was also a member of the committee investigating the case. Yeivin met him on 28 June 1949 and suggested adding a lawyer to the committee because legal guidance would surely be required (GL1342/22, 30.6.49). The committee finished its work in April 1949 and issued two reports, one official and one secret, to the Ministry of Defence. Copies were sent to the Ministry of Foreign Affairs (USA Department) and to the Minister of Public Works (GL44864/14 no. 11). Later, another committee, of which Yeivin was also a part, was formed to estimate the damage (GL44864/14 no. 790: p. 3). Damages were finally paid to the Oriental Institute of the University of Chicago (GL1342/22 no. 9). In a letter to Dr Moshe Avidor (Director-General of the Ministry of Education, 1954–1960) of 31 October 1956, Yeivin wrote:

> I need to remind to you, that at least in one case handled personally by me, the state paid more than 10,000 Lira compensation and repair money because of a grave robbery and damage to buildings done in the houses of the American expedition at Megiddo. A huge public scandal was avoided only with great difficulties and with the active help of the Chicago Oriental Institute. (GL44880/13)

In 1952 the University of Chicago returned to Israel to dig, but not to Megiddo. Yeivin mentioned that the team had 6,000 Lira in Israel: "damage payment that it received from the government of Israel" (GL1430/14, 1.8.52).

In a letter of 30 July 1954 to Dr Pinhas Delougaz of the Oriental Institute, Yeivin noted that at the time all government property was registered and kept by the Department of Governmental Property, and that the expedition buildings at Megiddo came into this category, but that the IDAM would have a say in the affair (GL44880/13 no. 4426a). In 1955 the Americans bequeathed the expedition houses at Megiddo to the IDAM (GL44883/12, yearly summary of 1957–58: p. 4). In the course of works carried out in these buildings (for creating a small museum) by the Government Tourist Corporation (GTC, now officially called the Israel Government Tourist Corporation, or IGTC), Yeivin stated that they were a gift to the state of Israel, reserved for the needs of the IDAM (GL44881/13, 13.1.59). As proof he attached a copy of the certificate of gift:

> This Indenture Witnesseth
> That the University of Chicago, a corporation not for profit under the laws of the state of Illinois, USA (owing and operating the ORIENTAL INSTITUTE OF THE UNIVERSITY OF CHICAGO), in consideration of the sum of One Dollar ($1.00) … does hereby transfer and convey unto the GOVERNMENT OF ISRAEL all right, title and interest that the University may have in and to the buildings standing on the land of the Megiddo excavations area as shown on map attached hereby and by reference made a part thereof.
> Dated at Chicago – this 18th day of January, A.D. 1955.
> (corporate Seal)   THE UNIVERSITY OF CHICAGO
> Attest: By /S/W. B. Harrel
> S/Howard H. Mare   Its Vice President in the
> Secretary   charge of business Affairs
>   (GL44882/9)

Yeivin recorded the history of this gift (GL44882/9 no. 3389, 19.11.59). Correspondence since March 1954 had been kept and the buildings were gifted in January 1955. Because of conflicts surrounding the GTC works in Megiddo in 1957–59, the IDAM wanted to ensure its rights by registering the buildings. Shimeon Nahmani (head of the guards battalion; see Ch. 5) visited Megiddo with a representative of the property division of the northern district to carry out the registration (GL44882/9, 21.12.59), so official registration in the *Tabu* (land registration) offices happened some time later.

For many years, the Megiddo expedition building – where hundreds of thousands of tourists passed through and gazed at the model of the ancient city – was the property of the IDAM/IAA, until finally in 2002 the IAA gave it to the parks authority responsible for developing the site.

ABANDONED PROPERTY AT TIMES OF WAR

On 28 September 1948, someone, probably Amiran, wrote to Yeivin that a certain Fritz (later Zeev) Goldman had handed in objects from northern Galilee for safekeeping, by orders of the unit of "enemy property" in Haifa (GL44880/4 no. 215). Yeivin was perplexed and wrote to Amiran on 31 October 1948, asking her:

> for further investigation on your next visit to Haifa. Do not commit to anything from our side. Just get information: what does he want? Who ordered him to save antiquities, a duty which is the business of the IDAM? What does he need and what can he do? Enthusiasm alone is not enough.
>
> (GL44875/9)

Dr Zeev Goldman was an official of the office of deserted property in Haifa. He was involved in the removal of objects from Tiberias (above). Later he maintained good relations with the IDAM, and was an antiquities guard (GL44883/12, summary 1957–58: p. 16) and the head of the Accho Municipal Museum. He also directed a few salvage excavations. Kahane wrote about him on 16 October 1948:

> Dr Goldman, a clerk in the office supervising enemy property, asks the IDAM to widen the authority he has. His special job is to collect and guard or protect antiquities, especially of the Arab period, in the area held by the army of Israel around Haifa. Since he can only dedicate 50 percent of his time to this task, and that, he thinks, is not enough time for the job itself as well as for writing reports, he believes that enlarging his authority will benefit the maintenance of antiquities in the said area. He is also sure that his superiors will agree.
>
> Since Dr Goldman is a scholar of the history of art and an archaeologist, reliable and really interested in keeping antiquities, I recommend backing his request … I asked him to send reports of his actions, as far as they concern us, also to the IDAM, and to continue writing his reports.
>
> (GL44875/9)

Other collections in danger included a folkloristic collection in Haifa; the Lawrence Oliphant collection and the collection of Spiridion at Beit Jimmal monastery (see Segev 1984: 85). Amiran asked Yeivin to move them to the IDAM for safekeeping (GL44880/4). Yeivin answered that "the system [for moving] is very complicated from a legal position, especially when it relates to churches and monasteries" (GL44880/4, 28.11.48).

Hundreds of thousands of Arabs left the area that became Israel in 1948–49, leaving behind some 94,000 rooms and about 6.5 million *dunams* (1 *dunam* = 0.1 hectares) of land, including about 4 million *dunams* of agricultural land and hundreds of villages (Golan 2001: 12). In early 1948 several units responsible for "enemy property" operated in chaotic circumstances. A supervisor of Arab property in Haifa was established in April 1948 (Golan 2001: 13; Fischbach 2003: 15). In July 1948, Dov Shafrir was appointed Custodian for Abandoned Property

(Apotropos al ha-Rekhush ha-Natush), and the various units were gradually placed under him (Segev 1984: 84–94; Fischbach 2003: 16–27). The Jerusalem unit remained independent until August 1948. In December 1948, under new legislation coupled with the decision not to allow the return of the refugees, the office changed its name to the Custodian for Absentees' Property (Apotropos al Nichsei Nifkadim) (Golan 2001: 14–15). Influenced by this system, antiquities were also seen as "abandoned" or "deserted", and after the cessation of hostilities, the IDAM acted to collect them for safekeeping. These objects were brought to the Tel Aviv office of the IDAM and, in accordance with the request of the Custodian for Absentees' Property, many vessels from antiquities shops, abandoned by their owners, were taken to Jerusalem. Other antiquities were collected in Jerusalem (e.g. GL44864/14 no. 4: p. 3; GL44864/14 no. 8; GL44880/4, 8.9.49).

The IDAM tried to bring order to the chaos. The scientific secretary, Avi-Yonah, wrote to the Custodian for Absentees' Property in Jerusalem on 10 January 1949. He explained that the IDAM was responsible for antiquities and was trying to take care of antiquities shops, both damaged and undamaged. Kahane was made responsible for the matter, and Avi-Yonah asked for the Custodian's help (GL44875/9 no. 25). Nothing was done; the strange consequence, at least in one documented case, was a sale of antiquities by the Custodian. Yeivin mentioned this case when he wrote to the Custodian on 31 March 1949:

> Following my conversation yesterday with the secretary of your unit, Mr Reisel, I wish to ask you to remind all the branches of the unit, especially those that deal in the sale of deserted property, that nothing of the follow-ing categories is to be sold without the prior advice of the Antiquities Unit: antiquities, religious objects and works of art.
>
> To my regret, a sale of antiquities recently took place in your store at Herzl Hill. Mr [Haim] Reisel [Director of the Urban Property Unit in the office of the Custodian for Absentees' Property] assured me that steps will be taken to return the [objects] sold. I only ask that if legal measures are likely to ensue, nothing will be done without first consulting with us …
>
> (GL44880/4 no. 516)

On 8 May 1949 Reisel replied that, unfortunately, they could not retrieve the objects sold by mistake. If Yeivin intended to use his authority to get the objects back, the Custodian's office would be ready to refund the buyers. Reisel again passed the order not to sell antiquities without permission, and suggested that the value of the objects held by the Custodian should be estimated, and the objects should be delivered to the IDAM for safekeeping, "against an acquittal of budget under the treasury's approval" (GL44880/4 no. 698). Yeivin did not intend to use legal measures and Ory was sent to estimate the values of objects in three stores at Haifa, Tel Aviv and Jerusalem (GL44880/4, 19.5.49; no. 767 of 29.5.49).

In 1948–49, the Custodian sold whatever domestic property survived looting or was found after the war (Segev 1984: 85–7; Fischbach 2003: 27–8). The IDAM's reaction to the sale of antiquities, with its hint of legal proceedings, ensured good cooperation later between the IDAM and the Custodian. On 13 June 1950 the Minister for Education, the Custodian for Absentees' Property (Shafrir), his representative in Jerusalem (Avraham Engel) and Yeivin met (GL44882/2). At this time, the Custodian for Absentees' Property ruled a vast conglomerate of abandoned land, villages, pastures, orchards, urban quarters and quarries, which he tried to put to use by renting (Fischbach 2003: 28–40). At the meeting, Shafrir promised to supply data about any quarry or mine that he intended to rent, to ensure that they were not part of antiquities sites, and asked for maps with the location of all historical sites. Six copies of such maps were prepared for him.

Not long after that, the Custodian disappears from the files of the IDAM. His scope of activities became limited after he delivered one million *dunams* of land to the Jewish National Fund (JNF) (Keren Kayemet) in January 1949. In 1953, after legislation created the Developing Authority, he sold all the land and retained responsibility mostly over frozen bank accounts (Segev 1984: 92; Lehm 1988: 132–3; Golan 2001: 15–18; Katz 2002; Fischbach 2003: 54–7, 63; Sandberg 2002).

THE *SHATZ* (שא״ץ): ARCHAEOLOGICAL MILITARY SERVICE

One early suggestion for a way of dealing with the damage caused during the war was that a military unit of archaeological officers should be created to supervise and coordinate the guarding of sites and antiquities. The first written mention of this idea is in a handwritten letter by Yeivin of 8 August 1948 (GL44875/9, no. 5, letter to Yadin, Chief of Staff). He conceived the idea of using Friends of Antiquities as "contact officers", and suggested nominating Avraham Bergman as an archaeological officer at General Headquarters. In the meantime the army should issue orders because antiquities such as the Crusader tower in Zar'in (Jezreel) were still being ruined. Yeivin gave Yadin a draft of the orders and asked him to add to it that if antiquities were discovered, work should stop and the appropriate department should be notified. If work had to continue, the nearest archaeological contact officer or a civilian Friend of Antiquities should be informed. Yeivin also asked Yadin for a favour, which illustrates the situation at that time. He and Ben-Dor shared the management of two offices, in Tel Aviv and Jerusalem, requiring them to travel between the cities every fortnight. Yeivin consulted Ya'akov Pat, the Consul of Jerusalem, and as a result wrote to Yadin: "He thinks the only possibility is for you to issue us with a permanent pass allowing travel between the two cities" (GL44875/9 no. 6).

Additional pressure for an archaeological unit in the army came in a letter from Mazar to Yadin, Chief of Operations, dated 23 September 1948. Mazar suggested the formation of "an archaeological unit" under the cultural unit of the army, to be headed by a chief archaeological officer, with a deputy and a secretary, and located at General Headquarters. One archaeological officer would be nominated at each front, with more officers in the brigades and the engineering forces according to need. The roles of the unit would include: supervising remains, monuments and museums; preventing destruction and robbery; exploring the land archaeologically and historically; and checking chance finds related to military activity. The chief archaeological officer would be in constant contact with the IDAM. The archaeological officers would also lecture on the value of antiquities and issue guide books. Mazar suggested Adolf Reifenberg (a numismatist) for the position of chief archaeological officer and Abraham Malamat (later a professor at the Hebrew University) for his deputy (GL1342/20 no. 4).

On 25 September 1948, Yadin announced to Yeivin:

> In the next days a special unit of archaeological officers under the General Headquarters is going to be established, headed probably by B. Maisler [Mazar]. Its aims will be to handle problems of antiquities in occupied areas ruled by the IDF.   (GL1342/20 no. 49=1294)

Amiran commented on the proposed unit (GL1342/20, 3.10.48), calling it "archaeological military service" (*sherut archeologi zeva'i*), which was given the military acronym *Shatz*. Amiran suggested some nominations: Zecharia Kleinman (later Kallai; professor at the Hebrew University) and Trude Krakawer (later Dothan) to the centre front (Jerusalem–Ramla); Moshe Hammer (later Dothan) to the southern front; Nehemya Zimbalist (later Zori) to the northern front – Malamat spoke with him and he was ready to enlist; and finally Shineon Sharoni, currently "a private soldier in the region of Karkur", to the eastern front – Sharoni "does not know yet about our intentions, but my heart tells me he will rejoice" (GL44889/3).

On 5 December 1948 Ben-Dor met Yadin, who suggested that the cultural unit should start a widespread educational effort. Ben-Dor told him that would not be enough; a regular service was needed that would be able to issue and carry out orders. According to Ben-Dor, Yadin agreed and decided that the *Shatz* belonged with the engineer forces, who often stumbled into antiquities and were mostly well educated. Furthermore, they could help by making plans and performing temporary restoration. Yadin promised to discuss this idea with the commander of the engineering forces (GL1342/20 no. 3). Nothing came of this, and the last mention of the idea for the next few years was that, according to Lieutenant Colonel Shahar, the commander of the engineering forces, the formation of the *Shatz* was temporarily postponed (GL1342/20 no. 5, 20.1.49).

The issue resurfaced in relation to the 1956 (Sinai) War, in one of the most interesting letters written by Yeivin. It was sent to Avidor at the Ministry of Education, marked "urgent", "confidential" and "[delivery] by hand":

In continuing our conversation from this morning I enclose two copies of my letter to the Chief of Staff of 1 May 1956 and his answer of 27 June 1956 … The main point is in section B of my letter, discussing the establishment of a special military authority at General Headquarters for protecting sites and historical monuments, as well as collections, libraries, etc., throughout the country and mainly in areas that might be conquered in enemy countries.

You surely still remember what happened during the war of independence, how many difficulties and international scandals these events brought, and how badly the honour of Israel would have been smeared abroad, especially by circles that could have been of great help to the state … [reminding him of the Megiddo affair]. On damage and payments in other places I do not comment, since I did not handle them, but they happened [mentioning the Notre Dam monastery, the Dormition monastery and the Cunaculum building].

According to all one might think today, such acts might possibly reoccur, and in more force when the IDF enters Arab Jerusalem, Bethlehem, Hebron, etc. Who knows as well as you the number of ancient buildings, mosques, monasteries and private and public collections that are found in the areas that might be conquered, and the huge knowledge gained in them; and, on top of all that, there is the former Palestine Archaeological Museum, known to the public as the Rockefeller Museum. Incidentally, at least officially it is an international institute. Without any exaggeration I must say that my hair stands on end from fear [*somer*] when I think about what might happen in such places unless immediate steps are taken to treat the coming danger [literally "bad thing"].

During the war of independence at least one had the shabby excuse, in my view without justification, that it was difficult to foresee such things, especially with an army organized overnight in a state that had no military and political experience; but today even this poor excuse will be lacking. We know beforehand what might happen and we must, both for the actual subject and for keeping the good name of Israel unblemished, take all possible measures to prevent such damage. The air of tranquility of General Headquarters in this regard is especially worrying. I am certain that it is true that [quoting the Chief of Staff's letter] "The issue is, under orders from headquarters, relegated to the department of manpower, which has the authority and disciplinary means to handle it effectively. All the orders exist, and a section concerning this issue appears within other disciplinary issues in the orders of operations."

Practically, we know what little value such orders have in reality, and how little attention local commanders can give to such matters at times when they are occupied by military operations and are ordered first, with justice, to succeed in them. I need only note that despite severe orders not to damage historical sites during training, each year a few cases of minor and serious damage reoccur, for several reasons: lack of knowledge, lack of interest, slovenliness on purpose and inattention to orders. Finally, as long as there is no special body whose sole concern is to treat these matters, there is no guard and keeper who will see that the strict orders of the head-quarters are executed ...

I want to mention one more detail. In nearly all the armies of the cultural states during the Second World War there was a special body whose purpose was to look after cultural assets, especially in occupied territories. In most countries this body existed already in the days of the First World War. I know from my special experience about the existence of such a body in the German army during the First World War, called Denkmal Schutz Kommando [written in Hebrew letters], which achieved a great deal in saving and studying historical monuments in the areas of the former Ottoman Empire.

It seems that this matter is extremely urgent at the moment ...

(GL44880/13, 31.10.56)

But Yeivin's influence was declining; and the last time he raised the issue concerned UNESCO's 1954 Convention for the Protection of Cultural Property in the Event of Armed Conflict (Hague Convention). Yeivin referred to its implications for Israel in a letter to Avidor. In one section he referred to "the matter of the army":

It is not that simple. Dozens of orders from General Headquarters exist on paper. The orders are good and admirable and exact; but from years of personal experience I know that orders do not have the power to maintain effective implementation. Very many soldiers and officers ignore them, whether out of neglect or out of malice. As long as the IDF will not have a specific body, whose role is to supervise this matter, no orders will help ... I must draw your attention to section 7(2) of the [Hague] Convention, which says: "the honourable signers of the convention take it upon themselves to plan or prepare in times of peace, among their armed forces, services or bodies of professional employees, whose aim will be to assure an honourable treatment of cultural assets and cooperation with civilian authorities responsible for their preservation" (the translation is mine and I am not responsible for the accuracy of the terms common in Israeli law, but the content is clear). This sub-section must be seen together with sub-section 1, which speaks about educating the army to maintain the orders of the convention.

This is highly important for the cultural assets in our own state, but even more so if, as we all hope and expect, the arena of battle during an armed conflict is transferred outside the limits of the state ...

(GL44880/12 no. 3992, 22.3.57)

Although such catastrophes did not happen in 1967, one has to admire the moral position of Yeivin, who saw wars and conquests not as wishful dreams, but as nightmares. If the 1950s was the age of a ruthless national Israeli archaeology, Yeivin, the highest archaeological official in the land, was not a good example of it. This was not from lack of Zionist ideology; nor did he hold radical political views. It was because Yeivin was, first and foremost, a scholar of the humanistic profession of archaeology, as well as an official in the service of the state. His integrity permitted him to combine these two roles. An archaeological military service was formed in the West Bank and Gaza strip after their conquest in 1967, but this is beyond the scope of this book.

For quite a while the IDAM remained preoccupied with the war. It helped that Yadin, the son of Sukenik, was Chief of Operations; he was promoted to Chief of Staff in November 1949 (GL44880/17 no. 1257). In one incident, a soldier named Eli Rothschild discovered a mosaic at Selbit (Sha'alabim). He took photographs and even managed to read the Samaritan inscription, found in the courtyard of a house in the deserted Arab village (see Fig. 4). Rothschild notified Yadin on 3 August 1949 (GL44846/14, press announcement; 44875/9 no. 5). Rothschild was later asked to join the Friends of Antiquities (GL1342/18 no. 78).

The IDAM started to repair what it could. The first repairs, costing 300 Lira, were made in the Tiberias citadel (GL44864/14, 14.10.48), which the IDAM hoped to turn into a museum (GL44864/14, 21.11.48). At Safad, repairs were made to a Mamluk tomb (GL44864/14 no. 10; for Safad in 1948 see Abbasi 2003). In Ramla, the IDAM carried out salvage excavations in the court of the white mosque in cooperation with the Ministry of Religious Affairs and the military governor (GL44864/14 no. 11). It tried unsuccessfully to prevent pipes being placed through this site (GL44864/14 no. 790).

MILITARY CAMPS, STRONGHOLDS, PRACTICE GROUNDS

With the end of hostilities, more mundane problems of military camps, training areas and so on became dominant. The files contain quite an extensive correspondence about several ancient sites that the army occupied. Yeivin tried to prevent damage to them. The letters hold no military secrets: the names and locations of these sites and the fact that they served the army are well known. It is sufficient to describe a sample of them here.

Susita, on the border with Syria (east of the Sea of Galilee), was used as a defensive position. Yeivin managed to enforce some limits and to issue a salvage excavation under Amiran (44880/13). There were many problems: lack of transportation, misunderstandings and debates about financing. Negotiations about the excavation's scope, duration, transportation and so on involved senior IDF officers Haim Laskov, Meir Amit and even Itzhak Rabin (later Israel's prime minister; GL44880/13 nos. 5996, 6339, 6390). Yeivin had to explain to Rabin that archaeological work is done by hand so it takes time. He even stopped the dig and announced that he would not resume it. When the army wanted to plant trees "for camouflage as well as for all the other benefits", Yeivin retaliated:

> I am not especially an expert in security, and I do not know if such a grove will help the security of the location or not, but I know one thing for certain: this tree-planting will be the complete ruin of this entire site.
>
> (GL44880/13 no. 3901a)

Another site, Arsuf–Apollonia (Rishpon, north of Tel Aviv) was severely damaged and many efforts were made to protect it somehow. Yeivin stated in one letter that all the people in the neighbourhood were well aware of the military use of the site. He did not know and did not want to know anything about the camp, because he did not want to slip up and reveal something by mistake (GL44880/13 no. 3265, 17.7.50). The army did not honour its agreement with the IDAM not to damage the site; they fenced the ancient site and dumped earth on it (GL44880/13 no. 3791).

On 27 April 1953 Yeivin complained to the Minister of Education. He had called several times for attention to be paid to the occupation of ancient sites by the army, and now thought that a definite solution should be reached:

> The problem is becoming more and more acute. The Ministry of Defence occupies a large part of the historical site of Arsuf (Apollonia). I have tried to convince its representatives that the area does not fit their needs, but they refuse to hear. They promise that they will not damage the historical remains and that most of the site will remain open for visitors and scholars. I must emphasize my sorrow that these representatives of the Ministry of Defence have not kept their promises; they have damaged and ruined many remains, without even notifying the IDAM. They have enclosed the entire historical site in the military zone, which is forbidden to scholars and visitors … In addition, the entire area of Athlit was closed by orders of naval headquarters. There, too, there was damage, not to the site itself but to the property of the IDAM. As far as I know there are plans for this area too that may ruin

large parts of this important Crusader city ... There was a plan, later found not to be based on necessity, to close a significant part of the ancient site of Caesarea near the port; so far the IDAM has managed to postpone this plan, but it seems to me that in this case also we have not yet reached the end of the affair. And there are plans for closing more areas ...

On the other hand, a few buildings were erected on the ruins of Susita. I must state, though, that in this case it was done with the complete agreement of the IDAM and all our conditions were met; but this agreement was given not wholeheartedly but under the pressure of the circumstances. An entire book could be written about what happened in the Negev, and I must note that not everything is known to the IDAM because, owing to the special conditions in this part of the country, it is difficult to reach all the ancient sites ...

(GL44880/13 no. 1030a)

In May 1954 Yeivin wrote to the Chief of Staff, Dayan, about an air force firing range in the Negev, the area of which included the ruins of the ancient city of Halusa. Yeivin arranged a tour, which found that Halusa was not part of the range itself, but clarified that the range had already been active for more than a year: Halusa was saved by chance (GL44880/13 no. 3837a).

Yeivin also campaigned for the Crusader site of Athlit. He complained that the navy had confiscated and wasted the steel rails of a small train, formerly the property of the Mandatory Department of Antiquities (GL44880/13 nos. 3246, 5558, 29.4.51). The navy claimed innocence. The information came from the antiquities guard at Athlit, who later changed his story. The guard's reliability was questioned and further inquiries brought no results. In June 1952 some agreement was reached about plans for Athlit: the navy declared that the area around the Crusader fortress was to be closed for a limited time, and that it was ready to arrange visits of IDAM employees (GL44875/10 no. 9973; GL44880/13 no. 9063). Yeivin refused to agree to the final closing of Athlit to visitors (GL44880/13 no. 10184, 28.10.52). On 19 March 1953 he informed the Department of Governmental Lands that:

> Under no conditions will the IDAM agree to hand this area to any authority for development, unless the developing institute will first finance a full excavation of the whole area ... Only later, if no monumental remains that require conservation are found, will it be possible to give the area to the planners of the development to do as they please. (GL4480/13 no. 723a)

On 1 June 1954 Yeivin complained to Dayan that the road to the site was being blocked without a fixed schedule. Some visitors could enter, but others could not (GL44880/13 no. 4042a; cf. 1013a, 24.5.56). Thus, the IDAM could neither plan visits nor inform visitors that the area was closed. The "battle over

Athlit" ended when it was declared a closed area in April 1957 (GL44880/13 no. 5409, 9.6.60).

A final category to be discussed here is excavations. Often the army helped excavations (e.g. at Masada and the Judean Desert Survey). Yet in one case Jean Perrot, excavating Bir Abu-Matar in the Negev, was taken by surprise by army manoeuvres. Yeivin wrote to Dayan, complaining:

> After much training with rifle shots the unit moved to mortars, and as a target found no other place than a nearby historical site, known as Bir es-Safadi … First, the impact of shells and their explosion needlessly ruin and destroy this site. Secondly, many shells do not explode at all, yet the site is supposed to be excavated soon by the same team … Thirdly, the shock-waves resulting from the shooting and explosions have an impact on the present excavation of Mr Perrot. The buildings Mr Perrot exposed have been partly ruined by this and the sides of one fairly deep trench in the area have caved in and collapsed. Only by some miracle were no workers in the trench then … I ask you to take the necessary steps required to stop training that targets historical sites, or even in the proximity of archaeological excavation areas … (GL44881/19, 29.12.53)

INDEPENDENCE WAR MEMORIALS

Because of its history Israel is home to many memorials to those fallen in war. Antiquities came to be involved even with that aspect of the 1948 War. In May 1949, Ben-Dor saw a newspaper report that an ancient pillar from Caesarea had been used as a memorial at Zemah (south of the Sea of Galilee). "This is a serious injury for antiquities", he wrote to the Unit for the Commemoration of Fallen Soldiers at the Ministry of Defence. He also heard a rumour about plans to set a memorial (*massebah*, "standing stone") on ancient Susita. It would destroy remains and the ability to excavate the area. Ben-Dor requested that ancient pillars not be used for memorials and that the IDAM should be consulted about their location (GL44875/9 no. 660, 19.5.49).

THE 1956 WAR

The 1956 War was planned in advance (Bar-On 1991, 1994; Golani 1998). A governmental committee was set up before the war to discuss emergency security measures. The IDAM was asked to participate and Yeivin prepared a list of places that required protection. He attached calculations of the sums needed for the building works and for the materials required. Some of the preparations would need to be made in advance. His list included sites owned by the government and by Jewish authorities. The property of foreign institutions was not included in the calculation of expenses: he thought they must take care of their own properties. He wanted to know whether the government would reimburse the expenses for all the works, including those sites under the jurisdiction of local authorities or in private hands.

For the IDAM, a shelter would be needed to safeguard finds and employees, and boxes for packing objects would need to be prepared. Collections of art and antiquities in the museums were considered next. Yeivin attached a list of museums of antiquities, and of the most important finds in the exhibition of the IDAM. The final sum he came up with was considerable. He asked:

> Can you notify me as early as possible who will finance this expense and out of which budget, so that we can immediately start securing the essential [collections]? Preparations in the IDAM have already started, but we need to acquire the necessary boxes immediately; this alone comes to *c.* 3,500 Lira. The department has not one penny for these acts in its regular budget; and from nowhere else can it save such a sum ...
>
> (GL44880/13 no. 957, 14.5.56)

Yeivin took it very seriously and attached five lists of various places or antiquities for protection. However, the 1956 War did not cause damage in Israel because its battles were fought in Sinai. Yeivin remembered later:

> I do not think that it will be possible to be once again in the ridiculous position of helplessness that we found ourselves in on the eve of the Kadesh operation [1956 War]. Then orders were given to secure certain assets, including cultural assets, but immediately we found that nothing could be done because no budget was given for that purpose, and no preparations were made in advance for such a case. Thank God that such special precautions were not needed. (GL44880/12 no. 3992, 22.3.57)

2 ABANDONED PLACES, NEW PLACES

When weapons operate muses are silenced, but not excavators ... From ruins,
broken vessels and crumbs of the past that disappeared you draw the eternal
spirit of man.
> Minister of Labour Mordechai Ben-Tov (*BIES* **15** (1949/50): 55)

Two years, ten years, and passengers ask the conductor:
What place is this?
Where are we now?
I am the grass.
Let me work   Carl Sandburg ("Grass", 1918)

The war left hundreds of abandoned places in its wake. The huge wave of immigration in 1948–52 resulted in extensive development of new places. This chapter discusses how these affected budding Israeli archaeology.

ABANDONED PLACES

The reasons why so many Palestinian Arabs left during the 1948 War have been the subject of heated debate in recent years among historians and "new historians" (Morris 1987, 1994: 1–18; Bligh 1998: 123–4; Karmi & Cotran 1999; Gelber 2004). The facts are not disputed. Plan "D" of the Hagana (the organization that preceded the Israeli army) from February 1948, formulated by Yadin, among others, aimed to conquer enemy bases (i.e. villages), destroy them and deport the residents. However, it aimed at a limited number of what were considered to be military targets (Morris 1987: 61–3; Benvenisti 2000: 108–10; Golan 2001: 204; Tovi 2002: 18). Shortly after the event, major Israeli leaders of the period spoke of the departure of the Arabs as an unexpected miracle (Fischbach 2003: 7–8). Thus there was no general intention of, or plan for, ethnic cleansing, although this did happen in a few cases late in the war (e.g. Majdal/Ashkelon; see Segev 1984: 68–9; Morris 1994: 323–48; Benvenisti 2000: 124–7). There was no need for such a plan: fear of war and the (relatively few) atrocities performed by both sides were strong enough reasons for the Palestinian Arabs to leave.

In the Ottoman period conquerors had come and gone, and the local population had always been able to return after escaping. The decision made by Israel not to allow refugees to return is at the core of the Israeli–Palestinian conflict (Morris 1987; 1993; Gelber 2004; Porath 2004). It was reached gradually. One of its first expressions was endorsed by a committee of the JNF (Lehm 1988) headed by Yosef Weitz, Ezra Danin and Eliyahu Sasson in spring 1948. They suggested that refugees should be prevented from returning and that 90 new settlements should be established in abandoned villages, the remaining villages having been destroyed (Segev 1984: 98–9; Morris 1993: 133–5; 1994: 103–53; Golan 2001: 209; Fischbach 2003: 7–8). At this stage Ben-Gurion wavered, and the final decision was postponed until June 1948 and the next few months (Morris 1987: 132–3; Benvenisti 2000: 150–52; Golan 2001: 15, 206–9).

The refugees deserted 360–430 villages (see Fig. 6); the estimate varies because of different definitions of what constitutes a village (Golan 2001: 12; Fischbach 2003: 3–4). Most of these villages remained whole and untouched by war. Today almost all are destroyed; for some there are no traces except for a change in the spread of vegetation. Some traces or buildings remain from 52 villages, especially in the Tel Aviv area (Benvenisti 2000: 131–42; 169–70; Morris 1987: 155–6). According to Weitz, Danin and Sasson, 180 villages were deserted up to June 1948. Most of these were small rural villages, but there were also urban quarters and cities, such as Accho, Ramla, Lod, Beersheba, Safad, Ashkelon and Jaffa. With the fresh memories of the 1948 War, and with the arrival of a million

Figure 6. Abandoned village of Khartiyeh, November 1948. Mud houses with tools. (Photograph by Ory, IAA 143)

newcomers in a few years, Israel felt no warmth towards the abandoned places. The abandoned villages were silent reminders that the country had not been empty before the war, which was a cause of embarrassment and even fear; they contradicted the common ideology of return to an empty land. As for the cities, the aesthetic potential was not understood; the living had their claims, and life was very hard for them. Many reached the brink of starvation under the *zena* (food rationing) economic regime of 1949–52, and children suffered malnutrition and health hazards (Segev 1984: 280–305; Rosin 2002: 68–131).

Newcomers and demobilized soldiers required housing. Almost all the newcomers were themselves refugees of the holocaust from war-torn Europe or from Arab countries (Shulewitz 1999). They had few financial resources. During 1948–49, deserted houses in or near existing cities were occupied. It was a very chaotic process: sometimes those who came first took the accommodation and sometimes those who had power or connections (Segev 1984: 89–90; Fischbach 2003: 9–11). The authorities hesitated when faced with *polshim* (intruders) in abandoned flats. Later, abandoned houses were allocated in order and also improved for the new residents. Thus officials were housed in luxury flats at Talbiyeh and newcomers were placed in the not so affluent Musrara, two areas of Jerusalem (Segev 1984: 91 n.). The availability of large numbers of abandoned undemolished houses in some towns was a considerable economic benefit (Golan 2001, 2003).

Late in 1950 Ben-Gurion addressed the issue at the IES conference:

> We do not comply with the fate of our land, even the part in our control. Foreign conquerors have made our land a desert; waste is large and extensive parts became unsettled. The war of independence enlarged the waste. And we must know: it will not be so under Israel's rule. We will not keep the Negev plains and coastal sands and bare mountains for long. Maintaining our independence forces us to build ruins, to re-erect waste, to settle abandoned areas and populate them in the nearest possible time.
>
> (*BIES* **15** (1949/50): 120)

In the countryside, some abandoned villages were resettled in late 1948. Between May 1948 and June 1949, 26 Israeli settlements occupied the locations of former villages (Segev 1984: 98–9; Morris 1987: 179–88; Fischbach 2003: 72–3, 103); two villages in western Galilee were later used to settle Arab refugees (Bligh 1998: 136). Meanwhile it was found that establishing a new settlement was often more effective than improving a deserted village. The densely built remains did not fit the architectonic ideals of most Israeli planners of that period (Golan 2001: 245), so most of the villages were left abandoned.

To the acts of war was added the demolition of abandoned houses and quarters by bulldozers and explosives. The first documented act of demolition (apart from military acts related to the war) included 8–12 villages demolished before July 1948 with JNF funding on the initiative of Weitz. Scholars give different data for the cost of this operation: 1500 or 5000 Lira (Morris 1987: 137–8, 161–2; Fischbach 2003: 12–15). There were more demolitions in June–July 1949, ironically as a result of the truce talks that started in April 1949. In May 1949, Zalman Lif (Lifshitz), a representative at the talks and a member of Weitz's "transfer committee", prepared a list of 40 villages, suggesting ruining all their clay-constructed houses and levelling the ruins in order to prevent the return of refugees. In June the Department of Public Works started to destroy 41 villages in the south and the Jerusalem corridor; the action continued into early 1950 (Segev 1984: 98–9; Morris 1987: 159–63; Golan 2001: 209–11, 243–5). At this stage, the IDAM was still affiliated with the Department of Public Works, responsible for the demolition. However, State of Israel Archive (Ginzach Leumi) (GL) documents studied here do not reveal an awareness of this operation.

Demolition by the army started in April–May 1948, mostly for military purposes (Segev 1984: 99 n.; Morris 1987: 112, 158–9; Golan 2001: 211–12, 244–5). Gradually, demolition became widespread, performed for all kinds of reasons. For example, the IDF blew up abandoned houses as part of explosives training (GL44875/9 no. 16, 9.11.49). Training with abandoned houses as targets became common, and at times historical monuments served the same purpose. Thus one commander used Kh. Miniah, an Ommayad palace not far from Kefar Nahum, as a shooting range (*Masa* newspaper, 2.12.53). Yeivin said that the damage was small (GL44875/10, 9.12.53). Sometimes local municipalities took the initiative to rid themselves of what they saw as houses in danger of collapse, or unfit for development and falling short of sanitary requirements. There was some political objection to the destruction of villages in 1948–50 (Morris 1987: 159–63). Settlement organizations had reservations too, but only when the destruction seemed to hamper plans for new settlements (Morris 1987: 163–9; Golan 2001: 244–6).

Yehezkel Sahar, the first Chief of the Israel Police, took credit for an operation that demolished 50 villages. He did not mention an exact date, but discussed the affair shortly before the events of 1952. Infiltrators (*mistanenim*) were allegedly using abandoned villages near the borders for shelter. The infiltrators were mostly refugees who cared for their abandoned property, or wanted to find some work or products in abandoned fields and orchards; but some came to kill (Segev 1984: 66–8; Morris 1993; Benvenisti 2000: 217–22). Israel regarded infiltration as opposition to the "sacred" sovereignty of the state over its land. Sahar wrote:

> When I learned the situation and received a list of about 50 villages, I approached the Minister of Labour, Golda Meir, asking that she order the Department of Public Works, under her disposal, to destroy these houses. My request was fulfilled and this considerably eased our war on the infiltrators. (Sahar 1992: 98)

Later, tourists started to ask questions about deserted villages. To solve this problem demolition continued, and more general operations were carried out in 1965–67 by the JNF and after 1967 by the army near Latroun and in the Golan Heights (thus Masalha 1999; Shai 2002).

The official position was that there was no demolition after the 1948 War, only demolition in legitimate military acts during the war. This was part of the myth of "the empty land", a land that was or became desolate by itself. For example:

> The war of independence brought ruin and destruction on hundreds of settlements, and when the state came into being there stood only the Jewish villages established in the last seventy years and a few which were not Jewish. The truth is that the state inherited a wasted and deserted land.
>
> (Ben-Gurion 1952: 15)

FACELESS ABSENTEES

To most Israelis the absentees were a faceless group (similar, though to a lesser degree, to the way veterans saw newcomers: Segev 1984: 155). This was true also for the IDAM, despite the fact that many of its first employees came from the ethnically mixed (not really integrated) Mandatory Department of Antiquities. Some absentees were mentioned in reports just by name, for example in relation to abandoned collections.

One absentee occupied a more prominent place, although fleeting and cold, in the files of the IDAM. This was Na'im Makhouli, the former Inspector of Antiquities of Galilee. On 28 January 1949 Yeivin wrote to Major Elisha Soltz, the military governor of eastern Galilee at Nazareth. He had heard that some of Makhouli's family members were still in Nazareth, and as far as he knew they held files from Makhouli's office, and a few other articles of government property. Yeivin asked Soltz to investigate, and deliver this material, if found, to Amiran, the supervisor of the northern district (GL1340/9 no. 302). However, Ben-Dor read this letter and wrote to Yeivin on 31 January 1949 that he had "very important reasons" against seizing the property, which "I will offer to you verbally". He asked Yeivin to tell Soltz to cancel the investigation (GL1340/9). Yeivin agreed and Ben-Dor sent Amiran an urgent telegram requesting her to postpone action (GL1340/9, 31.1.49). Amiran complied, and on 10 February 1949 reported: "Mr Makhouli is known as an absentee [ne'edar] and if he asks to come back to Nazareth his request will be carefully considered" (GL1340/9). This was still a period of uncertainty, when people were not yet sure whether refugees would return; later, only immediate family members were allowed to be reunited.

In 1950, S. Makhouli asked for his cousin Na'im to be allowed to return. Apparently Yeivin was asked to give his opinion about the request, but he declined to recommend agreeing to it. He informed the administrative manager at the Ministry of Finance that "as far as the IDAM is aware, Mr Makhouli left his home town of Nazareth and went out to Lebanon during the rule of the bandits of Qawukji [the leader of the Arab Liberation Army] in Nazareth and its vicinity; his fate [*dino*] is surely like that of all the Arab refugees, who left the country of their own free will, before the state of Israel was established" (GL44880/13 no. 2380). The IDAM, he wrote, was not very interested in returning him to his post. Yeivin hinted that "you would surely know what answer to give to S to his request about his cousin" (GL44880/13 no. 2380): that is, find some excuse. Why prevent the return of Makhouli? Apart from the reasons given above, a clue comes from the fact that the letter was sent to the Ministry of Finance. Presumably Makhouli, if allowed to return, would continue at his former post, following the rule of continuation in government bodies, but that position was now occupied by Amiran.

In other cases Yeivin showed sensitivity to the Arab minority in Israel (GL44880/13 no. 1903, 16.12.49). He wrote to Walter Eytan, the Director-General of the Ministry of Foreign Affairs, who later published accounts of events relating to Israel's foreign policy (Eytan 1958), recounting a conversation he had with Professor Grégoire (probably Henri Grégoire, scholar of Byzantine culture at Brussels University) and his secretary (GL44880/13 no. 4493, 17.1.51). Yeivin had defended the official position on refugees: that they had left for no reason, since those that stayed were not harmed; that they were not pressured or deported, but left before the Israeli conquest; and that some were allowed to return (although Yeivin added to their number a group that had stayed in Israel's territory). Yeivin's letter was termed private and confidential. He was under no obligation to report such a conversation, but he explained that the foreign scholar was a friend of Israel and an important person, so perhaps the Ministry of Foreign Affairs wanted to continue the discussion with him. There is something of a desire to impress, to prove efficiency, here; but Yeivin seemed to be disturbed that he had not convinced his guests.

In August 1951 the IDAM discovered various files from Makhouli's archives in the Prime Minister's Office (forerunner of the State of Israel Archive). How the files reached there was not explained (GL44875/9 no. 6368). Surprisingly, Makhouli wrote at least four long letters to Ben-Dor in late 1951, pleading for help from his former colleagues:

> My dear Dr Ben-Dor
> A very long time has passed since we heard from each other or knew each other's whereabouts. Thanks to Mr [Gedric Norman] Johns [Assistant to the Director of the Department of Antiquities of Palestine, 1945–48] who only

recently told me of your present post as Assistant Director of Antiquities and your exact address, which, I notice, does not appear much changed except for rubbing out "Palestine" and replacing it with ISRAEL. Hearty congratulations for everything!

I spent more than three years in an adjacent territory to the north of you. All that time, my condition was miserable and lamentable, [I was] racking my brains in order to devise some way to relieve my small children and my wife, who is always very anxious and longing to see and be near her very elderly parents ... but in vain.

Mr Johns was in Maresh as the last appointed Controller of Antiquities for Tripolitania and Cyrenaica in N. Africa. Having heard of my dreadful financial condition he at once started working hard with the Govt. of Cyrenaica to appoint me to the post of Surveyor of Antiquities ... I accepted the offer as a temporary remedy and joined him about 2½ months ago.

Can you now, my dear doctor, imagine what kind of life I have to live here? Let me tell you that I was stationed at a village known locally as "Shahat"; its ancient name is Cyrene. For about a thousand years in the Greco-Roman period [it] was the capital of the whole country, yet it is now a very poor and small village. About half of its 2,000 souls [population] currently take refuge in the rock-cut burial chambers ... In this poor place at present, rich in the past, I have nobody to talk to, so I spend my time in work, study and food preparation ...

So you find that under the present circumstances I am compelled to be separated from all members of my family and live an isolated existence. Is it not sad for a peaceful man like me, who attained the age of 54 years, to suffer deeply with his innocent children and wife and be sacrificed for the fault of others on the altar of ignorance and fanaticism? Do not you feel it? Are you not in sympathy with me?

My colleagues in Israel, who are at the same time my best friends, are numerous. They are, with you as the first: Prof. L. Mayer, Prof. Sukenik, P. L. O. Guy, Dr Meisler, Mr Avi-Yonah, Mr Ory, Dr Steglits [*sic.*] and Mrs Simon. If you all join together and try with good faith to save me from my present troubles and sad condition I believe you will succeed.

I was very glad to know from Mr Johns that the young Sukenik (now called Yadin) is the Commander in Chief of the Israeli army. If invited, I believe, to join you and others in helping me, he would not hesitate ...

I am sorry to have been worrying you so much, and ask your forgiveness for that.

In any case I should be glad to hear from you ...

Yours sincerely [signed] Na'im Makhouli

(GL44880/19, handwritten, 18.9.51)

Ben-Dor replied that it was a pleasant surprise to hear that Makhouli was "in good health and working". He mentioned that they had hard times in Jerusalem during the siege "with water rationing and bombs exploding on houses and in the streets. A few of my best friends were killed." He gave some archaeological news and mentioned that Hamilton was a professor at Cambridge and Iliffe excavated in Cyprus. He promised to pass on Makhouli's request to the higher authorities, who make the decisions (GL44880/9 no. 6758, 3.10.51). Makhouli wrote again on 23 October 1951. He expressed interest in some excavations and asked if the Roman theatre at Beisan (Beth Shean) was being excavated. He asked Ben-Dor to mediate with the higher authorities, with which he was already in contact. He added:

> The trouble is that they like to include me in the general question of a solution for refugees, while I pray to have my case considered separately …
>
> May I ask you to do me another favour? If you happen to pass Nazareth, would you kindly call on my very elderly father- and mother-in-law (Mr and Mrs Costandi Kanage) who live in the house with a red-tiled roof, by the road to Tiberias, and next to the house where I used to live, and enquire into their condition and let me have their news …?
>
> (GL44880/19, 23.10.51)

Ben-Dor answered briefly: Beisan was not being excavated and he didn't know how the petition for return stood. He asked for a copy of the petition and promised to use it to investigate. He promised to visit Makhouli's parents if he happened to be near Nazareth. In the meanwhile, he passed this request on to "one of the inspectors in the northern area" (in fact there was only one: Amiran) (GL44880/19 no. 7023).

Makhouli wrote again from Benghazi on 3 November 1951 (wrongly dated 3 October 1951). He was doing "some clearance work" at Berenice. He asked again about various excavations and particularly the Roman theatre at Beisan: "I wish I could join your department in Israel and put myself at your disposal for doing the clearance work there." He reminded Ben-Dor that he badly needed help, asking Ben-Dor to see the official from the Visa Sector of the Immigration Department responsible for his case (GL44880/19). Yeivin read this letter (he initialled it), so presumably Ben-Dor consulted him. The last letter by Makhouli was written on 23 December 1951:

> I enclose herewith a copy of the latest reply I have received from the Immigration Department, Visa Sector, signed Jacob Giller … They want to let my case hang until there is a general solution to the problem of refugees. But I wish they could do me a favour and consider it separately, partly on humanitarian grounds and partly because of the circumstances that

compelled me to leave my house. The longer I have to stay outside, the more miserable our life becomes, especially for my wife, who left her parents who are advanced in age and have no other children to look after them.

The second copy I enclose herewith is addressed to the Custodian for Absentees' Property in Israel and explains clearly the circumstances that made my wife and I leave our home. I hope, after consulting the Immigration Department about my case, you will be able to take the matter up with the high authorities, endeavouring to do your best to help me secure permission to return home legally with my wife and my daughter. I wish it would be possible for you to visit Nazareth soon and call, on your way, on my wife's parents … My father-in-law had a higher education in Russia, so you will be able to talk to him in Russian.

I worry constantly about the future of my children and the life of misery that I am going to live with my wife if my case is not solved very soon. So any help you can offer me in solving the problem will be highly appreciated … (GL44880/19)

The letter to the Custodian for Absentees' Property, dated 18 December 1951, carried the title: "Issue of a Non-Absentee Certificate". Makhouli explained that he and his wife were compelled to leave Nazareth on 11 May 1948 for Lebanon. He asked for a visa on the grounds that:

A Fear that the local Arab Committee organized early in 1948 at Nazareth would cause me harm. In the beginning of May 1948, one of the committee members, Amin Salem, requested me to pay an immediate instalment of 5 Palestine pounds for the use of the committee. As I refused his request, he became violent and threatened me that if I would not pay he would force me to pay or otherwise I would have to leave Nazareth … [detailing two eye witnesses who are still living in Nazareth and can be asked to give testimonials].

B My three children aged 17, 15 and 12 years were attending American schools in Lebanon during the scholastic year 1947/48, and in addition the fear that my wife and I might come to harm through the action of the Arab Local Committee, I was naturally anxious to be near my children, as they were too small to look after themselves should I not be in a position to communicate with them, and I did not want them to interrupt their studies. Should you desire it I can obtain at any time from the American school authorities certificates corroborating my statement.

In general, I must honestly declare that at no time have I interfered in political life or activities, and have always only lived for my work in the Antiquities Department and my family, as well-known persons like Prof. L.

Mayer, Dr I. Ben-Dor, Prof. Sukenik and Dr Meisler [Mazar] can confirm
at any time ...   (GL44880/19)

Makhouli attached a copy of the answer from Jacob Giller, then Director of
the Visa Department of the Ministry of the Interior:

Sir,
We acknowledge receipt of your letter no. ___ regarding your request for
permanent residence or a traveller's visa to Israel and regret to inform you
that your request cannot be granted. As stated in our previous correspondence, your request may be considered when a solution has been found to
the question of the return of refugees in general.
                                                         (GL44880/19, 28.9.51)

On 22 November 1952 Ben-Dor wrote Makhouli the last letter found in the
file. He thanked him for sending a guide book on Tripolitania and added that
he had applied to the Immigration Department, but:

Unfortunately, nothing can be done at present, since the whole question is
"sub judice" and awaits its final solution. It is a shame that you are unable to
return to your house and we are unable to have access, even for one hour,
to the material in the Rockefeller Museum. I have not yet been to Nazareth,
but on my first visit there I will certainly call on your parents and transmit
them your salaams.   (GL44880/19)

Ben-Dor tried to equate Makhouli's situation to his lack of access to Rockefeller "for an hour". Whether Makhouli was truthful about his reasons for
leaving is not the issue; nor should we criticize Ben-Dor, who was a consider-
ate human being. Israelis do not have many opportunities to read such letters,
which give the first-hand testimony of an "absentee". Of course, Makhouli,
who found work in his former profession and could communicate in English
with the IDAM, was not a typical "absentee"; the fate of most "absentees" is
hidden by a wall of silence.

Most refugees were no doubt innocent individuals, but as a group they
were part of a struggle between two emerging peoples. The situation would
probably have been similar for Israelis if the Palestinians had been the victors
in the war. From Makhouli's letters I draw a human, rather than a political conclusion. Let these letters be a warning to all of us who think we are
secure in our life and our work. There is no security; we are all potential
"absentees".

THE POLICY OF THE IDAM TOWARDS ABANDONED PLACES

The IDAM under Yeivin was one of very few Israeli bodies that tried to prevent wholesale demolition of deserted villages and quarters. It did not do so from concern for the refugees, nor from lack of Zionist ideology, but from a professional archaeological viewpoint. Very early on Yeivin reached the conclusion that acts of demolition were spreading; they were not limited just to actions of war and had no concern for antiquities and sites. Yeivin wrote to the Minister of Public Works as early as 16 September 1948:

> *Urgent*
> In recent times, cases of blasting houses and whole neighbourhoods in the cities and villages by the IDF and by local municipalities have proliferated. Whether such acts are aimed at improving the cities, widening roads or are acts of punishment, one must stress that they are, in most cases, done without any concern for historical monuments and important architectural remains, and without consulting with the bodies authorized to protect them, such as the IDAM and the Planning Department. I will detail only two cases, typical out of a whole line of other cases.
> 1. An ancient three-thousand-year-old relief that depicts two lions (probably Hittite) was blasted to pieces last week (data given by chief supervisor Y. Pinkerfeld, who visited Tiberias in an explicit mission to save this relief).
> 2. In Caesarea, the major second temple period port, the army blows up various buildings without consideration for the ancient remains found everywhere there (data given to me this morning by our representative at Hadera, the Friend of Antiquities Dr Rosenbusch).
> Our applications to the army in private meetings have brought no results so far. Therefore, we ask that immediate steps are taken by headquarters, the engineering branch of the army and the municipalities, to ask them to inform the Department of Public Works before any act of destruction or blasting; so that our representatives can visit the place and mark the buildings or area that must be preserved for historic, archaeological or architectonic reasons.   (GL44875/9 no. 29; cf. GL44875/9 no. 6, 24.9.48)

On 9 November 1949, Ben-Dor wrote to the naval headquarters at Stela Maris, Haifa:

> We have discovered that a group of soldiers under your command is blowing up deserted houses on exercises. We are concerned about ancient buildings that have historical value, and are under our supervision. We therefore ask you to give orders not to blow up ancient buildings … At your request our

representative will come and mark the relevant buildings with appropriate signs. The intention is especially for the well-known historical places such as Accho, Caesarea, Tantura (Dor), but sometimes one also finds historical houses worthy of care in less well-known places.   (GL44875/9 no. 7)

At first the IDAM acted piecemeal to "put out fires". Very often it was too weak to make an impact, and the chronic shortage of supervisors meant that it did not have information about planned demolitions. Often it just faced the ruins of an accomplished fact.

Caesarea

There was a sad, if not strange, case of damage at Caesarea, with the blowing up of "the old bridge of the Caesarea aqueduct" by the army during a flood. It was briefly mentioned in reports for February and March 1949 (GL44864/14 nos. 4, 11). The Ministry of Defence refused to repair the aqueduct, which was demolished at the request of the Palestinian Jewish Colonization Association (PJCA). The opinion of the manager of the water company (later Mekorot) was that the aqueduct did not need to be blown up at all, and the IDAM tried to arrange for it to be reinstated through the PJCA (GL44864/14 no. 713a).

Tiberias

Tiberias was a "mixed" city, but during the war the Arabs fled despite promises made by the Hebrew authorities that they would not be hurt. At the same time, some Jews also fled the old city. The buildings of old Tiberias stood empty for about four months and suffered looting. Then Yosef Nahmani (the right-hand man of Yosef Weitz, Director of the JNF) and Moshe Weiss, Deputy Mayor of Tiberias, tried to bring about the destruction of the old city. Mysterious fires broke out, allegedly started by hooligans; and the Golani Brigade also wanted to cut wide roads through the city. The army started to destroy it in August 1948, with the support of Yadin (Segev 1984: 99 n.). Rows of houses were blown up using explosives. Residents protested to Ben-Gurion, who ordered the cessation of the operation. A government committee recommended destroying houses in dangerous condition and the houses of Arabs in general. Yadin favoured this as a means of preventing refugees from returning. So in February 1949 the army, with a lot of enthusiasm, resumed the destruction of Tiberias. In all, 477 (some say 624) houses out of a total of about 670 were destroyed. About 55 percent belonged to Jewish residents. The (by now mostly Jewish) residents were evacuated, despite protests that failed to stop the destruction. Ben-Gurion visited Tiberias in March

1949 and was shocked. When he asked that those responsible be found, he was shown a document in which the operation was agreed between the army and … himself. He said that he did not remember agreeing to this. One of the possible reasons for the destruction of Tiberias was that it could be considered an act of war, allegedly carried out for military reasons. In that case the government did not have to compensate owners for the houses and their content, but only for the land. But the ground in Tiberias was found to be full of archaeological remains and was unstable for large buildings (with the techniques current at that time). The area remained desolate until the 1970s (Paz 1998: 97–106; cf. also Golan 2001: 161–6).

Jaffa

Jaffa (Fig. 7) fared only slightly better after its Arab residents abandoned it. The IDAM made visits to the old city and documented it. Some buildings collapsed, starting in winter 1949. The Planning Department blamed the lack of maintenance, since the new Israeli residents were not familiar with such houses and did not know how to maintain their roofs. The collapses were certainly not planned; people died or were injured by them. However, the solid traditional construction would not fail in a few years of neglect. Nor would the use of modern materials (like cement) cause collapse in such a short period. Either

Figure 7. Jaffa, old city, November 1948. Excavations by Guy. (IAA 15220)

someone was "helping" a natural process of decay (e.g. by breaking into houses and stealing stones) or houses were already badly shaken by former explosions. The Tel Aviv municipality and the Custodian for Absentees' Property wanted to destroy the city, and use the area for modern buildings. Tel Aviv did not want Jaffa as a competing city; and perhaps there were fears of the return of refugees (Jaffa was strategically located on the coast). The British authorities destroyed houses in Jaffa in 1936 for security reasons, so why shouldn't Israel? Yeivin was one of the first, on 19 September 1949, to protest against the plans to destroy Jaffa. Large parts of it had been reduced to ruins in summer 1949. Protest from residents, including artists such as Marsel Yanco, managed to save some parts. Destruction slowed down between November 1949 and April 1950. However, on 16 April 1950 a building collapsed and 18 people died. A committee under Ya'akov Kosilov, manager of the Administration Department of the Ministry of the Interior was formed, and in August 1950 it recommended that most residents should be evacuated and the houses destroyed. One enclave on the slope above the port was listed for preservation in an appendix of a committee report from May 1951. Only the desperate efforts of Eliezer Brutzkus from the Planning Department, with the help of Yeivin, coupled with protests by architects and artists, managed to raise a second committee under Kosilov (with the participation of the IDAM). It recommended preserving some parts of Jaffa. In 1948 some 185,000 people lived in Tel Aviv; by 1953 there were 350,000. They included 120,000 inhabitants of Jaffa, nearby abandoned villages and southern Tel Aviv, which became areas of low status. This was a direct result of the chaos of evacuation, destruction and resettlement (*Alon Makleket Ha'atiqot* (*Alon*) **3** (1951): 4; Segev 1984: 88–90; Paz 1998: 106–22; Golan 2001: 75–133).

Paz (1998: 131 n.87) suspected that Yeivin was not averse to the destruction of some (more recent) buildings, which left open areas that could be excavated. This is unlikely to be true; in 1948 there was no shortage of major sites for excavation, so Yeivin had more than enough to choose from. Moreover, even in Jaffa there were available sites, and Guy started to excavate there in 1948. Yeivin condemned the destruction of houses marked for restoration in Jaffa. He blamed the Tel Aviv municipality for this "transgression" and even considered, and rejected, taking legal action (GL44889/2 no. 4465, 11.1.51; cf. GL44882/9, 31.3.56, 18.4.57). The parts of Jaffa that survived were restored gradually over many years.

Accho

The Mandatory government planned to restore Accho, but no funds were available. The city remained nearly whole during the war. About a third of the Arab population stayed. The new (Israeli) municipality wanted to unite the city, build new roads and develop it as a modern city. Yeivin was the first to warn against these plans, writing to the Minister of Education on 9 September 1949. He pressed for the establishment of an "interdepartmental committee" to handle the problem of "old cities". In any case, he wrote, there were many ancient monuments in Accho and elsewhere that the IDAM must preserve, which required additional budgets (GL44875/9 no. 955).

Yeivin was asked by the Prime Minister's Office to prepare a memorandum on the state's antiquities as tourist attractions, and he sent it on 18 December 1949:

> An initial problem is what to do with "ancient" cities. Can they be "frozen" as they are now, with all their "Eastern" form and exotic appeal, or should one try to develop them as modern centres of settlement by saving and restoring [only] some special monuments? First and foremost is the question of Accho; I attach a copy of a memorandum I sent at the time to the Minister of Education and Culture (a copy was also sent then to the Prime Minister's Office), but Mr Zalman Shazar [Minister of Education] could not handle it because of his illness.
>
> It is not the question of Accho alone. On a smaller scale it is also the question of the old city (al-Qal'ah) in Jaffa, the old Jewish quarter in Safad, a large part of the old city of Tiberias (mostly demolished before the government had the chance to decide a general policy for these problems), Migdal Gad [Ashkelon] and more. There are also some deserted villages that are very interesting in this regard, such as 'Iqrit in northern Galilee.
>
> One must understand that it is not only a question of "freezing" the situation. It is impossible to maintain empty buildings. If one puts people to live in them, changes must be made to fit them to modern use. If people are taken out, the buildings must be filled with new content: turn them into museums, libraries, cultural collections and places of scientific or cultural conferences. Of course, money is needed for this, in very considerable sums. There are also buildings that in the meantime other ministries occupied for unsuitable purposes. A notable example is the fortress (former jail) in Accho. Without consulting anybody or asking permission from anyone, the Ministry of Health occupied the building and turned it into an asylum [which remained for many years]. It is impossible now to bring any tourist to this building, which has plenty of Crusader parts (especially underground). I myself in my last visit had to wait about half an hour until I could visit it, because when I came the patients were in the courtyard and "were not calm", as one doctor there said. I was therefore forced to wait until the courtyard was evacuated. All this needs radical change.
>
> (GL44875/9)

Rural villages

Little is known about the destruction of rural villages since 1948. Golan (2001: 201–46) and Fischbach (2003) reviewed the takeover of lands, but not the destruction of villages. Most documents are not available for study (cf. Benvenisti 2000: 167–72). The IDAM files do not give a general picture, since most villages were destroyed without the knowledge of the IDAM.

According to Benvenisti (2000: Fig. 16), only 40 of 160 mosques in the villages survived to some extent. The JNF (Lehm 1988: 96–119, 130–38; Katz 2002; Sandberg 2002) appeared in a report from Yeivin regarding budget year 1955/6 in relation to archaeological works in the abandoned village of Parwana near Beth Shean (GL44883/12). Otherwise, the JNF did not feature much in the studied files. The reason was that the JNF pretty much ignored the IDAM (GL44875/9 no. 1523, 28.11.49; cf. GL1430/13 no. 9468, 16.8.53; GL44875/10 no. 2008; Fischbach 2003: 60–63). Yeivin tried to establish contacts with the JNF but to no avail (GL44880/13 no. 5917, 19.9.57; GL44875/9 no. 1523, 28.11.49; GL44875/9 no. 327, 18.7.50). The JNF even tried to claim that planting trees in ancient sites did no damage and restored the site to its ancient appearance (GL44875/10 no. 2016, 4.1.53).

Avraham Dothan of the Public Relations [*Hasbara*] Department in the Ministry of Foreign Affairs wrote to Yitzhak Eilam, the Director-General of the Ministry of Labour, on 13 August 1957. Copies were sent to the Advisor for Arab Affairs at the Prime Minister's Office (see Segev 1984: 79–80) and Yeivin:

> Subject: Removal of ruins [*pinuy horvot*] from Arab settlements
> According to the orders of the Minister of Foreign Affairs, we would like to draw your attention to the following and ask that the Labour Office take a leading role in this matter.
>
> The ruins from Arab villages and Arab neighbourhoods, or intact blocks of houses that have stood deserted since 1948, have difficult associations that cause considerable political damage. During the past nine years many ruins were evacuated, whether by development projects or by climatic factors; but those that survive protrude even more now in contrast to the new landscape. Therefore, it would be proper to remove the ruins that cannot be restored, or that do not have archaeological value (and restore what ought to be restored for development or for archaeological needs).
>
> First, one has to get rid of ruins in the middle of Jewish settlements, in important centres or along major routes of transportation. With all the development done at Jaffa, there is still an area of ruins at Manshiyah; the same at Azor, within a thriving settlement on a major route. The view of the ruins of Kolonia – at the foot of Mevaseret Jerusalem – where the dressed stones were "peeled off" and empty shells remain, is very bleak. One can

see such "peeled" houses also inside Jerusalem between the *mekasher* [bus company] and the university. Examples of this sort are numerous.

The ruins of villages whose inhabitants are found [elsewhere] in the country, such as Barva north of Shefar'am and the ruins of Zippori demand quick treatment.

A very depressing impression of cultivated land that has become a desert is given in areas that have no development, for example, along the railway from Jerusalem to Bar-Giora (such as the ruins of the village of Valaja and the ruins west of Battir [Bethar]).

Attention must also be directed to ruins in major tourist areas, such as the ruins of the Chercessian village in Caesarea, which stands almost intact but is deserted. Here one must decide whether to restore the village or to destroy it completely. The ruins in the village of Kastel [west of Jerusalem] perhaps require improvement as a historical monument [of the 1948 battles].

These are examples of just four types of ruins to present the issue. It is desirable that the Ministry of Labour takes upon itself the mission of removing the ruins. It is also desirable that you will estimate the presumed expenses. One can assume that local authorities and authorities such as the Development Authority and the JNF will also be interested in this matter; and perhaps even private contractors, who might in a few cases make a profit by collecting the building materials. In this sense one should take into account that the collaboration with non-governmental bodies requires caution, since politically it is desirable that the operation is done without anyone becoming aware of its political meaning.

It would be very desirable to complete the operation and improve the situation in that regard towards the decade year [1958]. We hope that the Ministry of Labour will see its importance and do whatever is possible to get it done.   (GL44881/13, 18.8.57)

In response, Yeivin noted "if this becomes practical … we should receive the details of places as soon as possible". But he also replied in a confidential memorandum, which is the fullest declaration of the IDAM's policy about this issue:

As to the core of the matter, regarding the IDAM, Arab settlements must be divided into four groups:
A. Completely new settlements, in which the IDAM has no interest. These are very few and are mostly ruined and torn to such extent that even their whereabouts are no longer visible. The small village of Almansurah between Hulda and Ekron can serve as an example. Today one cannot recognize the place as a former settlement.
B. Settlements in very close proximity to ancient sites. Here each case must be discussed on its own merits, for sometimes such settlements should

be treated as group A, and sometimes they are built above more ancient layers, which mark the expansion of the ancient site beyond the limits of the Tell in relatively later periods (Hellenistic/Roman/Byzantine/Old Arab/Crusader). In the last case, reducing the buildings to ground level makes it very difficult to investigate the deeper layers, for it adds another layer of a few metres depth, which is of no interest to the study of the antiquity of our land.

C. Settlements located on the surface of Tells or ancient *Khirbeh*s. This group is highly important for the investigation of antiquities, since the abandonment of the settlement provides an opportunity to investigate and excavate the site. Yet levelling the remains will add, as in group B, a thick layer of remains that holds no interest, which will have to be removed for excavation. Otherwise, in many cases it will also cover early remains that are at present exposed in a few villages, such as Zippori, Kefar Bar'am, etc.

D. Arab quarters in various cities, such as Accho, Jaffa, Ramla, etc. This is a difficult and complex problem that the IDAM has always faced, and still no agreeable solution has been found. A great deal of money is required to preserve them, while the IDAM and many other state bodies object to demolishing them. For example, it was decided to preserve ancient Accho and parts of other cities for economic reasons alone.

If a serious discussion about these matters is held by the interdepartmental committee searching for a way to solve the problem, it will be necessary to include the IDAM. I am certain that representatives of the IDAM can also raise a few practical points in the continuation of such a discussion.

(GL44880/13 no. 55765)

Yeivin was not opposed to demolition for political reasons (note that he was very willing to give practical advice if a committee were formed), but he was opposed to the removal (actually, destruction) of all types of abandoned places apart from completely new ones, type A, and some of type B. Since, in his view, type A ruins were "extremely few" and most were hardly visible any more, he questioned the necessity of the entire operation, but not explicitly. He was not in a position to decide, and tried to prevent damage only to antiquities within abandoned places. The notion that the past 200–300 years is of no interest to archaeologists was shared by everybody at that period, all over the Western world. For example, the British Mandatory regulations or the Israeli Law of Antiquities of 1978 defined an antiquity as an object dating to before 1700/1800.

A few settled villages were evacuated, thus becoming abandoned (Fig. 8). One example of a summary of a tour of 22 September–23 September 1949, involving the Planning Department, the army, the Jewish Agency, the Kibbutz Arzi, etc., runs:

Figure 8. Kh. Jalameh 1949. Some inhabitants are seen; the village was occupied. Today it is unoccupied, near Kibbutz Lehavot Haviva. (Photograph by Ory, IAA 956)

> *Jalameh*. VI.151.200 [coordinates of the site]. An inhabited Arab village on
> top of a hill. The N–W slope of the hill and part of the area free of houses
> on top of the hill were finally fixed on for a [new] settlement [*nequda*]. The
> dwellers of the village will be transferred elsewhere. I notified [Yaacov]
> Matrikin [manager of the Technical Department of the Jewish Agency]
> and the representative of the Kibbutz Arzi that the approval of the Director
> of the IDAM must be received for '*aliya* [literally, "going up", meaning set-
> tlement] at this site. I think one may permit '*aliya* with [our] supervision,
> once we have the plans approved by the IDAM, on condition that remains
> that will be found in further works will be preserved.
>
> (GL44875/9, handwritten letter 29.9.49; cf. Segev 1984: 75–6)

Figure 8 shows the village with some inhabitants. According to Khalidi (1992:
554) it had 70 inhabitants in 1948. The village was never resettled; the neareset
settlement is Kibbutz Lehavot Haviva.

Some opposition to demolition came from unexpected quarters, like a case
reported by the revisionist newspaper *Herut*:

> Concerning the fishing village Nakhsholim-Tantura. There are Arab
> houses in the place, which "do not permit [economically] the existence of
> a Kibbutz". In our mind, they could use these buildings for settlement of
> individuals. But those who act in national property as in their own private
> property decided: a Kibbutz. So the Arab houses are abandoned and money
> is wasted to build new buildings for a Kibbutz.
>
> (*Herut* 28.11.1950, copy in GL44875/9)

Bar'am village

This village on the Lebanese border was evacuated in November 1948. The residents were told that the evacuation was temporary, but in May 1949 Ben-Gurion refused to let them return. They started a public campaign, but at the end of 1951 and before a court could rule on their case, the army destroyed the village (apart from the church). The by now abandoned village was also bombed from the air on 16 September 1958 in order to prevent the return of the refugees. Later, the people of the village, who were now living in other parts of Israel, were allowed to bury their dead there (Segev 1984: 73–5; Morris 1987: 237–43; Benvenisti 2000: 161–2). In a letter to the press in early 1952 Yeivin answered a report about Bar'am. So far the IDAM had taken one stone for exhibition, to protect it, since irresponsible people had already damaged the remains despite warning signs. The area of the ruins of the ancient synagogue:

> is still not registered under any owners, simply because in that region the land has not yet been registered [*hesder qarqa'ot*] ... No historical monument will be registered under any body without approval of the IDAM.
> (*Herut* newspaper, 26.2.51, copy in GL44864/14)

In the late 1950s and early 1960s Bar'am was "improved" by the GTC. On 20 September 1957, engineer Asher Z. Hiram of the IDAM reminded the GTC "again" that:

> This village does not belong to [the Custodian for] "Abandoned Property" and its inhabitants are in the country. Therefore, care should be taken in demolishing the buildings. In case a problem arises during the demolition related to making an access road, the IDAM will bear no responsibility. The IDAM definitely objects to the demolition of the house opposite the main entrance of the synagogue ...   (GL44882/9 no. 5929a)

The village was mentioned in a budget proposal of 1961–62:

> In order to finish the works of restoration of the synagogue, the Arab houses surrounding it must be destroyed. Also arrange an entry road and parking ... [and] finish the restoration of the synagogue and plant a garden around it.   (GL44882/9)

The "improvement" finally resulted in the demolition of the Arab village in order to accentuate the ancient, restored synagogue. Compare Benvenisti's observations about "erasing" the Ottoman period and restoring Mamluk buildings as Crusader ones (2000: 270–305).

Kolonia (near Moza, west of Jerusalem)

The demolition of this village appears in correspondence from the GTC Committee for the Improvement of the Landscape and Historical Sites. In 1960 new land legislation was passed (cf. Yiftahel and Kedar in Shenhav 2003: 29–37; Barkat in *Haaretz* 4.2.2005: p. 4). Anticipating the legislation, Yaacov Yannay, formerly Deputy Director-General of the Ministry of Defence, and now Secretary of the Committee for the Improvement of the Landscape and Historical Sites, wrote to Weitz of the JNF, summarizing a meeting held between himself, Weitz, Tedi Kollek (Director-General of the Prime Minister's Office) and Daniel Ben-Shabtai (legal advisor to the GTC and the Prime Minister's Office):

1. We pointed out the necessity for the JNF, in its new guise as administrator for land matters, to undertake a significant part of the works of improvement of the landscape of the land, especially in the field of cleaning and planting.
2. We pointed out the plan of beautifying the road to Jerusalem … We raised the problem of the forest of the 40s, the farm at Shivta, planting at Avdat and the evacuation of ruins of Arab villages.
3. Mr Weitz expressed his interest in the said plans and claimed that his first job as head of the new administration would be to take care of roadsides …
4. It was concluded that Mr Weitz will handle the destruction of the village Kolonia and the planting in the area of the ruins. The GTC will transfer to the JNF the sum of 3,500 Lira for that aim. According to Mr Weitz, the above-mentioned sum covers two-thirds of the entire expense.
   [signed] Y. Yannay …   (G11-5451, 15.1.59)

In April 1959 Kollek wrote to Weitz:

A few days ago you told me that you had destroyed the village of Kolonia following what was agreed between us. To my great sorrow it is not so. Perhaps in relation to paving the road a few houses were destroyed, but the remains of dozens of buildings exist and nobody has yet touched them. I would be grateful if it could be done soon. I want you to understand that this financial effort is quite serious in terms of the meagre means at our disposal, and if it is to be done, we are interested in a full clean operation, as agreed between us.
   With Blessing, T. Kollek   (copy, G12-5451, April 1959)

So the ruins had to be cleanly destroyed. David Levinson of the GTC wrote to Weitz again on 7 June 1959. Following the agreement between Kollek and

Weitz to destroy the village and plant on its area, he had delivered 3,500 Lira to the JNF on 23 January 1959. Yet, despite several promises, the village was still "standing in its former condition". He asked that the money be returned, "and we will solve the problem of the evacuation of the ruins in another way". The letter was written on official Prime Minister's Office letterhead with copies to Kollek and Shemuel B. Yesha'ayah, director of the Jerusalem district (G12-5451). On 22 June 1959 an employee of the JNF replied:

> The fact that you state in your letter that the village stands in its former position is not accurate. The entire village was evacuated and levelled except for a few ruins, which cannot be approached because they are located inside worked agricultural land and on high terraces that prevented the tractor from reaching them. As for planting the area, one might assume it will be done in the forthcoming planting season.   (G13-5451)

Yannay thanked him on 28 June 1959, but added:

> We had only one goal in financing the demolition of the village, and that was to prevent passers-by on the Jerusalem road the pleasure of seeing the ruined landscape, which raised various questions with tourists. Perhaps there are things that make the destruction of the houses difficult (these are not a few ruins but many ruins). I ask you to understand that if we do not destroy all the said ruins we would not achieve our goal. We would be very thankful if you will give the order to destroy the ruins at that location.
>   (G13-5451)

A soldier wrote to the IDAM on 23 May 1951:

> On one more thing I must report and it is the situation in Ashkelon. Recently I happened to be there many times and saw the sorry state there. All the antiquities are deserted, without a guard, so anybody does there as he pleases. The capitals strewn in the area of Ashkelon are being taken by the people of Migdal-Gad [the new city] and the vicinity. The ancient Arab cemetery of the village El-Jora is full of tombs whose marble slabs carry ancient inscriptions on one side, and on the other side the name and glory of the Arab dead. Our nice friends take these slabs for use in their kitchens, since it is both the most expensive material [when bought] and the cheapest [when taken from the tombs]. Its value is great and its price is just punishment from heaven ...   (GL44875/9 no. 5623)

He was answered (it was true) that the El-Jora remains were not ancient, so the IDAM could not protect them.

Later, when new settlements dotted the landscape everywhere, the former settlements were conveniently forgotten. The official ideology dictated that new Israeli settlements were a direct continuation of the ancient history, with nothing in between. Thus, during the conference of the IES at Ashkelon in 1954, President Ben-Zvi said: "I use this opportunity to bless Jewish Ashkelon … the establishers of the new Hebrew city on the ruins of the old Philistine-Greek city" (*BIES* **19** (1954/55): 111).

One isolated call to preserve something from the abandoned villages was made by Levy Rahmani of the IDAM at a meeting of the Committee for Locating and Preserving Sites in Jerusalem. This committee looked for tourist attractions in Jerusalem, since the old city and most attractions remained under Jordanian rule (GL44889/2, minutes 17.12.62). They reviewed a plan for a quarter of artists, so first P, an artist, spoke before the committee: "they bring the tourists to Jerusalem in closed cars: to the university, to Mount Zion. At night they take them back to Tel Aviv, for in Jerusalem there is nowhere to go" (GL44889/2, minutes 28.12.62). When the committee discussed the abandoned village of Liphta, west of Jerusalem, Rahmani said:

> I know that very beautiful, old construction is concealed in some of the houses at Liphta. I suggest that we perform a survey, and act as they do in Switzerland, where, to preserve old cities, a plan of every old building is made regardless of whether it is destined for destruction or preservation. Photographs or plans of each building are filed. Architectonic parts of Arab houses destined for destruction could be entered into an Arab Museum, to be established in the future, after the houses are destroyed. The photographs will show what existed at the place that is going to be destroyed. Otherwise they will say about us that we have ruined all the antiquities barbarically, without even leaving documentation. (GL44889/2, minutes 24.2.63)

It seems that the committee was so stunned by such vision that no reply was made or recorded in the minutes of the meeting. In fact it was impossible to preserve hundreds of abandoned villages, even if it was desired. Their destruction, by man and by nature, was inevitable once the refugees were refused permission to return.

NEW PLACES

The huge wave of immigration throughout 1948–52 engulfed and changed the entire state and its landscape (Fig. 9). The IDAM had to cope with the proliferation of bodies that had a hand in the development process: the Jewish Agency

Figure 9. Sindiyanna on a tour. New settlers draw water from the ancient Caesarea "upper aqueduct".
(IAA 1511)

(Stock 1988: 90–191; Kanterovitch 1997), the JNF, the Planning Department, army governors, the Inspector of Quarries, the Custodian for Absentees' Property, municipalities, government offices, and so on. With some bodies, such as the Inspector of Quarries, the IDAM managed to reach reasonable agreements (GL44875/9 no. 2860, 9.7.50). When a plan was drawn up to establish immigrant villages near Tell es-Safi and Nebi Rubin, Yeivin wrote to the manager of the State Property Division on 8 November 1950:

> In these two places there are very important Tells, not to be touched. It is not a question of a [verbal] *promise* made by the manager of the Planning Department. To my regret I have learned from the experience of recent years that promises are worth little. Worse, the planner prepares plans and does not pass on the IDAM's conditions, which he considers while planning, to the bodies responsible for the developments. These bodies have their own planners, who completely alter the first plans. Finally, the initial conditions are ignored. It has happened a few times in the north, centre and south of the country.
>
> I think therefore, that the IDAM's conditions should be entered into the body of the contract of sale, rent or transfer [of property], as an impassable requirement ...   (GL44875/9 no. 6997)

Work camps

In early 1949, 26,000 newcomers were sitting idle in camps such as Sha'ar ha-'Aliya near Haifa; by the end of that year there were 90,000. The living conditions in these camps were appalling, with epidemics of disease, a shortage of work and constant hunger. It was inconceivable that there could be sights in Israel that brought the holocaust to mind (Segev 1984: 129–30). The authorities started to speak about "work camps"; Yeivin mentioned them in a letter of 21 November 1949. First, he discussed plans to flood parts of the Netofa and Yavneel valleys (Galilee) to create reservoirs. The two valleys included significant sites that required full excavation. Yeivin gave the example of Egyptian excavations related to dams on the Nile. The second example he gave was of:

> work villages, which are going to be located on lands of the JNF in relation to extensive works of forestation. This also involves extensive areas that include plenty of ancient remains that need to be checked and studied first. Of course, the limited budget of the department cannot carry the burden of all these enquiries and excavations ...   (GL44883/8 no. 1466)

On 28 November 1949, Yeivin wrote to the JNF. He had received from the City Planning Committee in the northern district a list of places designated as work villages in relation to forestation by the JNF. This list included several historical sites, where, by law, all acts were forbidden without prior consent of the IDAM. Many notices were appearing in the media about work villages for newcomers, mentioning historical sites as locations. Yeivin asked to meet the JNF to reach agreement about the plans. He noted that such cooperation existed already with the Settlement Committee (Makhleket ha-Hityashvut) of the Jewish Agency (GL44875/9 no. 1523).

The plans mostly remained on paper; some 10,000 newcomers reached work camps, and were occupied in abandoned olive groves and in forestation (Segev 1984: 140). Some work camps later became permanent settlements; others became *ma'abarot* (below).

Ma'abarot

When Levy Eshkol, speaking on 27 March 1950, suggested that immigrants should be placed in "immigrant fields" [*sdot olim*], he probably meant what was later to be called *ma'abarot*. The origin of the Hebrew word is not clear, but it comes from the verb "to pass, to move": hence "transition camps". Within two years there were some 250,000 people living in *ma'abarot*. Conditions of life were only slightly better than in the former camps. Most *ma'abarot* were built beside existing towns, but services and employment were very limited (Segev 1984: 139–53; Naor 1986; Hacohen 1994, 1996). On 11 November 1951, Yeivin wrote to the Absorption [*Qlita*] Department of the Jewish Agency:

> I attach herewith a report of the antiquities inspector, according to which a *ma'abrah* is built on the ancient Tell of Kh. Samuniyah (Shimron) [lower Galilee]. As you know, all ancient sites stand under the supervision of the IDAM. Existing law prohibits any construction on them or digging of pits without authority from the IDAM. Although you might say this time that the *ma'abarah* is temporary, even temporary structures require licence, especially when one instals cement floors and cuts 2 m deep sewage pits ... (GL44875/10 no. 7012)

Yeivin asked that a common procedure be fixed on for all future *ma'abarot*. This did not help, and on 16 January 1952 he wrote to Zalman Shazar, then deputy manager of the Jewish Agency (later Minister of Education):

> I am sorry to have to bother you, but believe me if I say that I tried to talk with anyone I could talk to, but after it did not help I was forced to apply to you ... The matter concerns the engineers of the Jewish Agency that deal with establishing *ma'abarot*. In order to set their location there is, so I am told, a special committee joined by representatives of the Absorption Department and the Technical Department of the Jewish Agency, and the following governmental offices: the Custodian for Absentees' Property, the Housing Department of the Ministry of Labour and the Planning Department of the Prime Minister's Office. All the governmental institutions mentioned above, as well as the Technical Department of the Jewish Agency, stand in close contact with the IDAM regarding all possible problems. So far we managed to reach agreements ... Only on the location of the *ma'abarot* have we failed to reach agreement yet. In many cases the representatives of these institutions also complained that the engineers of the Absorption Department set the location for new *ma'abarot* alone, without first consulting this special committee.
>
> The *ma'abarah* of Nahariya was located at the foot of an ancient site without asking for a permit from the IDAM. When we found it, I passed it in silence, for in the end the *ma'abarah* only touched the edge of an ancient site, and in any case it was already too late.
>
> One sunny day I passed near Tell Harbaj (near Kefar Khasidim) and saw that a *ma'abarah* had been built near the Tell, and its toilets were built on its slopes. I applied verbally to different officials in the Jewish Agency and was promised that nothing more would be done there. Shortly thereafter the inspector of the northern district visited the site and, to his amaze-

ment, not only were toilets left on the slope, but also the buildings of the *ma'abarah* itself climbed the slope. Again he talked with the *ma'abarah* secretary and the head of the Haifa office of the Technical Department (Mr [Yosef] Rabinowitz). Their official excuse was that they did not know that there was a Tell there. This is ridiculous. Every little boy in the country knows what a Tell is; surely engineers do. Furthermore, lack of knowledge of the law is no excuse for breaking it.

Around this time a new *ma'abarah* appeared nearly overnight on Tell es-Samuniyah, at Shimron (near Nahalal). I wrote an official letter about it (copy attached), but have yet received no answer. Again the Inspector of Antiquities applied to Mr Konigsberg of the Haifa office, and again the excuse was "I did not know". In the case of Shimron I received a letter from the Planning Department (copy attached) that the committee for placing *ma'abarot* was not asked about it.

The Inspector of Antiquities reached a verbal agreement with Mr Konigsberg about the Shimron *ma'abarah*; they also agreed that in the future no *ma'abarot* will be put on ancient sites. Yet a few days later when visiting the vicinity of Shefar'am he found a new *ma'abarah* being built at Kh. Er-Rujm. He was forced to stop the work and notified me about it. On the first of this month I phoned Tel Aviv and asked to speak to Mr Rotem, who is in charge of this. He was not in the office. I asked the secretary to get Mr Rotem to phone me as soon as possible to arrange the matter. So far no one has contacted me. Meanwhile I was told that the building in the areas of the *khirbeh* was not erected, because the land belongs to a private Arab [i.e. private land belonging to an Arab], who refuses to rent it.

I am certain that you would also agree that this is not a nice way to treat ancient remains ... To prevent complications and unpleasantness like this, I apply to you to ask for your involvement in finding a final solution to the matter of locating *ma'abarot* and ending the problems of the *ma'abarot* of Kefar Khasidim, Shimron and Kh. Er-Rujm near Shefar'am.

(GL44875/10 no. 7672)

Ports

On 16 November 1949 a certain Yitzhak Ziman published a letter in the newspaper *Davar*. He had been to visit the ruins of Caesarea, but was amazed to discover a scene of destruction:

From the [newly] built pier stuck out pillars of granite, cones of red granite, capitals of marble and marble pillars, and more. All this is used as building material for the pier, thrown into the sea and covered by layers of earth and

kurkar rock. I know the importance of a fishing harbour in our country, but could they not find another place along our shores? ... Cannot all the pillars, capitals and all the ancient building materials be taken out and arranged on a nearby hill? I ask the people in authority to handle this matter urgently.
(GL44875/9; cf. *Herut* newspaper 28.2.50)

Nathan Dunevitz told a similar story in *Haaretz*:

All the coastal area of the Crusader part of the city was declared a development area ... A pier was erected, supported by stones from Herod's houses
[and] Crusader walls ... Dozens of workers, new immigrants from a nearby
maabarah, are busy developing the new port and placing the lid on the past.
(*Haaretz* 26.12.52, copy in GL44875/10; cf. *Al ha-Mishmar*, 16.1.53)

Yeivin answered that "crucial and important circumstances" necessitated the choice of this site for a fishing harbour, and that it ruined only very few, unimpor-
tant remains. The IDAM allowed it after reaching agreement with the developers that they would document and report every remain discovered (*Alon* **2** (1950): 4–5; GL44864/14 no. 3311, 18.7.50). Surely, he wrote, the IDAM knew better what to preserve than a journalist (GL44864/14 no. 4527, 19.1.51). Later Yeivin explained that the concerns of the living come before those of the dead. The plans could not be changed because the location of harbours is determined by the topography of the coast, so new harbours naturally occupy the same locations as old ones (GL44875/9 no. 955, 9.9.49); in any other location a new expensive pier would have been required. Yeivin complained that the work caused "a hail of protests from the public about sacrilege of ancient remains" (GL44875/9, 18.12.49: p. 3). In this case it seems that the protestors – and not Yeivin – were right.

New settlements

Between May 1948 and June 1949, 89 new settlements were erected; the number rose to 345 by 1953 and 467 by 1958 (Fischbach 2003: 72–3; for the new towns see Greenberg 1989; Troen 1996; Ephrat 1997). The establishment of so many new settlements for immigrants, refugees and released soldiers was a huge undertaking in very difficult circumstances. A multitude of institutions dealt with settlement in various forms. The IDAM worked hard to gain some recognition. For example, it participated in tours to decide locations ("points") for new settlements:

Report on tours with the Settlement Committee on 22–23.9.1945 [typo-
graphical error – 1949]. Participants Mr [Heinz] Rau of the Planning

Department of the Government, Mr [Ra'anan] Weitzman, head of the Agricultural Planning Unit of the Jewish Agency, Mr Eshel, representative of the General Headquarters, representatives of the *Kibbutz Arzi* and the Agricultural Centre.

Kh. Burin (VI.149.191). The two points to be established in this region are quite close to the ancient site, so obviously the antiquities area is located within the agricultural land designed for the Kibbutzim … Hence it is desirable to maintain personal contact with the people of the place [the new settlements], and also investigate with the agricultural planning unit what purpose the area of antiquities serves [in the plans]…

Kakun. Rush visit. "Ahaz" group occupies the location and waits to start building ['*aliyah*] on the land, when the location of the settlement is finally decided. (This will be done only after the map of roads of the district, prepared by the government planning office, will be coordinated with that suggested by the district authorities.) We ought to get copies of the plans from them. I talked with Mr Rau about "centres" [*rikuzim*]. Kakun, in his view, needs to serve as a sort of a "centre" to settlements established in the vicinity, so as to save expenses. Mr Rau thinks that "centres" can be located according to an arrangement that will be acceptable to the IDAM.

(GL44875/9, 28.9.49)

THE INTERDEPARTMENTAL COMMITTEE

Through his various contacts with so many bodies about abandoned and new sites, Yeivin became better recognized. A point of contact was formed between him and Alexander Altman of the Prime Minister's Office, Ben-Gurion's adviser for tourism. On 18 December 1949 Yeivin sent Altman a memorandum on antiquities of the state as a focus for attracting tourists (GL44875/9 no. 1911). He explained the need for a new survey and the economic value of sites drawing tourists (#1–3). Making sites attractive for tourists demanded investment: cleaning, fencing, placing guides (#4). Abandoned cities and some villages had aesthetic value and could serve as tourist attractions, "frozen" in time; but other people wanted to destroy them and develop modern cities. The IDAM did not have a budget for any cleaning and restoration work (#7–8). Could development be postponed in the meantime? Yeivin gave Caesarea harbour as an example; and noted that even the Planning Department did not always find a listening ear for all its plans (#10). Hence:

I suggest establishing first an interdepartmental committee to decide about all the said problems and to draw principal lines of governmental policy.

The Planning Department and the IDAM could count on them later in order to place complete authority upon all those who plan development projects.   (GL44875/9 no. 1911)

He recommended including in such a committee the IDAM, the Ministry of Religious Affairs, the Ministry of Absorption, the Prime Minister's Office (Planning Department), the Ministry of the Interior and perhaps the Ministry of Finance, which must set the budget. Success depended on three things: more workers, many more guards for antiquities and harsher punishments under new antiquities legislation, which was in preparation. For example, "Today there is no legal authority to destroy illegal buildings built without permission in antiquities sites and no possibility to force criminals to pay even for damages made on purpose" (GL44875/9 no. 1911).

Following more discussions, on 23 February 1950 the Prime Minister's Office nominated an interdepartmental committee: the Supreme Committee for Holy and Historical Places and Monuments in Israel (Paz 1998: 128). It made six tours, and held eight meetings, starting on 21 April 1950 (Fig. 10). The committee finished work in August 1951, and delivered a 147-page confidential report on 13 October 1951 (kept as GL44864/18).

It was a prestigious committee, with 13 representatives from many ministries (GL44864/18: p. 1): Dr Alexander Altman (Chair, Prime Minister's Office); Yohanan Beham, later replaced by A. Perlman (Finance); Moshe Shilo (Defence, representing handicapped soldiers); Dr Shemuel Kahana and Dr Haim Hirschberg (Religious Affairs); Mordechai Gazit (Foreign Affairs); Dr Noah Nardi (Education); Yeivin (IDAM); Gad Asher and later Avraham Reifer (Ministry of Labour and Social Insurance); Aharon Propes (Department of Absorption); Ya'akov Kosilov alternating with Shemuel Yesha'yah (Interior); Dr Leo Adler (Planning Department) and Na'ami Zuckerman, the only female representative, later replaced by Moshe Nevo (Transportation). Seven of the 13 representatives had PhDs (Paz 1998: 129; Katz 2004: 59–69).

Figure 10. The interdepartmental committee at Suq el-Khan, Galilee, 3 May 1950. Yeivin is standing at the centre (wearing a tie). (GL44864/18)

The committee established several sub-committees, for example, for Accho and Safad, and discussed many basic questions, such as the preservation of antiquities, aesthetic aspects, political consequences (what was worth restoring), finances and priorities. The committee discussed cases from the United Kingdom and India (*Alon* 3 (1951): 1–3). Yeivin realized that empty buildings would not survive, and was opposed to destroying the old cities. He joined Brutzkus, who understood the need to preserve entire units, not just separate buildings here and there, maintaining the general "atmosphere" of a place. This was a novel idea for that period (Paz 1998: 111, 131). Since many old cities were already too badly damaged, the new ideas could be tested mainly in Accho. Yeivin believed that it should be turned into a cultural complex with museums, libraries, artists's galleries and so on, and the private owners evacuated (Paz 1998: 126). The committee was divided about "foreign" sites. Shilo thought that Israel should preserve as few Arab remains as possible (GL44864/18: 38–9, 47, cf. Walter Eytan's words, p. 19). The committee accepted a sort of middle ground for the old cities: to restore as much as possible, but to recognize modern needs of sanitation, health and transportation (GL44864/18: p. 22; Paz 1998: 132–3).

The report was cumbersome: Yeivin (who edited it) included all kinds of material (even letters to guards of antiquities about organizing tours, probably to impress the authorities about his powers). The conclusions alone took up five pages. However, a page of shortened conclusions survived in the confidential report (GL44864/18):

1. Abandoned sites and monuments, including sites of recent history, should be defined as public property and delivered to the state or to recognized public bodies.
2. Prioritized sites should be preserved as entire units. They should be restored in their general outlook and outer walls and facades, with improvements inside and better sanitation systems. These included eight sites: Accho; some quarters of Safad; small parts of Jaffa and Tiberias; small parts of Ramla and Lod; some parts of Tarshikha (Me'onah – the parts with a non-Jewish population) and the entire village of Iqrit (GL44864/18: appendix A).
3. The government should forbid: destruction of holy buildings without authority; unauthorized acts by governmental bodies (such as occupying buildings); inclusion of sites in development plans, unless authorized by the government and supervised by it.
4. To increase tourism, a conservation expert from abroad should be invited and a general survey of the country should be made in 5–6 years. Plans for improving sites should be prepared and a special fund established for the work. Guides and publications should also be prepared.
5. Activities should be handled by a performing body with a council and a

committee [note how this duality was copied in the structure of the GTC; see Ch. 12]. It should nominate experts to decide priorities and estimate expenses. Work should be done by a special unit within the Department of Public Works. The performing body should have a permanent secretary.

6. Until a decision is reached, a temporary committee should handle urgent matters. Swift creation of this committee is needed.

(GL44864/18: general conclusions, p. 4)

Ha'aretz newspaper published a notice about the committee on 31 October 1950. In the report Yeivin warned:

One should note that besides the positive attitude towards Israeli [period] remains, an attitude of utter disregard is taking root towards ancient cultural and artistic non-Israelite remains. Restoration works may also … encourage relations of respect and tolerance [*sovlanut*] to the cultures and spiritual assets of the other [*zulat*], and calm down the spirit of national and political extremism that shows worrying signs recently, especially among the youth. (GL44864/18: p. 4)

The same words appeared in the interdepartmental report, crossed out by hand, so Paz (1998: 95) could still decipher and quote them in his thorough study. Yeivin repeated similar words in an interview with Nathan Dunevitz (*Ha'aretz*, 26.12.1953). There he expressed shock that the idea that only Israelite and Jewish remains were worthy of preservation had been heard from the manager of a governmental department. Yeivin repeated this view in a memorandum about the central museum (later the Israel Museum, Jersualem) in January 1952 (GL44873/10; see Ch. 10). Paz rightly stresses that Yeivin was a very significant member of the committee. With Brutzkus and others, he saved part of Jaffa and the old city of Accho. His leading role is evident in that he organized the committee and its tours in addition to editing the report. Yeivin reached one of the peaks of his career but, unfortunately, reaching conclusions was one thing and implementing them another.

FOLLOWING THE INTERDEPARTMENTAL COMMITTEE (1951–55)

The report was not published (cf. GL44865/1 no. 88/4279). The first obstacle to its implementation was the criticism it received from Kahana, one of the committee members (Ministry of Religious Affairs). He wrote bluntly to Altman that he could not support the report and its content. He (quite rightly) criticized its form

– a sort of diary – and claimed that the report did not reflect all the discussions. The core of the matter was the rift between secular and religious:

> I knew that men allegedly of science, who continue the Mandatory tradition of contempt for places of Jewish traditions, objected to certain projects. I saw the objection as something natural and understandable in terms of the common difference between religion and archaeology; and I saw it as one of my aims to explain the traditional attitude. It seemed to me that members of the committee understood us and agreed with us in principle. How astonished I was to read in the report the minutes on "the use of Mt. Zion for aims of commerce for expanding export of religious objects abroad", and the objection of some members to a number of works done at Mt Zion with the consent of the Ministry of Religious Affairs and the Chief Rabbinate of Israel ...   (GL44865/1, 25.1.51)

Kahana complained that his lecture on Mount Zion was not mentioned in the report. Worse, wrote Kahana, while religious Jews identified the tomb of David on Mount Zion, a letter by Avi-Yonah included in the report (GL44864/18: p. 75) defined this as "a scientific atrocity" [ma'aseh zeva'ah]. Avi-Yonah expressed the view that the site identified by religious Jews as David's tomb was used for Christian burials. Only a sick individual with blind hatred of religion, wrote Kahana, could see religious beliefs as scientific atrocity:

> Anybody can treat the traditions of generations and of a nation with contempt and rejection. However, it is completely not at the liberty of an editor, a collector and stylist of an official interdepartmental report to publish there a letter by a private individual who has no relation to the matter, just in order to show contempt for the nation's tradition and to prove that we have no relation to David's tomb. Who does the editor want to serve in this publication? It is very possible that we shall have to stand again in front of a UN committee about the holy places in the land, and have to explain our position about Mt Zion. Do you think such official publications like these will be helpful? For me, and for tens of thousands of other Jews, this place overseeing the Temple Mount is dear and holy, so I cannot agree with the report ...
>
> One of the important problems of the discussions was the matter of Jewification of places. I saw it as one of my major aims to influence all bodies in favour of "Jewification" of the places as far as possible. In the meetings of the committee, I and others objected to those who continue the tradition of the Mandatory authorities to blur [le-Mashmesh] the content and Jewish nature of many places in the name of pseudo-scientific sources, presented as basic sources not to be doubted, in the eyes of men of science of the old school, who are far away from Jewish sources.

I dared to doubt this "dogma" and demanded to re-pass a survey of all archaeological places in the land, with the cooperation of people who know first-hand – not fifth-hand – the Mishna, Tosefta, the Babylonian and Jeru-salem Talmud … I was happy with the decision to encourage the numbers of excavations of Hebrew remains, but I do not understand why and when that decision was related to a decision about cooperation with foreign insti-tutions …, a connection that in my view lowers our honour …

In my view, there is enough certainty and faith in Persian, Greek, Roman, Byzantine, Arab, Turkish and Crusader sources and very little faith in Jewish ones. We lack Jewish things, knowledge of the [Hebrew] sources and a warm attitude towards a nation's tradition, which continues an ancient tradition and strives to see everything in the land as Israeli and Jewish.

I innocently believed that I managed to influence the responsible bod-ies … but this report makes me very worried, hence I ask you to bring my position about Mt Zion and the "Jewification" problem to the attention of all the addressees to whom you sent the report of the IDAM …

(GL44865/1, 25.1.51)

Note how the report was identified with the IDAM here. Yeivin replied on 3 April 1951. Obviously, he did not feel threatened. He used irony: the delay was owing to urgent work, which was more important than a debate with a member of a committee that had finished its work six months earlier. Yeivin defended the structure of the report, hinting that Kahana had not read it carefully enough. As editor he had made only slight stylistic changes, based on the detailed minutes of meetings. These were given to all the members before publication of the report and nobody complained about them. Kahana had not submitted his lecture on Mt Zion; Yeivin had even asked the Prime Minister's Office and been told that it had not arrived. Then Yeivin lost his subtle irony:

As for the rest of Kahana's letter, I have nothing to answer for. Dr Kahana is probably not mature enough to understand that even a person who does not wear a small *talith* and a *kippa* on his head can be a dedicated and loyal Jew; and that there was no need to fight in the committee about – an alleged – *Jewification* of places. My colleagues and I, who during all our days have fought and will fight for recognition of the importance of the people of Israel in world culture and in the history of this land, do not have to hang on Kahana's every word. We do not require his *kosher* certificate. Never in our lives did we treat religion or its assets with contempt; but we have objected and will continue to object to conspiracies [*knuniya*] about holy sites, and the invention of new holy sites each morning. Dr Kahana already said the same things in the committee meeting, and then several members (including me) protested against these words of contempt towards

Hebrew science and its flagbearers. Nobody has asked for Kahana's opinion of whether there are enough foreign monuments in our land or not. What there is we will keep, and with the honour they deserve. We have and always will strive to understand the knowledge and value of Jewish remains, but Kahana will not teach us a lesson about it; nobody placed him as supervisor of the sources of our knowledge … a little respect in the face of a Jewish man of science would not hurt him …

(GL44865/1 no. 5379; on Yeivin's objection to new
holy places that "our fathers did not know",
GL44865/1 no. 4962, 26.2.51; cf. Hallote & Joffe 2002)

The committee was finished; the report placed on some shelf. On 2 December 1951 Yeivin warned the Minister of Education about Accho:

The conservation and restoration of the city called ancient in Accho … is needed to preserve a monument unique in all Israel, but it can also be a pressing factor for international tourism as a source of foreign currency and also propaganda for the cultural level of our state … I hardly need mention the value of [Accho] as an irreplaceable cultural and educational asset. The problem was discussed in several memoranda, and was one of the main subjects of the discussions of the interdepartmental committee … [attaching a marked plan and list of buildings for restoration].

I must add that the situation has deteriorated recently, for cracks and openings appeared in some buildings that demand thorough repairs and a significant investment of money, in order to protect them for the future and make them a worthy place to exhibit to tourists and visitors. Furthermore, the new city of Accho is developing rapidly. It will affect the old city for sure. The mayor demands – in my view, correctly – that matters should be decided once and for all. Either maintain the old nature of the old city and take it out of development plans, in which case special plans are needed for its conservation and restoration; or leave it to development and let the municipality approve projects that will ruin the old and build new in its place. Moreover, there are ancient quarters outside the walls of the old city. We know that the Crusader settlement of Accho extended far to the north of the walls, but precisely there the new centre of Accho is planned. Now the municipality stumbled upon a vast area of ruins when it went to prepare grounds for an industrial quarter. All these require checking … and, if monumental buildings are found, preservation and protection … This also demands a large investment of money, which the municipality in its current state and the IDAM with its current budget cannot supply.

Since the property belongs to the state, a governmental investment of capital is needed. From the report [of the interdepartmental committee] you will see that it is not just the problem of Accho alone … On a smaller scale the same problems remain at Safad, Jaffa (as much as the IDAM and other bodies managed to save some of the old quarter), Lod and Ramla, and even some rural settlements (Iqrit, etc.) …   (GL44865/1 no. 7194)

The actions Yeivin demanded were:

1. Invite an Italian expert in the restoration of ancient cities for six months to study the problems and teach local students.
2. Allocate a very large sum for restoration for 5–6 years. The IDAM should have 40,000–50,000 Lira immediately to begin repairs that cannot be postponed in old Accho, and to check areas of development outside it.
3. Reach a decision in the government that forbids acts of development and give authority to supervise and to restore to the IDAM, or to the special body recommended by the interdepartmental committee.
                                        (GL44865/1 no. 7194)

The report with all its drawbacks was still the result of many hours of work by a considerable team of high-ranking officials. However, there was no budget and little awareness of the value of the "old" towns. For some time Yeivin continued to ask for an annual fund of 50,000–100,000 Lira earmarked for urgent works (GL44875/10 no. 9536, 20.8.52). Yeivin pleaded with Remez, the Minister of Education, and with Sheref, the government's general secretary (who told him that he could not place "problems" in front of the government, as only ministers could). Remez promised to convince other ministers (GL44889/2, n.d.).

On 30 April 1953 Yeivin wrote a long memorandum to Altman on the "problems of guarding historical sites". He started by noting that there were at least 2,000 sites. A new survey was needed to locate all sites, but there was no budget for it. The wider public or tourists would find only 200 sites of interest: those containing monuments or visible remains (GL44875/10, #1–2). How could they be protected, restored and prepared for public visits? The ideal would be to keep all 200 sites clean, fenced and guarded, but in the present reality it was impossible. Still, the IDAM tried to do something with the help of Friends of Antiquities and antiquities guards. Even a permanent guard was not enough when large organized groups appeared at once or when the sites were extensive. For example (Figs 11–12):

In Ashkelon we placed signs three times, and three times they were stolen, until the IDAM despaired and stopped putting signs there … Four times the locks were broken … After cleaning the Sanhedria tombs, boys came in one evening and scribbled graffiti on the walls. This is in guarded sites.

More so in unguarded sites: at Beit Jubrin there was a building above an ancient mosaic, which had already been discovered during the rule of the Mandatory government. At our demand the roof was fixed and a new door was placed. But the roof was mended with rotten, corroded planks, so the IDAM mended it again. Again the planks were stolen and the lock was broken. The roof was fixed for the third time; a strong storm in early winter broke some of it. The roof was fixed for the fourth time; and again stolen, with the door. Now we are about to place a roof and a heavier door, harder to steal. We tried to interest the [nearby] Kibbutz in looking after the building; it agreed to guard and keep the key for some payment, but the door was broken immediately after the agreement was made and the roof stolen a few times. Naturally we cancelled the agreement, for they did not even notify us about the theft … Similar cases could be cited in their hundreds from all over the country.   (GL44875/10, # 9)

Figure 11. The house of mosaics at Beit Jubrin, 1949. (IAA 56)

Figure 12. Copying mosaics at Beit Jubrin, 1954. Seated at the front is Leah Ofer, who later funded the textile laboratory of the Israel Museum. The teacher (standing) is perhaps Teodoro Orselli. (IAA 10421)

Compare this with a letter of 23 May 1951 from a soldier:

> It was nice of the IDAM to put signs in certain places forbidding damage to
> antiquities. But is a "Rabbi" afraid of such sign? No, like a lion he takes out
> the sign, runs to his home and uses it in his goat shed or chicken den.
>
> (GL44875/9 no. 5632)

Yeivin's memorandum continued. He noted that the attitude of the police
depended on the officer in charge, but in general it was apathetic. In one case
that reached court, the offender was fined 3 Lira, so it became a kind of joke and
detrimental to the cause. There were only four district inspectors. Apart from
Jerusalem, the districts were far too large for one person to supervise. Supervisors
also had to tour with committees to choose new settlements, check plans for development, maintain contacts with all the bodies involved, excavate probes (*Khafirot
bdiqa*), visit local collections, and oversee guards and Friends of Antiquities. Very
little time was left for regular supervision while inspectors lacked cars, or gasoline
was limited. Development was hasty; higher authorities sometimes offered a
sympathetic ear and even allocated some budget, but not all were alike:

> The Absorption Department of the Jewish Agency and the JNF so far used
> to ignore the matter of antiquities, and caused considerable damage. In all
> cases, when things get down to those who actually do the work, the rules
> to maintain antiquities are not kept. Contractors and subcontractors are
> rushed for time and short of money, and usually prefer to destroy and
> ruin antiquities from fear that they will postpone their work ... Drivers of
> tractors and bulldozers do not show consideration. One can count hundreds
> of cases where damage occurred, including serious damage. It is sufficient
> to mention one major case: the project of deepening the Jordan, when
> the JNF stubbornly refused to show any cooperation in the research of the
> important prehistoric site (remains of ancient animals and stone tools of
> prehistoric man) [meaning Gesher Bnot Ya'acov?].
>   The problems will not be solved with tougher laws and even more guards,
> but with a wide education programme for the public, especially for youth,
> and detailed orders from the government to all bodies concerned.
>
> (GL44875/10)

This proves Yeivin's clarity of view. He identified the basic problems and was
aware of his inability to solve them with the means at his disposal. The solution
lay in long-term education and a change of public and governmental attitudes.
Salvage archaeologists all over the world could no doubt understand Yeivin's
feelings. On 4 June 1954, Yeivin briefed the Minister of Education about the
destruction of Lod (Golan 2003), which was unrelated to the 1948 War:

It touches the general principle that the government of Israel wants to take in regard to the few places where quarters called "old" still remain, with their special atmosphere, unique style of building and the expression of certain living conditions that belong to that period and place [avoiding the term "Arab period" because it would not help his cause]. Although mostly these quarters are not ancient according to the definition of the antiquities law, the IDAM as well as several other bodies such as the Planning Department think that there is a special interest to preserve such entire units as places for visitors and tourists. Furthermore, they have significant value as cultural and educational assets and as living historical documents that every cultural state must preserve.

To my great sorrow, not all military authorities understand this cultural value. Some officials in municipalities, some district governors and especially the Custodian for Absentees' Property, do not want to or cannot understand it. Their attitude is too simplistic: "these ruins must be demolished, in order to tear from them the inhabitants, who live there in unsanitary conditions". Since these authorities always hold the permits for action, a few places have already been damaged and I am afraid that the rest will also be damaged without notifying the IDAM or the Planning Department.

I did not want to bother you so far … but now I think that the matter will not be made right without a special order from the government on how to deal with these remains … (GL44875/10 no. 4062a)

Yeivin was not motivated by political reasons; in the case of "new" Arab villages he was not opposed to their demolition or use as building materials (e.g. GL44875/10 no. 10052, 16.10.52). But his attitude to the old cities should be applauded, given their widespread and at times futile destruction.

A Committee for the Improvement of Historical Sites and Holy Places was finally founded in winter 1954, that is, three years after the interdepartmental committee. It included the senior officials: Yitzhak Eilam (Chairman; Director-General of the Ministry of Labour); David Levinson (Tourist Centre, Ministry of Commerce and Transportation); and representatives of the Planning Department and the ministries of Labour, Religious Affairs and Finance (*Alon* **5–6** (1957): 4). The budget was considerable: about 200,000 Lira. As long as it existed, the committee was responsible for several works in Accho, Caesarea, Tiberias, Beth Shean, Beth-Alpha and Jerusalem. It prepared detailed plans for other sites and designed road signs for historical sites (GL44883/10, 16.3.55; GL44892/9 no. 7282a; GL44882/9 no. 422–1859; GL44865/1 nos. 422–1859, 7669a). The IDAM was a leading force on this committee. It suggested the sites, made the plans for improvement and supervised the work. Unfortunately, Katz (2004: 75–7) failed to mention this committee in a recent study.

In 1954 Teodoro Orselli, Director of the Ravena Academy of Art, arrived for six months and presented a course for 12 people on the restoration of mosaics (see Fig. 12); he also made plans for Accho and Safad (Yeivin 1960: 58–9; GL44883/10, 16.3.55).

In late 1955 the GTC was established (see Ch. 12). Tedi Kollek, the manager of the Prime Minister's Office and chairman of the GTC, swiftly abolished the Committee for the Improvement of Historical Sites and Holy Places:

> With the establishment of the GTC, certain changes in the activities of the department that handles historic and other sites have occurred. Therefore it seems to us that the Committee for the Improvement of Historical Sites and Holy Places will not continue to exist in its current form.
>
> Our thanks for the work that the committee did while it existed is hereby sent to you. (GL44865/1 no. 7020, 28.11.55)

Later, the GTC actually followed many of the recommendations of the interdepartmental committee, but Yeivin would not reap the rewards of his work. It took 50 years for his contribution to the salvage of old cities to begin to be recognized (Paz 1998).

3   FOREIGN AID

The Second World War stopped almost all excavation in Palestine, and the post-war situation did not permit the speedy recovery of archaeological enterprises in the Near East. The disintegration of the British Mandate in 1947–48 and the prolonged war halted foreign archaeological fieldwork in Palestine. Furthermore, most of the active archaeological institutions remained in East Jerusalem, so there were no foreign expeditions to Israel for a few years.

In March 1949 the Finnish scholar Aepeli Saarisalo (cf. Junkaala 1998), unde-terred by the war, appeared in the offices of the IDAM and asked for permission to continue his survey of western Galilee. Not really ready for such a request, the IDAM suggested that he postpone the idea for several months, because of the danger of "Arab mines and of Arab militia groups from the rescue army of Qawuqji" (GL44864/14 no. 11).

The first foreign scholar to resume evacuations in Israel was René Neuville at Qiryat el-'Anab (Kiryat Anavim) near Jerusalem in 1950. It was a small-scale project and he did not receive even an official excavation licence. Neuville, who died in 1952, was Consul General of France in Jerusalem (*IEJ* **2**(4) (1952): 255). In 1950, Jean Perrot excavated at Abu-Ghosh near Jerusalem and Gush Halav in Galilee. From 1952 the American School of Oriental Research initiated a fellowship in Israel (*Alon* **4** (1953): 3).

The IDAM strived to encourage the resumption of foreign expeditions. As early as 27 September 1948, when it was barely one month old and still under the Department of Public Works, Yeivin found factors that would convince his superiors to support foreign teams:

> In relation to the excavations at Jaffa, the manager of the IDAM raised the
> problem of wages. It is difficult to assume that any foreign expedition will

be able to excavate in the state of Israel as long as it will have to pay such high wages to daily workers, whereas in the Arab part of the land of Israel and in neighbouring countries one may pay a quarter of that wage and perhaps even less to a daily worker. On the other hand, no governmental budget can support the general activities of excavation on its own. Moreover, this is undesired scientifically, for all are keen to participate with scientists from other nations in large-scale researches of the antiquity of the land. Even the national scientific societies (two – the Israel Exploration Society and the Hebrew University) are not enough, and they also do not have very large sums of money at their disposal, to bear on their shoulders the whole burden of archaeological exploration. Therefore, we have to consider what to do about this matter in the future. With time, people will not pay attention to the fact that high wages are involved, but will acquire the impression that Jews do not allow foreign teams to work in their region, whereas the work in the Arab region will continue and thrive. Is there a possibility of arranging "conquering-work" groups [*kibush ha-'avodah*, referring to the former struggle of Jews to enter the workforce], with certain supporting regulations, as was done formerly in the governmental works of [building the] Tel Aviv harbour, etc.?

The manager of the [Public Works] administration explained that the conditions for "conquering the work" in former days are no longer valid or fitting to this case. He suggested as a first thought locating certain sums in the IDAM's budget for supporting excavation works of scientific societies. Anyway, it was agreed that the problem is important and must be discussed seriously ... (in GL44864/14)

Yeivin summarized the continuation of this discussion in a letter dated 18 November 1952:

Almost from the establishment of the IDAM this issue was treated, considering the high cost of work in Israel as compared to neighbouring countries. In the summer of 1950, under Minister of Education Shazar, discussion reached a practical stage, but owing to changes in the government the final decision was made only in the days of the late Mr Remez, who was then Minister of Education, and the late Mr [Eliezer] Kaplan, then Minister for Finance. Based on an agreement in principle with Mr Kaplan, the IDAM entered into negotiations with the Near Eastern Institute of Chicago University, which were completed with success; so now an expedition from that institute is excavating at Tell Beth Yerakh [Kh. Kerak].

Meanwhile, Mrs [Kathleen] Kenyon visited the territory occupied by the government of Jordan and published a notice in the Palestine Exploration Fund *Quarterly* that resuming excavations in the land of Israel is possible only in the occupied territory mentioned above, while it is impossible in the area of the state of Israel because of the high cost of work. I consulted Mr Moshe Sharett [formerly Shertok], then Deputy Minister of Education. With his consent I published a letter in the next volume of the same quarterly [*PEQ* (1951): 176] notifying readers that support will be given to foreign archaeological expeditions coming to work in Israel … On the basis of this notice, the University of Leeds applied to the IDAM and it was agreed that such support will be given to their expedition in Israel. This expedition already excavated at Jaffa [in 1952; see Bowman & Isserlin (1955)] and intends to return next summer and excavate on a larger scale. Also, the representative of the [Centre National de la Recherche Scientifique] CNRS applied asking for support from this "comparison fund" [fund for comparison of labour costs for foreign expeditions] for a large-scale excavation near Beersheba, after an exploratory excavation this summer had positive results. This exploratory excavation did not receive governmental support … [Minister of Education [Ben-Zion] Dinur talked with David Horowitz, Director-General of the Ministry of Finance, who promised to meet this obligation].

When the 1952–53 budget of the IDAM was planned, it included a special budget, of which one item was a sum of 30,000 Lira for this comparison fund. I do not know why it was not entered into the budget, but was told at the time that the matter would be taken care of.

I have to stress one more point. The foreign teams that come to work in Israel bring with them considerable sums in foreign currency to cover their other expenses (apart from the cost of work) and to pay their part of the cost of work. Also from this aspect, the approval of the said comparison fund out of the state finance is important …   (GL1430/14, 18.11.52)

The comparison fund (*keren hashva'ah*) was, then, a "bait" for luring archaeologists from abroad to Israel. It was accepted by the government, which realized the financial value (income in hard currency), and the cultural value (foreign contacts and a kind of small-scale tourism). At that period, the economic constraints were such that citizens were not allowed to hold foreign currency and there were several official rates of exchange for different commodities and bodies. The government agreed to finance two-thirds of the team labour costs, up to 2,000 work-days per year. The first teams arrived in 1952. They included, in 1952–53, Benedict Isserlin and John Bowman at Jaffa (July–September 1952) and Delougaz at Kh. Kerak (October 1952–March 1953). Meanwhile, the French continued their work, and Perrot of the CNRS excavated three Chalcolithic sites in the Beersheba valley (*Alon* **3** (1951): 28; *Alon* **4** (1953): 2). He did not apply to the comparison fund at this time because of the restricted scope of his work. Italian teams arrived in 1955 (Bellarmino Bagatti in Safad) and in 1959 (Luigi Crema in Caesarea). In 1959 Americans returned again to work in Israel.

Yeivin had the approval of the Minister of Education from March 1952 to negotiate with foreign teams up to a general sum of 25,000 Lira per year (GL1430/14
no. 82060). On 1 August 1952 he reported that the efforts had borne their first
fruits with the teams from Leeds and Chicago, but now they were obliged to
pay these teams:

> The Leeds expedition brought 160 pounds sterling for wages, which at
> today's exchange rate gives them 448 Lira. The IDAM must therefore hand
> them 896 Lira. To the Chicago team was promised funding for a maximum
> of 2,500 work-days. They have 6,000 Lira (received from the state of Israel)
> in a bank account in Israel. I do not know if they will bring further sums,
> and to what extent. In any case, the IDAM must be ready to give its support
> in full. The current wage for a simple worker is 5.050 Lira + 0.808 for social
> insurance (16%), that is, 5.858 Lira per day. If 2,500 days were promised,
> it means funding of 14,645 Lira. The total sum needed to support the two
> teams is therefore 15,541 Lira for the present year.
>
> (GL1430/14 no. 11656)

It was difficult to predict the exact scope of work and expenses each year. For
example, in 1952–53 the Leeds expedition was smaller than anticipated, so the
IDAM paid it only 300 Lira. As a result, the comparison fund for that year was
expected to be less than 13,000 Lira.

An official IDAM budget line item (no. 304), called "fund for comparison of
labour costs for foreign expeditions", was defined and inserted in the regular
budget of the IDAM from 1953–54. The IDAM was later permitted to exchange
US dollars to Lira on a 1:1 basis. For several reasons, the line item was not placed
in the budget of 1952–53 and the money – 7,500 Lira approximately – was paid
out of the IDAM's regular budget (GL44883/9, 13.5.53).

Reports and budget papers indicate the development of the comparison fund
(Table 1). Budget years started in April. Since most teams worked in summer,
excavation permits mostly came into the same budget year (e.g. permits for 1953
came into the budget year 1952–53). In 1962 the first fully combined Israeli–
foreign team appeared (Amiran and Richard A. Mitchell); such combined teams
are not included in the table.

The dearth of foreign teams in 1955–57 was not a failure by the IDAM, but a
result of the political tensions surrounding the 1956 (Sinai) War. I do not give the
details of minor changes in the budget. For example, in the budget year 1961–62
the IDAM initially requested 21,000 Lira, as it expected a large American under-
sea excavation at Caesarea, a new and unknown field. This was later reduced to
15,000 Lira, intended to fund teams from Milan and the CNRS only, with a further
2,000 Lira for unexpected expenses. Only 11,000 Lira was approved, but then
3,000 Lira was added from a general reserve in the state's budget. Then the sum

Table 1 The development of the comparison fund.

Budget year	Requsted fund (Lira)	Approved fund (Lira)	Fund as used (Lira)	Foreign teams in Israel	No. of sites excavated by foreign teams
1953–54		10,000	4,000?	1 (CNRS)	3
1954–55	10,000	9,500	5,747	2	3–4
1955–56	9,500	8,500	3,550[a]	1 (CNRS)	2
1956–57	4,500	4,500	3,297	1 (CNRS)	1 (Enan)
1957–58	5,000	5,000	c.3,500	1 (CNRS)	1 (Enan)
1958–59	12,000	12,000	4,000	1 (CNRS)	1 (Azor)
1959–60	16,000	16,000		5	6
1960–61	13,000	11,000		6	7
1961–62	15,000[b]	13,000	11,900	7	8
1962–63	15,000	15,000		4	4
1963–64	15,000	15,000	14,158	5	7
1964–65	15,000	15,000	8,568	6	10
1965–66	15,000	15,000		5	6
1966–67	15,000	9,000		6	8
1967–68	9,000	9,000		6	9
1968–69	9,000	9,000		7	9
1969–70	9,000	9,000[c]	5,966	8	9
1970–71	9,000	9,000		11	15[d]
1971–72	9,000	9,000[c]	6,000	12	15[d]
1972–73	9,000	9,000		10	18[d]

a) 4,500 Lira used by the IDAM, mainly to buy antiquities.
b) Original request of 21,000 was reduced to 15,000.
c) Later cut to 6,000 Lira.
d) Rise in numbers largely due to Professor Anthony E. Marks from the Southern Method-ist University in Texas, who excavated 4–5 prehistoric sites in the Negev. Files in the state archives for the past 30 years are not yet open to the public.

was reduced to 13,500 Lira, because there was "no pressure" from foreign teams apart from those expected at the beginning of the year. In the next stage 500 Lira went to support bringing in a UNESCO expert from Italy. Finally, 1,100 Lira was taken out of the comparison fund and used to buy antiquities (GL44884/5, various documents).

A letter of 18 March 1958 from Dr Moshe Prausnitz (an IDAM supervisor and excavator) to the Ministry of Labour clarified that the 12,000 Lira approved for the comparison fund for 1958–59, equalled 4,465 work-days (a misunderstand-ing, see below). The foreign teams were to pay for a further 3,735 work-days from their own budgets, and these days would also be calculated at the rate for relief workers (a system of relief work had been devised by the Israeli government to employ, mainly in hard manual labour for modest wages, the many unemployed newcomers; see Ch. 7):

> For example, if a foreign team receives a rate of ⅓ and 600 days were used, then the team has to pay for 200 days [with an attached list, from which the sum of 4,465 days of support for that year was estimated].
> (GL44888/12 no. 7715)

The procedure was roughly as follows: once the IDAM received the approved budget, the Ministry of Labour supplied a certain quantity of work-days for foreign teams. The IDAM paid the Ministry of Labour for two-thirds of the days. That was an internal governmental transaction, but it seems that the transfer was not just made on paper. The foreign teams paid for a third of the number of work-days (probably directly to the Ministry of Labour). Yeivin wrote on 14 January 1958 (GL44880/13 no. 6249) that in summer 1958 he expected 12,000 Lira as expenses for the comparison fund, that is, about 2,000 work-days "according to relief workers' wages". He suggested that the IDAM should ask the Ministry of Finance to exempt the scientific and some other equipment, mainly cars, of foreign teams from customs and other taxes: "of course, this letter must be kept confidential so that *Ena Bisha* [evil eye] cannot affect it" (GL44880/13 no. 6249).

Looking at the above data, it seems that the comparison fund enjoyed a very long life. In the 1950s it varied between about 5,000 and 10,000 Lira. It jumped to a level of about 15,000 Lira between 1958 and 1967. Then the sum declined and became rather fixed at 9,000 Lira, and part of it was occasionally lost to budget cuts. "Leftovers" were used by the IDAM to close holes in its regular budget. For example, 1,300 Lira from the comparison fund (line item 10.50.304) was used in favour of an urgent survey in the Judean Desert caves (GL1430/14, letter from Kahane 28.3.1960).

The development of the fund is especially interesting when compared to the number of sites excavated by foreign teams every year. In the 1950s until and including 1958, very few teams arrived each year (1–3) and they enjoyed the fruits of the fund. The scale of work was relatively modest and the fund was significant. From 1959 the fund rose considerably, but so did the number of foreign excavations, which varied from four to ten each year, with an average of seven per year between 1959 and 1967. The comparison fund was becoming marginal and most teams were not benefiting from it.

In the third phase, after 1967, the fund became an *idée fixe*. The IDAM often detailed the names of the foreign teams expected to use the comparison fund in its budget estimates to explain the need for that line item. In 1955–59, between three and five teams were usually expected to use the fund, but in practice only one or two finally reached Israel. For the budget year 1966–67 two teams were expected to use the fund and for 1971–72 only one team was. Yet the numbers of teams and excavated sites grew significantly. This shows that by then, the comparison fund was allocated to a minority of the teams that arrived in Israel; it was not available to most foreign teams.

Among the many documents that concern the comparison fund, none mention criteria for allocating the money. Why give to one expedition and not to another? Furthermore, the habit of cooperation blurred the divide between locals and foreigners. There was no reason to give the fund to foreign teams if they incorporated Israeli partners. A good example is the expedition of the University of Rome. It started in the late 1950s in cooperation with Yeivin at Tell "Gat" (Sheikh Ahmed el-'Areini). The Italians contributed US$4,000 to the excavation budget for two years. In 1963 the team returned and was interested in working at a few other coastal sites. They offered US$10,000 to the IDAM for cooperation at those sites (GL44884/7, letters from Hannah Katzenstein 10.2.63, 3.5.63). Avraham Biran (Director of the IDAM, 1962–74) asked that the expedition be given the usual allowance from the comparison fund (GL44884/7 no. 5208, 22.12.63), indicating that helping others was often richly rewarded as the funding benefited the IDAM, the partner of that team. But there was no obvious reason for rewarding this particular team, since the offer of $10,000 showed that they had means.

There were more teams asking for financial assistance for excavations, so in 1961–62 the IDAM requested permission to add a line item to its budget for "income for initiated [yezumut] excavations" (GL44884/5; cf. GL44884/7 no. 3336). As far as I know, this was the origin of the term "initiated excavations" still used today. At present this term means excavations that are not designed only to salvage remains from destruction or development. The IDAM explained that foreign institutions sometimes agreed, through scientific interest, to add to the budget for "salvage" excavations (which were part of the duties of the IDAM), when the regular budget of the IDAM was insufficient.

For these reasons, coupled with the development of Israel's economy in the 1960s and the end of relief work around 1970, the comparison fund became redundant. The picture becomes clear when comparing the fund with the regular budget of the IDAM. In 1956–57, the budget for IDAM activities was 145,850 Lira, and the budget for excavations and surveys 29,000 Lira. A decade later, in 1965–66, the activities budget was 521,400 Lira and that for excavations and surveys 162,100 Lira. The budget of the IDAM increased fourfold over this decade, but the comparison fund did not match this growth. Furthermore, in the 1970s Israeli scholars became dominant in excavations in Israel, outnumbering by far foreign teams. Quantity is not a sign of quality, and quality varied in both local and foreign excavations. My point is different: a feeling of competition for sites started to appear. With so many excavations, there was less inclination to encourage even more.

Did the comparison fund fulfil its role? How significant was it in luring back foreign expeditions to Israel? Some scholars were friends of Israel, others would be lured by the "Holy Land", and still others had ample means of their own. In the circumstances in Israel in the early 1950s, the concept of the comparison fund was legitimate. Yet very few teams arrived in the 1950s, and their numbers rose rapidly only in the 1960s. It seems that teams were more impressed by the general political and economic condition of the region than by the reimbursement of labour costs.

Why was the comparison fund continued for so long? We don't know when exactly it was cancelled; perhaps it is lurking somewhere as a forgotten line item! The only people to recognize that the fund had become redundant were working in the IDAM; but it still existed for them. The IDAM could use it for public relations with foreign scholars, shared cooperation and (seldom) for other pressing needs.

My final notes in this chapter are twofold. First, I marvel at the romance of small line items of budgets. Secondly, looking at the data again, in the shadow of the façade of governmental bodies, research institutes and scholars, I see the bent backs of Israeli relief workers, generously supplied by the state of Israel to support foreign expeditions.

4 FROZEN FUNDS

The tower of Cairo, a prominent feature by the Nile, epitomizes Egypt's lost architectural identity. No one knows for certain what it is. Built by CIA money, reported to have been a bribe to Abdel-Nasser that he didn't accept, it rises meaninglessly in Cairo's skyline. Hassan (1998: 212)

Data on the "frozen funds" were pieced together from many bits and pieces; the picture is far from complete and the conclusions are tentative. Still, nothing could prepare me for the surprise that US intelligence funds were frozen in Israel and used for Israeli archaeology.

THE IDAM'S DREAMS ABOUT FROZEN FUNDS

I found the first mention of frozen funds in correspondence between Yeivin and Delougaz of the Oriental Institute of the University of Chicago. Delougaz was the first American excavator in Israel (in 1953) and he knew Yeivin personally even before the Second World War. The earlier correspondence is missing. On 30 July 1954 Yeivin sent a confidential letter to Delougaz:

Dear Pinhas
I was happy to receive your letter of 28 June and if I have not answered you so far, this time I am free of any guilt. It was owing not to the pressure of urgent work or lack of time, although that also existed, but the need to find out a few details before answering you. Although the things I saw fit to find out had not yet been clarified, salvation and help came from another place and cancelled the need for the above-mentioned searches, as you will see from the continuation of my letter.
    Let us start with the most important thing, about the sums frozen in Israel. I immediately applied to the secretary of the Prime Minister, and demanded an urgent interview with the Prime Minister on that matter;

but unfortunately it could not be arranged until now, since I have been excavating for three weeks now and come to Jerusalem only on Fridays and Saturdays. Indeed, the Prime Minister has not been available until now. I hope that I will meet him in the near future and ask him to give the right orders to our embassy in Washington.

However, as I said at the beginning of my letter, in the meantime salvation came from elsewhere. It seems that this problem already occupied the government's offices, and an agreement has already been made about the use of this money, or at least a major part of it, for cultural projects. As far as I understand there was a suggestion by the Americans to limit the use only to certain areas of study. The Ministry of Education and Culture objected, and it was agreed that it would suggest a more general use for various cultural matters. This week Dr Avidor, who in the meantime was appointed Director-General of the Ministry of Education and Culture, spoke with me about including expenditure for foreign teams within the framework of the suggestion put forward by the Ministry of Education and Culture. In a preliminary discussion we agreed between us that in the first phase, in the present year, an allowance of 100,000 Lira would be requested for the work of three archaeological expeditions from the United States in Israel. This expenditure of c.33,000 Lira per expedition will include work in the field over 3 to 4 months with an average of 50 workers per day (5 days per week). The team would stay in Israel for 5 to 6 months in order to prepare the fieldwork and finish the early preparation of the material after excavation. Expenditure for wages in such a case could be as much as c.23,000 Lira; and according to the present situation it seems to me that 10,000 will suffice for the rest of the expenses (salaries of four or five people, accommodation rental for the team, petty cash and living expenses, transport and haulage [of finds], photographs, writing needs, etc.). Possibly, with certain cuts, the money may even be enough to buy return tickets from here to the United States with Israeli currency. Of course, travel expenses to Israel, paid by foreign currency abroad, as well as some of the wages of temporary workers that need to be paid by foreign currency, are not taken into consideration. Equipment and supplies acquired with foreign currency abroad are also not taken in account.

Since this is demanded by the Ministry of Education in agreement with American institutions, I do not think there will be competition or objection from other Israeli bodies when things get into practical discussion. In any case, we shall try to meet in the near future with the Prime Minister…
[Yeivin mentioned the Megiddo affair of 1948 and news on his excavation at Caesarea].
With friendly blessings,
[signed] Sh. Yeivin   (GL44880/13 no. 4426a)

As we shall see, Yeivin was wrong about the lack of competition. Anyway, Delougaz answered in Hebrew on 13 August 1954:

Dear Shemuel,
I was very happy to receive your letter of 30.7.54 in which you notify me that the Director-General of the Ministry of Education and Culture applied to you regarding the taking out of some of the "frozen" American money for funding American excavations in Israel.

Of course, you know better than anybody else the cultural needs that can be served by this money, its relative value from both Israeli and US government points of view, and what sums you would like to allocate for the various purposes. The first "rounded" sum of 100,000 Lira for the first year seems reasonable also to me "in the first stage". If permitted, I would like just to note that in my view it is better at this stage of negotiation not to fix all the details in a committed inflexible manner. Thus, for example, I would not set in advance the number of teams and the sums allocated for each of them exactly to "a third", i.e. 33,000 Lira. You know like me the beaurocratic plague involved in "budgets", budget managers and accountants, and you know how hard it is to change even the smallest detail once a certain sum appears in a document. I would like to ensure just the general sum and leave the committee to which all those who want to enjoy funding for their archaeological work in Israel will have to apply some flexibility. I would suggest a mutual committee somewhat similar in composition and role to the committees that approve the "Fulbright" prizes from American money in various countries … [Thus] there will be no limit to the number of expeditions, and several teams with different natures and compositions can work side by side. This is very important if you want to attract to the field small teams whose supporters (a small university or a theological college, for example) do not have enough people and money for equipment and travel to manage a 4–5-month excavation with an average of 50 workers per day …

I hereby attach sections from my memorandum to Washington on this subject, and you will see that I had the same point of view there. To their question about a specific plan I answered that the matter must be accepted in principle at this stage, for the several reasons I have detailed, but freedom of action must be kept for the future regarding different circumstances and needs. You will see from this memorandum that I stressed the need for allocating 30–35% of the budget for each team for conservation of the site and publishing the material. I think it is very important to insist on it. On my side I would even enter a similar commitment for it in any excavation licence, but maybe it is not practical.   (GL44881/13 no. 5085a)

Delougaz sent his regards to Avidor and gave some news from Chicago: the summer was hot and tiring, and Carl H. Kraeling, then Director of the Oriental Institute at Chicago, had returned from Libya and had now gone on holiday. He had been briefed about the funds and promised to maintain relations with Washington. Hopefully, he would show "more enthusiasm to the matter" when he returned. Delougaz added:

> The news about the death of Frankfort [the great scholar, author of *Art and Architecture in the Ancient Near East*] surely reached you by now. You can imagine that for me, personally, it is a great loss. Not only was he very close to me as a friend and colleague, but also he was of those very few unique ones [*yekhidey segula*], with whom I could work for many years out of complete mutual understanding and without any conflict.
> With warm regards to Batya [Yeivin's wife]…
> In friendship, [signed] P. Delougaz   (GL44881/13 no. 5085a)

Perhaps Delougaz had been asked by Washington to test the waters. It is known that archaeologists in the Middle East at that time often served in various secret services. (For example, American archaeologist Nelson Glueck worked for the Office of Strategic Services (OSS) in 1942–45, in the rank of lieutenant colonel; see Smith (1981) and Fierman (1986). Gordon Loud, one of the Megiddo excavators, was Glueck's contact in the OSS; Fierman (1986: 22).) Perhaps this is why this channel of communication was chosen. Delougaz's memorandum is interesting for his take on Israeli archaeology at that time (although he was not a real outsider):

> I wholeheartedly and enthusiastically support your idea that the frozen funds, which have accumulated in Israel as a result of the US Information Office activities there, should be released for American archaeological work in that country. In fact, the more I think about this idea, the more merit I see in it from any angle of approach. First, it provides an extraordinary opportunity to further American scholarship in a field of great intrinsic value, a field in which traditionally international competition for achievement and prestige has always been very keen. Secondly, this opportunity would come at the most appropriate time, when financial support for archaeology from other sources is on the decline …
> From my recent experience at the head of the only American expedition to Israel since the establishment of the new State, I can testify that the Antiquities Law of Israel is by far the most liberal of any Near Eastern country, and that it is administered not only in a fair but most generous manner. It may interest you to know that the IDAM of the Government of Israel contributes ⅔ of our labor expenses, and that in the final division of the finds we are allowed to take home not only the most important finds,

93

but approximately 90% of the rest. This extraordinary generous attitude is prompted no doubt by the keen awareness of the IDAM of the pressing need for extensive archaeological activity in the country, where a sudden increase of the population with the consequent stepped-up agricultural, industrial and building activities imperil many of the archaeological remains which were in no danger for many centuries, while the country was under-populated and inactive. As you undoubtedly know, other and more pressing needs preclude adequate funds being spent by the Israeli government for archaeological activities. Any outside resources that could at this time be diverted to archaeological work in Israel would help to save and bring up to light archaeological monuments which are the concern not only of Israel but of the whole civilized world.

In addition to these scholarly considerations, archaeological activity would have some very real practical results, for as you know (A) archaeological sites are among the best tourist attractions and (B) archaeological excavations are often carried out in regions where the additional employment of even a relatively small number of men may considerably affect the unemployment situation (again from my own experience, the employment of some 40–50 men out of 140 unemployed in Tiberias in the winter of 1952–53 was appreciated by the whole community). Finally, archaeological work and discovery have a considerable popular appeal and "news value" and this too could be used to a best advantage. In other words ... the realization of your plan would further in the best possible way the fundamental aims of your organization from the point of view of goodwill, public relations and favorable news. The employment of the frozen funds for archaeological work in Israel would in my opinion bring the best possible dividends on your initial investment.

As to a specific program, it should seem to me that one should not try at this juncture to tie the funds ... to a single site or project. Rather I would envisage these funds being made available for "bona fide" archaeological work in Israel by accredited American institutions. Any institution which is interested ... could submit a detailed program together with the names of an adequate and competent staff and the sums which it is prepared to spend in dollars for salaries, travel, equipment, supplies, etc., in order to have funds in Israel made available for it. I would think that the funds in Israel should be expected to provide all labor costs, local salaries, housing, transportation, household and other expenses within the country, as well as the cost of preservation of the antiquities discovered, and of their eventual study and publication. From my own experience, I would estimate that at least 30–35% of the funds spent in Israel should be budgeted for the last two items. I know of more than one site which would probably produce magnificent results from the point of view of archaeological information, as well as tourist attractions, but that cannot be touched for fear that once exposed, its monuments will deteriorate for the lack of funds and facilities for their preservation. I know also of some important archaeological results obtained decades ago which have never been published for the lack of adequate provisions for publication at the time the excavations were undertaken.

As to the body that would decide on application for allotment of funds, I envisage it to consist of a competent American group (scholars and officials) which would work with consultation with the IDAM of the Israeli government, somewhat along the lines [of] the Fulbright Awards board ...   (GL44881/13)

On 17 September 1954 Yeivin wrote to Kollek, the Director-General of the Prime Minister's Office. Yeivin attached Delougaz's memorandum, noting that "as you can see, he does not say in his letter to whom particularly his memorandum was sent, but just mentions generally that it was sent to Washington" (GL44881/13 no. 4709). In a meeting of the Committee for the Advancement of Archaeological Research in Israel (see Ch. 12) on 28 December 1954, the Minister of Education suddenly announced that:

Money can be found from the USA for archaeological works in Israel, but we need to put before the people [in America] our detailed plans, according to various periods and in relation to known historical sites. He asked Mr Yeivin to prepare such plans and bring them ...

Professor Mazar: he does not believe that this money will be seen ...

Mr Yeivin: he mentions the USIS [US Information Service] money frozen in this country. Part of those huge sums is guaranteed for the use of American teams; it is desired that part will be used to prepare stores for cultural assets in times of war. The remaining part could be used for a new large excavation, or to continue one of the large unfinished excavations: Lachish, Maresha, Beth Shean, Gezer. What is missing is manpower, and certainly it will be necessary to bring to the country scholars from abroad ...

Professor Mazar: very doubtful about the American money. He talked about it a lot with Mr Tedi Kollek and also with the Americans. It must also be considered that one can interest the Americans not only in Jewish antiquities, but also in other periods, including the Crusaders. Mr Kollek will soon visit the US and the State Department in relation to this question.

Minister: noting to himself that he will invite Mr Kollek to meet him before his visit to the US about this matter; Mr Yeivin asks to be a party to this conversation.

The minister adjourns the meeting at 12.15.

(GL44889/2, minutes 28.12.54)

Perhaps Mazar knew something; but he did not explain it. Several months later, a meeting was held in Israel. It is described in another confidential letter from Yeivin to the Minister of Education of 17 January 1955 (at first I thought it was dated 17 January 1956, but the letter mentions June 1955 as a future date):

> Dear Minister
> In relation to our last conversation about the use of the frozen funds of the US Information Service I wanted to summarize the situation today.
>
> During your stay in the US last autumn a suggestion was made, simultaneously by American institutions (the people of the Oriental Institute of the University of Chicago, who notified me about it, and as far as I understand other institutions too) and on behalf of local government offices [in Israel], to use the above-mentioned funds in order to encourage archaeological activities of all kinds in Israel. These funds have been set aside to finance cultural projects only, and their use for aims of archaeological research will be appreciated [ahada] by those in charge of them in the USA. After consulting with Dr M. Avidor, it was agreed to suggest that 100,000 dollars from these funds would be devoted to the funding of three archaeological expeditions from the US. According to Dr Avidor's offer, I contacted Mr T. Kollek, the Director-General of the Prime Minister's Office, to discuss the question of the use of this money for archaeological work in general. Out of this conversation two things became clear:
>
> A. There will be a possibility to use a far greater sum from these funds, not just for financing teams from the US, but also for things that are difficult to finance on a large scale out of the regular IDAM budget: first and foremost, improving existing monuments and those exposed in excavation, and also improving and restoring them to encourage international tourism. In this regard, I suggested later to Mr Kollek to take into consideration the building of regional shelters, where various cultural assets can be collected and protected in cases of armed conflicts, as required by the international convention in that matter, signed also by the Israeli delegates at The Hague in May 1954.
>
> B. It was clarified that this money will not be available ... even if approved, before 1.6.1955, which is the beginning of the fiscal year in the US ...
>
> As you surely remember, the matter of the so-called frozen funds was also raised in the last meeting of the Scientific Committee for the Advancement of Archaeological Research in Israel. At the time you said that you would invite Mr Kollek to discuss that matter before he leaves for the US. It was suggested in the meeting that you would also include me in such a conversation. I would be very grateful if you could kindly notify

me whether you still have this idea; also if you set a meeting with T. Kollek
about it, if you will be ready to invite me.
Respectfully yours, with hearty blessings,
[signed] S. Yeivin   (GL44880/13 no. 5604a)

A typed copy of a handwritten letter from Yeivin to Delougaz stated:

> ... a few words about the use of the USIS funds frozen in Israel. I believe
> that I already notified you that the matter couldn't be realized before the
> beginning of the new fiscal year in the US, that is, after the next 1 July.
> All relevant sides here agreed to allocate $100,000 for three archaeologi-
> cal expeditions from the United States, but this needs the approval of the
> American senate within the timescale for the 1955/56 budget. A short time
> ago a meeting was held in the Prime Minister's Office between the bodies
> concerned. I was not present since the details were not discussed but just
> the general outline. I was told that the recommendation to use these funds
> for archaeological aims was approved, and the matter was transferred to the
> care of the proper authorities in Israel and the United States. So chances
> are good that a resolution that benefits us all will be reached.
> (GL44881/13 no. 5934a, 24.2.55)

The fact that Yeivin was not invited was not a good omen for the IDAM.
However, Kollek initiated a meeting with Yeivin on 28 June 1955 "to speak
about the possible uses of the frozen funds". It was summarized in a confidential memorandum written by Yeivin and sent to the Minister of Education,
Avidor and Kollek. Yeivin wrote that Kollek had announced that there were
good chances for allocating considerable sums, especially in summer 1956,
for various archaeological matters. The proposed uses were: (a) excavations
by US scholars in Israel; (b) restoration and improvement of sites, especially
in order to encourage tourism; (c) establishment of a central museum (which
would involve "official problems that first require solution"). Kollek thought
about a project of "improving visits" at Beit Jubrin (Hebrew Bet Govrin); Yeivin
suggested preparing shelters for antiquities and art objects in times of war. He
added:

> A committee of four members was set up to discuss the correct and valid
> use of this money: two to represent the US and two to represent Israel. Each
> national delegation will include as one member an archaeologist special-
> izing in the scientific problems. The other [member] will be a specialist in
> economic and organizational [mishqiyot] problems, yet an enthusiast for
> archaeology and knowledgeable in its problems, such as a banker. Possibly
> the specialist archaeologist to be nominated to represent the USA will be

Professor Albright. As for section C, I told Kollek about the plan of HE the Minister of Education and Culture to establish a complex of museums … [cf. Ch. 10].

As for membership in the committee to discuss the general plans for the financial expenditure and supply them for approval to the US Secretary of State, I raised the candidateship of Dr A. Lahman [spelling uncertain] as the economic member of the Israeli delegation. Dr Lahman, who runs the Himoskai bank, is well known in Israel as someone who likes antiquities and is interested in archaeological matters. Mr Kollek raised the candidate-ship of Mr Vitkon (the brother of the judge [Alfred Vitkon]), who also runs a bank and is probably interested in matters of archaeology in Jerusalem …   (GL44880/13, 4.7.55)

Lahman was later one of the managers of Bank Leumi, and Yeivin recom-mended him to the Archaeological Council in 1959 (GL44865/9 no. 1122; cf. *BIES* **15** (1949/50): 60). Yeivin wrote to Kollek on 4 July 1955 saying that he had not raised the issue in his previous letter only because he was certain that the organizational member in the Israeli delegation must be the Director of the IDAM, who was:

the only governmental official versed in all sides of the problems and who knows the needs of the state from this aspect in all their levels of urgency and priority. I find it necessary to mention it now, since perhaps during the discussion of the make up of the committee some side might raise the notion that it should be a neutral person, not a member of the govern-ment. Apart from doubting the existence of such neutral people, I see nobody else in Israel who is knowledgeable about all the problems and their details as discussed in the attached memorandum.
                              (GL44881/13 no. 7042, confidential)

Yeivin did not seek just personal status, but the power to direct the funds according to his priorities (and not just for excavations – he also saw preser-vation and protection of sites and old cities as a top priority). Yet, at the same time, Kollek was already involved with the establishment of the GTC (declared in August 1955), and wanted the funds for its use. He used Yeivin's arguments against him:

Concerning candidateship as a member in the Israeli delegation that will participate in the bilateral committee, I have to note that it has been discussed that the committee will include two Americans and two Jews, none of whom are to be governmental officials. This explicit condition came from the USA State Department and there is no chance that we can change it because the money comes from the US Treasury and not from the treasury of our state.

Of course, in due course it will be possible to discuss nominations. Sincerely, [signed] Tedi Kollek

PS. After I had written, a letter arrived from the US that puts the whole idea of a committee in question and perhaps one will need to find another way to distribute the money. I shall let you know the details.

(GL44881/13 no. 651/1354, 18.7.55)

Yeivin answered in a letter marked "confidential" and "delivery by hand" that he had not known about the condition regarding government officials. Of course, neutral experts were required, without "a preconception about the roles of various archaeological institutions in the land" (GL44881/13 no. 7257a). He was referring here to the emerging conflict between the IDAM and the Hebrew University and IES: the only other Israeli "archaeological institutions in the land" at that time (Ch. 11). Unfortunately for Yeivin, Kollek had no intention of placing Yeivin in a position where he could influence the use of the frozen funds. If two Israelis were finally selected for the delegation their identity remains unknown; they were not from the IDAM.

The available details indicate that there were USIS frozen funds in Israel, in sums "far larger" than US$100,000. Israel acted as a kind of custodian, but not one appointed voluntarily by the US. Apparently the US, for reasons not detailed in these documents, could not remove the funds without exposing their origin. The solution to this embarrassing situation was the release of the funds for "special cultural projects" in Israel.

FROZEN FUNDS AND FROZEN ACCOUNTS

What was the origin of these frozen funds? How did Israel come to freeze US funds? It seems strange for a young, small state, desperately in need of foreign support. Also, the US was a friendly state. It seems reasonable, although there is no proof, that the funds were frozen "by accident", in relation to the 1948 War, as part of the freezing of the property of absentees, namely, Palestinian refugees. The definition of "absentee" altered as a result of changing legislation in Israel. Basically, an absentee was anybody who left Israel for whatever reason between 29 November 1947 and the end of the war and stayed for even a short time in a neighbouring Arab country, or was a citizen of an Arab country (Fischbach 2003: 20–25). If US agents had mingled with the Palestinian population and left Israel at some time during the war through an Arab country such as Jordan, they were technically absentees. The property of Western foreigners who absented themselves to an Arab country was also declared absentee property, but Israel usually agreed to compensate such foreigners, unless they were Arabs with dual citizenship (Fischbach 2003: 24–5).

Several million Lira of absentees' money in bank accounts was sequestered by the Custodian for Absentees' Property, mainly in 1948 from the Ottoman Bank and Barclays Bank. It took several years and difficult negotiations to arrange the release of the frozen accounts by the UN Conciliation Commission for Palestine (UNCCP). Israel was at war with the countries where most of the refugees were living. In 1952 it agreed, as a token of goodwill, to start releasing the accounts. On their part, the refugees saw it as a natural act and many even refused at first to demand their assets so as not to acknowledge the existence of Israel. The money was returned in three stages. In the first stage, 20 percent of the accounts in two banks (the Ottoman Bank and Barclays Bank) was released only for individuals who were residents of Palestine before 19 November 1947 and who fled from it before 1 September 1948. Payment started in June 1953 and continued for several months (Tovi 2002: 276–83; Fischbach 2003: 195–202). A second phase began on 25 May 1954, when Barclays Bank agreed to lend Israel £5 million, of which £3 million was intended for releasing absentees' frozen accounts. Israel officially announced its willingness for this phase on 27 September 1954; it also included corporations, bonds and the contents of safe deposit boxes. Applications were collected in early 1955. Most of the requests were approved and most of the money was released by August 1955. This phase lasted, though, into 1957–59. By 1959 the Custodian for Absentees' Property had released £2,781,164, and yet "some outstanding accounts" remained. Then a list was made public in the whole region from Egypt to Lebanon, so that potential owners might find their assets (Fischbach 2003: 203–7; Tovi 2002: 283–9). Discussions about a third and final phase of release, for the much fewer remaining accounts in other banks, started in February 1956. The growing tension and the 1956 (Sinai) War delayed the issue until late 1959. The release took place from May 1962, lasting until 1966. In total, about £3.6 million was released (Fischbach 2003: 207–8).

If the funds called the "American frozen funds" in the GL documents studied here were part of the propery held or seized by the Custodian for Absentees' Property, the first phase of release happened too early, leaving them frozen, and the last (third) phase was much too late. The documents suggest that the release of the USIS funds was expected in early 1956 (it was spoken about using them in summer 1956). By early 1955 most of the second stage of release of absentees' accounts was over. However, Delougaz and Yeivin were corresponding about the release of the USIS funds from June 1954. This fits exactly the date of the decision by Barclays Bank in May 1954 to lend Israel money to release absentees' frozen accounts. This decision set the wheels in motion for the second stage. The long delay in releasing the American frozen funds was caused by the negotiations over their use and by the tension in US–Israeli relations surrounding the 1956 (Sinai) War. The USIS funds were finally released in August 1957. Perhaps the details will become clearer when more files are made available.

Various plans for the use of these funds, such as the Beit Jubrin improvement, did not materialize. I also found no evidence for the use of the frozen funds for US excavations in Israel (but maybe such evidence lies outside the scope of the files studied). There were no American excavations in Israel in 1954–58. Brandeis University excavated two sites in 1959 and Princeton University started to work in Caesarea in 1960. Between 1963 and 1966 Delougaz (and others) returned to several sites, and from then the number of American teams in Israel rose. There is no record of the sudden appearance of three American teams, as discussed between Yeivin and Delougaz.

FROZEN FUNDS AND IMPROVING SITES

One segment of the mystery can be solved with the help of documents related to the GTC Committee for Improving the Landscape. It was established at the end of 1955 under Kollek and included also Yadin and Yannay (Ch. 12). The committee discussed IDAM plans to improve Megiddo (GL44882/9 no. 471, 14.2.56). The minutes of one meeting included the following report:

> Furthermore, the plan of the GTC [is] to interest Mr Katzen [spelling unclear, but see below] of the American State Department, in doing restoration at Megiddo, Monfort and Zebita [Shivta in the Negev], using foreign currency accumulated by selling American [books? one word not clear] to Israel. It was decided by the Americans to dedicate it to a cultural purpose in Israel ... (GL44882/9, 25.2.57: p. 1)

For about two years the GTC Committee for Improving the Landscape worked with the Israeli government budget alone, because the Katzen funds remained frozen due to strains in Israel's relations with the US. The transfer of the Katzen funds occurred in November 1957, and then Kollek and the GTC created a committee for improving the landscape of the land and for developing historical sites as a non-profit-making organization; its English name was Israel–America Archaeological Foundation. This was a fictive creation. The articles of this association, following the rules set for such bodies, stated that it must have an annual general meeting, keep a register of members and have a supervision committee nominated from among the members (G11-5451, c.10.11.57). But there were only three members – Kollek, Yadin (Chairman) and Yannay (Secretary) – and therefore no supervision committee for lack of members to occupy such a committee.

Katz (2002) barely mentions this body, although he does write that it was created just to enable "monetary transactions".

The Second Secretary of the American embassy in Tel Aviv and "Officer in Charge of Program" Harold G. Williams, wrote to the Israel–America Archaeological Foundation on 1 November 1957. Added to the letterhead for "The Foreign Service of the United States of America" was the heading "American Special Cultural Program with Israel" (Fig. 13). The letter read:

> Gentlemen:
> The United States Government authorized in Public Law 85–170 the expenditure of funds for certain specific cultural, educational, and scientific projects in Israel. Your organization presented a project for the restoration of the historical sites of Megiddo, Montfort [*sic*.] and Subeita which was approved in the amount of IL 600,000, subject of course to negotiation and implementation within a reasonable period of time … (G11-5451)

US Law 85–170 of 28 August 1957 concerned the supplementary budget for the year ending 30 June 1958 (I thank M. Kersel for this information). Under the heading "Educational, Scientific, and Cultural Activities", in Chapter XI, which relates to the State Department, the law stipulated:

> For expenses to carry out the provisions of the United States Information and Educational Exchange Act of 1948, as amended (22. U.S.C. 1442(d)), $3,525,000: Provided that the amount shall be used for the purchase of foreign currencies for the Informational Media Guarantee [IMG, as mentioned in GL documents, see p. 104] program … (71 Stat.: 426)

The sum of 600,000 Lira was also mentioned by Levinson of the GTC, when refusing a request for help in building a memorial by the Menashe Regional Council. He explained that the 600,000 Lira was to be spent according to a contract with the Americans on improving five specific sites, so it could not be used for other purposes, even if they were noble (G11-5451, March 1958). The contract for Avdat and Shivta is later mentioned under "section 10-Katzen" in a letter from Levinson to Yaacov Ofer (a GTC employee, and later Director of the GTC Northern District) (G11-5451, 8.10.58). Williams asked the Israelis to provide details about their association, dates for the start and finish of the work, a detailed description of it, and so on. These details were transmitted to the American embassy, together with a plan to use the funds for Megiddo, Subeita (Shivta) and Monfort. Avdat and Athlit were mentioned as possible replacements:

> The regular budget of the society [for improving the landscape] is provided by the government of Israel … The government of Israel will supplement

THE FOREIGN SERVICE
OF THE
UNITED STATES OF AMERICA
American Special Cultural Program
with Israel

November 1, 1957.

Israel-American Archaeological Foundation,
    Jerusalem, Israel.

Gentlemen:

   The United States Government authorized in Public Law
85-170 the expenditure of funds for certain specific cultural,
educational, and scientific projects in Israel. Your organization presented a project for the restoration of the historical
sites of Megiddo, Montfort and Subeita which was approved in
the amount of IL 600,000, subject of course to negotiation
and implementation within a reasonable period of time after
negotiation of a grant-in-aid agreement between your organization and the United States Embassy in Tel Aviv.

   In order that the Embassy may have current information
on which to proceed with the negotiations, it will be
appreciated if the following will be transmitted as soon as
possible:

   (1) Official name of organization, address, and principal
officers.

   (2) Brief outline of the purpose of the organization
sponsoring this project and its affiliations.

   (3) Full description of the project as presently contemplated.

   (4) Earliest date project can be started.

   (5) Estimated date of completion of project.

   (6) If additional funds are required to complete this
project other than those provided under this Public Law,
please give full details, i.e., total amount required, whether
now available and, if not fully available at this time, when
will such funds become available.

- 2 -

   Your replies should be addressed to Mr. Harold G.
Williams, Second Secretary of Embassy, U. S. Embassy, Tel
Aviv.

                    Very truly yours,

                    Harold G. Williams
                    Second Secretary of Embassy
                    and Officer in Charge of Program

Figure 13. The frozen funds. Letter from Harold Williams to the "Israel-America
Archaeological Foundation", 1 November 1957. (G11/5451)

from its regular and development budget the work that will be initiated with
the aid of funds furnished by the American Special Program for Israel.
(G11-5451, Yadin to Harold Williams, 20.11.57)

On 22 January 1958 Kollek wrote to Yeivin:

Subject: Crusader fortresses at Athlit and Monfort
Considering the decision of the USA government and the fund it has allocated for that purpose, it was decided to [start] restorations in the two
above-mentioned fortresses. The work will be made through constant
consultation and supervision of Mr Avi-Yonah and Professor Prawer [both
of the Hebrew University].
   I will be very grateful if you notify me if you wish to receive more details
about this matter, or if you have comments about it.
[signed] T. Kollek   (GL44882/9 no. 5145)

Yeivin replied on 28 January 1958 (GL44882/9 no. 7097), writing that he was
happy to hear about it. The use of "funds" for Monfort and Megiddo was even
mentioned by Yeivin in public (*Alon* **5–6** (1957): 4). Later, on 19 November 1959,
the secretary of the IDAM, Hannah Katzenstein (1908–2004) (*Qadmoniyot* 2005:
64), reported to Avidor:

Discussions about improving the site [of Megiddo] began in May 1955
with the "Tourist Centre" … the money was allocated from the frozen
American funds (the Katzen fund) [the "a" in Katzen is written using the
Hebrew aleph, א] …   (GL44882/9 no. 3389)

The works at Avdat and Shivta proved to be far more expensive than originally planned. The cost was *c*.100,000–120,000 Lira above the planned budget;
so Yannay asked Kollek to convince the Americans to transfer 25,000 Lira from
Monfort, as otherwise work at Shivta and Avdat would have to be stopped before
completion (G12-5451, 8.4.59). Kollek explained to Dr Howard P. Backus, Special Assistant to the Ambassador, that the lack of roads to Monfort prevented
its immediate improvement (G12-5451 no. 220/13/3, 14.5.59; mentioning the
program under the initials "IMG", i.e. US Informational Media Guarantee). Backus
sent Kollek "the most recent report by Mr Bernard Katzen" (a US Republican
candidate in elections in New York in 1926, 1928 and 1932; www.political-
graveyard.com) on 6 May 1959 (G12-5451). Backus was probably responsible
at the time for the "American Special Cultural Program with Israel". Katzen's
eight-page report is missing from the file, but exists under the title "Mission to
Israel: Report and Recommendations to the Secretary of State, Washington" (see
www.chabadlibrary.org/ecatalog/EC01/EC01028.htm). It may also be found in the

Table 2 American payments to the GTC for site improvements (G13-5451, letter from Backus to Yannay, 27.10.59).

Date	Payment	Details
14.02.58	Payment 1, Biblical section	IL180,000 to Megiddo (plus IL22,500 for Monfort)
16.10.58	Payment 2, Nabatean section	IL90,000 for Shivta IL67,500 for Avdat
28.01.59	Payment 3, Crusader section	IL90,000 for Accho IL22,500 shifted from Monfort to Avdat
27.10.59	Payment 4, Crusader section	IL90,000 for Accho
Anticipated	Payment 5	The remaining 10% for Megiddo and Shivta, until IL40,000

collection of Senator Jacob Javits at Stony Brook University (www.stonybrook.edu/libspecial/collections/manuscripts/javits/, Container 8SS3, Box 4). I stress these sources because they are open to the public, so eventually the story can be told from the American side too.

The funds were used to improve Megiddo, Accho and Avdat for tourism. Work at Megiddo started in 1957 and the site was opened in a ceremony in October 1959. Work at Shivta ended in August 1958 and the site was also opened ceremoniously, with a speech by the American ambassador (GL44882/9, letter by Yannay, 18.8.59). Avi-Yonah was responsible for the archaeological work there (GL44882/9 no. 9228, 22.8.58), and he was the excavator responsible for Avdat (GL44882/9, memorandum of meeting, 23.6.60). When discussions took place about Athlit, Avi-Yonah was mentioned as a manager (but this plan did not materialize).

Letters in G13-5451 from Kollek, Yannay and Backus show that the Americans defined three types of sites: Biblical (Megiddo), Nabatean (Avdat, Shivta) and Crusader (originally Monfort, replaced by Accho). They kept back 10 percent of each payment until they received satisfactory written reports on the conducted works. The contract (not traced) probably stipulated that Israel must invest at least as much as the Americans. Details of the payments are shown in Table 2. The total allocation was 600,000 Lira, as mentioned by Williams on 1 November 1957 (above). The Americans tried to avoid including relief workers (called "unskilled labour force") in this budget, but their reason was not stated (G13-5451, Backus to Yannay, 27.10.59). The allocation of payments and the timetable went according to plan.

The Committee for Improving the Landscape also enjoyed its archaeological roles. In February 1959 Kollek arranged a study visit to Cyprus to see Crusader sites, with noted experts of Crusader archaeology such as Yannay and Dayan (G12-5451, letter from Dayan, 20.6.59, offering to return the expenses). In June 1959 Yannay reported that the Americans were ready to give 50,000 Lira for a Crusader Museum in Accho, so he would have to go to Italy and France to find out what items they might lend. He also specified that they would have to erect the museum by the end of the year; perhaps this was the final date for the Katzen program (G13-5451, 5.6.59). To the Americans Yannay wrote:

> We have pleasure [in] confirming the sums invested by us for improvement of the historical sites of Avdat and Shivta … We have already exceeded the sums allocated by you. Nevertheless we continue with the improvements as we feel that the completion of the work is highly desirous …
>
> (G13-5451, 1.1.59)

However, he wrote to the Ministry of Finance just a week earlier complaining about the poor Israeli budget for "his" committee. A very similar version of this complaint appeared in another letter he wrote on the same day to Kollek, with a copy to Yadin:

> Perhaps the Budget department will claim that we received money from the Americans. As is known, this money is for specific aims which are not included in the list of our works, and they would not have been made from the regular budget; these sites are not at the top of our list of priorities. Without the funding of the Americans, we would not have performed these works but only after several years …   (G11-5451 dated 24.12.58)

Yannay did not deceive the Americans about the value of the improved sites; he just tried to wangle more budget from Israel by arguments that were far from accurate.

The history of the frozen funds was not mentioned in the many archaeological textbooks, excavation reports and studies written in the past half century. A ten-year gap existed in the history of our major sites between 1948 and c.1958. The GTC's version prevailed, for example, in a report about Megiddo (GL44882/9, "Prime Minister's Office: Report of the Commissioner for Landscaping and the Preservation of Historic Sites", c.1960). Similarly in the little "brown" guide for tourists to Megiddo, issued in about 1960 by the GTC:

> Megiddo. Original archaeological excavations on this site were carried out by the Oriental Institute of the University of Chicago between 1926 and 1939 … Since then, the site was neglected, its matchless relics disappearing under weed and bramble. In 1958 it was chosen as a site for clearance and restoration by the department for landscaping and the preservation of historical sites [of the GTC]. The project was made possible by the generosity of the United States Government under the American Special Cultural Program with Israel.

THE ESTABLISHMENT OF THE GTC

Perhaps the entire establishment of the GTC was related to the USIS funds. The GTC was officially established by the government in August 1955, while the unfreezing of absentees' funds became evident in May 1954 (when Barclays Bank offered the loan). It could have taken some months to complete the beaurocratic and legal procedures. The GTC was oxymoronic: a "private governmental company". It had articles (*taqanon*) of the usual format for a limited company with shareholders, but it was a rather peculiar company. The articles of the GTC stated that it was registered as a private company, but the government held all the shares:

> We, the persons whose names and addresses are listed below, wish to associate in a company following the articles [*tazkir*] of this association and agree to maintain the number of shares in the fund of the company registered against our names written below:
> The Development Authority .... One share
> The State of Israel............................Ninety nine shares
> (GL44882/9, returned from Staner 5.12.55)

The "persons" was the State itself. Perhaps the Development Authority was added because just one "person" could not form a "company"; but the Development Authority was hardly different from the state. GTC workers could not be considered government workers, although in practice they came from among government workers and worked under the same conditions (G-7/5451, letter from Yitzhak Levi, Deputy Director Prime Minister's Office, to Kollek, 8.9.55). The GTC managers signed a declaration like this one:

> I, Theodore Kollek, declare hereby that I hold shares of the GTC and rule as chairman of the board of managers [*mo'ezet menahalim*] in the said company not as a governmental employee personally, but as delegate of the government and its representative. I sign the ordinance and articles of the company with authorization; following the law of governmental properties (*nichsei ha-Medinah*).
> [signed] _____   (G7/5451, unsigned copy, October 1955)

On 12 October 1955 Ben-Shabtai, the GTC legal advisor, applied to the register of companies:

> Subject: GTC
> The said company is established by decision of the government; its managers will be appointed by the Prime Minister; all its shares will be held by the government; its entire budget will be accepted from the government; all its

employees will be governmental workers. Therefore, I humbly request you
to register the said company without the words "limited warranty" [initials
for *be'eravon mugbal*].   (G7-5451)

The number of shareholders was limited to 50. Under section 1, no. 7, the
managers of the GTC had the right to refuse transfer of shares. Even if someone
legally inherited a share, they could refuse him or her, and they were not obliged
to explain why. Why was all this needed when GTC articles stated that the capital
of the new company amounted to 100 shares worth 1 Lira each? This was not
much capital.

Of course, the government financed the GTC. If so, why all the fuss about a
"private company"? Was the "private" side needed as a source of jobs for "our
men"? This is a much too cynical explanation. Was it done to enable more flexibility in activities, spending budget and so on? This is what Katz (2004: 78)
seems to think. If flexibility was the reason for establishing the GTC, perhaps it
was needed to spend the expected "Katzen funds" without too many questions
being asked. However, the documents I studied do not prove this; and a detailed
history of the GTC is beyond the scope of this book.

FROZEN FUNDS AND THE ISRAEL MUSEUM, JERUSALEM

Perhaps by this stage readers should not be surprised to discover that another
major portion of the "Katzen funds" served as the basis of the Israel Museum,
Jerusalem. Tamir (1990), most probably unaware of the "frozen" origin of
the funds, tells the accepted story of the creation of the museum. According to
her, Mordechai Narkiss, the director of the Bezalel art school, had the vision
and Kollek was the hero who made it real. She conveniently ignores Yeivin and
the IDAM, who conceived it earlier (GL44880/13, 4.7.55 proves that in 1955
Yeivin told Kollek about the plan for "a complex of museums"). This is what
Tamir wrote:

> Tedi Kollek took up the idea with full gusto ... It was Narkiss' last point,
> that the donation of gifts was being held up, that spurred Tedi Kollek ...
> to even greater efforts to actualize the dream of a unified Israeli National
> Museum. For Kollek was aware that American Jews were prominent among
> the donors to major museums in the United States ...
>
> These prospects did not become more concrete until 1956, when Bernard
> Katzen, special representative of the United States government, came to
> Israel on behalf of the America–Israel Museum Fund – the fund that enabled
> initial realization of the project – to recommend how the sum being supplied

could best be allocated. Two years later, when Narkiss was no longer alive, Katzen told Walter Eytan, the chairman of the Bezalel [art school] executive, that the single greatest influence on his decision to support the project had been Narkiss' well-reasoned argument for constructing a new building for Bezalel ...

In March 1957 Kollek informed Narkiss that "with the improvement of our relations with the United States, there is every chance that we will get the money for the Museum" ... (Tamir 1990: 8–9)

A Committee for a National Museum was established in 1957, directly connected with the American funds. Kollek, Yadin, Yannay and others were nominated for membership of the committee, later joined by Beham of the GTC and Biran (nominated in October 1958). Yeivin was never invited. Tamir admired Kollek, who:

would travel, conduct negotiations and generally advance the project ... It was Kollek's unbounded energy that ultimately fueled the bulldozers that leveled the rocky slopes of Neve Sha'anan, the site chosen for the museum complex after protracted debate ... In a letter dated 26 August 1957, Bernard Katzen formally apprised Walter Eytan and Tedi Kollek that the United States Congress had endorsed his recommendation regarding establishment of a comprehensive museum in Israel. (Tamir 1990: 9–10)

Katzen informed them that the US would "contribute" 7 million Lira, equal to US$1.5 million for that aim (see more below). In 1958 the agreement was signed between the American government and the America–Israel Museum Fund. (Care must be taken not to confuse this with the America–Israel Cultural Foundation (AICF, formerly the American Fund for Israeli Societies; see Ch. 10) chaired by Raphael Recanati, which also gave donations to the Israel Museum in the same period. To the best of my knowledge it had no relation with frozen funds.) The America–Israel Museum Fund was, unsurprisingly, registered as a non-profit-making organization. The Ambassador to Israel, Edward B. Lawson, signed the agreement on behalf of the American side (Tamir 1990: 10). Another document from 24 September 1961 states that the American government allocated 1.5 million Lira, while Israel contributed the land (GL44871/10 no. 9398, 24.9.61). The American funds were used to build Phase A of c.6100 square metres (GL44871/10, minutes of meeting 20.3.61); in fact the area was somewhat larger. Phase A was the central building. Its plan was agreed in April 1959 and construction started in 1960. As in the procedure for handling the funds for improving sites, the Americans first gave 1,350,000 Lira, keeping back 10 percent. On 23 February 1962 the museum committee decided to ask the Americans to allocate the remaining 150,000 Lira (GL44871/10, minutes of meeting: p. 2). Of course, the museum received other and even larger donations later.

Even the name of the museum was chosen by Katzen or one of his colleagues. From 1957 onwards, the museum in the making was called by various names, but most commonly "the national museum". For example, in the minutes of the meeting of the "technical committee for the national museum" of 30 August 1959, the first section reminded the members to take care – following the requests of the Americans – to call the museum the Israel–America Museum Foundation (GL44871/10). The name Israel Museum, Jerusalem appeared in a meeting of 20 March 1961 (GL44871/10). When Kollek confirmed with Charles Bronfman a donation of one million dollars, the agreement stated that the museum in general would be called "either the Jerusalem Museum or the National Museum of Art and Archaeology" (GL44871/10, copy of a draft dated 27.2.61, #2).

As Tamir (1990: 13) notes, the museum "has always been regarded as the country's national museum". Indeed, the committee for the establishment of the museum wanted to name it the "National Museum". However,

> Professor Yadin reviewed various conversations about it with the American embassy. The government of the United States is opposed to calling the museum the "National Museum" and suggests on the other hand naming it the "Israel Museum, Jerusalem". It was decided to adopt this suggestion. It may take a while until the change will become valid since it involves a few administrative changes …
>
> (GL44871/10 no. 9863, minutes of meeting
> of the museum committee 20.5.63, #4)

The Americans chose a beautiful name; it seems that Katzen and his colleagues worked with considerable intelligence. On the other hand, by May 1962 the museum committee had spent about 3.3 million Lira for Phase A, which was supposed to cost about 1.5 million Lira (the total American funding for the museum). The excess was due to changes to the original plans and additional components. The State Comptroller warned that phases B–C would cost much more than their planned budget of about 7 million Lira (GL44871/10, letters to Beham 3.3.62, etc.). The museum committee, in its meeting of 20 May 1963, discussed a plan to ask for a US government loan of 3.5 million Lira for 20 years, an idea conceived by Billie Rose, but:

> The Ministry of Finance is not interested in another discussion of the affair of the Katzen funds in the US senate; and the American embassy [in Tel Aviv] received a notice that, indeed, such a discussion might be necessary unless there was a special order from the President of the US. Mr Beham asked to go to Washington to find out the various possibilities there. No

doubt the presence of Tedi Kollek in the US at the same time will ease the
work ... (GL44871/10, minutes of meeting 20.5.63, #2)

The committee started to cut the budget (GL44871/10, minutes of 10.7.63).
News from the US about a possible loan of the money from the "revenue funds"
(*temurah*, see below) were not encouraging, in view of changes in US legislation (GL44871/10, minutes 16.33.64, #5). In July 1963 a deficit of 3 million Lira
existed (GL44871/10, draft attached to a meeting from 9.9.63). On 23 February
1965 Kollek wrote to Beham from abroad in English:

> Dear Yohanan,
> On the day before my departure, you told me that you have sufficient funds
> until the end of March, and that you would need another IL2,000,000 for
> the opening between 1 April and 15 May.
> Now, to my astonishment, I get a cable from you calling for additional
> funds immediately ... I was quite willing to accept personal responsibil-
> ity for IL1,000,000, pledging, so to say, my personal credit, but I think it
> would be unwise for us to repeat such a procedure before we have a clear
> undertaking of major donations indicating how and when we shall be able
> to repay these debts and so far we have none ...
> If it is discovered that a large amount of money is required soonest, and
> none is in until then and none is likely to be forthcoming quickly, I urge
> that the Hanhala [= management], armed with the financial statement,
> approach the government for help. Such help is surely justified, for we
> have not exactly sat back with our arms folded ... Moreover, I want all
> governmental bodies concerned to know that they may be called upon to
> help us out, and the time to prepare the ground is now; for the fact is that
> we may not be successful in our endeavours here and in the United States,
> and we may be faced with huge disbursements before the opening with no
> funds to cover them. (GL44871/10, 23.2.65)

In the next museum committee meeting in July, Kollek said that the situation
was fairly complex and they were "in the mud". There were pressing debts mainly
from the construction. A sum of 4.5 million Lira was required up to December
for survival; but at that time not a penny of it was available. Yet he was optimistic
about more donations. Yannay thought that Kollek was too optimistic though.
Perhaps only 2.5 million Lira was missing, he said, but salvation could come
from just two sources: governmental-municipal, or a loan (GL44871/10, minutes
of meeting 26.7.65). Biran told the committee in August not to be under any
illusion about donations: 3 million dollars was needed to cover the deficit. By
getting rid of any idea of donations they could:

"... direct our steps to convince the government, the municipality [of Jeru-
salem] and the Jewish Agency that, really, they carry the responsibility for
daily maintenance at least for 2 million Lira. Our demand to these institutions is justified in view of the large enterprise that was erected ...". Yadin
added: "In a meeting with government representatives, it was agreed that
we would demand immediately that the municipality, the government and
the Jewish Agency take part in the regular budget in appropriate sums."
(GL44871/10, minutes from 23.8.65: p. 5)

There are excellent studies about the architecture of the museum (see Kroyanker
1991: 143–8), but none about its budget troubles. Kollek never revealed anything
about it, always maintaining the façade of glamour (e.g. Kollek & Goldstein 1994:
320–27). However, the mayor of Jerusalem in 1959–65, Mordechai Ish-Shalom,
had his own misgivings. Ish-Shalom (1989: 317–20) claimed that Kollek abused
the museum, using it as a springboard to gain public positions; Although far from
playing first fiddle in the creation of the museum, Kollek planted in the minds
of the public the idea that he alone had created it. Kollek even tried to omit Ish-
Shalom from the list of speakers at the opening of the museum. As Ish-Shalom
obviously had an account to settle with Kollek, one should take his words with a
pinch of salt. However, more important, and amusing, is Ish-Shalom's revelation
about the "Katzen funds":

> The first donation was from US government money. There was then a
> settlement between the government of the US and the government of Israel,
> about transferring revenues [*temurah*] of American books sold in Israel. It
> was agreed that the money would be left in Israel to encourage cultural and
> public institutions in Israel. The person who suggested the idea and who
> pushed to implement it was Bernard Katzen, a Jewish politician [*'askan*],
> member of the Republican Party. This money also received the nickname
> "Katzen funds". Katzen came to Israel for a visit in February 1956 to advise
> the US government how to use these funds. Until then, 7 million Lira
> gathered in Israel, destined for allocation. We won one million Lira. We
> received the cheque from the US ambassador, Mr Ogdan Rid ...
> (Ish-Shalom 1989: 317–18)

The "books theory" was a bit too clumsy a cover story, for immigrants from
Arab countries did not read English. Other immigrants originated mostly from
central and eastern Europe where German, Polish and Russian dominated; but
books are the stuff that dreams are made of.

The further history of the Israel Museum is beyond the scope of this study.
What should be pointed out is the way the GTC operated. In both cases (the
museum and the ancient sites) the GTC formed "sister" bodies, registered as non-

profit-making organizations. Their key players were the GTC managers, with very few others (notably Yadin). There were no private shareholders or supervision committees and annual assemblies, if held, were a formality. The English names of these bodies were "America–Israel" funds. In both cases they used frozen funds, supervised by the US embassy. The funds were given following a strict and orderly procedure, keeping 10 percent until the Americans were satisfied with the work. Israel was committed to matching the same sum for each project. The works had a rigid timetable, explaining perhaps some of the haste in their execution. In both cases, the GTC and its sub-bodies did not maintain the budget, nor did they consider the need for daily maintenance once the projects were ended.

THE GENERAL SCOPE OF THE FROZEN FUNDS

So far we have traced the use of about 2.1 million Lira of frozen funds. Today it seems a minor sum, but in 1957–58 the budget of the IDAM was 310,000 Lira; so even this figure was enough to fund the IDAM for nearly seven years. When Yeivin first heard about the funds in 1954, they seemed imaginary to him. Why the Americans kept such large amounts in Mandatory Palestine is a question for military historians, not archaeologists, but it probably started in the Second World War as part of the war effort in 1942. The documents sometimes mention dollars, but usually Lira, and the sums remain fixed, although the documents range over several years during which time the rate between the two currencies changed. Consider Tamir (1990), who thought that the American Katzen would surely hand out dollars, and probably translated the sum of 1.5 million Lira given to the museum into dollars, and then back as 7 million Lira. Not knowing the origin of the funds this was a natural conclusion. It is likely that the funds started as Mandatory pounds and then at the end of Mandatory rule, when frozen, they became Israeli Lira (at first equal to pounds and stronger than dollars). The Lira deteriorated against foreign currencies, but the funds remained fixed in Lira. Confirmation comes from documents from the American embassy in Tel Aviv, which refer to Lira. Furthermore, one letter specified how to deal with a cheque coming from the Americans – in Lira (G11/5451, 8.10.58). The fact that American funding was handled in Israeli Lira is a strong indication of its unusual origins, for the US government would normally have dollars, not Lira, to give (exactly what Tamir expected).

Ish-Shalom mentioned the general scope of the frozen funds as about 7 million Lira (1989: 318). However, one can doubt his accuracy (he remembered one million Lira when the museum eventually received 1.5 million Lira). Another clue about the general scope of the Katzen funds comes from an unlikely source: the mayor of the city of Safad. The story goes like this. In the summer of 1958 the American ambassador and Kollek made a tour of the north. They reached Safad and met its mayor, who learned something about the American funds. During this meeting or slightly later Kollek promised to help Safad. The Mayor of Safad, Avraham Hacohen, explained in a letter to Yannay of 14 April 1959 that while Kollek was on holiday in Safad they agreed "clearly" that the municipality would perform works in the old city to encourage tourism. Kollek committed to invest up to 20,000 Lira. The municipality sent Yannay plans, marking streets that they would "pave, fix and improve". The mayor added:

> I asked Tedi to confirm it in writing since I have bitter experience with governmental institutions when I do not have written confirmation. Tedi reconfirmed that there is no need, and that I must start work immediately. In his second visit during the [IES] conference of the archaeologists, he raged at me for my talk with the President's entourage [after I approached it]; ... saying "really I approved a sum for the old city, why do you complain?" [By this] he reconfirmed what was agreed upon in summer.
>
> I now apply to you asking you not to fail me, for my monetary situation is already difficult and complex because of the recent things we have done in the past two years mainly for tourism, such as enlarging and improving the fortress ... [and] building a swimming pool, for which we did not receive any support from the government ... I must remind you that the Safad municipality did not receive a penny from the American Cultural Foundation (KAZ"N) [writing as an acronym]. Actually Tedi agreed to do the improvements in the old city [only] because of my talk with the American ambassador ...
>
> I appreciate your [moral] support, but it cannot absolve you from your commitment, which was already made ... I end my letter calling: please do not fail me!   (G12-5451 no. 1130-59)

Yannay claimed that there was no commitment; so Hacohen wrote again on 26 April 1959:

> So still it was found that justice is with me, and there is no reason to ignore Tedi Kollek's promise. Instead of sharing my sorrow, I would ask you to share our pressured financial condition, which came as a result of performing works for you without any monetary cover ...
>
> Incidentally, I told you and also Tedi Kollek how much I am criticized by the members of the municipal council for not applying at the time to Mr Kazin to ask for help for cultural aims. The truth is that I am amazed that out of 6 million Lira you did not see it worthwhile to allocate anything for Safad ... In no way can I give up the agreement made between Tedi Kollek and myself (in front of quite respectable witnesses). I therefore ask

you to hand out the necessary orders for reimbursement in our favour …
If you still cannot comply with this request, I shall exert no more pressure,
and shall understand that you [in plural] have failed me and caused the
financial distress in which I find myself without an escape.

(G12-5451 no. 1280/1/59)

Yannay answered that one allocation of 10,000 Lira, intended for Safad, could
not be transferred as money since equipment was already ordered, and:

> The section in your letter about not applying to Mr Katzen about allocation
> to Safad is not clear to me. We never prevented you from such application.
> I also do not understand your claim that out of 6 million Lira "you did not
> see it worthwhile to allocate something for Safad". The money is not ours
> and the list of institutions, to which money was allocated, was arranged by
> the United States government – like institutions in Haifa, Jerusalem and
> Tel Aviv. Perhaps under certain treatment, institutions at Safad could also
> receive endowments. All this, of course, if the United States government
> would have approved the aims.   (G12-5451)

Yannay was sarcastic. The sites were suggested to the Americans by the GTC and
Safad was never included. Furthermore, in the tour with Kollek, after meeting the
Mayor of Safad, the American ambassador told Kollek that he would be happy to
allocate a small sum to Safad. However, Kollek wrote to Yannay that he thought
that "this would not be necessary" (G11-5451, October 1958).

The Mayor of Safad mentioned 6 million Lira as the sum of the "Katzen funds".
In his answers Yannay never corrected this sum, which fits well with Ish-Shalom's
reckoning of 7 million Lira. Apart from the $3.535 million intended for the IMG
programme according to US law 85–170 (see above), the same law mentioned a
further sum of $2.745 million assigned to the President as the "President's Special
International Program", which was "to remain available until expanded". Out of
this sum, $0.545 million was to be allocated for an international exhibition. The
sum seemingly available to Israel was $6.27 million (3.535 + 2.745), perhaps
another indication of the provenance of the frozen funds, if the Lira–dollar
exchange rate is taken as 1:1.

So far we have traced the use of about a third of these funds. It should not
be too difficult to find the rest following the period 1957–59, looking for the
involvement of: the GTC and Kollek; cultural institutions in the cities of Haifa, Tel
Aviv and Jerusalem (mentioned by Yannay above); non-profit-making organizations called "America–Israel Foundations"; and the "American Special Cultural
Program with Israel". It is also possible that the programme was halted because
of changes in American legislation (referred to above).

Tamir (1990: 11) praised the establishers of the Israel Museum for their success in creating a "museum consciousness". On frequent visits to the Israel Museum, I have pondered on the basis upon which proud national symbols stand, watching the modern statues in the Billie Rose Sculpture Garden, poised in suspension in thin Jerusalem air. The story of "frozen funds" does not change my appreciation and affection for the Israel Museum. It is a wonderful museum, an architectonic miracle, full of unique antiquities, and staffed by distinguished experts and their colleagues. But exhibiting the past cannot be done properly by silencing parts of it. The museum consciousness must now accommodate frozen funds, or else the cement walls of the buildings will forever dominate the antiquities inside.

5   A BATTALION OF GUARDS

When will the stern fine "who goes there"
Meet me again in midnight air?
And the gruff sentry's kindness, when
Will kindness have such power again?

Edmund Blunden ("The Watchers", 1930)

On 27 December 1948 Yeivin wrote to the head of the Public Works Administration. The bitter experience of the previous months, and especially the case of Megiddo, had shown him that without taking action it would be impossible to prevent sites and monuments being damaged and collections being robbed by soldiers. He and Pat, the army officer responsible for liaison with the public, devised a plan:

> The IDAM will prepare a detailed list of 40–50 places that need guarding against damage and destruction, and special armed guards will be nominated, a kind of *Notrim* (Geffirs) battalion, as existed formerly in Mandatory times. They will be placed under the local army or police commander, according to need, and will act under the order of the IDAM. These *Notrim* will be responsible for guarding the monuments or collections, or any other property under their supervision.   (GL1342/22 no. 1)

Yeivin suggested a budget of 3,000 Lira per month for 50 guards, shared by four ministries: Public Works, Defence, Religious Affairs and Foreign Affairs. A meeting was arranged with Kahana (the Ministry of Religious Affairs); Dr Mordechai Ettinger (later Etter) (General Secretary for Interior Affairs at the Ministry of Transport), Yeivin and Ben-Dor (GL1342/22, 17.1.49). The Ministry of Foreign Affairs refused to join in. Kahana objected to the idea of a shared budget and suggested that an army unit should do the guarding. Yeivin answered that this was impossible. Ettinger wondered about a special police force, and asked what the custom had been during the Mandatory period. Yeivin explained that the Mandatory Department of Antiquities had used Arab guards (paid 3–4 pounds per month), but this arrangement had only been partially successful.

The Israeli police were not available for such missions. It was decided to meet again, inviting also the ministries of Defence, the Interior, Foreign Affairs and the Department of Tourism (Figs 14–15).

Meanwhile, the IDAM prepared a tentative list of sites (GL1342/22) based on a Mandatory period list that named 21 guards with their sites and salaries. Yeivin suggested having 20 guards in sites under military rule (Ashkelon, Beit Jubrin, Caesarea, Beth Shean, Megiddo, Zippori, Ramla, Lod, Jerusalem and Selbit) and in civilian jurisdiction. The same people met again on 31 January 1949, together with representatives from the mMinistries of the Interior, Immigration and Tourism, Religious Affairs and Defence.

The result was a four-page memorandum from Yeivin (GL1342/22). He reported that since most of the sites were in military areas or far from settlements, the Friends of Antiquities could not solve the problem. Pat (Ministry of Defence) asked whether the number of places could be reduced. Yeivin replied that the list could be reduced by at most one or two sites. Kahana (Ministry of Religious Affairs) suggested adding more religious sites; his office had made a list of 250 holy sites, and had already posted guards, nominated by military commands in places lacking civilian settlements. Yeivin explained that the problem was not one of supervision, but that full-time guarding through the creation of a battalion of guards was required. Pat warned against mixing civilian and mili-

Figure 14. Ashkelon "museum", 1949. The sign says "Out of Bounds by Order". (Photograph by Ory, IAA 496)

Figure 15. Ashkelon, 1949. "The family of the antiquities guard" with Ory's daughter (behind). Note the basket of oranges on the left. The first IDAM guards started work in 1951. This, then, is the family of the former guard, Mohamad Ismail Radi (according to an undated Mandatory period list), who lived at the site at least until 1949. (Photograph by Ory, IAA 941)

tary authorities; guards should be like *Geffirs* with special uniforms and arms, but perhaps (to save budget) without cars at first, or Arabs could be appointed (although officially wages were equal for all citizens, in fact Arabs were sometimes employed for lower wages). He suggested appointing only 16 guards for a trial period of half a year, with a budget shared by all offices. Yeivin concluded that a list of 15 sites must be made and the participants must seek the support of their ministers. The question of who would administer the guards remained open (GL1342/22).

Yeivin sent the following memorandum to all concerned on 8 February 1949:

> The experience of the IDAM during the few months of its existence shows that damage is caused by military acts to the dear remains of our past in the land and also to holy places that belong to the state or to various religious churches, sometimes out of ignorance and carelessness and sometimes even on purpose. The fact that so many non-Jewish residents left their settlements and in some places abandoned [them] for military reasons also caused damage to sites and to collections in the deserted areas.
>
> The experience of the last months shows that it is impossible to prevent destruction by memoranda and orders issued by the Chief of Staff and various brigades, or by agreements with local commanders, or by explaining or preaching to soldiers. As long as there are no special persons to supervise the carrying-out of such orders, it is difficult to ascertain whether they have been fulfilled. Local commanders change occasionally and appealing to conscience has no immediate impact …
>
> In two meetings … it was found that there is no alternative but to establish a special battalion of guards, whose members will be placed for the time being at the most important places in order to guard them continually …

1,000 Lira will be needed per month to maintain 20 guards, or 6,000 for the first half year, and a further 1,000 Lira for organization … However, this sum will prevent much larger expenses incurred paying compensation and damages, which will be caused if guarding is not arranged.

(GL1342/22, 8.2.49)

The first Chief of Police, Sahar, agreed to take care of the administration of a guard unit. It was the *zena* period of severe shortages and food rationing, and Sahar mentioned that a similar arrangement existed for "supervisors of food" (GL1342/22 no. 8, 31.3.49), who, although not policemen, had some similar powers, including searching private homes. On 6 May 1949 Yeivin informed Pat that he had spoken with the Chief of Staff, General Yadin, who had suggested a unit under the civilian police. Sahar agreed in principle, but asked for a budget. Yeivin applied to the Ministry of Defence, because guards would also be needed at border posts or army camps (GL1342/22 no. 9). The IDAM tried to include an item of 12,000 Lira for guards in its 1949/50 budget; and campaigned for this among other ministries (Ben-Dor, GL1342/22, 15.6.49). The army admitted that it did not have the ability to guard ancient sites, especially since "the soldiers do not always distinguish a ruin [*khirbeh*] in general from what deserves protection" (GL1342/22 no. 2041, 20.6.49; cf. 28.6.49). However, Pat told Yeivin that the Ministry of Defence would not provide a budget. They applied to the Ministry of Finance (GL1342/22, summary 2.6.49, letter no. 17835).

Meanwhile, word about the new unit spread. On 18 July 1949 Amiran suggested that the guards appointed should be interested in antiquities. On 22 July 1949 Yeivin wrote to Sahar (GL1342/22 no. 11, copy in GL44869/3) asking for 16 full-time guards and 6 part-time guards at 22 sites and one commander for the unit. Some guards could supervise more than one site, but the Negev, the coast of Accho and the Galilee required guards with motorcycles. The list included the most important sites, of all types and periods. Further talks were held with the police, and a search for nominees began (GL1342/22 nos. 12, 14; 998). Yeivin informed the Ministry of Education on 16 September 1949 that the battalion needed a jeep for the commander and five motorcycles, but the police could not supply vehicles (GL44869/2 no. 1016). He drafted a budget of 600 Lira for a jeep and 350 Lira for a motorcycle. He speculated about the commander – "Pesah Bar-Adon? Munya Feldman?" – then added: "Careful selection – see Ruth's [Amiran's] suggestions" (GL1342/22, not numbered).

File GL1342/22 was closed when a budget was finally approved, and a search for nominees started (GL44869/3). Interesting ideas arose at this stage, as Yeivin wrote:

I talked with Y. Ory about the guards' battalion and he has a very reasonable offer. Clearly the guards will be, occasionally, busy supervising their sites and guiding visitors, but most of their time they will spend idle. This may exert in the long run a bad psychological effect on the people, making them used to a life of idleness and boredom.

He suggests compelling guards to perform four hours of work per day, that is, actually four hours of work in addition to the time spent guarding and guiding. One could find them work in the field, which would be very beneficial. They would be able to clear rubble from ancient sites, clear them of weeds, make paths, build roads, etc. ... They can also perform small acts of preservation, [such as] fixing ruined walls ... Even if they work a little every day, the months and years will join such hours of work into considerable amounts. They must also be committed to active help in nearby excavations ...   (GL44869/3 no. 980, 18.10.49)

In October 1949 Shimeon Nahmani from Jerusalem was chosen to be the commander of the new unit, but its exact form was not yet decided (GL44869 no. 1187). On 2 November 1949 *Ma'ariv* newspaper mentioned the battalion, and as a result some people applied for jobs (GL44869/3 no. 1139, 8.11.49). On 13 November Nahmani told one candidate that, indeed, a battalion of guards (*Notrim*) was being formed under the conditions:

Salary level like a policeman; equipment provided (shoes, clothes); licence to carry weapons (you have to acquire the weapon, for each guard is responsible personally for his weapon and its use). From a guard we demand, in addition to guarding, maintaining the site, for example keeping it clean, weeding, and a favourable attitude to antiquities in general.   (GL44869/3 1384)

Yeivin finally decided that the battalion would be part of the IDAM, but that its equipment and police authority would come from the police (GL44869/3 no. 1408, 16.11.49). He asked about the salary of a "simple policeman" for the guards and of a sergeant (*samal rishon*) for the commander. Yeivin wrote to Yadin that guards would be involved with soldiers, and should be able to handle them. Colonel Shimeon Avidan (one of the first Friends of Antiquities; see Jackier and Dagan 1995) was then Chief of Operations at General Headquarters, and he promised Yeivin that he would find out how to arrange matters with the military police. Yeivin wanted the guards to be able to "bring criminal soldiers in front of the military police" (GL44869/3 no. 1409, 16.11.49). However, Yadin clarified that the army would not delegate the authority to arrest soldiers to the guards of antiquities, unless they had the authority of the police. Since the guards were to be civilians, they would have to have the authority of a "civilian policeman". Therefore, he suggested that antiquities guards should be sworn in as "added [*musafim*] policemen". This would give them the authority to arrest soldiers (GL44869/3 no. 1493, 20.12.49).

On 2 December 1949 the police agreed to draft guards on the condition that they would be chosen by the IDAM with the consent of the police and that women would not be drafted. The IDAM would pay salaries through the police for three months in advance, and an additional 25 Lira per guard for equipment provided by the police. Sodom and Beit Jubrin could not come under this arrangement (they were probably still under military rule; GL44869/3 no. 1393). The IDAM issued a form of registration, which was completed by one applicant as follows:

Family name: *R.*   Private name: *Aharon*
Date of birth: *1903/15/5* [*sic.*]   Birthplace: *Tiberias*
State: *Israel*
Immigrated [*ʿAlah*] to Israel: *immigrated to Israel*
Family status: *5 souls*
Finished elementary school: *Alliance school*
High school classes: —
Language knowledge: *French Hebrew Arabic*
Speaking: —   Writing: —
Profession: *without profession*
In addition, worked in the following jobs: —
Service in foreign army: *no*
Service in the Hagana: *member of Hagana*
Service in IDF: *no*   (GL44869/3)

It is a sad form; the man was not recruited (GL44869/3 no. 1569). On 23 December 1949 Nahmani held a meeting with the police. Seven people were chosen as the first guards, including Fritz Berger, Yariv Shapira and Nehemia Zori. The police promised to draft them once the budget arrived. However, Nahmani reported to Yeivin on 28 December 1949 that his unit was the only one of its kind in the country. The holder of a position with the Mandatory title *Noter* had the duties of a policeman but few rights; the *Noter* did not receive additions to salary like a policeman. The sergeant of the unit was a *Noter*, with the addition of rank but without out-of-base expenses, or the use of a car to move from place to place:

> This made me realize that the problem must be reviewed from scratch. I believe that none of our guards will agree to work for a salary of 36 Lira [per month] ... Furthermore, if our unit is given the status of *Noter*, it is inconceivable that a Mandatory period status will please the men ... I suggest employing what was called in the Mandatory period "special policemen", who besides the oath and uniform are not part of the police ...
>
> (GL44869/3)

A whole year passed, and the appointed guards started to have doubts. One of them wrote to Nahmani:

> At the time Ruth Amiran applied to me about my consent to serve in a police brigade for supervising and keeping antiquities ... I announced my consent for it was my sole wish to move to work in one of the fields of archaeology. I received several notices about the progress of the matter ... [and] on 25.12.49 you announced that work would soon start. Since I am still a member of an agricultural cooperative, leaving my agricultural work requires certain formal arrangements. I must know: is there certainty about the existence of this battalion and my work in it? When will work start?
> ...   (GL44869/3, 21.1.50)

In March 1950 the budget was transferred to the police. The guards were defined as "added policemen" (GL44869/3 no. 2359). Yeivin asked the police (GL44869/3 no. 2358) to employ the first guards immediately. Guards would be supervised by police officers, but employed only as antiquities guards by orders of the IDAM. The police would receive 7.5 percent of the budget for its services. There would be two types of guards: permanent guards at sites, mostly with the status of simple policemen; and "mobile guards" responsible for several sites in sergeant grade B status. Seven mobile guards were needed, but police regulations allowed only two sergeants in a unit of 20 men, so the additions to the salaries of five mobile guards would be financed by the IDAM.

It became reality; and now all kinds of correspondence started. For example, in March 1950 a certain functionary from Tiberias recommended Izhak K. as a guard, explaining that he "wants to leave the police because he is afraid of difficulties in the examination of written Hebrew, which any policeman now has to pass. He speaks fluent Hebrew but has difficulties in writing ..." (GL44869/3 no. 1986). The questionnaire attached showed that Izhak was married with three children. Born in Berlin, he finished high school studying the exact sciences in Kitzbühel and came to Israel in 1935. He spoke Hebrew, English, French and German and could write in English, French, German and "a little Hebrew". He served in the British Royal Air Force for six years and was a member of the Hagana organization for eight years. I mention all these details to demonstrate how, despite an impressive curriculum vitae, this man felt so threatened by the written Hebrew test that he was prepared to give up the authority and prestige of a job in the Israeli police force to become an antiquities guard.

Difficulties with drafting the first guards were endless:

> I have to inform you that the men came to enlist on the days and at the times set for them by [Eli] Dekel, but the recruiting officer did not show up on time. The men wasted a day of work and now several more days

> have to pass until a new date for making the oath is set. I too was sent from
> Jerusalem to Tel Aviv, and there told that I must report in Jerusalem on
> Tuesday.   (GL44869/3, Nahmani on 10.4.50)

On 19 April 1950 Yeivin asked the general secretary of the Ministry of Education to speed up the supply of vehicles for the unit. They required: a transport
car "not very low so it will be possible to drive on dirt roads, at least in summer";
five motorcycles for mobile guards and four jeeps for guards in difficult terrain
such as the Negev. These dreams never became reality; no vehicle was ever given
to the guards. Even Nahmani had to join Yeivin's tours as means of transport.
In February 1950 the IDAM received one green Willis Tender (GL44866/8 no.
1987). By 1953 its condition was such that it remained in the garage for 84 days
between April and October (GL44866/8 no. 2241a). It was replaced in 1954/55
with a car that served until 1959 (GL44866/8, 16.12.58).

The first eight guards were sworn in as policemen in April 1950. They were
intended for Natanya, Tiberias, Jerusalem, Hadera, Caesarea, Athlit, Safad and
Megiddo (GL44869/3, 27.4.50). On 11 May 1950 Yeivin had to complain to the
police. The salary of 46.170 Lira per month was not attractive and no nominees
had been found; so a salary of 51 Lira was agreed and 14 guards were enlisted.
Yet, the first guards received just 41 Lira per month … (GL44869/5 no. 2726).
Yeivin could not overrule the police, since without them the guards would lose
police authority (GL44869/3 nos. 3251, 3655, 3087, 3757).

Working conditions were also difficult. Some guards had to fill 47 hours a
week (GL44869/7, from 30.6.57, etc.). Nahmani wrote to the Athlit guard, Arieh
X, on 16 August 1950:

> The manager of the IDAM visited three times and did not find you there.
> It is impossible. As a guard of antiquities you must be present at all times
> at the site. You have permission while on holiday to leave the site … If you
> cannot do what is required of you notify us soon. It is impossible to get the
> salary but not be at the site …   (GL44869/3 no. 3502)

Matters became worse and Nahmani concluded that Arieh did "not fulfil his
duty". On 29 October 1950 Nahmani asked the police to dismiss him, yet he
visited him in November and reported:

> These are the reasons [for his absence]: he has to bring fresh water and
> food from the [nearby] settlement, but it is some time until he gets his
> foodstuff and rations, which the shopkeeper only delivers on fixed days
> and hours. His salary he must get from the Hadera police station. Since the
> officer there does not notify him when to come to get his salary, he must
> travel a few times until he gets it. This also takes time, for to reach Hadera

[*c.* 30 km] and back takes more than half a day. Also he has to travel once in a while when a camp officer is exchanged [Athlit was occupied as a military camp], since the new officer asks him to leave the building and then both of them go to the main headquarters [until] the officer in charge says that Arieh can remain at his place. This is because he does not have a letter from the authorities with permission to sit in a military area ... Also, since he is on duty on Saturday, he takes a free day on another day of the week. From what I heard I realized that he was not absent from the place out of malice, but to make arrangements needed to carry out his duty.   (GL44869/3)

The police force was worried about other matters, as the following letter from Yadin Frumkin (manager of the police quartermaster department) indicates:

Subject: repairing shoes
1. At the time we decided that guards' shoes would not be fixed by the workshops of the Israeli police, and as a result the guards neglect their shoes and wear them until they reach a state that does not allow repair.
2. In relation to shoe rationing, and to prevent excess, we are ready to repair guards' shoes at official rates set by the government, on these terms:
A. You will agree to pay for the repairs;
B. You will supply us with coupons to buy leather to repair the shoes from the supervisor of reserves.
3. Clearly, we will fix only those shoes supplied by us, not private shoes.
(GL44869/5 no. 1763)

Some early diaries of guards survived in GL1340/2, but most just repeat entries such as "work runs in order", "Sh. Nahmani came to check". Nahmani issued the following orders on 22 October 1950:

Subject: APPEARANCE AND BEHAVIOUR
1. Guards on official duty must be fully dressed and carry weapons.
2. Guards who supervise fixed places in addition to guard duty must also maintain the cleanliness of the entry road and the near vicinity of the antiquities.
3. Guards who live in buildings within the antiquities area must keep the rooms and courtyard clean.
4. All guards must run a work diary and send a copy each month to the IDAM.
5. Guards at fixed places must also register names of visitors.
GUARDS WHO WILL NOT OBEY THESE ORDERS WILL NOT BE ABLE TO CONTINUE THEIR WORK   (GL44869/3 no. 2972)

This direction did not pass unnoticed. Nehemia Zori answered in the least militaristic fashion:

> My Friend Nahmani, Hello!
> About your letter 2972, arranged in five sections, its meaning and nature are not very clear to me. For, as you know, your faithful servant has worked for over two months now at the excavation at Beth Shean courtyard 151, and naturally it is impossible when excavating to serve any other matters except excavating. "A wise person will be satisfied with a small hint" [an Aramaic idiom]. Fare well and see you soon, yours,
> [signed] Nehemia Zori
>
> [Added in handwriting] On the other hand, one must express a general note about the payments we receive from the police paymasters. For the second time I have had to go to the regional police station in Tiberias because of their claim that the payroll sheet does not arrive on time. Needless to say, this is, especially for me, a waste of money and time (which is, during an excavation, dearer than money and not measured in gold) ...
> With blessing [signed], Nehemia Zori   (GL44869/3 no. 3756, 4.11.50)

Guards were often involved in excavations near their sites. On 28 May 1951 Nahmani mentioned that two out of eight guards were involved in excavations (GL44869/4). This was especially true for the more senior regional guards, who were in fact "assistant district inspectors". They checked places of discoveries and "for many years now they have dealt with the direction of small excavations" (GL44880/13 no. 5726a, Yeivin to Avidor). This was despite their lack of formal education in archaeology. At best, guards completed a three-month seminar in 1952 (Yeivin, GL44883/1, letter of 1956). In 1961 regional guards were required to have only an undergraduate education and an unspecified level of "archaeology and knowledge of the country" (GL44869/7 no. 1491, 2.5.61).

Nahmani summarized the first year of the unit as a history of difficulties (GL44869/3, 3.11.50). Actual work began in May 1950 with poor salaries. It took a whole month for the police to approve a candidate, and often a person had to appear three times until he was sworn. It took two months for the first guards to receive uniforms; they did not fit and the police refused to alter them, so some guards could not wear uniforms. The police did not supply proper weapons. Many guards had rifles, which did not fit the nature of work. The Megiddo guards lacked weapons for a month because of a dispute between two police stations. Police stations displayed notices giving payment dates on noticeboards, so to learn the date guards had to keep visiting until the notice had been displayed. Finally, there were no vehicles and Nahmani could not supervise the guards properly. Still, the guards proved to be loyal, helped in excavations and prevented damage. Nahmani's conclusion was that relations with the police had failed, and in fact were not necessary. Most visitors were polite if guards explained that they were working to save antiquities; this was better than a stiff "police" presence. For the money paid for uniforms to the police one could easily buy better ones (GL44869/3 no. 3999).

As a result, from 1 April 1951 the guards ceased to be *Notrim* and became volunteer policemen employed by the IDAM. They were released from police service for the main reason, stated openly, that their salary as *Notrim* was not sufficient in the eyes of the IDAM. On the day of release they were sworn as volunteers and continued their work as usual. This turned guards into permanent government workers instead of temporary policemen. It was a large and significant increase to the IDAM's permanent workforce (GL44869/5 nos. 5085 and 5063; GL44869/4 nos. 5011, 5131).

There were 15 guards in late 1950 (GL44869/3 no. 4274) and 17 from February 1951 (GL44869/4), and they eventually received rifles (GL44869/5 no. 4756, 11.2.51). From August 1952 the guards became workers (*po'alim*) instead of officials (*pkidim*) (GL44869/3 no. 9592). They were supposed to have special berets with a symbol (GL44869/5 nos. 5096, 5127), but as for complete uniforms, the authorities quarrelled:

> How to supply antiquities guards with uniforms? The old ones that they received from the police when starting work (when the police still had a few khaki uniforms at hand) are already worn and old. New workers have been accepted in the meantime and have not received uniforms. I think the central office should speak with the Prime Minister's Office and demand approval for issuing uniforms to antiquities guards, so that the civil service can issue "coupons" to the supervisor of reserves … Or maybe you know another way? … Please handle this matter urgently, for winter is approaching and the guards are ill-equipped for it.
>
> (Yeivin, GL44869/4 no. 10185, 28.10.52)

Termination of the *Notrim* status did not end the involvement of the police force. The police brought the "volunteer policeman N. from Safad" to a hearing in front of the Safad police commander. He was accused of ruthless behaviour:

> He squeezed and pushed his way between people who stood in a queue for the bus at Haifa and entered the bus without queuing, claiming that he is a policeman and need not wait in line. He was fined five days' salary. Since this volunteer policeman receives salary from you [IDAM], please reduce from his salary five days of work … and deliver the sum to the [police] for item "income – general police fund".   (GL44869/5 no. 6262, 9.8.51)

Ben-Dor complained (GL44869/5, 9.8.51): the man had been judged in his absence and the fine should be used for the benefit of antiquities guards, not the police in general. The police answered that volunteer policemen were very rarely judged for disciplinary offences, however, any fine must be paid. The constitution ruled that fines were given to the general police fund; if one wanted to use them for antiquities guards, it would necessitate special legislation (GL44869/5 no. 7185).

In April 1953 nearly 2,000 registered sites existed in Israel and many more as yet unregistered (GL44875/10). The guards helped to save the sites. Six guards were stationary, at the "Sanhedrin" tombs in Jerusalem, Jerusalem in general, Caesarea, Athlit, Bet She'arim and Accho. It was impossible to appoint guards to Beit Jubrin and the Negev for security reasons. Two guards (at Safad and Beth-She'arim) were later dismissed because of budget cuts, and 15 remained in 12 places (Nahmani and three guards were employed in Jerusalem, where two guards served in the IDAM's museum). One guard was not enough for extensive sites such as Caesarea or Ashkelon. Guards worked the usual eight hours each day, so early or late visitors found an empty site; and most sites were not fenced (GL44875/10, 30.4.53; cf. GL44868/7 no. 6308a of 10.4.55).

In November 1953 the position of guard at Athlit became free. A certain Izhak from the transition camp (*ma'abarah*) applied, but was rejected. On 11 November 1953 the labour office at Athlit complained bitterly to Yeivin:

> Following my conversation with you during your visit yesterday about the application of Izhak to the position of guard in the Athlit fortress, I have to remark that the argument about his being a father of three children as denying the right to have the said position cannot be accepted, not in my mind and not in the mind of any institution. I must state that in the course of my duty in the position of secretary of the labour office, it is the first time that I have faced a strange argument like this. I am sorry that such a first case appears from a high and responsible official in our government.
>
> To prevent a serious reaction by the unemployed and to keep the rights of anyone who looks for work I would ask that the said argument not be considered, and that the candidateship be approved …
>
> (GL44869/4 no. 2521a)

The mayor of the regional council of Athlit joined in on 12 November 1953:

> We would like to add that employment conditions at the place are very bad, for about two-thirds of the population are residents of the *ma'abarah*, while for the time being there is only one factory that can employ unprofessional workers. Despite this, thanks to energetic actions by all involved, we have

succeeded to run matters without disturbance in the *maʻabarah* and among the unemployed; for as much as they suffer from lack of employment, they know that we on our side do whatever we can to ease the situation for them.

We also welcome with thanks your involvement in our favour, in that you got us the 150 work-days [for a former excavation] and we thank you for that from the bottom of our hearts. But on the other hand, the fact that a head of a family will be refused work in the government because he is blessed with three kids will cause a lot of resentment. Until today the people thought that our government strives for inner *ʻaliya* [immigration, literally "ascent"], and will in no way understand how a proliferation of children can be an obstacle to them getting work. (GL44869/4 no. 2538)

Yeivin backed down, although still claiming that it was not the business of the IDAM to "care about the comfort of arrangements in the *maʻabarot*". He ordered Nahmani to accept the man for a trial period (GL44869/4 no. 2521a); in 1961 the man was dismissed for reasons not related to the IDAM (GL44880/13 no. 7543).

In June 1954 Nahmani wrote to the police to ask why, since 1951, papers certifying that the guards were volunteer policemen had not been renewed, and why guards who had asked for the papers certifying their status had been told that this status no longer existed (GL44869/5 no. 4197a). The police assured him that the arrangement was valid and that certificates would be renewed (GL44869/4 no. 5086a; cf. no. 5270a). Yet in late 1954 the police pointed out that giving the guards the status of the police was not necessary; it only complicated the work through the need to enlist them, fill in forms, and so on. Eli Dekel, manager of the Manpower Department of the Israel Police, explained that the institution of "volunteering policemen" had been important in the past, when it made possible the distribution of weapons to groups of civilians. But this situation had been changed by new firearms legislation in 1950, which recognized special collective weapon-holding for the defence of villages, factories and so on. Hence, the police intended to stop the service of volunteer policemen in the IDAM (GL44869/4 no. 5988). Yeivin checked the issue and discovered that, based on the Mandatory regulations, the Minister of Education had the legal power to nominate antiquities guards (GL44869/4 no. 5409a, 28.12.54). But the Mandatory government had never issued such regulations and it would take a few months for them to be prepared. He asked the police to postpone the change. Dekel answered politely on 5 January 1955 that the preparation of such regulations might take a long time, but the discontinuity of the service of volunteer policemen would not change the existing situation, except regarding the expense to the police. Therefore, the police would stop the service of the guards (GL44869/4 no. 6356a). Yeivin asked for this not to affect the guards' right to prevent damage and to arrest criminals "in order to hand them to the police" until the new regulations came into force

(GL44869/4 no. 5716a). The police answered that antiquities guards would not have, once their status as volunteer policemen was cancelled, any authority to arrest criminals,

> However, I must state that we know of no cases in which those who damaged antiquities were arrested by antiquities guards in order to be taken in front of the police. So, therefore, no change will occur in the status of these guards when they cease to serve as volunteer policeman, and we intend to perform it starting on 1.4.55. (GL44869/4 no. 7001)

This was true, although Yeivin tried hard and found one case at Afulah (so marginal that the offenders were not prosecuted; their offence was entering and photographing the site). Yeivin asked that "in the meantime ... the police will not be very orthodox about the details. If an offender is brought in front of the police by a guard, let them investigate and not be strict with the guard about his legal authority to arrest the offender" (GL44869/4 no. 5973a).

The 1935 Antiquities (Enclosures) Ordinance allowed employees of the Palestine Antiquities Department to remove from departmental premises persons who offended the regulations and "to arrest or detain without a warrant any person found stealing or doing damage, or reasonably suspected of having stolen or having done any damage to any antiquity, furniture or equipment". The premises included historical sites and monuments; the regulations also forbade betting and gambling in historical sites (Palestine Official Gazette 1935: c–d, copy in GL44869/5). Yeivin prepared modified Hebrew regulations (GL44869/5 nos. 6697a, 7259).

The guards continued to work, although they now lacked the legal basis for any action against transgressors. Yeivin tried several times to solve this problem. He wrote to Avidor on 18 October 1956: "The matter of regulations about antiquities guards ... I must stress again that the situation is unbearable; all the actions of the guards, in fact, have no legal basis as long as regulations are not published" (GL44889/2 no. 2611). This was underlined by Ruth Staner, the legal advisor to the Ministry of Education. When asked about it, she informed the IDAM that when an antiquities guard discovered thieves, even if he caught them in the act, he could do nothing except notify the police. Indeed, he could ask them for their names and addresses, but they did not have to answer ... He even had no right to take from them the stolen items. This right was afforded to the Director of the IDAM only, and perhaps only if the thieves were found guilty when tried. This situation would change only through new legislation (GL44869/7, 22.12.58).

Guards initially had power as *Notrim* and later as volunteer policemen (until 1955). Although that right was almost never used, it was once more delegated to the guards in the Regulations of Antiquities (Enclosures) of 1959, section 10 (3). These regulations allowed certain employees of the IDAM to arrest anyone suspected of stealing or damaging an antiquities area, as long as the arrested person was handed over to the police as soon as possible (Israel Government 1959: 1072). As a result, the guards could carry the official certificates of antiq-uities guards (GL44869, 19.6.59, 26.6.59).

In the late 1950s, documentation relating to the guards dwindles, while their position deteriorated. The GTC started to improve historical sites such as Megiddo, Avdat and Shivta in 1957/58. The GTC dominated sites undergoing improvements, used IDAM guards for its needs and later placed guards and guides of its own. It did not help the IDAM that the guard at Megiddo was the target of various accusations of corrupt behaviour. He allegedly took money from tour-ists and sold stones from the site. Yeivin did not believe it at first, but later the man admitted the charges (GL44880/13 nos. 286 of 28.12.58; 1173 of 20.3.59). By 1959 there were 15 guards (GL44869/7). When the first "improved" sites were opened to the public in 1959, the IDAM lost them to the GTC. In 1960 Kahane, then Deputy Director of the IDAM, decided not to return the Megiddo guard to work. The nature of the site changed; it was improved, a museum was opened, thousands of visitors used guides from the GTC, so an antiquities guard was no longer required (GL44869/4 no. 5336).

The need for site guards was questioned. In March 1960 Nahmani complained that since Yeivin's retirement he had been unable to visit the guards every couple of months, as he had done previously by joining Yeivin's tours. He now used pub-lic transport and walked, but some places were some distance from bus routes (GL44869/7 no. 3844). In January 1961 three guards' positions were vacant (GL44889/7 no. 7263). The Ministry of Education suggested giving the position at Beersheba to the municipality, quoting Biran, the new Director of the IDAM: "the problem of guards in general is one of the most painful ones in the IDAM and we must give our mind towards a general solution" (GL44889/7 no. 7564, 16.2.61). How did an achievement that almost doubled the number of workers in 1951 become a painful problem? This was not explained. Most probably the military nature of the guards, important in 1948/49, was no longer necessary for the IDAM. Still, the IDAM refused to give up some guards (GL44869/7 no. 7564).

The solution came in 1962 when Biran suggested that local institutes (munici-pal or regional) would be responsible for guarding sites "for promoting tourism and for li-shmah [not for profit]". Site guards would become mobile "regional inspectors". They would have a fixed plan for supervision; arrange meetings and initial negotiations with developing bodies; and check new discoveries. They would also carry out salvage excavations in emergencies. The necessary quali-fications were "elementary knowledge in archaeology, including identification of sherds; high school education desired" (GL44869/7 no. 1804). It was decided to leave stationary guides only at Mazor and in Herod's Tomb in Jerusalem, and to try to find another "owner" for the latter site (GL44869/7, 18.7.62). In 1965 the IDAM's museum was amalgamated into the Israel Museum, so the guards there were transferred to the Israel Museum (GL44869/7 no. 7114). The large historical sites, such as Megiddo, Caesarea and Ashkelon later became national gardens under the parks authority.

The only "legacy" of the battalion of guards of the 1950s is the authority of antiquities inspectors to arrest transgressors of the Antiquities Law. This right was reaffirmed in the IAA law of 1989 (LIAA 1989: 88, §25b). To the best of my knowledge, arrests have never been made by supervisors of antiquities, perhaps with the exception of the unit against robbery, established in 1984 (Zissu 1996; Ganor 2002); but it belongs to a later chapter in the history of Israeli archaeology.

6   RELIEF WORK

> *And whatever I do*
> *Will become forever what I've done*   Szymborska (1997: 170)

INTRODUCTION

In the New York of the 1930s the economy was crushed and salaries for those who still had them were at rock bottom. Fifteen million Americans were unemployed. The federal government, facing tremendous difficulties, issued a policy of relief works. Roosevelt's ideology was that earning a living is a basic human dignity, preferable to handing out money and letting people sit idle. The first Relief Act was passed on 31 March 1933, and six weeks later a Federal Emergency Relief Administration was established. The emphasis at this stage was on supplying work immediately, so in November 1933 Congress established the Civil Works Administration, which created 4.2 million jobs in the space of just nine weeks. The jobs included laying sewer pipes and building and improving roads, playgrounds, schools and so on. By 1935 the government had put more stress on social and human values, with priority on fitting jobs to the skills and trades of the workers.

In April 1935 Congress approved a budget of $4.8 billion for the Emergency Relief Act. From this enormous sum some 5 percent – $27 million – was set aside for arts projects. A project called the Federal Theater received about $6.8 million for providing work to unemployed theatrical professionals, through "production units": theatres. As a rule, each production unit could choose up to 10 percent of its workforce from professional actors, to ensure good standards of performance. The remainder had to come from the unemployed. The Federal Theater, headed by Hallie Flanagan, employed thousands of people across the US. New York, the centre of American theatre life, took the lead with more than 4,000 employees in 49 theatres. The previously unemployed received $21–$55 per month, while professional actors could receive up to $103 per month (Flanagan

1940: 15–44; de Hart 1967: 35; Buttita 1982: 25; Gill 1988). The Federal Theater gave Orson Welles his first taste of fame (Bazin 1978: 42; Leaming 1985: 98–9). In the Negro People's Theater in Harlem, Welles produced an adaptation of Shakespeare's *Macbeth*, staging the play with African-American actors. It was a *tour de force*. Ten thousand people stood in the queue for tickets on the opening night (Flanagan 1940: 74; de Hart 1967: 75; Leaming 1985: 113).

The Israeli government of the 1950s also had to step in to create jobs for large numbers of unemployed people. Let us consider a day like any other outside the small village of Rosh-Pina in the Galilee. A group of people is boarding a bus in the dark. They are of different ages, badly dressed and look tired. The bus follows a narrow road to a hill near Kibbutz Ayyelet Ha-Shahar, just east of the large Tell of Hazor. Two men eagerly wait for it, one of them smoking nervously. The bus is late, and work must start immediately, but the workers are not in a hurry as they step down, sleepy, trying to postpone the day that lies ahead. The Kibbutz is building a new cowshed, and trenches for foundations are everywhere, surrounded by heaps of materials.

The IDAM has investigated and a salvage excavation has been organized. Philip Guy, formerly from the American expedition to Megiddo, and Moshe Dothan, a young archaeologist, head the work, but the workers get instructions mainly from their deputy, who supervises the work. The supervisor works in the excavations wherever help is needed, and often carries out small excavations himself. He shivers in the early morning cold, the small diary where he keeps his excavation notes quivers in his pocket. The workers gather around him and his frustration rises. Only 16 turned up today, although the employment office promised 25. Worse, they promised good workers, but some men look too weak, while two youngsters are not in the mood for work. They joke and mess about when handling tools, throwing heavy picks at the feet of the men. The supervisor has to shout at them; the silence of the new day is hopelessly broken. The supervisor must register every tool he issues, every day, or a worker might be tempted to hide a tool and sell it later in the *ma'abarah*. One man complains: his lower back is aching; he wants a lighter job, such as washing sherds, perhaps. The supervisor hardens his tone. If he gave a cushy job to everyone, who would be left to do the work? The man grumbles to himself and walks away. He will manage, work slowly and sing or chat to make the hours fly. There is no such relief for the supervisor: a third of those who came today are new. It is useless to ask what happened; the workers neither know nor care. Perhaps one was ill; another was sent to a more urgent job, yet another just missed the bus. This means that the supervisor has to teach the new workers from scratch: how to hold a *turiya* [a large square-headed hoe] and how to fill a bucket with sherds. Some nod, but do not understand, for he speaks Hebrew. Finally he despairs, and shouts at them to get moving and start work. It is 7.10 am on Thursday 30 November 1950. Forty minutes later than usual, excavation starts. A boy steps forwards. His Hebrew is better, and he has learned to write numbers on finds, earning the post of clerk. I would like to tell you his name, but I do not know it. Today we find him pictured standing at the site in a faded photograph.

In 1994 I was sorting through an archive of drawings in Jerusalem. I was surprised to find a file marked "Ayyelet ha-Shahar". The site is famous: Guy and Dothan discovered an Iron Age palace. Sadly, Guy died in 1952, and this was his last excavation, so the site remained largely unpublished (Guy 1957; Reich 1975). Another excavator who worked at Ayyelet ha-Shahar under Guy and Dothan, Shalom Levi, later published the Nirim Synagogue (Levi 1960). A final report is in preparation (Kletter & Zwickel forthcoming), but that is another story. Let us return to the 1950s and to the many relief workers who served Israeli archaeology.

THE WAVE OF IMMIGRATION

In barely four years (1948–1951), a huge wave of immigrants doubled Israel's population, which had been about 650,000 when Israel was first established: they numbered 101,819 in 1948, 239,576 in 1949, 170,215 in 1950 and 175,129 in 1951. The immigrants came for various reasons: through Zionist ideology; to escape life-threatening situations; or owing to economic pressures. At first, many European Jews arrived, survivors of the holocaust, but soon, newcomers from Islamic countries became a majority. Many of them were illiterate: in Israel in 1952/53, 17 percent of men and 31 percent of women were illiterate. By 1954 the figure was 28 percent of men and 49 percent of women. It was estimated that in 1954 61 percent of all Israelis spoke Hebrew as their primary language, but only 16 percent of the immigrants knew Hebrew, and only 0.4 percent of them spoke it as a daily language (Bachi 1957: 665–81; Zur 1997: 80–81).

Israel could not find housing and employment for all the newcomers. Arab houses from the 1948 War and the former British military camps were occupied, crammed full, and the immigrants were forced to stay in the horrible camp of Sha'ar ha-Aliya near Haifa (Segev 1984: 129–30). The JNF planned "work camps" (JNF 1950, GL44879/9 no. 2937; Segev 1984: 140), but not much came of this plan. Then *ma'abarot* (transit camps) in the form of tent cities and shack neighbourhoods were erected. The first ones were built in spring 1950 and by the end of the year there were about 40 of them. Their name was a euphemism: *ma'abarah* comes from "to pass, to move", but many remained for years, becoming slums. They were often located near or within veteran communities, which were supposed to absorb them and to supply their needs. The plan failed, because camps were hastily built, often facing rejection by veteran settlements. Many camps lacked basic facilities; some were located on badlands, and even on areas flooded by rainwater each winter. Camps were often much larger than the veteran villages or towns in their vicinity. By September 1951 there were 87 *ma'abarot* containing 170,000 people (Hacohen 1994; 1996; Segev 1984: 139–53).

Believing that the central cities were already too crowded and that sovereignty over every square mile demanded a dispersion of the population, the government decided to build new towns in peripheral areas and place immigrants in them. It was probably unavoidable in a new state with disputed borders, surrounded by hostile neighbours and built on an ethos of "conquering the land" piece by piece. So "development towns", such as Beth Shean and Kiryat Shmonah in the north, and Dimonah and Sderot in the Negev, were erected. By 1951, 18 new towns had been established, with some 120,000 inhabitants (7.1 percent of Israel's population). By 1961, 273,322 people lived in these new towns. In 1964 there were 27 new towns housing 16 percent of Israel's population. Like the *ma'abarot*, most of these towns suffered from a severe lack of services and jobs (Troen 1996; Ephrat 1997). This traumatized many newcomers, who described their difficulties only years later. For example, they accused the authorities of misleading them with promises of a better life. A typical story describes the first morning at Zomet village in the western Negev, which had been funded in 1949:

> I lift the rag of this tent and think, listen God! Only sand hills up to the sky; no green branch, no no no bird, no greenery, no car, no road, no houses, nothing. What is this? From where? What is this? Eight tents, perhaps ten ... and one little wooden shack. I told them: what is that? They said: *zarchaniya* [small general shop]. I said: what is *zarchaniya*? ... I had nothing to do. I sat near the shack; sat to cry, to cry, to cry ...
>
> (in Shelli-Newman 1996: 292)

Shelli-Newman noticed that those who remembered arriving in daylight were better prepared to face the challenges. Many newcomers came from cultures that differed greatly from the bourgeois–socialist ideology of the leaders of Israel at that time, and went through a severe culture shock. The authorities failed to realize this, and were convinced – as David Ben-Gurion allegedly once said – that the immigrants were "human dust" that the state must renew. This could be done only in a "melting pot", a crucible moulding a new persona: Zionist, socialist, Israeli. The vision was too idealistic and its implementation was extremely painful. In the camps and development towns, the so-called "Second Israel" was born (Zur 1997; Greenberg 1989). Rather than just melt in the pot, the immigrants melted parts of it after their own image. They rejected the efforts to imbue them with local history and archaeology, keeping some of their own cultural traits (Feige 1998). The encounter between veterans and newcomers entered Israel's literature, although much later than the 1950s. There, varied opinions are voiced. Perhaps the best picture of Israel in the 1950s is given in the 1986 epic "Heart Murmur" by Joshua Kenaz (Holtzman 1996).

THE SYSTEM OF RELIEF WORKS

It was in these circumstances that a system of relief works was formed in Israel. The ideology stated that relief work would teach the "human dust" how to work. Manual work was preferred, for it was supposedly good for health and the soul. The authorities believed that supplying work, even if unproductive, contributed to the melting-pot ideology and to national aims, such as road-building, planting forests and improving agricultural lands.

Basing her writing on a study that focused on welfare, Merom (1997, 2003) sharply criticizes the relief works system and especially its ideology. According to Merom, the Israeli Welfare Law, accepted only in 1958, was outdated and based on Victorian British laws. It did not guarantee the rights of the poor, and included no clear criteria as to who deserved aid and how much. Decisions were made by local social workers. The law was extremely restrictive: it recognized relatively few people as unemployed. Relief workers were often given just 2–3 days' work per week, mostly hard manual labour. All family members (not just the closest) had to be fully unemployed; otherwise, the right to aid was annulled. Also, no additional work was permitted: only full unemployment was considered appropriate for welfare. Even those who were considered unemployed received only 1–8 Lira per month in the late 1950s, despite the minimal living wage being acknowledged as 56 Lira per month. Philip Klein, an advisor to the UN, reported in 1961 that a family of eight people in Israel received just 25 Lira per month welfare, whereas a hired worker received an average monthly salary of 365 Lira. Merom claimed that the government was angered by this report and pressured the UN to suppress its publication. The Ministry of Labour asked a Zionist, Harold Silver, to produce another report, which was delivered in 1965 but this was no better. According to Merom (1997: 31–49, 121–6; 2003; cf. Kimmerling 2004: 295–6), policy-makers did not want to pay welfare. They devised the system of relief works because they believed that Eastern Jews (who made up most of the immigrants) preferred welfare money to earning a "decent" living through work. This was a prejudice without any valid basis. Furthermore, withholding welfare from the unemployed meant that they could be used as a cheap work-force. Israel became a modern welfare state only in the middle of the 1970s and early 1980s, when laws of insurance against unemployment and a guarantee of income (*havtakhat hakhnasa*) were issued.

What was the scale of relief works in Israel? It did not compete with the US, of course. A summary for the decade 1948–58 was published in the official journal *Avoda u-Bitu'akh Le'umi* [*Labour and National Insurance*] (Ministry of Labour 1958: 9/107). Average registered unemployment was 10,800. This was not the real number of unemployed, because many did not register or were not recognized as unemployed. During this decade, some 300,000 persons were employed in relief works, with a total of about 22 million work-days. Relief works included restoration of 3,500 hectares of citrus groves, preparing 4,000 hectares of old citrus groves for other agricultural aims; restoring 4,500 hectares of olives, vines, and so on; planting 8,000 hectares of forests; planting avenues along 800 km of roads; and stabilizing and preparing 35,000 hectares of grazing land. In 1957/58 alone, a total of about 4.25 million work-days was allocated for land restoration; fruit trees plantation (600,000 work-days); forest plantation (850,000 work-days); work for local municipalities (550,000 work-days); road construction and improvement (150,000 work-days); work by handicapped and old persons (950,000 work-days) and various other works, including archaeological digs (1,150,000 work-days).

The daily life of relief workers was rarely described in the 1950s, and not from their own viewpoints. A description of the work on a new road from Beersheba to Sodom in late 1951 is fascinating, although it was written by the supervisors of the work (Ministry of Labour 1951: 6–10). This project employed 600–800 relief workers, of which 45 percent were newcomers from Iraq; 20 percent from Iran; 8 percent from North Africa and 18 percent from the Druze minority in Israel. They had one day off per week at home, or three days every two weeks, living in temporary camps. At first, they were given an extra 0.450 Lira per day for food, but the authorities discovered that "newcomers from Arab countries saved from this money, ate only meals of bread and oranges or olives, so their work production declined". It was then decided to give free meals instead, although this cost slightly more, and "a large portion of the workers simply learned to eat, and it also shows in their work" (Ministry of Labour 1951: 8).

Another problem was the high turnover of workers. This forced the authorities to raise the salaries of workers who maintained their positions for at least three months. Allegedly, relief workers did not share the cultural ethos of veteran Israelis. They just did not know how to work:

> Work so far considered simple, such as lifting a stone on to a wheelbarrow or levelling earth with a *turiyah*, is complex for those exhausted [*tashush*] people that lack any feelings for work [*sic*.]. Lifting a stone of 8–10 kg is a difficult act for them and the *turiyah* is a strange instrument of torture.
> (Ministry of Labour 1951: 9)

Perhaps even worse was the notion that the newcomers did not know how to behave, although at times it was also a source of amusement for veterans: "One day when there was enough water, a camp commander told four workers that they could take a shower. The four went immediately and showered – without taking off their work clothes" (Ministry of Labour 1951: 6–10).

The veterans' lack of understanding of life in transition camps is found in the case of a man from the *ma'abarah* near Athlit, who applied in late 1953 for a job as an antiquities guard. Yeivin refused to accept him at first, on the grounds that he had three children (see Ch. 5).

RELIEF WORK IN ARCHAEOLOGY

In March 1951 Yeivin wrote to Shalom Cohen, a civil servant in the Department of Employment in the Ministry of Labour, about the possibility of using unemployed people "in the realm of public works, which perhaps do not carry real wages [*sic.*], but might be a blessing to the state" (GL44875/9). Yeivin suggested that employing them in archaeological work would be beneficial to the archaeology and heritage of the state, as well as enhancing a link to "our past in the land" and the possibility of attracting tourists. On 17 November 1952, the government of Israel decided to allocate 500,000 Lira to finding work for the unemployed. The IDAM suggested using part of this sum for archaeological projects, but it was not approved (GL1430/14 no. 10385).

When relief workers became available free of cost to the IDAM, it "indulged" in excavations that were not strictly for salvage, although, from the beginning the IDAM had not conceived its duty to be in salvage only and had wanted to carry out scientific excavations of its own. However, the limited budget quenched the first attempts at independent excavations (such as the one in Jaffa in 1948). Relief work brought a second opportunity. Thus for several years Yeivin carried out large-scale excavations at Tell Sheikh Ahmed el-Areini, near the new city of Kiryat Gat in the Negev (wrongly identified with Gat of the Philistines). In a letter of 20 November 1956, Yeivin explained the budget for this project in plain words:

> The workers were supplied by the Department of Employment of the Ministry of Labour of the Lachish region. In fact, the whole excavation was planned and carried out in order to supply work for the people of Kiryat Gat. Indeed, up to 120 people were employed in this work for approximately three months. The expedition itself was also financed by the Ministry of Labour with a sum of 25,000 pounds, which was barely enough to cover the employment of additional workers among scientific and technical staff related to excavating, and to process the material after the end of the field-work … (GL1430/14 no. 2865)

This is mentioned elsewhere. One document explained that the project was conceived from its beginning to supply "work in the dead agricultural season to the inhabitants of Kiryat Gat, from early May to early August" (GL44883/12: 5). As was often the case, the arrangement failed to ensure that there was a budget for the study of the finds and their publication. Yeivin's excavations at this site remained largely unpublished.

At first the term "relief work" did not appear in IDAM documents, although excavations already used unemployed people (Fig. 16). A summary of the budget for 1949–54 (GL44883/9, 13.5.53) gives prices of work in Lira for an "average" worker (not specified further). Due to rapid inflation, the wage rose from 2 Lira to 5.630 Lira per day, so that despite a growing budget, the IDAM's capacity to employ workers was reduced from 13,000 work-days in 1950/51 to 10,500 in 1953/54.

Relief work was first called *"avodot dhak"* in Hebrew. This was replaced in favour of the euphemism *"avodot yezumot"*, meaning "initiated work"; the ingenious inventor remains anonymous. Documents related to salaries prove that until 1953 the IDAM recognized several grades of workers. In the most developed form there were four grades of "archaeological assistants" (*ozer*) and three grades

Figure 16. Rishpon, 1951. Hired excavation workers, before the relief work system. (IAA 1302)

of "archaeological workers" (*po'el*). They earned, depending on the grade, 2–4 Lira per day in November 1950. An early example of the use of the unemployed is found in the excavation of Nehemia Zori at Beth Shean (GL1342/8, 3.51). The workers were supplied by the work office at Beth Shean. Yeivin hoped that they would be paid 1.800 Lira per day, since they were simple manual workers, equivalent to agricultural workers. The representatives of the workers demanded 2.300 Lira per day, since the official rate for a "simple worker" was 2.500 Lira. The IDAM protested, but on 24 March 1951 the Beth Shean office clarified that this was the regular rate for ordinary work and that they took orders from the worker's organization, not from the Ministry of Labour. By May 1951 workers allocated from a *ma'abarah* at En Ha-Naziv were defined as "simple, temporary agricultural workers", and their daily salary was 3.155 Lira, including social insurance (GL1342/8, 22.5.51). During the same period, "archaeological workers" received 3.824–4.824 Lira, depending on the grade. So unemployed workers who found temporary work in archaeology were earning considerably less than the lowest IDAM salary. The creation of the large-scale system of relief work did not improve this situation.

A grade of "excavation workers" (*po'el khafirah*) first appeared on 16 March 1953 in a handwritten addition to a table of salaries of temporary workers at the IDAM (GL1342/8). The IDAM also used "archaeological assistants" (such as students of archaeology who joined excavations for short durations) and "archaeological workers" (part of the regular staff, such as surveyors). The documents are summarized in Table 3. It proves that the salary for excavation workers was about 70 percent of that of the lowest grade of archaeological worker. Excavation workers also were the only ones not entitled to increases when acquiring experience or if they were married and had families. One type of worker, guards at excavations, received even less at 3.730 Lira per day: it was not seen as "real work". Even cleaners received more than excavation workers.

On 31 January 1954 the Ministry of Labour announced that from 1 February 1954 the full salary for "relief work" would be 3.900 Lira per day (GL1342/8 no. 22123; cf. GL44883/5, list attached to letter 3283 of 15.2.54). The full salary included social insurance, which was deducted. This was about 30 percent

Table 3 Daily salaries of IDAM workers, 1953–55 (Lira).

Date	Archaeological assistant (*ozer*) lowest grade A	Same assistant, married and experienced	Archaeological worker, lowest grade A	Excavation worker	Cleaner
16.3.53	4.550	5.460	5.994	4.355	4.550
16.6.53	4.775	5.730	6.280	4.570	4.775
16.9.53	5.025	6.030	6.600	4.810	5.025
16.12.53	5.200	6.240	6.838	4.977	5.200
16.12.55	5.900	7.080	7.803	5.650	5.900

lower than the lowest IDAM salary (excluding perhaps guards in excavations). The salary of relief workers, based on many documents in GL44883/5, grew with inflation, from 4.100 Lira per day in May 1954 to 4.600 in March 1955, 4.930 in March 1956, 6.140 in April 1958 and 6.360 from 1958 to 1960. In 1967, the pay was 11.390 Lira per day. Compared with other workers in the Jewish sector (e.g. Riemer 1957: 738), it was much lower than the average salary. Merom (2003) also concluded that the relief work salary was about 30 percent lower than the *lowest* daily salary of hired workers. Still, the IDAM did not have a regular budget to employ relief workers; the money came from the Ministry of Labour, which paid the workers directly (e.g. GL44883/5 no. 897 of 10.5.56; cf. GL44883/11, 11.1.57). The IDAM usually paid for the transportation and in some cases for social benefits. Each month the IDAM sent requests for relief work-days needed, and the Ministry of Labour sent back a list of approved work-days. Flexibility was required from both sides, since excavations were not always foreseen.

The documents studied for this book do not show "ethnic" tensions between the veteran employers and the relief workers (Fig. 17). Workers were graded into two major categories of fitness: healthy workers who worked the usual eight hours per day and "limited workers" (*mugbalim*), that is, elderly or handicapped workers, who worked five hours daily (often called "8-hour workers" and "5-hour workers" or 8/8 and 5/8: GL44881/14 no. 8520; GL44883/5). Some of the problems of using "limited" and unprofessional workers in excavations appear in a summary of a meeting with Arieh Levi, the manager of the labour office of the district of Tiberias. He reported that he was ready to supply 1000 work-days for the IDAM in the region of Tiberias, on the condition that only "limited"

Figure 17. New immigrant from the Atlas Mountains working at Ozem in 1956 as a relief worker. (Photograph by Gophna, IAA 14866)

workers would be employed and replaced every ten days. The IDAM objected: limited workers were not very productive; the work required lifting very heavy stones; and excavation managers could not repeatedly teach new workers. The IDAM asked the labour office to show consideration and supply limited workers as only 40–50 percent of the total. Levi replied that "unlimited" workers were sent to works that were really needed. Naturally this angered the IDAM, which retorted that "we are not a welfare office, which must deal with social cases" (GL44883/5, memorandum by Yeivin 16.3.55). Often, work-days could be given only during "dead seasons"; for example, relief workers were not available during the cotton-picking season (cf. GL44883/5, 26.9.58).

After a visit by the President and his wife to Yeivin's excavations at Caesarea (Fig. 26), the workers sent Yeivin a handwritten letter (punctuation added):

> To Mrs [and] Mr Yeivin Shalom. From Eliyahu Z., Caesarea.
> In answer to our conversation about the workers, on the day that you visited me at Caesarea, I approached the [labour] office and we talked with a large number of the workers. We explained to them [that] if [they] want land the lady [of the] President can help them. They claim that they lack means. Water they have only for a few hours per day and they say that they do not work even the part of the land that is now in their hands. They all ask the wellbeing of the President and his lady, and they ask that they will help them only by the way of work. They say that even [if] they get 15 days of work per month, they will have enough for survival.
> The workers of Caesarea   (GL44880/19, 29.9.55)

On 19 October 1956, Dothan wrote to the labour office at Tel Aviv about the troubling "unpleasantness" at Barkai and Mezer. Work started in September with workers from Karkur. The IDAM wanted to continue with them in October because the excavation could not be postponed. But the Ministry of Labour allocated people from somewhere else. The IDAM found itself in a weird situation: it had to dismiss the first group and accept new workers. It found a "compromise", keeping half of the former group (GL44883/5 no. 2604), but straining the relations with the labour offices. Dothan threatened to break off relations with the labour offices altogether (GL44883/5, 5.11.57). When he suggested that the labour office at Beth Shean "needs us more than we need them", they surprised him by saying that they did not need the help of "antiquities work" at Beth Shean because there were no unemployed there (sic.). Dothan remarked to Yeivin that if this were true, relief work was not assured anymore, and:

> If their attitude to our work is so negative, we shall have no alternative but to break up the cooperation. I think that we cannot go on for a long time counting on the Ministry of Labour as supplier of work-days and must

search for other sources of funding, or give up completely part of our
work.   (*sic.*; GL44883/5, 5.11.57)

The IDAM also employed relief workers for other tasks. Six workers were
permanently employed in Jerusalem in gardening works. They were not supervised properly and the situation was discovered by Avraham Levanon, Regional
Supervisor of Work for the Ministry of Labour; at each of the places visited he
did not find a worker (GL44883/5 no. 42904, 11.57).

A summary from 1955 stated that there were some 30 excavations in addition
to a large one at Caesarea. They all:

> Became possible ... because the IDAM did not have just its own regular
> budget but also a further 9,150 days supplied mostly by the Department of
> Employment of the Ministry of Labour (7,300); the Housing Department
> (100); the Public Roads Department (200); Israel Trains (600); Barne'a
> Company (100); Ayyelet ha-Shahar ... (600); Beersheba Municipality (200)
> and Mekorot [Water] Company (50).
>   (GL44880/12, summary of budget year 1954/5)

A summary of April–December 1956 listed a total of 16,680 work-days in
excavations. Of these, relief work-days accounted for 7,537 work-days at Tell
"Gat", 6,740 at other excavations and 850 through other sources (GL44883/11).
During this period, there were 26 excavations. A report for 1956/57 detailed
8,926 relief work-days given by the Ministry of Labour, used in 20 excavations;
900 relief work-days came from other sources (GL44880/12). Another report
summarized April–December 1957: 18 excavations were performed using about
8,000 relief work-days (GL44883/12). In 1959/60, there were 21 excavations using
more than 10,000 relief work-days (GL44884/3). Adding the secondary bodies, a
reasonable estimation would put the IDAM's use of relief work in the late 1950s
at about 10,000–15,000 work-days per year.

The few large "relief" excavations (*khafirot yezumot*), which were not salvage
excavations, took a heavy toll on relief work-days. After all, this was their intention. For example, at Caesarea alone 2,432 relief work-days were used in 1955
and 2,734 work-days went to Tell "Gat" in 1957 (GL44883/5). One can imagine
the large gangs of inexperienced workers, inadequately supervised owing to the
limited professional workforce available at that time (today, the norm is up to
20–25 workers per archaeologist). Relief work was also used, to a lesser degree,
in restoration and cleaning works.

Relief work became the backbone not just of IDAM excavations, but also of
excavations in Israel by the IES and the Hebrew University. Best known is the
Hebrew University's expedition to Hazor. The first season in 1955 lasted four
months with an average of 110 relief workers, mostly from the Rosh Pina camp,

the rest from Safad. Buses brought them to Hazor each day, where they worked for 8 hours and 20 minutes (Yadin *et al.* 1959: 15). In the second season in 1956 some 180 daily relief workers were employed (Yadin 1957: 118–23). Yadin (1972: 24) dedicated only one sentence to the labourers "provided by the government labour exchange": mostly new immigrants from North Africa living in the "new town" of Hazor. No data exist for many other excavations, since relief work was a matter of fact, not considered worthy of mention. Acknowledgements were offered to the Ministry of Labour, never to the workers themselves, as at Ramat Rahel (Aharoni 1955: 127), Bet She'arim (Avigad), Teluliot Batashi (Kaplan), the Temple of Nahariya (Dothan) and many other excavations.

Relief work was used also by the GTC for improving historical sites. It was even offered to foreign expeditions. The IDAM served as a kind of mediator and arranged relief workers for them. The arrangement covered labour expenses: foreign teams provided a third and Israel two-thirds of the labour expenses in the field. The number of relief work-days used by foreign expeditions reached a few thousand each year. Payment was the same as for any other relief work (GL44880/13 no. 6249, 14.1.58; GL44888/12 no. 7715).

As the salary was poor and relief workers were not allowed to have additional jobs, the system encouraged all kinds of fraud. Documentation for one case concerned a relief worker in Perrot's excavations. He worked more than the hours allocated to him and "for covering up signed three additional work cards" (probably under different names). The labour office refused to pay and asked the IDAM for instructions (GL44883/5, 30.1.59).

The extent of reliance on cheap relief work for Israel's archaeology was absolute. In a letter of 6 December 1957, Yeivin explained how "in all the works of excavations the Employment Department of the Ministry of Labour supplies, from years ago, relief workers to perform the work". When the Ministry of Labour refused to finance workers at Mezer (see above), it caused a shortfall of 3,000 Lira in the IDAM's budget. It was partly covered by "abolishing a trial excavation at Azor" (*sic.*, GL44883/5, 6.12.57).

Another report from late 1957 admitted that almost all the work-days for excavations are "produced by the Department of Employment of the Ministry of Labour". Without its help, it would have been impossible for the IDAM to perform any excavations (GL44883/12). IDAM excavations were possible only because workers' salaries were paid by the developing bodies (GL44880/12, annual report for 1956/7; cf. Yeivin 1955b: 19; 1960: 51–2; *Alon* **5–6** (1957): 4). When proposing the budget for 1960/61, Yeivin noted how vital the relief work was for the IDAM (GL1430/14).

The "hard currency" of the 1950s was relief work-days (today we sometimes base economic comparisons using the price of a McDonald's burger; Primo Levi concluded that bread was the hard currency in Auschwitz). When Yeivin asked the GTC to give priority to improving the synagogue at Hefzibah, Yannay answered that the Ministry of Labour provided the budget for relief work alone. Since the work at Hefzibah was "entirely based upon cash and almost does not require relief work" (it was restoration work that demanded professionals), Yannay was sceptical about whether it could be done that year (GL44882/9, 18.4.57).

The IDAM's official budget did not acknowledge relief work. Within the budget for "Excavations and Surveys" there was one small line item for salaries of workers in excavations. It was meant for manual workers, but the IDAM used it to pay temporary professional workers, since manual (relief) work was usually paid by others. For years the Ministry of Finance never queried how such a tiny item sufficed for scores of excavations using thousands of relief workers each year. Finally, on 14 October 1960 a clerk wrote to the IDAM asking for confirmation that there was no mistake. The IDAM explained that this line item was used for students and similar assistants (GL1430/14 no. 6477). The Ministry of Finance protested: item 304.4 should be used for manual workers. Archaeological staff should be paid from the regular budget (GL1430/14 no. 991, 30.10.60). I could not find documents showing how the affair was resolved.

Merom rightly criticized the attitude to new immigrants, but her appreciation of relief work is too negative. It was not an organized plot against "eastern Jews". True, the rigid ideology of the period consecrated work and the veterans looked down on the immigrants. Yet, under the severe conditions of the early 1950s, Israel had no other option: there was no magic solution. Similar concepts were adopted earlier in the US and in Mandatory Palestine. The US did not employ relief work because of a sudden socialistic impulse; it was a matter of necessity.

Relief work brought some undesired consequences, such as becoming accustomed to the availability of large numbers of cheap workers. Many large excavations could be carried out, but there was no comparable budget for post-excavation work and publication. The result was a backlog of many unpublished excavations.

THE END OF RELIEF WORK?

In 1960/61 the Ministry of Labour cut down the number of relief work-days allocated to the IDAM (e.g. GL44883/5, 29.11.60). In 1962, Biran faced a new situation: full employment in Israel. It "made it difficult to find 'gratis' labour of the ordinary type for excavations" (Biran 1962: 175). The solution was to use pre-military youth groups (*gadna*) as volunteers, but this was only a temporary measure. Later, relief work became available again without difficulty (GL44883/5, GL44881/14).

According to Merom (1997, 2003), Minister of Labour Yoseph Almogi abolished relief work in the late 1960s, "because he realized that it is impossible to maintain such an archaic system in the conditions of a modern economy" (Merom 2003). Officially, relief work stopped in September 1970 (Statistical Yearbook of Israel 1971: 271). If Merom is right, why did Israel renew relief work in the 1990s, despite its modern economy? The answer is not that relief work became "archaic", but that it was no longer required. In the 1950s, prior to the development in the economy, Israel could not do without some sort of relief work. The problem was not the idea itself, but the way it was implemented.

It seems to me that it is not just a coincidence that the abolishment of relief work came soon after the 1967 War. This war brought the West Bank and Gaza strip under Israel's control. Palestinian workers occupied, at least partially, the place of former Israeli relief workers. If this is true, it was a change of workers more than an abolition: only the terminology "relief work" was abolished. This conclusion is tentative and demands study by economists. How did the IDAM cope with the new situation? One does not see any trauma; some excavations in the 1970s and 1980s used unemployed people, since the abolition of relief work did not abolish unemployment. Sometimes youth groups or other sources of cheap labour (Palestinians, Arab-Israelis) were used. In most cases, developers continued to finance the expenses of labour in the field, and many salvage excavations in the 1970s and 1980s were also performed with volunteers.

While relief work officially ended in 1970, it continued for some time in the people's minds. For example, Yosef Aviram of the IES administrated Mazar's excavations near the West Wall of Jerusalem after 1967. The Ministry of Education paid part of the budget. In 1971, 50,000 Lira above the allocated budget was spent on labour in the field. So on 23 March 1971 Aviram formally asked the Ministry of Education to update the allowance to cover "salaries of relief workers" in the following year's budget to 300,000 Lira. This was approved on 27 July 1971, although officially there were no more relief workers (GL44884/12).

RELIEF WORK IN THE 1990S

The story cannot be complete without a short reference to the renewal of the system in the 1990s, under very different circumstances. As a result of the demise of the former USSR, mass immigration to Israel took place. Between 1990 and 1999, 956,319 persons immigrated to Israel, of which 821,763 came from areas of the former USSR. In 2000, a further 61,192 immigrants arrived, 50,776 of which came from the former USSR (Statistical Yearbook of Israel 2001). Later the numbers dwindled as economic recession set in. The 1990s immigrants were much better educated and had high self-esteem. The very high number of immigrants from former Russian-speaking lands enabled cohesion, and led to what is sometimes called "Moscow in the Holy Land". Enterprises for and by these immigrants developed, from delicatessen shops to theatres and newspapers in Russian. Still, the problems were severe and painful: immigration is a very difficult process even under the best conditions.

At the peak of the wave of immigration, fearing housing shortages and perhaps trying to avoid temporary camps like the *ma'abarot*, camps built from prefabricated small caravans or hastily built houses were erected. This was very expensive and a few of these places remained much longer than anticipated, deteriorating rapidly.

There was also a severe unemployment problem and relief work was again used, although on a much smaller scale. The IAA employed a few hundred workers in archaeology under what was named "project 500" (Sheri 1998; Fishbain 1999). At times, there were more than 500 workers; suggestions to expand the system were made in 1997 by some governmental offices headed by ministers David Levi and Eli Yishai. They suggested employing 1,500 workers in archaeological digs, forest planting and tourist-related projects, such as the celebrations planned for the jubilee of Israel. They also suggested financing small businesses in development areas and professional courses for the unemployed. In 1999, the manager of the Employment Service (*Sherut ha-Ta'asuka*), Moshe Dimri, suggested a plan of relief works, although the term "relief work" was not mentioned explicitly. He proposed employing 10,000 workers in road construction and tourist projects, but this time those who refused would lose their welfare payments. This was a much-criticized new component. Dimri hoped that this plan would have educational value; it would give the unemployed "working habits and … improve their self image and their occupational and social status", supposedly turning "employment-handicaps with low self-esteem" into motivated workers (Fishbain 1999). In recent years, with the economic recession and policy of cutting social welfare, the plans to employ relief work were shelved. Few workers of project 500 are still employed by the IAA. At the time of writing the continuation of their employment is not certain.

In conclusion I should like to return once more to the 1950s, to read the daily page of the Kibbutz Ayyelet ha-Shahar. In 1950 the members were told: "For the attention of smokers, we still have enough for one more allocation of 'Amir' cigarettes. Smokers must realize that getting cigarettes is difficult, and they must accept 'Amir' cigarettes" (Kibbutz archive, daily page 2, 1950). Slightly later, the following story appeared:

> Regarding the tension between the clothes storer and member K, the committee heard a thorough explanation and decided that there was no serious basis for such a relationship, and one must avoid, as much as possible,

spreading undesired rumours. On the matter of the store, and of supplying the needs of the members, a special discussion must be held. And as for the affair itself, it was decided that a smaller committee must check Pasiyah K's clothes store and reach conclusions based on this investigation.

(Kibbutz archive, daily page 4, 1950)

Alas, gone forever are the facts behind this affair; we shall never know who was responsible for what. Gone are the days of the strict Kibbutzim, with committees ruling every minute detail of the life of the individual. Gone also are the infamous "Amir" cigarettes; only their imagined smoke lingers in the memory for a while.

7 MAN ROBS HIS LAND: "AGREEMENT" WITH GENERAL DAYAN

Gabriel Garcia Marquez (1967: 106–7) describes the glorious Colonel Aureliano Buendia, who organized 32 rebellions, had 17 children with different mothers and survived 14 murder attempts and 73 ambushes; the only thing left was a street named after him in Macondo. Almost every major city in Israel has a street named after Moshe Daya, a general and politician with enormous status and influence. Born in May 1915, he was jailed by the British authorities in Accho in 1939, lost an eye in an operation in Syria in 1941, served as commander of an army division during the 1948 War, and was head of the Jerusalem Front. In October 1949 he was appointed Commander of the Southern Front, and in December 1952 Chief of Operations at General Headquarters. From 1953 to 1958 he was Chief of Staff, leading the army to – and during – the 1956 War. After a short year of studies at the Hebrew University of Jerusalem, Dayan was elected to Parliament and became Minister of Agriculture (1959–64). On the brink of the 1967 War he was appointed Minister of Defence, and the 1967 victory turned him into a national hero. He held this post until 1974, after the shattering crisis of the 1973 War. Although many Israelis blamed him for it, he prospered by deserting the Labour Party to join Begin's government in 1977 as Foreign Minister. In this post he conducted the talks with Egypt's President Sadat that led to the Israeli–Egyptian peace agreement. Meanwhile his health deteriorated, and he died in October 1981 (Slater 1991).

Over three decades (1951–81) Dayan established a vast collection of antiquities acquired through illicit digs, and bought, exchanged and sold antiquities in Israel and abroad. In a recent study I tried to analyse his deeds and separate the facts from the many wild rumours left in his wake (Kletter 2003). There is a pressing need for this, because of the persistent view that he was a great explorer of sites and a saviour of antiquities: a romantic Robin Hood who ignored stupid bureaucracy (Taslitt 1969; Slater 1991: 161–2; Ben-Ezer 1997: 121, 218–19). The only biographer to have seen that Dayan's claim of having saved antiquities is paradoxical is Falk (1985), perhaps because as a psychoanalyst he is trained to recognize deceptive statements. Israel's inability to limit Dayan's "narcissistic greatness complex" by ending his wrongdoings is "sad evidence to its lack of maturity at that time" (Falk 1985: 246; cf. Adler 1987). I use the term "digs" in relation to Dayan, and "excavation" for work by archaeological scholars, which involves registration, stratigraphic analysis and scientific publication. In Hebrew there is no distinction, but the two types of activity are very different.

DAYAN'S ILLICIT DIGS

Dayan robbed dozens of sites in Israel and the occupied territories. The evidence is still accumulating: recently I found that *Ma'ariv* of 28 June 1957 published photos of Dayan digging at Tell Jerishe, a "new" site on the list. Dayan was caught in person on at least four occasions, but two examples will suffice here.

Serabit el-Khadem, Sinai

Dayan robbed the famous Egyptian temple at Serabit el-Khadem at least twice. In 1956 he landed with a helicopter and carried away Egyptian stelae, using military vehicles and personnel. He described the visit, but not the looting (Dayan 1978: 56–8). This story may sound incredible, but many independent sources confirm it. Naftali Lavi, a journalist who worked for Dayan in his later years, testified that:

> There was the famous story about Serabit el-Khadem, that he brought army officers to carry a pillar [meaning stele] for him from there. I once asked him about it. It is an artistic-archaeological valuable, he said. The Egyptians don't deal with it. Instead of it being destroyed there, let it be in a museum. (in Cohen 1991:16)

No destruction threatened this site except Dayan's acts; the finds were not stolen for any museum. When asked about the incident in Parliament in 1971, Dayan admitted taking one stele in 1956, but claimed that he was just a delivery boy. The stele, he said, was "chosen by a senior Israeli archaeologist and delivered to the IDAM in Jerusalem" (*Divrei Ha-Knesset* (parliamentary minutes) 7/62

(1971): 532); this was a composition of half-truths. A private soldier named Ido Dissentchick, who happened to be the son of the editor of *Ma'ariv*, was an eyewitness to the robbery in July 1969. Dissentchick's unit was ordered to provide protection for Dayan at Serabit el-Khadem. Arriving there, they found:

> "Dayan and his friend for archaeological matters [not named] busy on a tour. It was not a regular military tour, but an archaeological one. The pilots … took aboard the helicopter the treasured antiquities that Dayan desired." They watched in amazement, said Ido, and on the way back one of his unit suddenly said: "We provided security for a crime. Just like in the movies: the robbers inside the bank, the covering men outside. We are accessories to a crime".
> (Slater 1991: 284; Dissentchick 1981: 12–13)

Dissentchick tells how his father refused to publish this story, saying:

> "What you tell does not surprise me. No story about Moshe Dayan will surprise me. He's capable of any bad deed. But we will not write such things about him. Moshe Dayan must be accepted as he is, with the good and the bad in him, because we need him … When D-day comes, he is our hope and our saviour." In response Ido asked, "Regardless of the cost?" His father's answer was unequivocal: "There is no price for the independence and safety of a nation."
> (Dissentchick 1981: 12–13)

Uri Yarom was the pilot who carried Dayan's loot from this site. In his autobiography, he describes the 1956 "Steiner operation" (from the German for "stone"). Dayan is explicitly mentioned as responsible for it. Yarom landed at Abu-Rudeis, where:

> Over a picnic lunch the commander of the camp described our next mission: to reach the ruins of Serabit el-Khadem … and carry a load of stones of archaeological–historical value, already marked by Shmaryah Gutman, and to land them at Abu-Rudeis. The booty [*shalal*] will be loaded on a Dakota plane, to be taken to Israel.
> (Yarom 2001: 171)

Yekutiel Adam and Uzi Narkis, two high-ranking officers, were present. Yarom made at least three round-trips, taking an inscribed stele, a large obelisk and "a few other pieces". Some 20 soldiers helped to transfer the "booty" to a plane going home, hoping to get a ride on it. At least one stone "found its way to the private collection of Dayan" (Yarom 2001: 173). A photograph of the helicopter lifting the obelisk printed in Yarom's book provides evidence for this act. Much later, the finds were returned to Sinai (Miberg 1991: 20; Ben-Ezer 1997: 209; Amitai 1998: 8; for more photographs of looting see Yurman 1968).

Azor, south of Tel Aviv

Dayan robbed this site continually from 1957 (Perrot & Ladiray 1980: 27, 43). He claimed that he was saving antiquities that would otherwise be ruined by construction (Dayan 1978: 132; Ben-Ezer 1997: 217–22). In January 1965, Moshe Brosh (formerly Busheri), an IDAM supervisor, caught Dayan robbing the site. I quote from a report by Brosh dated 13 January 1965:

> While driving on the bus from Tel Aviv to Ashdod on my way home, I saw someone who seemed to be digging at the site. I asked the bus driver to halt at the nearest bus stop, and walked on foot to the site of the Philistine cemetery. Upon arriving, I saw Moshe Dayan digging at the site and taking out parts of vessels. I greeted him, and addressed him with a question:
> Question: Do you know that you are digging in an antiquities site?
> Answer: To the best of my knowledge the antiquities site is in the fenced area, and here are neither a fence nor a sign to indicate that this is an antiquities site.
> Question: Do you think that these sherds, taken out by you, are ancient?
> Answer: Undoubtedly.
> Question: Do you know that a dig in order to take antiquities is an offence even in an area not defined as an ancient site?
> Answer: I did not know that.
> Question: According to the law one who finds antiquities must inform the IDAM … To the best of my knowledge you gave no notification about finding antiquities at this site.
> Answer: No, I did not know that I should have done so.
> (IAA archive, Azor administrative file)

Brosh explained to Dayan that the fence was built to protect later burials and a sign about the site was posted by the IDAM on top of the hill. He took the broken vessels that Dayan had exposed. On 11 January 1965 Brosh went to the Jaffa police station to complain:

> To the lieutenant's question about against whom the complaint was directed, I answered, "Against MP Moshe Dayan". He went to the officer in charge of the station, who explained to me that one cannot file a complaint against an MP unless the presidency of Parliament rescinds his immunity. One needs first to apply in writing to the presidency of Parliament, and only then will the police deal with the case. (IAA archives, Azor administrative file)

According to Shabatai Teveth (1972), on 15 January 1965 Dayan was summoned to the police following the complaint and declared that he was ready to forgo his parliamentary immunity. He was questioned on 25 January, but reached an agreement with the IDAM (headed by Biran; Teveth 1972: 321; Slater 1991: 326–7). The exact circumstances are not clear. On 20 July 1965 the tabloid newspaper *Bul* claimed that its photographer, Avi Naveh, had photographed Dayan robbing Azor on 9 July 1965. Gad Peri, a reporter for *Bul*, asked Dayan why he had not notified the IDAM about the finds, but Dayan retorted, "If you want, you can notify them." The journalists complained to the police. So it seems that Dayan had continued looting and was caught twice in the same year, and nothing was done by the authorities in both cases.

Dayan was not brought to justice; the case was closed (Ben-Amotz 1974: 32, Ilan 1986: 7). Yet he returned again to loot this site. In 1968 Dayan was badly injured by a landslide while robbing a cave at Azor, and was hospitalized for three weeks as a result. It could not be hushed up because the failure of the dig coincided with the failure of an army operation at Karameh in Jordan (Teveth 1969: 262–7; 1972: 320–21, 356; Elon 1971: 284; Dayan & Dudman 1973: 224; Dayan 1976: 337–42; 1978: 132; 1985: 195–7; Falk 1985: 262–5; Slater 1991: 304–5; Amitai 1998: 8). Ido Dissentchick knew that Dayan was injured during looting and phoned Biran, head of the IDAM, to ask: "Are you going to file a complaint against him? Biran, having heard that Dayan might be dying, retorted: Do you think that my only worry is to charge the Defence Minister with something like this?" (Slater 1991: 305–6).

AN "AGREEMENT" BETWEEN DAYAN AND THE IDAM

Documents about the 1965 Azor incident refer to some agreement between Dayan and the IDAM, which allegedly allowed him to dig. Dayan referred to this "deal" with the IDAM: "I was less happy having to part with the vessels I had collected [at Azor]. It was with no ease of heart that I handed them all over to the IDAM. I was left with only a few sherds" (Dayan 1978: 132). The "few sherds" were only from this one looting; Dayan's collection included many robbed objects from Azor (Dayan 1978: 40, 43; Perrot & Ladiray 1980: 27, 41, 43; Ornan 1986: 32, 72). Yael Dayan (1986:15) claimed that Dayan's "alibi" for digging was a letter stating that the IDAM had free access to his collection and the right to visit and confiscate items that were "valuable for a museum". She claims that the IDAM also took items. Slater (1991: 326) wrote that in the 1960s Dayan proposed that IDAM officials "cart off whatever part of his collection they wanted. They removed half the collection." This is a strange myth: where are the objects? Which IDAM workers took part in the confiscation? The Minister of Education confirmed in Parliament that the IDAM had not visited, registered or confiscated anything from Dayan's collection during eight years between 1963 and 1971 (*Divrei Ha-*

Knesset (parliamentary minutes) 7/3 (1971)). Nothing was confiscated except those vessels taken by Brosh in 1965 from the scene of the robbery. Dayan's loot from all the other occasions remained in his hands.

Formerly, I have been sceptical about the entire affair (Kletter 2003). I thought it inconceivable that the IDAM would hand Dayan an official permit to dig illegally. However, documents from several files in the state archive in Jerusalem shed new light on the matter. At first, the IDAM had cordial relations with Dayan. His digs started in 1951 and it took time for the IDAM to realize the nature of them. In 1955 Dayan sent the IDAM a letter, allegedly on a "private" matter:

> I am writing concerning a private matter ... as you (and all Israel) know, I collect in my garden a mixed lot of remains of pillars, capitals, troughs, etc., which I often find among the ruins of deserted Arab villages. None of these objects is taken from among the remains of a building or settlement to which they originally belonged; I would see it as vandalism to dismantle the remains of a historic building in order to acquire a part of it.
>
> I am certain that you have no interest in the objects collected by me, but as I told you verbally – and I wish to repeat this in writing – I am ready to hand to you, at each and every hour when asked, every object that you are interested in. I shall also be happy to make a catalogue and note the place names from which the various stones, pillars, capitals, etc., were taken ...
> Moshe Dayan, COS   (GL44864/9 no. 1291-19/144 , 25.8.55)

The letter mentions a former memorandum "between us" (probably related to a case when the army newspaper *Bamahane* published details about an IDAM excavation). Dayan did not mention digging: only collecting items from the surface. Yeivin replied kindly:

> I suppose that most of the things collected by you are not of interest to the IDAM at the moment. I noted before me your promise to see them as objects temporarily loaned (*be-hash'alah*) to you. One of these days I shall ask one of the IDAM supervisors to visit the homes of people who hold such antiquities in order to check and register these remains. Possibly they may include rare objects, which we shall be forced to collect in secure places or museums.
>
> I should be most thankful if you could kindly notify other IDF officers who might hold such collections.   (GL44864/9 no. 7544, 5.9.55)

At this early stage cordial relations were maintained. Yeivin "supposed" that most of the items would hold no interest, without asking what those items were. He failed to act, perhaps because he did not yet have a clear picture of Dayan's deeds. After all, the authorities collected "abandoned" antiquities in 1948 as well. The extremely limited workforce prevented efficient supervision of sites. One can understand – although hardly justify – Yeivin's reaction. This first "agreement" between Dayan and Yeivin allowed collecting, but not illegal digging. More importantly, Dayan acknowledged the full authority of the IDAM over the finds. He explicitly stated that they belonged to the state. If only someone had found this letter when the collection was sold as Dayan's private property …

There was even some cooperation with Dayan, for example about a robbed Byzantine period grave with drawings at Burir (GL44880/12, 25.11.55). The IDAM had no reason to suspect Dayan in this case. Gradually, however, the IDAM discovered what Dayan was doing and the cordial relations were shattered. By late 1957 the situation was explosive. Behind the change in relations were the many sites robbed by Dayan between 1955 and 1957, including an unnamed site near Ashkelon; Muntar, Sheikh Zuweid, Tel Ali, Serabit el-Hadem, Hazav (Saluja); Benaya near Gederah, Ashdod and Azor. These are just the documented sites (Kletter 2003). Dayan's digging became widespread and savage; the victory in the 1956 War seems to have freed him from any constraint.

Yeivin couldn't remain idle. After some correspondence (which we lack), he wrote a letter labelled "confidential" directly to the Prime Minister:

> Honourable Prime Minister,
> When I returned from abroad a month ago I found your kind answer waiting (no. 2053, 2 August this year). I was very sorry to read the words of the COS [Dayan], who did not address the issue at hand at all, and also did not reply accurately.
> Meanwhile, I discovered that you are going on holiday and I could not and did not want to disturb you by asking for an interview. However, as the time is nearing for your return to office, I should be grateful if you could spare me, when you return, a few minutes of your time so that I can inform you about all the accurate details of the affair.
> I hear that the COS is returning soon from abroad, and I fear the renewal of his archaeological activity. Therefore, I ask you by all means to see my request as a most urgent one and to set a date for an interview at your earliest convenience.   (GL44880/13 no. 5975, 29.9.57)

Ben-Gurion probably intervened immediately, since a day later, on 30 September 1957, Yeivin wrote again to say that the matter was resolved; an agreement had been reached:

> Honourable Prime Minister,
> In regard to my last letter to you (no. 5975, yesterday), I am pleased to inform you that yesterday afternoon the COS, General Moshe Dayan, visited my home, and after a short conversation we have reached the following agreement:

A) From now on the COS gives up any idea of digging on his own in any historical site;

B) Only where he, by chance, happens to see various development projects, such as quarrying, hewing, excavating for building foundations or for laying pipework, and finds that the workers of the project are about to damage ancient remains whose presence at the site was unknown will he be allowed to act immediately to save those remains from oblivion, and then only on two conditions: 1. he will try, as best he can, to notify immediately or as early as possible the IDAM or one of its workers closest to the site; 2. he will prevent publicity in the press about his actions to save antiquities.

Allow me to thank you for your active help in settling this problem, which has caused great sorrow and not a little damage to the IDAM.

I sign in feelings of honour and blessing,

[signed] Sh. Yeivin

[copies to Dayan, the Minister of Education, M. Avidor]

(GL44880/13 no. 5988)

This was the famous "agreement" later cited – after Yeivin's days at the IDAM – as official permission for illicit digging. One must note that it was not a true legal agreement in the sense that Dayan never signed anything. The letter forbade any further digging and demanded Dayan to immediately notify the IDAM about each endangered site. Unfortunately, the letter left open the fate of damaged sites, where Dayan was allowed to collect finds. It also did not address the issue of ownership of such finds. Moreover, the wording that suggested "saving" antiquities was unfortunate. Yeivin's true feelings about Dayan's digs were expressed in the last section: "great sorrow and not a little damage".

The letter was a grave mistake – one of Yeivin's darkest hours – but only because he expected a gentlemanly agreement with someone who had proved his ruthlessness in many fields of life. The ink had hardly dried on this letter when it became clear that there was no agreement; Dayan never kept to the terms. Again, we miss the full chain of events, but on 24 March 1958 Yeivin wrote to Dayan:

Honourable Dayan,

I asked Mrs Katzenstein [Yeivin's secretary] to phone you, to ask that in your next visit to Jerusalem you will kindly visit the IDAM. I wanted to ask you about several matters regarding Bney-Braq, Ashdod and Elnahar. I thought it might be best to talk in person rather than describe them in writing.

I understand that you are not certain whether you will visit Jerusalem before the renewal of studies at the [Hebrew] University. Since matters are very urgent, I should be very grateful if you could find time to visit the IDAM at least before Easter. Unfortunately, the pressure of work here is so

great that I cannot see any immediate opportunity to visit Tel Aviv or its
vicinity.

However, please notify me if you are at home as usual in the afternoons.
If I am forced to visit Tel Aviv and its vicinity next week, I shall try to find
free time some afternoon to come to you; although this is not very likely.

(GL44880/13 no. 7770 [marked "personal and confidential"])

Although the letter does not specify much, we know that Dayan robbed
Bney-Braq and Ashdod; Elnahar is now called Kabri (Khalidi 1992: 27–8) and
there is a large ancient Tell there, but the details are unknown. Yeivin tried to
avoid another written "agreement", but still hoped that a face-to-face meeting
would solve the problems. The suggestion to meet Dayan at his home was a sign
of weakness, rather like having tea with the poacher while the game is displayed
all over the house. The necessity of such a meeting was explained a few months
later, when Yeivin sent Dayan another letter:

My Dear Honourable Dayan,

In view of various complaints recently received by the IDAM that, despite
what you have promised me, you are not keeping the agreement that you
made with the IDAM a few months ago, I have no other choice but to
conclude that a misunderstanding occurred concerning the nature of the
agreement.

When it was agreed between us that you could save what was possible to
save in places where mechanical tools have been operated and have ruined
ancient remains, it was clear to me that this referred only to the parts of sites
that have already been ruined by the mechanical tools, where no scientific
excavation can produce any new evidence for study. In no way did I imagine
allowing the additional destruction of parts of sites that have survived the
teeth of mechanical tools, for scientific excavation might give scientific
knowledge of the highest order, both in relation to these parts themselves,
as well as to parts that have already been lost and ruined.

It seems that you have understood that our agreement refers also to parts
of sites that have not been damaged by mechanical tools.

I must therefore make it clear to you that this is a mistake. At places
where bulldozers or other tools have passed and ruined anything, the
settlement between you and the IDAM is valid. Places not yet ruined by
bulldozers (etc.), even if parts of them have been ruined, are not covered
by the settlement. The IDAM cannot allow any private person or public
body to continue to poke [le-khatet] in its ground without a methodical
archaeological excavation and without a permit for excavating as required
by the law. Such actions do not answer to the principles of either science
or the law, and also sets a bad and dangerous antecedent and an exam-

ple to all kinds of saboteurs [*mekhablim*; a negative word now used for Palestinian terrorists], who lust after antiquities for private inclination or for commercial greed.

I am assured that no further correspondence in this case will be necessary following this explanation, and that you will be careful to maintain the agreement as explained in this letter.

With feelings of respect and in blessing,

[signed] Sh. Yeivin, Director of IDAM

(GL1430/14 no. 9299, 29.8.58)

Copies were sent to the Prime Minister, to the Minister of Education and to Avidor. The wording is very peculiar: if scientific excavations may produce important data from both ruined and intact parts of a site, one must forbid any illicit digging in any part of a site, but how does one know beforehand if a certain part is completely or only partially ruined? Yeivin reserved his anger more for the "saboteurs" than for the person who gave them the example: Dayan. Yeivin also clung to the former "agreement", finding excuses for why Dayan broke it: it was just a "misunderstanding". Dayan, however, broke the "agreement" without either scruples or excuses. Yeivin even assumed that sending this letter would be enough to ensure the desired solution. He expressed the groundless hope that further correspondence, not to mention legal acts, would be unnecessary. It is a sad letter, reflecting lack of the will or power to confront Dayan. Still, the letter never gave authority for illegal digging. It allowed collection only from the surface of destroyed parts of sites, never altering the earlier requirements (immediate notification, giving up "wild" digs, etc.).

CONTINUED VIOLATIONS OF THE "AGREEMENT"

It is understandable why Dayan or his supporters never exposed this "agreement" in public. A shrewd lawyer could use it in court, but it was far from complimentary (especially the second letter with its mention of saboteurs). Israeli archaeology suffered for years from Dayan's cynical abuse of this "agreement". The ill effects are evident in a letter from Rahmani of 13 August 1959 (GL44880/13), carrying the handwritten reference "TL/I/COS". This signifies that the letter originated from the notorious "Complaints File Chief of Staff", kept by the IDAM. What we have here is a copy taken from this file (which perhaps still exists), that was sent to the Ministry of Education:

On 10 August 1959 Dr Kaplan of Tel Aviv notified [us] that a Middle Bronze Age II tomb was discovered on Abba Hilel Silver road [in Ramat Gan], opposite the pharmacy. According to Dr Kaplan the work was stopped and the Israel police placed guards there.

On 12 August 1959 at 09.15 we – Mrs Varda Sussman and me – were there. We found no guard, but a large number of children. They and the manager of works on behalf of the contractor, E.B., revealed that Mr Moshe Dayan was there on 10 August 1959 and took from the remains of the tomb a small jug [juglet?], a green [=rusted] knife [spear head?] and coins [probably scarabs]. He left a large jar (a picture of which appears in the attached *Ma'ariv* report) and asked the works manager to cover the tomb with wooden logs.

The works manager did place a few logs there, but on the evening of 10 August 59 children from the neighbourhood came, broke the jar and took its parts out …

Kaplan and Sussman thought that there was no room for a salvage excavation because the road was right above. However:

Today, 13 August 1959, Dr Kaplan appeared in Jerusalem and told me that the tomb was not filled in. At noon Mr Moshe Dayan arrived, re-dug the tomb and took out a few scarabs and fibulae. With that aim in mind, he did not avoid digging about one metre under the [modern] road. Asked by Mr Kaplan to explain his actions he said that he had an agreement with Mr Yeivin that he was authorized to dig at any place forsaken [*mafkir*; this word is used to describe the IDF ethos of never abandoning a soldier on the battlefield] by the IDAM. Attached is the clip from *Ma'ariv*. It should be pointed out that there is no truth in the [newspaper's] story suggesting that Mr Dayan notified us about the find. [Actually, the newspaper reported with sympathy how Dayan changed his clothes and excavated jars, and the headline was "M. Dayan discovers antiquities". There was not one word of criticism.]

RECOMMENDATIONS
There is no doubt that Mr Moshe Dayan transgressed the Antiquities Law. If he is by chance at a place where antiquities have been damaged, it is his duty to see that the work stops, to immediately notify the IDAM, and – if it is in his power – to see that the Israel police place adequate guards there … No doubt Mr Dayan's public status is strong enough to ensure that all these things could be done – if he wanted them to be. In fact, he did not notify the IDAM but himself conducted a savage dig with the sole aim of acquiring a few finds … Finally he came again and dug without any concern for public safety: the traffic on the road above his dig; the safety of the children at this open site; and finally his own wellbeing.

It is hard to find any justification for such a savage sort of dig … The justification of securing the ancient objects does not apply in this case, since Mr Dayan did not hand the objects to the IDAM; there is no reason to assume that his intention during the time was to hand them to the IDAM.

The over-publicity of his actions in daily newspapers and on Kol Israel [radio] places the IDAM in a very difficult situation. There are two possibilities. Either Mr Dayan … broke the law, which the IDAM is responsible to maintain, in which case the IDAM must issue a complaint against the transgressor. Or one must assume that Mr Dayan has received a special permit of excavation by the IDAM now or in the past; if so, this must be made public knowledge. Not doing one of these two things will by necessity be used by anyone who wants to break the Antiquities Law …

(GL44880/13, not numbered)

The letter reached several officials, but there is no evidence for action taken in line with its recommendations. After Yeivin's retirement in 1959 the IDAM lacked strong leadership. A younger generation of supervisors took the opportunity to write a letter to the management of the IDAM, marked "confidential". It was also deposited in the Complaints File Chief of Staff, but a copy reached the state archives:

Subject: transgression of the Law of Antiquities by General Moshe Dayan.

The signed below, antiquities supervisors of the IDAM at the Ministry of Education, see it as their duty to bring to the attention of the management of the department the repeated comments about the matter under discussion. General Moshe Dayan has publicly transgressed against the Antiquities Law for years now, and this has become a matter of notoriety. Attached are newspaper cuttings …

There is no truth in the reports suggesting that Mr [altered to General] Dayan notified the IDAM about discoveries. The truth [is] that he dug and re-dug the sites, and added the finds to his collection. The IDAM acted on a message received from another source. From all these sources it seems that General Dayan is digging in view of the general public without any licence or permission, without any [archaeological] method or registration – against the law and the rules [i.e. ethics] of archaeological excavations. Furthermore, General Dayan adds the finds to his private collection; of course this too is in contravention of the law.

This open contempt towards the Antiquities Law by a prominent person who is loved by the public is used as an excuse for any person in the land who does similar deeds. Thus ancient sites are destroyed with no possibility of repair; moreover, supervisors of antiquities no longer have control over other transgressors.

All this makes it clear that the digs of General Moshe Dayan must be stopped once and for all, and it should be ensured that the finds of his illegal excavations are delivered to the state. If these goals are achieved, we recommend a public announcement by the press. Let this announcement serve as an answer to the above-mentioned letters and notes [of complaint].

(GL44880/13, 12.859)

The letter was signed by Ram Gophna (later a professor at Tel Aviv University), Joseph Leibowitz, Yosef ("Sefi") Naveh, Dr Moshe Prausnitz and Levy Yosef Rahmani. Their petition was ignored. Katzenstein, the IDAM secretary, wrote to Dr Fritz Berger in Natanya on 19 August 1959:

On behalf of Dr Kahane [Deputy Director] and myself I thank you for your good wishes in your letter. Nevertheless, I also thank you for directing our attention to the letter in the "*Ha'aretz*" editorial of 4 August about the antiquities collection of General Moshe Dayan. The matter has been entrusted to the care of the appropriate authorities.

(GL44880/13 no. 2551)

Who were the "appropriate authorities" if not the IDAM? Kahane admitted the lethargy in a "confidential" letter to Avidor of 26 August 1959:

I have not yet found a reasonable solution to the problem of the "excavating" of Moshe Dayan [note the quotation marks, to distinguish this from other legitimate excavating]; any offer on our side he will only interpret as giving him acknowledgement of the authority to continue his digs. Since Mr Moshe Dayan often bases his acts on an "agreement" with Mr Yeivin of 30 September 1957, without himself keeping to the terms of this agreement, we must annul the "support" of this agreement by the IDAM; unless we find in the near future a general solution to the problem.

The questions to be asked are when to abolish it, who [should abolish it] (I suppose the IDAM, as Dayan rests his case on an agreement with Mr Yeivin), and how. I hereby attach a draft of a letter [of abolishment] addressed to him.

I wait your decision in this matter ...   (GL44880/13 no. 2613)

I did not find a reply to this letter.

CONCLUSIONS

The IDAM failed to take legal action and was more worried about hushing up the scandals than stopping the culprit. It is especially true for the period of Biran, for by then Dayan's deeds and their damage to Israeli archaeology were horrible. Yeivin at least tried to do something.

Dayan's deeds continued to haunt Israeli archaeology long after his death. A conference was organized in 1988 to discuss a suggestion (that failed) to abolish the legal basis for trade in antiquities. The subject of Dayan kept coming up. Martin Weil, the manager of the Israel Museum, placed the blame squarely on the IDAM (Zemer 1991: 9). He was backed by Yaacov Meshorer (a numismatist, and for many years Chief Curator of the Israel Museum, Jerusalem), but most archaeologists thought otherwise. Amnon Ben-Tor said that Dayan's collection "was a stumbling block and will be a stumbling block" (*ibid.*: 53). Moshe Kochavi of Tel Aviv University told Meshorer bluntly: "until the Israel Museum admits its large crime [in producing] the Dayan Exhibition, you cannot come with clean hands" (in Zemer 1991: 41–2). Most surprising was Rehav'am Zeevi, then head of the Eretz-Israel Museum:

> When Dayan died at the end of 1981, there was immediately an offer to sell his house and its content to the Eretz-Israel Museum and display the Dayan house … We said it did not interest us. First, I did not have the money, but they said not to worry about the money … I said I was also not interested because it was not educational to bring school children to the museum and tell them: look, all these things were excavated in Israel's earth, with the nation's means, but it became the property of one man … They tried to persuade me. Meanwhile the house was sold. Then they tried to convince me to buy just the contents. I said I did not want them; we were interested in three items only. We applied and asked for the three items promised to us … but we did not get them, for someone else paid and someone else got them … I go back to Dayan. They tried to intimidate me. One of our board members came and said: I shall find the money, or else the collection will go abroad. I said it would not go abroad and in my view the widow must donate it to the nation … I will not say what I think about my colleagues from Jerusalem, who bought and displayed the collection … We also could have been candidates to fail in this matter.
> (Zemer 1991: 60)

Dayan also corrupted many others who followed his example (Ariel 1986, 1987; Segev 1986). Consider the case of a couple from Kefar-Yehoshua. They collected some metal finds and brought a few to the IDAM for treatment. The IDAM wrote to them that "after hesitations we decided that, because of the rarity of the bronze sword and bronze vessels, we will have to save them for our national collection", offering reimbursement (GL44864/9 no. 5076). The couple responded:

> We answer that we do not like it … First we want details about the finds; later, something about this national collection and where it is found. You must understand that maybe we also want to establish a national collection of our own, like the "Dayan collection"; then there will be a respectable place for our finds.   (GL44864/9 no. 6446, 13.5.68)

It seems that Dayan conducted his worst looting in the late 1960s and early 1970s. This was his period of glory, between 1967 and 1973. He was the "cat that got the cream", in charge of all the occupied territories, far from democratic institutions and the media in Israel. Precisely for this reason, sources about his looting in the occupied territories are scarce.

How far was all this from the allegedly harmless "playing with jars" that the man wrote in an innocent book of children's poetry:

> To Yonathan
> I explained to you what a limerick is
> So let's together write one;
> On Moshe and Yonathan, who both like
> To play "hide and seek", and in the store with jars.
>   (M. Dayan in Ron-Feder 1986; my translation)

Yeivin was responsible for reaching the "agreement" with Dayan, but Dayan was responsible for the total abuse of this agreement and for savage digging and looting. The only consolation of this grim story is that today the situation is much improved. There is still looting and trade, but supervision is better and public figures are not immune. Most importantly, the people have accepted the view that antiquities, like endangered flower species, are a public treasure that should not be molested by private individuals.

8 "GOLD OF OPHIR FOR BETH-HORON":
3,000 SHEKELS

Everything the dead predicted has turned out completely different.
Or a little different – which is to say, completely different.
Szymborska, "The Letters to the Dead" (1997: 118)

The late Iron Age ostracon "Gold of Ophir for Beth-Horon 30 Shekels" is famous. It was first published by B. Mazar (1951: 66–7, Fig. 19.3), and has received considerable attention ever since. I have nothing to add to its reading or historical significance, but wish to present its tortuous journey after it was found.

Most inscribed Hebrew seals and ostraca are not found in scientific excavations, but are acquired through the antiquities markets. Any data provided, if at all, by dealers about their origins are doubtful. The reasons are clear: if the object was found after 1978, its trade is forbidden since it is the property of the state, under Israel's Antiquities Law (AL 1978). The honest finder must inform the IAA immediately and, if required, deliver the find into the hands of the state for examination, and in certain cases acquisition. Hence revealing the source may result in supervision or excavation, preventing accumulation of other finds from the same site. Antiquities dealers claim that all objects for sale were found before 1978, and are thus not under jurisdiction of the 1978 Antiquities Law (see Amikam 1983; Ariel 1986, 1987; Borodkin 1995; Zissu 1996; Bisheh 2001; Davies 2001; Herscher 2001; in general also Vitelli 1996).

If we choose to believe so, there were no finds in Israel in the past 26 years except in licensed excavations, and the information supplied by dealers is at least 26 years old and comes secondhand (the dealers were not present at the find). The information comes from the unknowns who made the finds, who for similar reasons are not interested in revealing their sources. As a result, data about the origins of unprovenanced ostraca and seals, regardless of the place and type of publication, cannot be trusted. Even if the object reached a museum and was published by a scholar, the period between discovery and exhibition is rarely discussed. As for price, it is a dirty word, never to be mentioned. We are expected to admire the beauty and rarity of an object, its importance for art and history; but the art and the history of acquiring it are too subtle for the public. This lends some interest to the story of the "Gold of Ophir" ostracon.

The IDAM became aware of this ostracon thanks to a letter from a certain Mr Gefen from Tel Aviv, written in May 1951:

> To the attention of your honour, a sherd carrying an ancient Hebrew inscription ("Gold of Ophir", etc.) like the one found in the recent excavations of Tell Qasile, is offered for sale by the antiquities dealer Shemuel Harari, Allenby 81 Street (in the window), Tel Aviv. I wonder! How did such governmental–municipal property come into private hands? Does the government (the IDAM) know about the above-mentioned case? If it is a forgery, why not forbid its selling as an original?
>
> (GL44873/10 no. 5797, 3.5.51)

The writer had heard about the famous Tell Qasile ostracon, but was uncertain whether the sale concerned a second example "like" it or a fake. He did not assume it to be the same object, since the first was surely a "governmental–municipal" object by nature, so who could imagine that it would reach private hands?

A second request for action was sent to the IDAM on 4 May 1951 from the IES, which carried out the Tell Qasile excavations (GL44873/10 no. 5488, signature unclear). For the writer the object was an important Hebrew antiquity, directly related to Israel's past in the land, and it was the duty of the IDAM to investigate the case. The writer did not think that the IES should buy the ostracon (and the budget of the IES was extremely limited at that time). When these notifications arrived, Yeivin went to salvage the ostracon. On 7 May 1951 he wrote to the dealer, Shemuel Harari:

> I visited your shop today and sadly did not find you there. In the window of your shop a sherd is displayed, found on the surface of El-Khirbeh (Tell Qasile), "Gold of Ophir for Beth-Horon S[hekels] -=" [typewriter representation of the numeral 30, three horizontal lines].
>
> I wish to notify you that the IDAM is going to purchase that sherd and therefore it must not be sold at present to any other buyer. I will visit your shop again next Friday (11.5.51) afternoon, and ask you to be there between 2–4 p.m.
> (GL44873/10, 7.5.51)

In a memorandum of 13 May 1951, Yeivin explained the history of the ostracon. It was discovered on the surface of Tell Qasile between 1943 and 1945. Dr Robert Hoff (an architect), who found the ostracon, did not notify the Mandatory Department of Antiquities, although this was required under the Antiquities Law. The "circle of Jewish archaeologists" learned about the find and saw it, but "in those days they were not interested that it would be taken out of

Jewish hands into the governmental museum". The memorandum implied that the IDAM had known about the whereabouts of this find since 1948, but had not seen any reason to act "as long as the sherd was in the hands of its finder" (GL44873/10 no. 5661). In reality, the IDAM was notified about it only ten days earlier on receiving Gefen's letter of 3 May 1951. According to Mazar (1951: 66), the sherd was found in May 1946. Ben-Dor, Yeivin's deputy, also met Hoff and wrote to Yeivin on 13 May 1951:

> I met Architect R. Hoff, the owner of the ostracon "Gold of Ophir" at his house in Gotlieb 9 Street, Tel Aviv. I saw the sherd there; he gave up the idea of selling it after he learned about Yeivin's letter to the antiquities dealer Harari (of [7.]5.51).
>
> I negotiated with Mr Hoff about acquiring the ostracon for the IDAM. I named a price of 200 Lira and added while talking that a larger sum might also be considered. According to Mr Hoff's words, he is not interested in selling because the economic reasons that drove him in this direction have now been removed. He is ready to sign a commitment by which:
> A) he will not sell the sherd without the IDAM's consent;
> B) he will hand the sherd to the IDAM for scientific aims, photography, copy, etc., and from time to time even for exhibitions;
> C) if at any time in the future he decides to dismantle his small collection of antiquities, the IDAM will have the first right of purchase.
>
> (GL44873/10 no. 4, signed IB)

This meeting was held with Yeivin's consent and he did not comment on its results. Hoff seemed very reasonable and the sherd was removed from the shop to his home, so the danger of immediate sale was removed. Still, Hoff did not sign a binding agreement, so Yeivin rightly sought legal advice, sending a memorandum on 13 May 1951 to Ruth Staner, the legal advisor to the Ministry of Education and Culture. Yeivin mentioned his visit to Tel Aviv on 7 May 1951 and attached the note he had left at Harari's shop. Then he described a second visit he made to the shop with these words:

> Last Friday (11th this month) I revisited Harari's shop. In answer to my questions he informed me: (A) that Mr Hoff wants to receive 2,000 Lira in return for this sherd; (B) that after my above-mentioned letter [of 7.5.51] he (Mr Harari) did not want to take upon himself the responsibility of keeping the sherd in his shop and returned it to Mr Hoff. As far as I know the sherd is now kept by Mr Hoff's attorney.
>
> The IDAM is interested to: (A) receive this sherd for the benefit of its governmental museum (by buying it or in any other way possible by law); (B) prevent its transfer to other hands for fear that it will be taken out of the

country … I must stress that any step taken must be taken immediately, in order to prevent the sale of the object in the meantime to a buyer, whom it will be difficult to trace later.   (GL44873/10 no. 5661)

Strangely, Yeivin did not mention here Ben-Dor's direct talk with Hoff. Ben-Dor saw the sherd in Harari's shop on or before 13 May; perhaps without knowing about Yeivin's meeting with Harari on 11 May 1951. This would explain why, although Yeivin learned that Hoff wanted 2,000 Lira on 11 May, Ben-Dor still suggested the much lower price of 200 Lira (writing on 13 May, although as a basis for further negotiation). When writing to Staner on 13 May, Yeivin was probably already holding Ben-Dor's report. It seems that the "salvage" efforts of the IDAM were not well coordinated, and perhaps Yeivin's enthusiasm, based on the notion that the ostracon was a supreme Hebrew item in danger, caused the price to soar. It would have been cheaper to buy it *incognito*; however, this was not in Yeivin's nature. Two unsigned handwritten drafts were attached to Yeivin's letter to Staner. One draft shows that the writer struggled considerably to find the correct wording:

> In continuation to your talk with Mr XXX I thank you for our conversa-tion [added above the line: on 13.5.51], I am glad to hear [changed to: in which you notified me] that you give up the intention of selling the ostracon "Gold of Ophir".
>
> Clearly, this historical ostracon belongs in a public museum; therefore the IDAM will object to its transfer to private hands or from hand to hand. The IDAM reserves to itself the right to confiscate this sherd at any time when circumstances require this, but it does not intend to do so yet, hoping that its transfer to the hands of the IDAM will be based on negotiation.
>
> In your talk with [Mr Ben-Dor?; two words were erased] you men-tioned your agreement to sign certain obligations about the sherd, and we will be thankful if you will return to us a signed obligation letter attached hereby.

The amended draft mentions a "talk" with Hoff on 13 May; on that date only Ben-Dor met Hoff, but the date is an amendment. One could also assume that Yeivin conversed by phone with Hoff. However, the writer of this memorandum remains in question. The handwriting of the amendments is similar to that of the original; perhaps both were written by Ben-Dor. In the two places where the name was erased, there is a clear final "n" (nun in Hebrew). This could fit Yeivin, if it was not entered on purpose to deceive, since the names were erased in a way that makes their reading very difficult. However, in both places the final "n" is located too close to the word "Mr" to allow for the name "Yeivin", but would fit Ben (with final n)-Dor. It thus seems that the draft originally mentioned

Ben-Dor's meeting with Hoff, and the changes avoided mentioning this meeting. In the first version the (now erased) Hebrew words translated here as "I am glad to hear" indicate that the writer was not personally present for the conversation, although this is not as clear in the English translation. These words do not fit and were replaced by words that imply personal presence at the meeting ("in which you notified me"). Similarly, at first the writer mentioned "your talk with [Ben-Dor]", but then erased the name. It seems that Ben-Dor prepared this draft, to be used or authorized by Yeivin; then Yeivin (or the two together) altered it. Still, why make the changes that erase Ben-Dor's part in the negotiation? The reason could be related to the unexplained rise in the price of the ostracon. Yeivin, if responsible, was not keen to mention the different negotiators to the higher authorities. Yeivin's integrity is his most important and admirable characteristic; I have never had reason to doubt it in the thousands of documents of his that I have read. Even if this memorandum was altered, it is an exception that should not be judged harshly; note that the draft was kept in the file.

The second draft ran:

> To: the IDAM.
> Honourable Sir,
> In my ownership I hold the sherd inscribed with the words "Gold of Ophir for Beth-Horon Sh. ---", which I discovered at El-Khirbeh (Tell Qasile) a few years ago. Considering the historical value of this sherd, I hereby promise that:
> A) I will not sell the sherd ~~nor transfer it~~ out of my ownership to any other authority, unless I receive the consent of the IDAM.
> ~~B) I will keep the sherd in a safe place at my house.~~
> B) I will place the sherd at the disposal of the IDAM for making copies, photographs, drawings, or any other purposes required for the goals of the IDAM;
> C) I will hand the sherd to the IDAM for certain periods for exhibitions;
> D) I will notify the IDAM before I decide to dismantle the antiquities collection that I own. In such a case, as in any other case, the IDAM will have a first right to acquire this sherd from my hands.   (GL44873/10)

Again there was some effort to find precise wording; the writer is probably Ben-Dor again. This is the letter that Yeivin wanted Hoff to sign. Knowing already that the sherd was not in Hoff's house, the letter was altered (by Yeivin) by erasing point B and by many minor points of wording (not all marked above).

Staner sought the advice of the government's legal advisor, and Yeivin wrote on the lower left of Ben-Dor's report of 13 May that they agreed not to send the letters to Hoff in the meantime. On the right Yeivin wrote (adding the date 23 May) that Staner had received a draft of a letter of commitment for Mr Hoff and returned a corrected, printed document (also found in the file). Staner was quick and decisive, writing to the government's legal advisor barely a day after receiving Yeivin's letter:

> *Urgent*
> Subject: Antiquities Ordinance 1929 Section 3; 22 (1)
> Hereby attached is a letter from the manager of the IDAM to me, of 13 May 1951. In my view the following actions are possible:
> A. Publish a notice in all newspapers, according to the attached suggestion;
> B. Tell Dr Hoff that, if within __ hours he will not hand the sherd to the IDAM, the attached notice will be published;
> C. At the same time that the said notice is given to the press, a criminal offence will be presented at court against Dr Hoff, based on section 22 (1) of the antiquities ordinance. In this case also section 5(3)(a) of the antiquities ordinance will be activated.
>
> However, it is possible to suggest to Dr Hoff that if he agrees to hand the sherd to the government immediately, it will not use its rights according to section 5(3)(a) of the antiquities ordinance but its rights by section 5(1) and (2) of the same ordinance. If the archaeological council estimates [the value of] the sherd in a sum that the government is ready to meet, then Dr Hoff will be given the fitting compensation … If the government cannot pay the value of the sherd, according to the decision of the archaeological council, Dr Hoff will be allowed to offer it for sale, as long as it will not be taken out of the country. (GL44873/10 no. 5541)

The following draft of notification was attached:

> *NOTIFICATION*
> Antiquities Ordinance 1929
> Public Warning
> SINCE Dr Hoff from … , Tel Aviv, found on the surface at Tell el-Qasile a sherd carrying an inscription in the ancient Hebrew script: "Gold of Ophir for Beth-Horon Sh(ekels) 30";
> AND SINCE the said Dr Hoff never notified the IDAM of his discovery according to section 3 of the said ordinance;
> AND SINCE the Minister of Education and Culture intends to acquire for the IDAM this ostracon based on sections 4 and 5 of the said ordinance;
> AND SINCE Dr Hoff, against the warning of the IDAM, concealed this sherd, refused to hand it to the IDAM and put it up for sale;
> AND SINCE a criminal prosecution was brought today against the said Dr Hoff, under section 22(1) of the said ordinance:

Therefore we hereby warn the public that no person shall buy the said sherd from the hands of Dr Hoff or from the hands of any other person, for Dr Hoff has no right of ownership over the said sherd according to section 4 of the said ordinance; anybody that buys or tries to buy this sherd from him, or from any other person, puts his money for naught [a Hebrew idiom, literally: "puts his money on the deer's antler"] and may be prosecuted with a criminal offence.

[to be signed] Manager of the IDAM

One must understand the legal background. Despite many expectations in 1948 Israel had not yet ratified a new constitution (Yannai 1988; Rosin 2002), and had meanwhile adopted the existing Mandatory laws. In the case of antiquities, there was the basic ordinance of 1920 (Palestine Official Gazette 1920) with several amendments (especially Government of Palestine 1929, Palestine Official Gazette 1935; used by Staner, above).

Hoff was living peacefully, oblivious of the clouds of governmental wrath gathering on the horizon. In the meantime, a certain A. Alprin, Municipal Superintendent, sent a letter to Yeivin with a copy to the Mayor of Tel Aviv. He told Yeivin that the ostracon had been offered by Harari, and its owner, Hoff, "wanted to sell it for a sum of 200 to 300 Lira. I now hear that *c.* 2,000 Lira are requested for it." The superintendent feared that this ostracon would be sold abroad and Israeli archaeology would lose "a very expensive commodity". The man demanded to know what measures the IDAM intended to take (GL44873/10 no. 5617, received 22.5.51). The interest of this person remains a mystery. The government's attorney general came to a decision and notified Staner:

Unfortunately, I cannot issue a criminal prosecution against Dr Hoff, since the offence, which is a sin [*avon*], became obsolete a long time ago. I also hold the opinion that the notice for the press attached to your letter of 14.5.51 should not be published, since:

A) it may lead to a trial for slander;

B) it has no legal value since section 4(1) of the antiquities ordinance states that no person has any right over an ancient object provided the manager [of the IDAM] has not given up the government's right to buy the ancient object.

I therefore maintain the opinion that the owner of the sherd should be warned that if he does not hand it over to the manager of the IDAM he will be prosecuted in court. If he does not hand over the sherd I will give all the necessary orders to start a civilian trial.

... The Government Attorney General   (GL44873/10 no. 1733, 21.5.51)

Figure 18. The permanent exhibition of the IDAM, Jerusalem 1951. Between 1948 and 1956 the museum had 36,000 visitors. (IAA 4502)

Staner stuck to her guns, maintaining that "every day that the sherd is not handed to us, a new offence is committed" (GL44873/10 no. 5632, 25.5.51). Yet, she realized that even if this opinion were accepted in court, the sentence might be light, so presenting it as a criminal offence would be a mistake. Therefore, Yeivin proceeded to reach a peaceful agreement with Hoff, who apparently did not suspect all this. He willingly signed the suggested commitment on 31 May 1951 and meanwhile kept the sherd. On 15 July 1951 Ben-Dor wrote to him to ask for the sherd for an IDAM exhibition (GL44873/10 no. 61921) (Fig. 18). The sides agreed on a final sum of 3,000 Lira, to be paid partly in antiquities. The IDAM did not have this full sum available in its regular budget, so arrangements were necessary with the Ministry of Finance. Eliyahu Katzenelbogen, Deputy Manager of the Ministry of Education and Culture, suggested to Kahane (then head of the IDAM Museum) that he should explain the situation to Hoff. If the Ministry of Finance refused to finance the acquisition, perhaps Hoff would agree to postpone the last payment of 500 Lira until April 1957. Katzenelbogen promised to pay 200 Lira (altered by hand to 2,000) immediately, followed by about 500 Lira in antiquities, and the remaining 500 Lira later (GL44873/10, 20.7.51).

And so it was. As part of the payment Hoff received a collection of prehistoric flint tools from Gesher Bnot Ya'acov, defined as duplicates (GL44873/10 no.

1843). Katzenelbogen summarized the deal in a letter of 18 September 1956 to Dr Bergman of the Ministry of Finance:

> The IDAM notifies us that in the course of acquiring ancient exhibits to enrich the museum we now have an outstanding opportunity to acquire an object of exceptional value: the famous ostracon from Qasile, from the period of the Kings, with a Hebrew inscription, "Gold of Ophir to Beth-Horon … 30 Shekels". The price of the object is 3,000 Lira, which is, in the opinion of the IDAM, not exaggerated at all. The owner of the object agrees that part of this sum up to 1,000 Lira can be paid with antique objects (prehistoric tools) from the museum, and we suppose that we could give him objects in the value of 500 Lira. (GL44873/10 no. 120–364)

There is a discrepancy in the amount to be paid in antiquities: 500 Lira or 1,000 Lira. Hoff probably agreed to accept antiquities to a value of 1,000 Lira, but the IDAM was reluctant to give antiquities valued at more than half that sum. Hoff and Kahane signed the final agreement on 24 September 1956 (GL44873/10), and the ostracon became the property of the state.

There was another Hebrew stamp found by Hoff at Tell Qasile before the start of the excavations (Mazar 1951: 8–69). Furthermore, another ostracon was found at Tell Qasile before the excavations by Dr Yaacov Kaplan, inscribed: "To the king, 1100 [units of] oil …" (Mazar 1951: no. 2). This ostracon was recently placed on the market by an antiquities dealer (Deutsch 2001: cat. no. 337), and its present whereabouts is unknown.

One wonders what would have happened if Staner's recommendations had been followed. Perhaps the authority of the IDAM could have been demonstrated; perhaps some of the later looting by "heroes" such as Dayan could have been avoided.

9   THE BUILDING BEYOND THE BORDER: THE PAM, 1948–67

Much has been written about the establishment of the Palestine Archaeological Museum (PAM), commonly called the Rockefeller Museum, during the British Mandatory period, but very little about its fate after 1948. In this chapter some parts of this unknown history are described. In some aspects they bring to mind V. S. Naipaul's marvellous tragi-comic story "A House for Mr Biswas" (Naipaul 1969: 7).

The establishment of the PAM was a landmark in the history of archaeology in Palestine. In 1917 the Ottoman authorities planned to transfer about 6,000 antiquities from Jerusalem to Istanbul. Failing at the last moment, they left them packed in Jerusalem. The British decided to exhibit them and this became the kernel of a museum for Palestine (Phytian-Adams 1924). In 1929 John D. Rockefeller Jr. donated 2 million dollars for the museum. He first offered his donation to Cairo, but the negotiations there did not succeed. The PAM was built in 1930–38 with Austen St Barbe Harrison as architect and with Eric Gill doing some of the interior design. Their genius is still evident today, after seventy years. The building was made of quality materials in a neo-Gothic style, mixing Eastern and Western features. The museum was supported by an annual endowment and served all ethnic groups in Palestine (Harrison 1935; Iliffe 1938, 1949; Reich 1987, 1992b, 2001; Sussman & Reich 1987; Reich & Sussman 1993). With the deterioration of relations between the factions in Palestine the joints were severed. The little-known fate of the museum after 1948 is the subject of these pages.

THE ROCKEFELLER MUSEUM, 1948–51

In late 1947, senior Hebrew archaeologists met for "unofficial consultations" about the PAM. They wanted to keep the museum unified, since it was "a unique centre of knowledge", which included nearly all significant finds from Palestine. Dividing it would disrupt the scientific completeness of the collection and compromise its cultural and public merit. The participants added:

> Whatever the future of the land of Israel, there is no doubt that its past is one and united, and must be learned as one unit. This is possible archaeologically only in a central museum of the entire land … Dividing the museum will be against Jewish interests, for the study of the past of the land is important in maintaining the living, organic relations between the people and its land. This connection is one of the sure means to induce Zionist conscience in the hearts of the people … We need to act in the best way possible to ease that study, and not to burden it. Furthermore, we must strive to maintain and develop our cultural positions in Jerusalem… Dozens of thousands of tourists and immigrants will visit Jerusalem in the future. By keeping our interest in the museum, which thousands of foreign people will visit, we maintain a valuable means of propaganda and influence.
>
> (GL44868/7, report by Mayer 8.1.48)

The participants suggested that the museum would form a separate legal body under a board of trustees, with representatives of the Arab and Hebrew states, UNESCO and Jerusalem (at the time there was a plan to make Jerusalem an international city under a UN regime based on UN Resolution 181 (Bialer 1985)). Holy sites would be governed by another body, thus Jewish officials, who formed the majority of PAM workers, could continue running the museum (GL44868/7, report 8.1.48). Yeivin later explained that in those days there were still talks about having some united services for the Hebrew and Arab states, such as a combined postal service or customs (GL44880/13 no. 4867, 18.2.51).

The Jewish workers left the PAM on 14 December 1947, when conditions had deteriorated. The museum was closed to the public on 1 April 1948, and shut down completely on 10 May 1948. On the brink of the termination of the British Mandate, on 20 April 1948, the Mandatory government published an ordinance (Palestine Official Gazette 1948; copy in GL44874/16) that assigned a committee of eleven representatives headed by Iliffe to take care of the PAM. From the Jewish side, only Sukenik was nominated. The IES complained to the High Commissioner on 10 May 1948 (GL44868/7, Zalman Lifshitz (later Lif), Chairman of the Executive Committee of the IES), to no avail, probably because Mandatory rule would terminate five days later. Iliffe wrote in English to Ben-Dor (Fig. 19):

IN REPLY PLEASE QUOTE

No. ....

XERXXXXXXXXXXXXXXXX
JERUSALEM

2nd September, 1948.

Dr. I. Ben-Dor,
  4 Rashba Street,
    Rehavia - Jerusalem.

Dear Ben Dor,

      I rang you up to-day but you were away
(according to your maid).

                       far
      The Museum is intact so^I am glad to say, and
in fair shape. I have been living here myself when in
Jerusalem, with Dimitri and Yousef Saad and about 15
attendants. I also established a 'pied à terre' with Harding
in Amman, for the sake of communications with the outside
world, etc.. I shall be leaving in about 10 days en route
to the United Kingdom, but shall probably retain my capacity
as de jure Curator until the period of my leave expires
(several months). During my absence I am hoping to arrange
that Harding shall be Acting Curator in my stead.

      I should be very grateful if you could get
Guy to let Harding have the last packing lists of
Trans-Jordan antiquities. I asked him on the telephone to
do this, but nothing has yet come through. They could be
handed to Sheringham on one of his periodic liaison visits,
or be transmitted via the British Legation. Harding is
wanting them urgently to avoid unpacking the whole lot.
Next, were the Catalogue Cards ever microfilmed and sent
to London ?

      I hope you are keeping well under the
inevitable stress and strain; also the Kahanes, Kallners,
Avi-Yonahs and all. I had an attack of 'sandfly fever'
followed by an outbreak of boils and had to spend a few days
in hospital, but am now recovered from these.

      Dr. Sellers, as you may know, is here as
Director of American School of Oriental Research. We are
all most interested in the find of Hebrew manuscripts in
Palestine. Had I not been so pre-occupied with merely
mechanical tasks last March and April, I should have no
doubt gone and followed up Trever's photographic activities
at St. Mark's Convent and elsewhere. As things stand,
however, I understand that various institutions are in the
market for the manuscripts. I have pointed out to the
Americans, and should be grateful if you could do so to
anyone interested whom you may know, that as this find was
made during the period of the Mandate, the Department of
Antiquities should have had the first opportunity to
acquire some of them. I am not sure what the legal view
will be when an administration for Jerusalem is again set up.
I am sorry that experience of the last fifteen or twenty
years of the Museum's policy in regard to excavators, casual
finds, and so on, does not seem to have produced that mutual
confidence which I have always aimed at. It is disappointing
(to say the least) to find Big Business taking advantage of
our difficulties and in the market for things which were
rightfully the Museum's.

- 2 -

PALESTINE ARCHAEOLOGICAL MUSEUM.
~~GOVERNMENT OF PALESTINE~~

IN REPLY PLEASE QUOTE

No. ....

~~DEPARTMENT OF ANTIQUITIES~~

JERUSALEM.

    I have kept in mind the question we discussed
with regard to the disposal of a portion of the
Endowment income for the current year, (£P.500 in six
months) and am prepared to act accordingly, subject to
the conditions we laid down.

    I expect to be in London early in October, where
an address that will always find me is :

        Royal Empire Society,
            Northumberland Avenue, London W.C.2.

    I will try and telephone you again when I have
another opportunity. Meanwhile, all best wishes to
Mrs. Ben-Dor and yourself, the Reifenbergs, and all
old friends, and hope we may meet again under happier
circumstances ere long.

                    Yours sincerely,
                      J. H. Iliffe.

                    J.H.ILIFFE.
            CURATOR, PALESTINE ARCHAEOLOGICAL
                        MUSEUM.

P.S. - Could you also please stimulate Stekelis
        to return to Dikaios in Cyprus the flints
        which were sent to him about last April,
        and his notes on them. Dikaios wants them
        urgently for publication.
        Could you also please return to us here
        either the original or copies (5 & 6) of
        the additional sections of Megaw's Report
        on the Dome of the Rock which were sent to
        you for typing on 12.4.48. They will then
        be sent on to him, as he needs them urgently.

Figure 19. Part of a letter about the PAM from Illife to
Ben-Dor, 2 September 1948, written on "Government of
Palestine, Department of Antiquities" stationery (heading
erased). (GL44874/16)

Dear Ben-Dor,

I rang you up to-day but you were away (according to your maid).

The Museum is intact so far I am glad to say, and in fair shape. I have been living here myself when in Jerusalem, with Dimitri [Baramki] and Yousef [Yusuf] Sa'ad and about 15 attendants. I also established a "pied à terre" with [Gerald Lancaster] Harding [archaeological advisor to the Jordanian government] in Amman, for the sake of communications with the outside world, etc. I shall be leaving in about 10 days en route to the United Kingdom, but shall probably retain my capacity as *de jure* Curator ... During my absence I am hoping to arrange that Harding shall be Acting Curator in my stead.

...

I hope you are keeping well under the inevitable stress and strain; also the Kahanes, Kallners [Amiran], Avi-Yonahs and all ... (GL44874/16, 2.9.48)

Iliffe mentioned the Dead Sea Scrolls and asked for copies of the card index [of finds] given to the Hebrew workers before they left. He also offered help of £500 from the Rockefeller endowment for the next half year. This was the result of a verbal agreement made in May 1948 that the Hebrew employees would go on with research and the museum would then deliver this sum as a kind of advance on salaries. Ben-Dor explained to the manager of the Department of Public Works that the PAM had lost all governmental support, and its income had decreased from 40,000 to 10,000 Palestine pounds per year. He asked for instructions:

> Now a new situation has formed. Since we are officials of the [Israeli] state, we cannot receive a salary from an outside institution. On the other hand, it is very important politically and nationally not to sever relations with the museum and give up our positions there, should normal conditions return or should Jerusalem become an international city. If we answer Iliffe negatively, we give up participation in the [museum's] work and the share of Jewish officials in it. Therefore I suggest writing to Iliffe that:
> A. we are officials of the IDAM;
> B. we do not give up our rights to work in the PAM in the future;
> C. our work in the country [Israel] can help the PAM in both archaeological exploration and keeping monuments, objects and excavations;
> D. we will gladly receive the 500 pounds for half a year and use it for travel expenses concerning preserving antiquities, restoring monuments and excavations. (GL44874/16; cf. GL44864/14 no. 4)

Iliffe wrote in the tone of one used to giving orders; Ben-Dor, on the other hand, appears uncertain. Iliffe is still an authority, although Ben-Dor is the new Deputy Director of the IDAM. Ben-Dor wrote to Iliffe again (GL44874/16 no. 3508, 23.11.48) and the IDAM even received boxes with books and commodities sent for the PAM. These were held by the Haifa port authorities, and in order to release them, the Department of Public Works told the Ministry of Finance that the PAM was an international body, and that: "The national bodies agreed to this. Also the Hebrew University agreed, in an official letter, to participate in the board of trustees. Hence the Rockefeller Museum is an international body and its property does not belong to the Mandatory Authorities" (GL44874/16 no. 3246, 11.11.48).

As a result of the 1948 War the PAM remained in the West Bank. On 16 November 1948, in the period when there were plans to make Jerusalem an international city, Yeivin wrote to Walter Eytan at the Ministry of Foreign Affairs. He had learned from the press that Israel demanded to include "New Jerusalem" within its borders. He wrote that he did not yet know what this term included, but guessed that it would not include areas occupied at the time by the Arab legion, including the PAM, which was:

> given from the first as gift to the general population of the entire land of Israel. This museum has a very dear collection of antiquities from the land of Israel; and a major part of them is the legacy of our past in this land. Moreover, the building holds a rich library in the professions of knowledge of the land and archaeology and history of the Middle East, and also Biblical studies. Some arrangement is needed to ensure our rights in the antiquities collection and library there.   (GL44874/16, 16.11.48)

The Ministry of Foreign Affairs was not keen to interfere. They informed the military governor of Jerusalem, Dov Joseph, and agreed that the problem was very simple:

> If all the new city will be in our hands (that is, outside the walls), then we will have the Rockefeller Museum anyway. If, on the other hand, the city is divided by the present lines of occupation, we will have to demand that the museum is included in the international area. Finally, if an international regime is forced upon us, we will surely claim access to this important cultural asset.   (GL44874/16 no. 3633, 8.12.48)

This letter arrived at the IDAM on 18 December 1948, and in the meantime Yeivin had arranged a meeting with Dr N. Rodi of the Ministry of Foreign Affairs. Yeivin explained the history of the PAM and noted that Iliffe had left the country, and there was as yet no board of trustees. Harding, the archaeological consultant of Transjordan, was probably supervising the museum. If Jerusalem was to be divided according to existing borders, the PAM would be left in Arab hands. If an international regime was enforced, the IDAM demanded to include the PAM within it, because:

> The Hebrew state has great interest in the museum itself, and also … most of the officials of the IDAM are, in fact, officials that used to work in the museum or in its library or in its nearby archive. In fact, these officials have been lent to the IDAM until they can return to their jobs in the PAM. By all means Israel should be interested to return them to their work in the said institution …   (GL44874/16, 16.12.48)

Yeivin mentioned rumours about exchanging Sheikh Jarakh, now in Arab hands, with areas in south Jerusalem, to enable Jews free access to Mount Scopus and Arabs free access south to Bethlehem. If this was to happen, he asked that the PAM be included in this plan. If these arrangements were to fail and the museum were to remain in the Arab area:

> The IDAM believes that serious thought must be given about the possibility to buy from the Arab authorities all the antiquities collections (at least until the Arab period) in the museum; the library and the archive and the collections of maps and glass photographic plates. For, in the end, it is not the building and furniture that are of the most interest to the state of Israel, but the cultural assets kept inside them; assets that cannot even be estimated in terms of monetary value. The collections of antiquities are unique; and a large part of the volumes in the library are out of print, and can under no price be acquired; and the same is true for the archives.
> (GL44874/16, 16.12.48)

Yeivin's scholarly priorities should be applauded. This cannot be said of all his ideas, but it was a very peculiar and hectic period (cf. Pilowsky 1988). Meanwhile Iliffe was forming the international board:

> I have been in the throes of moving around the country seeing all sorts of people both in connection with the Palestine affairs and my own personal ones … When I came to England I left Harding responsible for the museum, with Baramki and Sa'ad in residence there; I have made Sa'ad "Secretary of the Museum" and he is keeping all the financial matters, as well as controlling the dozen or so attendants, who are being kept on to keep the building as clean and in good condition as possible. All are being paid out of the income of the Endowment Fund. The museum is safe, and its content, except that most of the windows on the south side were broken by the blast

of mortars or machine-gun fire. These have been repaired temporarily with
oiled beaver boarding against the rains …

(GL44874/16, letter to Ben-Dor 19.12.48)

Iliffe managed to secure £500 from the Colonial Office in London and sent
the money to Harding, who was to deliver it to Ben-Dor, perhaps through the
British consulate. Iliffe dryly noted: "you will appreciate that it takes much time
to get things done in a three-cornered show like this!", then added:

> I still approve of the original plan of an international board of trustees, and
> have taken steps to bring this about as soon as possible. When in Paris in
> October I saw Prof. Huxley, Director-General of UNESCO, and outlined my
> ideas to him. He agreed and said UNESCO would do its best … At the same
> time I attended … the inaugural lunch of ICOM [the International Council
> of Museums] NEES (i.e. the first issue of a periodical by the International
> Council of Museums). I was invited to the lunch, and gave them a brief
> outline of the situation and our plans. The Chairman (Prof. Huxley) said:
> "Here is your first task, Gentlemen"!…
>
> In brief, I proposed that UNESCO, through its Museum Section, should
> assume the task of setting up our board of trustees. Until it is done, I retain
> the responsibility for the museum … I shall [then] enter into discussion
> with the board re plans, staff, finance, etc. and as to whether I remain a
> keeper or not. In any case I should like to retain my connection with the
> museum, either as one of the trustees or curator emeritus! I certainly look
> forward to getting back to Jerusalem at no very distant future: there are
> many loose ends, which I left, needing to be tied up …
>
> Yours ever, J. H. Iliffe.
>
> PS. I told Sa'ad that I expected to make him the permanent "Secretary" of
> the museum. His knowledge of the finance will be invaluable … Baramki
> will not be a permanent member of the museum.   (GL44874/16)

The Jordanians had other plans. The *Jerusalem Post* of 12 May 1949 reported
the lack of agreement about the PAM between Sir Alec Kirkbride, the British
representative in Amman, and Abdallah Bey El-Tell, governor of the old city of
Jerusalem. Kirkbride held the opinion that both sides should share the museum,
but the Arab Jerusalem Congress demanded all Jerusalem for the Arabs. El-Tell
reputedly said that the British gave Israel all the places such as Ramla, Lod, Haifa,
Tiberias and Jaffa; if they returned them the Arabs would share the PAM with the
Jews. Yeivin heard from Sukenik that the international board of trustees, which
had ten members (Kelso 1950: 66), gathered to meet in Amman in December
1949. Sukenik tried through the British consulate to arrange for the meeting to
be held at the Mandelbaum Gate on the border, or to be given a travel permit,

writing to Harding but receiving no reply (GL44874/16). A state of war remained between Jordan and Israel but the board refused to meet on neutral ground, so Israeli scholars could not reach the "international" PAM. *Ma'ariv* newspaper reported on 26 December 1949 that Jordan had moved important antiquities from the PAM to Amman, but they claimed that it was only antiquities from Transjordan on loan. Professor James Leon Kelso of the Pittsburgh Theological Seminary, who was then chair of the board of trustees, agreed to the antiquities being moved.

Jordan actually annexed the West Bank early in 1950 (cf. Pappe 1988: 76, 110–14), yet the international board of trustees was retained. Israel accepted the new situation in silence. In 15 February 1950 the museum was reopened to the public (Kelso 1950). Carl Umhau Wolf of the American School of Oriental Research (ASOR) visited it and told Kahane (report dated 8.8.50) that only Sa'ad and a dozen assistants remained. There were few visitors and almost no readers in the library. According to Wolf, Kelso tried to prevent the taking of antiquities, but lacked the power; the Jordanian government wanted the antiquities for the then new Museum of Amman.

Yeivin refused to accept this situation. In March–April 1950 Israel and Britain held financial talks and the Rockefeller fund was mentioned (*Ma'ariv* and *Haboker*, 14.4.1950). On 5 May 1950 Yeivin was informed by the Ministry of Finance that the Israeli delegation demanded a share in the Rockefeller fund, which amounted to 289,955 Palestine pounds on 15 May 1948, as part of a financial commitment made by the Mandatory government, which was now the responsibility of the British government. The British government did not admit Israel's claim; but decided that it needed to be studied. In a letter signed by J. I. C. Crombie of 30 April 1950 it asked Israel to suggest new aims for the fund. Yeivin was asked to prepare, in cooperation with the Hebrew University, a concrete proposal for using the Rockefeller fund that still fit its original aims (GL44874/16 no. 10/35/0-32, by A. Bavli of the Ministry of Finance).

Yeivin searched for the original documents in London, finally finding copies in Israel's National Archive headed by Mrs Sophi Yudin (GL44874/16, 26.5.50 and nos. 2652, 3223a). However, the British government received the opinion of the PAM's board of trustees, backed up by a letter from Hamilton of 2 August 1950:

> The British Legation presents their compliments to the Israel Ministry for Foreign Affairs, and, on instructions of His Majesty's Principal Secretary of State for Foreign Affairs, have the honour to inform the Ministry of the following.
> *Rockefeller Fund*
> … The Israeli proposal has now been given careful consideration in the light of both the correspondence between the Palestine Government and

Mr J. D. Rockefeller at the time of the constructions of the Archaeological
Museum … and of the relevant Palestine Order in Council, 1948 …

His Majesty's Government are advised that, by the terms of John D.
Rockefeller's letter to Lord Plummer of 13 October, 1927, the Endowment
Fund is inseparable from the Museum itself and can only be used for the
maintenance of the existing Museum at Jerusalem. Moreover, the Endowment Fund having been vested by the 1948 Order in the Board set up under
that order, its disposal is now beyond the jurisdiction of His Majesty's
Government.

His Majesty's Government are also advised that, since the Museum is
situated in Jordan territory, only the Jordan Government is legally in a
position to pass legislation abrogating or amending the 1948 order. On
the other hand, it seems that, save in very exceptional circumstances, e.g.,
if the Museum and Board were quite unable to carry on under the present
order, it would be quite improper for the Jordan Government to interfere
at the present time...

The views of the Board itself are set in a letter dated 16 October, 1950,
from the curator to Mr J. H. H. Pollock of the Colonial Office … In the
circumstances, His Majesty's Government have decided with regret that it
will be impossible to comply with the proposal of the Israel Government.

(resolution 165, copy in GL44874/16)

Yeivin refused to leave the matter alone. In January 1951 he met Sukenik,
Eytan and Reuben Nal (deputy legal advisor to the Ministry of Foreign Affairs).
According to Yeivin, the purpose was to issue guidelines about Israel's position
on the PAM. Did Israel accept its international status, or did it have demands,
such as adding Israeli representatives to the board of trustees (GL44880/13, confidential)? When Ben-Gurion attended the IES annual conference in 1950, the
President of the IES, Professor Mayer, asked him to solve the problem of access
to the PAM (*BIES* **15** (1949/50): 119).

In the January 1951 meeting Nal explained that there were different legal opinions about the validity of the Palestine Order-in-Council ordinance (Palestine
Official Gazette 1948), and that the government's legal advisor would have to give
a binding opinion. Eytan suggested that this should be done before any political
action was taken. So Yeivin arranged a larger meeting, inviting also Schwabe
and Mayer of the Hebrew University (GL44880/13 no. 4781, 12.2.51). In a letter
of 18 February 1951 Yeivin noted that the situation had changed. There were
no more talks about an international Jerusalem, or collaboration with Jordan.
The PAM should not belong to one side only:

An institution like this has the right to exist only if it can grow and develop.
According to (albeit unofficial) information that has reached the IDAM, the

Jordanian government has ceased to send antiquities found in its jurisdiction, and even in Cisjordan, to this museum, but transfers them to its central museum at Rabat-Ammon [Amman]. Under these conditions, the former PAM will not be able to survive and develop. It has become a dead and mummified place. The relatively small sum that is received from the Rockefeller fund (10,000 Lira annually), cannot even support this mummified institution with honour and allow it to maintain the necessary body of workers, not to mention allowing the continuation of research and publication … I believe that there is justification, I do not know whether legal, but in any case moral and practical, to demand the division of the PAM and the fund between the two governments (Israel and Jordan). [Thus] both will give a continuation and future life to their parts of this property, as addition of cultural assets to their Departments of Antiquities.

(GL44880/13 no. 4867)

On 28 January 1951, in consultation with Schwabe, Sukenik and Mayer, Yeivin prepared "Guidelines for Discussion of the Formerly Governmental Museum (Rockefeller)":

A. Two possibilities: (1) Acknowledge the legality of the order [of 1948]. (2) Dispute its legality.
B. From A(1) it follows that the international board of trustees exists and the institution stays in its [present] condition. Our requests can be: (1) Give representation to the Israel (the IDAM) and to Israeli institutions (IES, Israeli Numismatic Society?) … ; (2) Site the meetings of the board where Jewish delegates can also participate; (3) Move the museum to a border location accessible to both sides.

From A(2) follow the inadmission of the legality of the board and a demand to divide the collection and the properties. This demand could also come according to A(1) (see the order [of 1948] section 4h), since the museum has no future, because the government of Jordan does not want to continue to give it antiquities. The revenue of the fund is not enough to sustain it in honour and develop it. There is also no hope for the growth of the library and the continuation of the journal [*Quarterly of the Department of Antiquites of Palestine*, or QDAP]. In such case our demands should be:

1. Division of the antiquities according to territorial basis; anything found in places now in Israel will be given to Israel; what was found in places within Jordan will be given to the kingdom of Jordan. Objects whose origins are unknown will be divided according to the extent of areas, approximately ⅓ to the Kingdom of Jordan and ⅔ to Israel …

(GL44874/16)

Yeivin further suggested dividing, similarly, the archive, the removable property and the immovable property. Movable property (antiquities and equipment) would be registered on Israel's side, which would be ready to pay the Jordanians for their part. Immovable property (the building) would be registered on the Jordanian side. Everything would be divided according to the territorial ratio: approximately two-thirds for Israel and one-third for Jordan (GL44874/16).

What a cumbersome, Talmudic document! The logic was clear. It would give Israel a general advantage (two-thirds to one-third) and force Jordan to pay for two-thirds of the building in order to keep it. Yeivin surely hoped that Jordan would prefer, or be forced, to give up the antiquities instead, since it could not give up a building located in its area. He also contacted Staner about it and tried to yoke the professors of the Hebrew University to this cart. However, the government's attorney general reached a final decision in March 1951: Israel could not dispute the 1948 ordinance. Despite Yeivin's continued efforts (GL44880/13 nos. 5126, 5127), the issue died out.

THE PAM, 1952–54

The grand idea of division had gone, but ideas of exchange appeared in its place. In the middle of 1952 Dr Itzhak Nebenzahl, who Yeivin described as Consul of Sweden in Jerusalem (although the Swedish consulate was in Tel Aviv, so Yeivin probably meant that Nebenzahl was an honorary consul in Jerusalem) passed on a letter from Gösta Hedengren, the Swedish consul, to Ben-Dor, asking about the materials of the PAM in Israel. Hedengren was the representative of the Swedish Royal Academy on the board of the PAM. Yeivin consulted Biran, and ordered Ben-Dor to reply that the matter had been passed on to Sukenik and himself. In June 1952 Hedengren visited Jerusalem, and Nebenzahl held a dinner in his honour. Not surprisingly, he invited Yeivin and Sukenik (who was ill and could not attend). After dinner Hedengren talked with Yeivin. He explained that the secretary of the PAM had shown him gaps in the archives and library; the missing files and books were now in Israel. He asked for their return to be arranged. Yeivin answered sharply: if the museum board thought that it answered to the Jordanian government, negotiations were out of Yeivin's field of authority and he could not even express his opinion. If the board was a purely international body, Israel also had certain demands of it:

> For example, the Israeli representative on the committee was never given a chance to participate in its meetings. The committee not only refused our suggestions to meet in a neutral place, but did not even find it necessary

to answer our letters. Moreover, we were not given access to this international institute ... I also hinted that especially because of the international status of the managing board, it was an unacceptable arrangement that the manager of the museum is a man who is, in fact, an official of the Jordanian government (Mr Harding). (GL44880/13 no. 8880, 9.6.52)

Yeivin explained that the files in Israel related mostly to sites in Israel. Israel needed information from the PAM too. Hedengren suggested exchanging materials or, better, copies of them. Yeivin viewed this idea favourably. Hedengren also explained that Harding was employed only because the board did not have sufficient funds to pay a prominent scholar just to manage the PAM. The two agreed to try to arrange the exchange. Still, Yeivin concluded from the talk that the PAM had financial difficulties and in his report to the Ministry of Foreign Affairs suggested that it might be an opportunity to raise the issue of dividing the museum between Israel and Jordan in "an international UN institution" (GL44880/13 no. 8880, 9.6.52).

In December 1953 a meeting took place at the offices of the IDAM with Yeivin, Arieh Aroch of the Ministry of Foreign Affairs (later Israeli ambassador to Sweden and Brazil, and today much more famous for his paintings) and representatives of the board Father Dr Roland de Vaux, then president of the board, and Dr Jens Malling (Swedish representative at Tel Aviv). The meeting was also connected to the Israeli Committee of UNESCO under the Ministry of Education, whose secretary edited its minutes. On 24 December 1953, Yeivin asked for several major amendments to be made to the minutes (GL44880/13 no. 2778a):

1. Mr Malling opened the proceedings by explaining that Father de Vaux and he had come on behalf of the board of trustees of the Rockefeller Museum to discuss the matter of certain files, card-index and catalogue of the museum and some other objects belonging to the PAM; but at present in Israeli hands. Father de Vaux would give details concerning the objects ... Mr Malling would like to know what Mr Yeivin's reaction would be to the request for returning these objects to their owners.

2. Mr Yeivin replied that [section added by Yeivin: this matter was already taken up with him by Mr Malling's predecessor on the above-mentioned board, Mr Hedengren, at a meeting arranged by Dr Nebenzahl. At that time he told Mr Hedengren that] as a government employee he could not give him a definite and final answer, before consulting the Minister of Foreign Affairs. This was also ... the reason why he asked Dr Aroch to be present today. He told Mr Hedengren that he could give only his private reaction, which could be summarized under two headings:

(a) He was sorry that the board of trustees did not seem ... to have taken any steps to enable the single Israeli representative on it to attend the meetings …

(b) Personally, he would be very glad to have the question of the return of files, etc, settled on a give and take basis, with a view to receiving back some Israeli material now in the hands of the PAM and information on sites at present within the territory of Israel …

3. Father de Vaux replied that as far as participation in the meetings of the board of trustees was concerned, neither he nor the board could do anything as long as the Jordan government was opposed to the crossing of the lines by any Israeli citizen. The matter of holding meetings at a place accessible to all parties was brought before the board, which unanimously resolved that the only place suitable for the meetings … was the premises of the PAM.

4. Mr Malling added that Father de Vaux and himself were only empowered to conduct these negotiations on a non-governmental basis, strictly as between two scientific bodies, the PAM, an international body on the one hand, and the IDAM as a scientific institution on the other.

5. Mr Yeivin replied that though [originally: even if] the PAM was an international institution, it was still a foreign body in Israel since it did not operate within Israeli territory [Yeivin added: and consequently within the purview of matters dealt with by the Ministry of Foreign Affairs; as on the other hand, though the IDAM was a scientific body, it was still part and parcel of government machinery, and he as the Director … could only function under the rules and procedure laid down for all governmental offices].

6. Father de Vaux thereupon suggested that the negotiations should be held between Mr Malling and himself as representing the board of trustees of the PAM and those former employees of the PAM who held the material under discussion.

7. Mr Yeivin answered this by saying that the material was no longer held by private people, but by the IDAM. He further added that he failed to understand the attitude of the board of trustees. They were an appointed body composed of representatives of various scientific and cultural institutions. One of these institutions which had the right to nominate its representative on the board was the Hebrew University. As an international body they were bound to see to it that all members are enabled to attend the meetings …

8. Father de Vaux regretted that owing to the present situation, as it is, nothing more could be done in the matter.

9. Mr Malling intimated that the board of trustees had no idea that objects belonging to Israeli citizens were in their hands, and he asked for more details …

10. Mr Yeivin gave the following enumeration:

(a) Some objects from the private collection of Professor L.A. Mayer, which they later loaned to the PAM for exhibition purposes. (b) Several objects belonging to Dr Stekelis, which he brought to the museum to facilitate his researches … (c) [Added by Yeivin later] Finds from some excavations undertaken by Israeli bodies, which had not yet been divided between the authorities of the museum and the Israeli excavators. (d) A very large number of potsherds brought by Dr Maisler [Mazar] and himself in the early forties from Sha'ar Hagolan to the PAM … (e) The files of the museum contained a mass of relevant material, concerning sites now in Israeli territory. Copy of such information was required. [Yeivin added a lengthy section here] The lack of this information hampered the proper functioning of the IDAM in connection with such sites. Mr Yeivin further mentioned that during Professor Mayer's stay in England last summer, he was approached by Mr Hamilton, the former Director of the Department of Antiquities of Palestine, with the same request for the return of the objects … Professor Mayer promised to take up the matter with the IDAM upon his return to Israel; he also used that opportunity to mention to Mr Hamilton the matter of the participation of the Israeli representative … and the presence in the hands of the board of certain objects belonging to Israeli citizens. [Mayer met Yeivin and wrote to Hamilton about the objects; Yeivin read extracts from his letter].

11. Father de Vaux said that both Mr Malling and he had thought on the same lines. They had not known of the objects owned privately, but assured Mr Yeivin that the museum had no intention of holding them … They, too, had thought of the files holding information on historical sites in Israel and would recommend to the board that copies of such files be submitted to the IDAM.

12. Mr Aroch was sure that though the board did not comply with the request of Israel's representative … to enable him to attend the meeting … The government of Israel would still show its goodwill by furthering such agreement on exchange of objects … but stipulated that this should not form in any way a precedent for any future dealings or prejudice any further steps of the government of Israel concerning the PAM.
This was agreed by all present.

13. Father de Vaux gave the following enumeration of the material requested by the PAM: (a) The card index of the PAM; (b) Files relating to certain sites within the former territory of the government of Palestine; (c) Some books belonging to the library of the PAM; (d) Certain exhibits belonging to the PAM …   (GL44874/16)

The sides agreed to the exchanges; also including copies of negatives. The amended minutes were sent to the participants. Yeivin wrote to Malling, reminding him of the 1,000 pounds promised by Iliffe in 1948, and approved by the board in 1950 (GL44874/16 no. 2833a, 29.12.53). But no further letters were exchanged according to the IDAM files. The atmosphere became less friendly: the *Jerusalem Post* of 16 June 1954 claimed that the Jordanian government recommended the removal of the Israeli representative from the board in favour of a Palestinian. The reporter suggested that Jordan was not able to look after the PAM, since the President of ASOR had to appeal to J. D. Rockefeller for help. Rockefeller renewed his support for the museum for three years. *Haboker* newspaper reviewed Israeli claims after more scrolls were found and taken to the PAM. The reporter insisted:

> It is impossible to revoke our rights to this institution just because it happens to be situated a few metres across the border ... Nobody knows when there will be peace between our neighbours and us; but even then the question of division of antiquities kept in the PAM will remain between them and us. It was a mistake not to raise this question during the ceasefire negotiation at Rhodes. Now, after five years, we have to fix the mistake. We are already permitting reunion of Arab families in Israel. Let the Jordanian Kingdom permit reunion of cultural assets in Israel!
>
> (*Haboker*, 19.5.1954, copy kept in GL44874/16)

Yeivin now tried to act through the Israeli Committee to UNESCO (GL44874/16 no. 1169a, 21.6.54; GL44874/16 no. 4713a, 19.9.54). He met J. K. van den Haagen of the UN in Paris on 19 August 1954 and raised Israel's claims about the PAM. He also wrote a memorandum together with the Hebrew University and the IES in preparation for a visit to Israel by Luther Evanns (Director-General of UNESCO, 1953–58). He expressed the view that the PAM did not operate in a vacuum. Iliffe had assembled the board with the help of UNESCO, so UNESCO shared some of the responsibility of the PAM, and Israel could demand its intervention to remedy the situation. Israeli representative/s should be added and allowed to attend the board's meetings. If these claims were not fulfilled, all the PAM's property, including the fund and the buildings, should be divided (he had not specified this in his Paris talks). However, the Ministry of Foreign Affairs in Israel answered on 10 November 1954 that they had already given their opinion, namely, that the Israeli Committee to UNESCO should not do anything for the time being, until the position of Evanns was clarified (GL44874/16 no. 14673).

THE PAM, 1966-67

The board of trustees remained until 1966, when Jordan took over the museum. This was the report given by Patrick Seale (reporter and acclaimed expert on the Middle East) in the London *Observer*:

JORDAN TAKES OVER FAMOUS MUSEUM

The Palestine Archaeological Museum, situated outside Herod's Gate in Jerusalem, last Thursday (December 1 [1966]) passed into the hands of the Jordan government from a board of international trustees which had run the museum for the last 18 years. The PAM is one of the finest museums in the world. Sober archaeologists say it is second only to the Metropolitan in New York and the British Museum [an exaggeration] ... They speak with delight of its laboratories, darkrooms and workspace. The handsome sandstone building, set in a four acre olive grove, houses a unique collection ... The atmosphere is of peace and scholarship.

Last August the Jordan government suddenly declared that it was taking over the museum from the board of trustees. The moving spirit behind the nationalization was Anwar Al-Khatib, the powerful governor of Jerusalem, who claimed it a triumph for Arab nationalism. The Jordanian charge was that the trustees ... had done little more than "keep the place clean". Funds were lacking to expand the library. New archaeological finds went instead to the Government Museum in Amman or to the museums on the sites at Jerash and Petra ... For all its beauties, the PAM had become a fossil. For 18 years it had stood still, faithfully preserved, as in aspic, since the day the British left Palestine. It had become a tourist attraction rather than a centre for live research.

None of the distinguished scholars on the board of trustees contested the right of the Jordan government to nationalize the museum. But some of them – taken aback by the sudden decision – expressed concern. Would the Jordanians be able to run this treasure house? Was there not a danger that the endowment fund ... might be milked for other purposes? Would the splendid olive grove be sold off?

There was particular indignation at suggestions in the Jordan press – believed to have been inspired by the Director of Antiquities, Dr Awni Dajani – that the trustees had not done their job properly and that some museum treasures had been "lost". Stung by these allegations, Miss Kathlin Kenyon, principal of St Hugh's and the British School of Archaeology in Jerusalem, exploded with wrath against her former pupil Dr Dajani, accusing him of incompetence, or worse. But these passions have now been stilled. The Governor [of Jerusalem] told me that the King had approved the granting of medals to the trustees ...

The trustees had prepared a document releasing them from all further responsibility, which they wanted the government to sign. But Aref Al-Aref, the new government appointed Director-General of the museum – a delightful septuagenarian, thrice Mayor in Jerusalem – was reluctant to sign without a detailed inventory being presented.

This is where the scrolls reared their head once more … In the museum vaults lie boxes of tens of thousands of scroll fragments, many smaller than a sixpence … It took a long day's discussion … – and a very good lunch – to convince the Jordanians to concede that scroll fragments, like sherds, cannot easily be inventoried. A compromise was reached in that Mr Yusuf Sa'ad – perhaps the most devoted servant of the museum over the past 18 years, who is reported to sleep with the key to the Scrollery under his pillow – is to stay at his post for a further month to finish with the catalogue
…   (reprinted in *Jerusalem Post*, Seale 1966)

Ironically, the Jordanians did not have much time to enjoy the museum. Barely half a year later Israel conquered the West Bank during the 1967 (Six Days) War. The dissolution of the international board of trustees served Israel's interests; Israel now took over the management of the PAM. The olive grove is still with us, but the atmosphere of peace and scholarship was replaced by the industrious activity of the Israel Antiquities Authority Management, which now occupies most of the building.

Figure 20. PAM, inner court with damage from the 1967 War. (Photograph by Burger, IAA 49239)

For those Israeli scholars who worked in the PAM before 1948, seeing it again in 1967 was an exciting moment (Fig. 20). Milka Cassuto-Saltzman, the librarian of the IDAM, started to work in the PAM in 1941 and became a permanent worker in 1942. She described her feelings in a memorandum of 5 May 1968:

> Since I knew the Rockefeller Library well after working there from 1942 until the end of the Mandate [period], I did not need a long time to assess its current state: the library and its arrangement have not changed since then. I have the feeling that for 19 years it has almost not been used. Very few books were bought – I estimate their number as 1,500 volumes approximately – and the buying was random and unplanned. The books and the catalogues were not damaged during the battle [in 1967].   (GL44875/8)

She wrote another report on 28 May 1968, after returning to work in the PAM's library:

> The arrangements have not changed, the collections are in place, almost without exception, and so are the catalogues, all meticulously clean and in order. Few acquisitions were made (I estimate not more than 1,500 volumes; possibly the management did not have sufficient budget) ... The library holds nearly 30,000 volumes. The main subject is antiquities of Israel, but there are also rich collections about neighbouring and classical countries ... All this treasure is up-to-date up to 1947. For example, "Rockefeller" library has all the volumes of the famous English journal *Archaeology* from the first in 1770 to the last volume before 1948 ...
> (GL44875/8; cf. GL44889/15, 9.73)

After 1967 the IDAM tried to establish some contact with Harding, the "erstwhile Director of the PAM", who apparently was in Beirut, through the courier services of the UN. J. P. B. Ross of the UN wrote to Hannah Katzenstein at the IDAM on 17 March 1968 (GL44888/6 no. 2-3-03/407). Ross explained politely that the UN delivered only official correspondence between Jerusalem and Beirut. Apparently the letter was not "official", and we can only guess about its content.

In the future, the PAM may again become a source of dispute between Israelis and Palestinians, and the documents and the questions discussed here will acquire a new significance. Hopefully, the view expressed so persistently by Yeivin, that the PAM was established for all the people of the region, will prevail.

10 A BUILDING OF DREAMS: A HOME FOR THE IDAM AND THE ORIGINS OF THE ISRAEL MUSEUM, JERUSALEM

There is nothing more deceptive than an obvious fact.
Sir Arthur Conan-Doyle, *The Boscombe Valley Mystery* (1891: 161)

A HOME FOR THE IDAM: THE REALITY

The IDAM's first premises for the week of 23–27 August 1948 was one room in the Public Works building, Hanevi'im Street, Jerusalem (GL44869/1). On 27 August 1948 the police left the building and the IDAM occupied the upper floor, which measured about 81 m²; the annual rent was 160 Lira (GL44869/1 no. 25). The office acquired the Post Office box number 586 (GL44864/14, report 14.10.48: 3). According to legend, Yeivin chose this number because it was the year of the conquest of Jerusalem by the Babylonians. I found no written evidence for this, but although the choice of the date of Jerusalem's surrender is awkward, the story rings true. In April 1949 government units were supposed to move to Jerusalem (to counteract the "international Jerusalem" plan), and they were allocated flats in abandoned property; but the IDAM was already in Jerusalem (GL44869/1 no. 29, 4.4.49).

A second office for the IDAM was found in the "Measuring House" in Tel Aviv. The government decided to settle officials in abandoned houses in Jaffa. In the summer of 1948 Ben-Dor applied for such accommodation, and the supervisor of the urban area of Tel Aviv, Yehoshua Guvernic, notified him that: "Before I issue a confiscation warrant I must be certain that it is needed and effective to the benefit of the public, or to the defence of the state, or to maintain public order or vital services and supplies for the public" (GL44869/1 no. 8, 10.10.48). Yeivin approved the application and the temporary government issued a warrant of confiscation for one of three rooms in flat no. 5, 33 Hanevi'im Street, Tel Aviv (GL44869/1, 11.10.48). It sounds dramatic, but in fact Ben-Dor already rented that room, and simply carried on paying the rent of 10 Lira per month: half to the lady who hired the flat from the owners of the building; half to the owners themselves (the said lady gave him access to the kitchen, water, electricity, etc.) (GL44889/1, 28.12.48).

In July 1949 the IDAM was transferred to the Ministry of Education and Culture (*Alon* **2** (1950): 7). Even before that, the IDAM had moved to its second home: the "Palace Hotel" in Mamila (now Agron) Street, Jerusalem. It had the central pavilion in the building, formerly the home of the Mandatory royal committee (GL44869/1, 7.4.49). The space was divided into nine working rooms and two stores, and the annual rent was about 300 Lira (GL44869/1, 11.7.49, 13.7.49). When the IDAM moved in, the state symbol had not yet been decided, so the IDAM was ordered to erect a sign saying "government office" near the entrance (GL44869/1 no. 75/5-5-0).

Shortly thereafter, the Ministry of Supplies and Rationing had increased in size and needed all the space available in the Palace Hotel, so the IDAM moved again to Olivet House on Shlomoh Hamelekh Street (formerly St Louise Street), remaining there until 1965 (Fig. 21). Later it served as stores for the Education Department of the Mandatory Government. Then it became Store "A" of the Custodian for Abandoned Property. At some point in between, the building became the property of Reuben and Albina Zilberstein, and was also called by this name (GL44869/1 no. 1164, 17.10.49; no. 1169, 17.10.49). When the IDAM learned that the Custodian was ready to evacuate this building, it applied to the regional housing committee. Reuben Zilberstein agreed to rent it to the IDAM (GL44869/1 no. 1039, 26.10.49). Before moving, Yeivin discovered that it was not exactly an improvement and wrote the first of many letters of complaints about this building:

> To my amazement, only this morning I was notified by officials from the Ministry of Supplies and Rationing that your committee [for moving government offices to Jerusalem] intends to place at the disposal of the IDAM only the second floor of the building known formerly as "Olivet House" on St Louise Street, and not the whole of it as I was promised earlier …
>
> 2. The second floor of the said building includes five rooms and a hall, which can be divided into three more rooms. As well as a corridor, which cannot be used at all because of this, and because of its darkness; so, all in all, eight rooms.
>
> 3. The number of officials that work in the offices of the IDAM today in Jerusalem is 16. In 1950–51 nine more officials were demanded, all in Jerusalem, so the IDAM needs a workplace for 25 people. The Director and Deputy Director at least need a room each … obviously one cannot find room for 23 officials in six quite small rooms.
>
> (GL44869/1 no. 2125, 17.1.50)

Yeivin continued: what about the library? Storage? Laboratories? Garages for the (still missing) two cars? His protests helped and in addition the IDAM was

21.The Olivet–Zilberstein
house, home of the IDAM
1949–65. (IAA 1264a)

given the basement, ground floor and one room on the first floor (GL44869/1
no. 5073). The IDAM shared the building with the "Institute for Dietary Education" (Machon le-Hadrakha Tzunatit) of the Ministry of Supplies and Rationing,
headed by Dr Sarah Bavli, so perhaps the IDAM officials could learn to diet to
take up less office space!

Yeivin constantly complained about working conditions in this building. He
wrote that he had five or six employees in each room; he did not know where to
put new staff. Instead of moving the IDAM with all its heavy antiquities, he wrote,
the Institute for Dietary Education should be moved, and their rooms given to
the IDAM (GL44869/1 no. 4095). On 10 February 1950 he wrote an urgent letter
to the Minister of Education:

> I am stressing the cramping and crowdedness in the present accommo-
> dation of the IDAM. There are rooms sized 4.5 × 4.5 metres where six or
> seven workers sit and work ... In addition the stores are nearly full, and
> finds keep flowing in from the various excavations; in no time we will not
> be able to accept them ...   (GL44869/1 no. 7873)

Yeivin asked permission to purchase wooden huts and use them as stores
in the courtyard (plans in GL44869/1), but this was difficult and did not suit
the building. And to make things worse the building was in a poor shape. The
official engineer's survey read as follows:

> Basement. Room No. 1. Stone tile floor – bad. Plaster mostly ruined by
> humidity. Whitewash – bad. Wooden door ... with external lock, two

handles and key and double window. The wood – bad, the rest – good. Double window to the street: the wood is rotten, two broken panes ...

(GL44869/1, 12.3.51)

Salvation came from elsewhere: the Ministry of Commerce and Industry, which took over from the Ministry of Supply and Rationing, was going to sack a considerable number of officials to "become efficient" (*hitya'alut*, euphemism for cuts). Hence many rooms would be freed in the ministry's main office. Yeivin "took the necessary actions with the greatest speed" to move the Institute for Dietary Education (GL44869/2 no. 59a, 7.1.53). But it took time and he complained to the general secretary of the Ministry of Education:

> With the start of the new budget year I see myself obliged to return and stress the worsening problem of accommodation. This question has been discussed now for nearly three years. The situation today is catastrophic by all accounts. Today Mrs. Pommerantz came to work for us as a scientific secretary instead of Mr Avi-Yonah, who resigned a while ago. I did not have anywhere for her to sit. Fortunately, or sadly, I. Dr Ben-Dor is not in Jerusalem today, so for now she sits at his desk. Tomorrow I will not be here, and she can sit in my room. But what about Sunday, when both Mr Ben-Dor and I will be in Jerusalem? Indeed, next week Mrs Amiran goes abroad, and then Mr Aharoni can move to the desk of Mrs Amiran, and Mrs Pommerantz be sited in the place of Mr Aharoni. But you will understand that such enforced "wanderings" from place to place are no solution to the problem. It must also be remembered that two of the employees are currently abroad (Dr P. Kahane and Mr Prausnitz). Eventually they and Mrs Amiran will return to work ...
>
> The stores have been full for months. Many objects are dispersed in temporary storage places across the country ... This is a serious danger to the safety of the finds, and also a psychological danger, for people in these places might get used to seeing the finds as their own property, and will be angry when these are taken away in the future ... I have not yet spoken about the exhibition, library and archive ... The area of the exhibition is both painful and funny in its tiny size ...   (GL44869/2 no. 3668a, 1.4.54)

In August 1955 the IDAM was officially named a Department (a larger unit, *agaf* instead of *mahlaka*) of the Ministry of Education (to which it had been affiliated since 1949), and it received more space: the upper floor (*Alon* **5–6** (1957): 3; GL44869/2 no. 7336a). This did not solve the problem of maintenance. The oil-heated hearths were smoking to the extent that the municipality issued a warning letter. The chimneys became blocked every fortnight. The municipality advised that the old heaters should be replaced with new "Oilomatic" ones, but this was expensive. The district engineer advised the IDAM to dismantle the oil burners and return to using coal for heating (GL44869/2, 3.56). In 1957 (for the second time) a piece of plaster fell from the roof of one room, and "by a miracle no one was injured"; the IDAM was forced to make repairs (GL44869/2 no. 3830, 1.3.57).

In 1965 a new home was prepared for the IDAM in the brand new complex of the Israel Museum. Shortly after 1967, the management and most other units returned to the PAM. Some units remained in the Israel Museum and others were located elsewhere.

HOME FOR THE IDAM: DREAMS 1948–53

Few people even within the IAA realize how old the dreams are about a permanent building for the IDAM. In 1948, after Israel barely managed to hold on to Jerusalem, the development and strengthening of the capital city were considered a top priority. The government was determined to move its premises from Tel Aviv to Jerusalem and with that aim was planning to build a governmental quarter (*Qiryah*) between Ein-Karem and Rehavya (Kroyanker 1991: 94–103). Plans for a building for the IDAM and a central museum began in 1949. In late 1949 Yeivin visited the government's planning department in Jerusalem, and talked with engineers Rau and Brutzkus about the inclusion of a building for the IDAM in the *Qiryah*. They asked for some specifications, which Yeivin gave as follows: a building with four or five large halls (100–120 m^2) and three or four medium-sized rooms (25–30 m^2) for exhibitions; a large storeroom and a large library; a large room (about 100 m^2) for the archive; a lecture hall for 300 people, built as an amphitheatre; storage for antiquities (handwritten later addition: "the storage will serve as a [bomb] shelter"); laboratories and offices (for about 50 staff members); a large roofed courtyard for work and garages for three cars; a large fabulous court to display very large antiquities. Rau promised to raise the question in a meeting of the *Qiryah* planners. He also told the IDAM that it must seek approval from Mordechai Schattner of the Ministry of Finance (GL44873/10, 16.11.49, 18.11.49). Schattner was an industrialist, and one of the signatories on Israel's declaration of independence. He occupied several senior positions, such as Custodian for Absentees' Property, and was responsible for the development of Jerusalem.

This was still a modest plan, mainly for an office building. Altogether the measured area totalled about 1000 m^2. It also seemed very easy; the buildings could be standing in a year or two. On 10 December 1949 Yeivin met Rau, who told him that there was a space of 8–10 *dunam* on the western side of the *Qiryah* (the Sheikh Bader hill). They met to look at the maps and Yeivin was supposed to prepare a general plan that would fit this area, with the cooperation of an architect from the planning department (GL44873/10). On 20 December 1949 Yeivin asked approval from Schattner of the Ministry of Finance. He now mentioned a museum, and not just offices for the IDAM. The museum must be located in a plot that enabled free admittance to the public, but the offices must be close to the *Qiryah* buildings. Thanks to Rau, an area was found close to the new congress hall (Binyanei Ha-'Umma). The offices could be ready the same year, if the required budget was available. Yeivin asked Schattner to bring the question up at the next meeting of the committee "that handles this matter" (GL44873/10 no. 1923).

Financing the dream was the problem, but it was not yet fully perceived by the IDAM. Schattner answered that he could only bring the request before the committee for development of the government quarter. He warned that the matter was not simple and he did not expect swift approval (GL4873/10 no. 1571). Soon he announced that the committee had discussed the request, but "did not find it possible to set aside a plot for a museum within the *Qiryah* area" (GL44873/10 no. 1648, 11.1.50). Yeivin did not despair, but met Schattner on 15 May 1950 and wrote to him on 6 June 1950, giving "further details" of the plan for a *Qiryah* building for the IDAM:

> For the time being these are meant not for a central museum for the whole state, the erection of which would involve huge expense, and the time for which has maybe not yet come for various reasons, but for a building that will include the offices of the department, a library, lecture hall, laboratories and exhibition halls for ongoing excavations and temporary exhibitions … The building should consist of:
>
> 1. Offices of the IDAM, 30 rooms, two of them large;
> 2. Lecture hall — 300 m²;
> 3. Reading room — 250 m²;
> 4. Store for the library — 100 m²;
> 5. Reading room reserved for scholars/research workers — 30 m²;
> 6. Archive room — 100 m²;
> 7. Five exhibition galleries, 120 m² each — 600 m²;
> 8. Six exhibition rooms, 30 m² each — 180 m²;
> 9. Six rooms for scholars and students, 25 m² each — 150 m²;
> 10. Eight storerooms 120 m² each — 960 m²;
> 11. Laboratory for fixing vessels, two rooms 30 m² each — 60 m²; [In a later version called "workshop for formatore"]
> 12. Photography studio and dark room — 80 m²;
> 13. Chemical laboratory, two rooms 20 m² each — 40 m²;
> 14. Carpenter's workshop — 40 m²;
> 15. Guards' room [in a later version 60 m² was added for toilets] — 30 m²;
> 16. Visitors' buffet — 50 m²;

17. Garages for four vehicles
18. Lift for [heavy] loads
19. Air-raid shelter for valuable objects, employees and visitors ...
20. A garden of approximately 3 *dunams* [10 *dunams* in the later English translation], to exhibit large objects, which cannot be exhibited inside;
21. A closed courtyard for various works, about 1 *dunam* ...

(GL44873/10 no. 2933, 6.6.50)

This was a far more ambitious plan than the plan from November 1949. Again, not all the parts were measured, but those that were added up to about 3000 m². It was a product of its time, for example planning garages for only four cars, and with details based on the PAM's design. Yeivin sent copies of this plan to the ministers of Education and of Finance. More interesting, the idea of a central museum found its way into the press:

> From our correspondent in Jerusalem.
> A large governmental museum will be opened in Jerusalem, where all the antiquities of the state will be gathered, we are informed by a reliable source. So far valuable antiquities, collected by the IDAM, have been kept in various storerooms. The valuable objects include pottery vessels, sarcophagi, jewels, standing stones and weapons from 5,000 years ago. The government strives to establish a large worthy building for the museum but lack of budget delays the execution of the plan ...   (*Yediot Akhronot* 11.4.1950)

Who could their source have been if not Yeivin? The same article continued with the IDAM's plan for new antiquities legislation. The only problem with Yeivin's tactics was that they did not work, for the *Qiryah* planners suggested that there was no location for the museum and the higher authorities provided no budget.

In October 1951 Amiran visited the office of the *Qiryah*. She saw the plan and model of the intended *Qiryah* buildings. An archaeological museum did not appear in the plans, although the area had sufficient space (GL44873/10). Yeivin should not have been surprised by this, given the negative answer of the *Qiryah* committee in 1950. On 21 October 1951 Yeivin wrote to Yeshaayahu (Isaiah) Avrech, the Deputy Director-General of the Ministry of Education. He gave details of the history of the idea and requested the Ministry of Education and Culture to arrange, before it was too late, the inclusion of the museum and IDAM offices in the general plan of the *Qiryah* in Jerusalem. He promised to send a detailed report about the museum "as we discussed it". As for the contents of the museum, it could be discussed later (GL44873/10 no. 6914).

Avrech (1912–88) was a journalist, translator and editor. In the 1948 War he served as the education officer at the Central Front, and was the first general secretary of the Ministry of Education. He was later to join the workers union (Histadrut) (in 1953), occupying several positions in the union, including representing it in the US and Canada. He went on to establish the Histadrut Department of Higher Education, which he directed until his retirement in 1984. He was a member of the *Davar* newspaper's editorial board, and received the Israel Prize for journalistic writing in 1986. Collections of his essays have been published (Avrech 1976, 1990, 1991).

Avrech reported that on 26 August 1951 he had spoken to Moshe Sharett, then Deputy Minister of Education and Culture, who agreed to submit to the government a proposal for establishing four central museums in the country: for Antiquities, Art, Ethnography and "The Independence Museum" (for the 1948 War). No details were given about the contents of each museum. The Ministry of Education would request a budget for this plan from the development budget of the state. Avrech asked Yeivin to draw up a general plan for the antiquities museum, which they would attach to their general plan for the government (GL44873/10 no. 4117, 12.9.51).

Avrech realized that the Ministry of Education could not finance the plan; it all depended upon the government. Yeivin sent him a five-page "Memorandum on a Governmental Museum of Antiquities of the IDAM" (GL44873/10, 10.1.52). This fascinating document shows Yeivin's ideology as addressed to the higher authorities. The document was translated into English in 1953 and I am using that translation here. Yeivin opened by stating that one of the main tasks of the IDAM is scientific research on finds from various excavations. This includes scientific publication and proper exhibition of finds. Exhibition would:

> enable the student as well as the public to see the collection of archaeological, artistic and cultural exhibits, and thus acquire an understanding of the life of the people in ancient times and the development of the material and spiritual culture in all its aspects during their long history within the confines of the State of Israel. (GL44873/10)

Exhibitions demanded a large space, so a museum was a necessity for the IDAM. It had a dual purpose:

> On the one hand, the museum offers to the public a display of the results of archaeological achievement in Israel [in Hebrew, "of Israeli archaeology"]; on the other hand, it constitutes a basis and foundation for scientific research and gives practical guidance in archaeological fieldwork. Hence, a very important conclusion is to be drawn in connection with the planning of a State Museum: there should be no separation – as far as administration

and location are concerned – between the museum and the Department of Antiquities, for they depend on each other and the work of one cannot be properly achieved without the support of the other.

True, in Europe and America there are both state and public museums, which are not affiliated with departments exercising there the functions of a Department of Antiquities; yet, conditions there are entirely different. First and above all, those museums are not usually concerned primarily with antiquities of their representative countries only, but give homes to large extent collections brought together from all corners of the globe, particularly from countries of the Near and Middle East. Consequently, their connections with the Department of Antiquities of their respective countries are rather tenuous. Secondly, the major part of these museums was founded and opened before the establishment of special government offices charged with matters archaeological. However, this is not the case in Israel. (GL44873/10, #4–6)

Yeivin pointed out that the national museums in all neighbouring countries (such as Egypt and Turkey) *were* directly tied with departments of antiquities. Israel was a bridge between cultures for many periods, so Yeivin suggested that its national museum should include exhibitions of antiquities from those cultures. His suggestion included, in fact, everything from Classical Greece to Egypt, Mesopotamia, Iran, Armenia, Ethiopia, South Arabia, India and even the Far East (*ibid.*: #12). The museum would, of course, have an immense value for the "edification of children and adolescents", including:

an invaluable influence not only on the widening of the mental horizon of the Israeli public, but also on jolting it out of the rut of a national and cultural provincialism [!]; a real danger, the first disquieting symptoms of which are already becoming apparent even in the dissemination of knowledge of the country and archaeology among the general public.
(GL44873/10, #8)

Scholars who claim that Israeli archaeology was overtly nationalistic in the 1950s, a willing tool in the hands of the state, may not have seen this document by the leading archaeological official in Israel. Yeivin mentioned (*ibid.*: #16) that a calculation made in June 1950 resulted in a price tag of 250,000–300,000 Lira. Now, in January 1952, materials and work had become so much more expensive that a budget of 500,000 Lira (or 100,000 per year for a five year plan) had to be considered.

A partial plan relating to this proposal was drawn up by architect Asher Hiram (IDAM Keeper of Monuments) and kept in an envelope inside GL44873/10 (dated 10.2.52). It is entitled "A temporary plan for the building of a museum

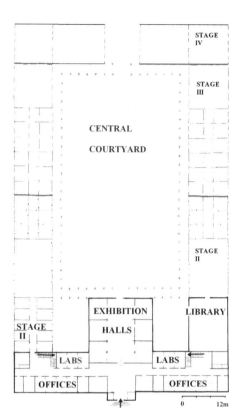

Figure 22. English rendering of the original Hebrew temporary plan for the governmental museum and IDAM offices, 1952. (GL44873/10)

and offices of the IDAM in Jerusalem" (Fig. 22). It includes several stages; the first, mostly that of the office building, is the most detailed. The plan is very symmetrical, with office rooms on both sides. Two larger rooms flanking the entrance were most probably planned for the manager and his deputy. The museum part included six galleries in two rows and a central large space in the centre. There was a very large library (on the right). Stages II–IV created a huge, closed rectangular courtyard surrounded by colonnades (reminiscent, perhaps, of an ancient synagogue). The plan is grand in scale, but quite modest in features. It seems Classicist in spirit. The rooms are mostly functional; the entrance has few stairs and no grand foyer; there is no excessive display of wealth.

Avrech was greatly impressed by this vision:

> My very dear Yeivin
> I thank you much for your memorandum about the museum. I need not tell you that I will not be the person who will deal with it any more, but I do find it interesting. With this letter of yours you have ensured that [the names of] those who initiated the idea will be remembered after the museum has been built.   (GL44783/10 no. 7615=10215, 10.1.52)

So Yeivin dreamt first about a central museum of antiquities in Jerusalem and Avrech was the first to have the vision of combining different museums in one complex. Sharett accepted the proposal, but he and Avrech left the Ministry of Education soon after that. The next Minister of Education, Ben-Zion Dinur (Minister of Education 1951–55), promoted the idea and contributed to it.

A few months passed and then an urgent announcement was sent by Eliezer Rieger, Director-General of the Ministry of Education, to all heads of units in the ministry. On 25 July 1951 the government had decided to create a committee to discuss land for government institutions. This committee would gather requests, and two phases must be considered: the first 2–5 years and the next 20–25 years. Requests for land must be sent immediately. Ben-Dor answered on 23 January 1952 that the IDAM had already provided a plan for a building and museum (as discussed above). But now the IDAM presented a different plan for the governmental committee. The first phase discussed an office building with 30 rooms and a branch in Tel Aviv with two rooms. The second stage included completion of the museum, but also:

3. Building centres for supervision of antiquities and excavations. Each with six rooms (for management, supervisor, engineer, excavator, secretary and guard); garage for two cars, storage, service rooms [i.e. toilets] and a courtyard. These buildings for supervision centres should be built at: 1. Upper Galilee; 2. Jezreel valley; 3. Sharon [plain]; 4. Tel Aviv area; 5. The Negev.
4. Twenty buildings for antiquities guards, each with two rooms, workroom, storage, and service rooms.
5. Two workshops for restoring mosaics and collecting antiquities; one at Beth-Shean and the second at Beersheba. Each workshop will include one large hall and four rooms.   (GL44783 no. 7719)

This plan was rather unimaginative, with the museum taking a secondary place. Then Shlomoh Arazi (manager of the *Qiryah* office) contacted the IDAM on behalf of the *Qiryah* office (GL44873/10 no. 728, 29.2.52): they needed more details on the administrative offices and the exhibition halls, laboratories, workshops, courtyards and so on. Apparently the plan sent by the IDAM was not specific enough. He also asked whether it was desirable or possible to accommodate the Hebrew University's Department of Archaeology next to the museum, without merging the two institutions. Yeivin responded only seven months later (the reason for the delay is not clear). Apparently he did not like the idea of accommodation too close to the university.

1. After reconsideration of the draft [Ben-Dor's letter] that we sent you, we found that such a great number of adjustments have to be inserted that

only two points from our previous proposal have practical value: a) the suggestion to build in stages; b) the arrangement of rooms and galleries round a courtyard ... In the first stage the building must contain halls and rooms as set out in the enclosed list.

As to the second question ... we have no objection about housing the Archaeological Department of the Hebrew University in the neighbourhood of the Archaeological Museum of the State of Israel, but we do not consider it advantageous. The two institutions are separate, indeed, the Archaeological Department of the University is an organic part of the organization of academic research and lectureship, and has nothing in common regarding organization, with the IDAM.   (GL44783/10 no. 9962, 3.10.52)

In April 1953, Hiram, the IDAM's Keeper of Monuments, prepared detailed specifications for the museum complex (GL44873/10). This was the most detailed and ambitious plan to date. It specified the size of each building and their parts; the estimated costs varied from 40 to 90 Lira per square metre. The scale was lavish. In the IDAM part alone, about 600–700 m^2 was suggested for IDAM offices; 200 m^2 for guards (so far 81,000 Lira) and about 1800 m^2 for stores and laboratories (72,000 Lira). The complex would have a lecture hall seating 2,600 people (2845 m^2, 180,000 Lira), as opposed to the former plan with room for only 300 people. For the antiquities museum, Hiram planned a large exhibition hall (1,400 m^2) and a few smaller ones, in total 3,700 m^2, as well as a building for special collections (2,880 m^2) in three storeys and "pillared buildings" (corridors and courts with rows of pillars) of 3,250 m^2. This part alone included a built area of about 10,000 m^2, with a price tag of about 600,000 Lira. The ethnography museum was slightly smaller, 5,800–6,000 m^2. The plan also included 6000–7000 m^2 for the art museum; as well as a gallery of portraits of about 8,000 m^2. Specifications were given for gardens, paths, fences, and so on, reaching a total of at least 80 *dunams* for the whole project, with a built area of about 36,700 m^2 and a total (estimated) price tag of 2,213,000 Lira. This included the cost of the land, 80,000 Lira, which by today's prices in Jerusalem would be a bargain! But this did not include the cost of furniture and special equipment.

The drawing of the plan was entitled "A general schematic plan for the museums" (Fig. 23; it is slightly modified and dates from 1955). It presented an array of rectangular buildings connected by roofed colonnades, and courtyards or gardens in between. Visitors, once they passed the entrance, would find themselves in a very large rectangular court, about 100 m × 50 m, mostly covered in grass, with a rectangular pool (27 m × 7.5 m) and a few trees. The various museums and offices were spread around this courtyard, having inner courtyards of their own.

One should remember that those who dreamt up this grand plan were themselves sitting in small, uncomfortable rooms, in temporary, makeshift housing.

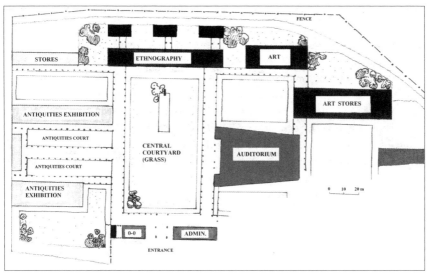

Figure 23. English rendering of the original Hebrew plan for a complex of museums by Hiram. This version is probably from 1955. The portrait gallery and some antiquities components are not shown here. (GL44873/10)

The state was fighting for survival under waves of immigrants, with food rationing and unemployment. Vivid descriptions of the reality of the conditions of work in the IDAM at that time are abundant. For example:

> It is an impossible situation that there is no allocated room or even corner for the manager of the IDAM, who often needs to speak to people about matters that should not reach the ears of all those present in the room. Of course, these applications have had no result. We are asked not to make any alterations and not to construct inner divisions in the rooms … and work suffers. (GL44889/3, Yeivin to Ben-Dor, 18.2.49)

In 1952 Amiran approached the supervisor of reserves: "We would be very pleased if you would approve urgently one thin sheet of wood ("*dict*"), 8 mm thick, needed for fixing a shelf in an exhibition cupboard for the exhibition in the museum of the IDAM" (GL44874/3 no. 9548, 22.8.52). Next she applied to the district engineer of Jerusalem:

> Attached is a permit for a *dict* sheet 8 mm thick for the shelf in the exhibition hall. S. of the Metal Department in the Ministry of Commerce and Industry notified us that glass will be [available] in the free market in October; therefore we will place a *dict* now. We greatly thank you for agreeing to do these two urgent jobs … (GL44874/3, no. 9546)

205

Yeivin wrote on 22 September 1952:

> I have a few times already drawn the attention of secretarial employees in my
> department to the use of State of Israel letterhead. On this I have received
> the answer that for some weeks now the administration has not supplied
> paper at all. Since stocks of plain stationery have been used; and we are
> forbidden to buy stationery except through the administration, we are left
> with only two choices: either not write documents or letters at all; or use,
> for drafts and copies as well, sheets bearing the State of Israel letterhead,
> which are still available ... I think you understand which option I chose.
> We use leftovers and any scraps at hand (reused memoranda, etc.), and I
> write on both sides of these scraps, but even they are nearly finished.
>
> (GL44875/10 no. 9858)

HOME FOR THE IDAM: ABROAD AND WITH
THE HEBREW UNIVERSITY (1953–55)

I could not trace an official rejection of Yeivin's plans; it seems that the matter
was left undecided because of the lack of budget. The state had more pressing
needs. Hence, after 1952 Yeivin shifted his efforts to outside sources; for that
reason some of the former plans were translated into English. On 11 June 1953,
Yeivin wrote to Izhak Norman of the American Fund for Israeli Institutions in
New York (later to become the America–Israel Cultural Fund; see Ch. 4):

> Dear Mr Norman
> I am writing to you about a matter that has been on my mind for a long
> time. The archaeological excavations carried out by our Department of
> Antiquities and by other Israeli institutions bring to light great treasures,
> which form the inheritance of our past. Chance discoveries caused by the
> increased pace of development and construction furnish additional mate-
> rial. And last but not least stand foreign archaeological expeditions, which
> are renewing their activity in Israel and most of whose finds remain in the
> country.
>
> All these discoveries foster archaeological and historical research,
> increase our knowledge of the essence of ancient art and civilization ...
> There is another side to it too: archaeological finds provoke great interest
> in the public and provide attractions for thousands of tourists, who come
> every year to Israel with the object of seeing the land of the Bible and its
> remains.

All the above reasons make it imperative to create a central museum, which would house the most important antiquities of the country and become a centre of archaeological research as well as a showplace for the public. The site of such a central museum has obviously to be in Jerusalem, the capital of the country, the seat of its cultural institutions and the town to which the visitors from all over the country and from abroad are mainly directed.

The State of Israel is involved in a difficult economic struggle, and is unable to carry out this plan out of its own resources. Help has to come from outside, and it would be the noble task of the American fund to sponsor this important undertaking. [Followed by a short, general list of the parts needed in the museum, including the IDAM offices.]

... I do not intend to go into further details at this stage ... [But] in addition to the cost of the building, means will have to be provided for the purchase of furniture, apparatus and tools.

I am confident that you will realize the importance of the project and give it your adequate consideration.

(GL44873/10; Hebrew and English versions,
both "draft", English modified)

The American Fund for Israeli Institutions had Albert Einstein as chair of its advisory board and other dignitaries, such as Leonard Bernstein and Abba Hillel Silver, on its board of trustees. Edward Norman was the President and Izhak Norman was Executive Vice-President (he lived in Israel and was a member of the IES, but died around 1957) (*IEJ* 7 (1957): 275). This fund helped the IES with modest contributions in the 1950s, especially for the Bet She'arim excavations (e.g. *BIES* **17** (1952/53): 78). Apparently the fund was interested and asked for details. On 14 August 1953 Yeivin sent an "air-graph" (i.e. aerogram) to Louis M. Rabinowitz (who had donated to the Fund for Exploration of Ancient Synagogues of the Hebrew University; cf. Sukenik 1952: 50) in New York. He discussed the plans with Norman, and they thought that the material should be taken to the US and handed over to Rabinowitz (GL44783/10 no. 1841a).

To the letter was attached a list of details of rooms for offices, exhibition galleries, laboratories and so on for the first stage of the plan alone, with a total of about 2000 m². It was more limited than the grand plan of four museums, and basically concerned only the IDAM offices. The five-page memorandum of 10 January 1952, translated into English, was attached (GL44873/10 no. 7367). Yeivin updated some details, such as the cost: now 800,000–850,000 Lira, including furniture and equipment.

On 12 November 1953 Yeivin reported to the Minister of Education that he had dined with Haim Ariav, honorary secretary of the Israeli committee of the American Fund. Ariav read long sections from a report by Norman, mainly on the "Land of the Bible" exhibition, which was then in the Metropolitan Museum in New York. Yeivin added:

> As for the erection of the central museum of the IDAM in Jerusalem, Mr Norman asks also for letters from the ministers of Education and Culture and of Foreign Affairs explaining the importance and necessity of the project. He also asked for a map, with the exact location of the plot secured for the building, and a few plans and photographs, which will explain physically the details included in the memorandum that I gave Mr Norman for Mr Louis Rabinowitz with that purpose.
>
> The IDAM is now handling the making of drawings and plans to clarify the details included in the said memorandum for building a central antiquities museum in Jerusalem. (GL44783/10, 12.11.53)

A letter from Ariav followed to Dinur, Minister of Education (GL44783/10, 11.11.53) (on Dinur see Zameret 1999: 45–61). He reminded him of the need for an official letter for the American Fund, asking for support for the museum to the sum of US$500,000, stressing the necessity and importance of the project. Ariav sent Yeivin this request and explained that Rabinowitz was a "prospective contributor", but Norman could not meet him because of the lack of detailed material and supportive letters. Yeivin drafted a letter of support and mentioned to Ariav that the minister had promised to act quickly (GL44783/10 no. 2538a). Yeivin wrote to Norman again on 28 December 1953 to tell him that the negotiation was continuing. He hoped that it would be settled quickly, and he would send the plan of the plot and first drawings of the building (GL44783/10 no. 2808a). Norman responded on 27 January 1954 (letter not traced), and Yeivin answered on 15 February 1954:

> I am sorry that the final location for the governmental museum in Jerusalem has not yet been decided, despite the efforts of H.E. the Minister of Education and Culture. Surely you know that it depends upon more than a few governmental institutions, and it is not easy to set their wheels in motion. In any case, I understand that the Ministers of Education and of Foreign Affairs have provided the letters required to start the operation
> … (GL44783/10 no. 3288)

As the decision about a *Qiryah* location remained unsettled, Yeivin tried to find a site on the Hebrew University campus of Givat Ram, which was then being developed (Kroyanker 1999: 115–30; 2002). He talked with Mazar (President of the University) and asked the Minister of Education to meet Mazar in order to locate an area (GL44873/10, undated). Yeivin wrote to the minister on 23 March 1954:

I happened to talk about it with Prof. Mazar, the President of the Hebrew University. According to him, place was allocated within the area planned for the university for several museums, to be concentrated in an area of 40 to 50 *dunams*. These will include the national museum [for art] Bezalel, a botanic museum and one other museum, whose nature I do not exactly remember. From his words I understood that the university would be prepared to include the IDAM museum in this plan also.

Indeed, the general area seems smaller than adequate. But perhaps one may reach an agreement to enlarge the general area allocated to the museums ... (GL44783/10, no. 3585a)

In April 1954 Avidor of the Ministry of Education asked Mazar to set up this meeting (GL44783/10 no. 992-440). It did not take place until July, and was attended by Mazar, Yeivin and Avidor. Mazar explained the situation and the general plans for the museums, and said that the university was ready to administrate and plan the IDAM building as part of the Givat Ram complex; but a budget of about 30,000–40,000 Lira would have to be allocated. The Ministry of Education would nominate a committee to negotiate the details. When this was finished, he would establish another committee "to put together a thorough strategy to realize the said plans to establish a governmental museum in the area of the university buildings" (GL44783/10 no. 4237a, 2.7.54).

According to Tamir (1990: 8–9), Mayer, Mazar and Yadin wrote a memorandum in 1955 trying to establish the university museum and the national museum in the planned campus at Givat Ram, and to affiliate both museums with the university. It is not clear if Yeivin knew of this plan. To raise funds from the American Fund he needed to show it a concrete location, wherever that would be. On 18 July 1954 the plan of the university's area was delivered by the IDAM to Avidor, who was going to meet Norman the same day. Two areas were possible, marked on the plan with red lines; Yeivin preferred the larger area of the two. The area available for building was about 20,000 m^2, half of it for the IDAM requirements; the IDAM wanted to have 3000–4000 m^2 at the first stage (GL44873/10 no. 4366). However, on 13 August 1954, Zvi Ventic, the secretary of the *Qiryah* committee in Jerusalem, intervened. He wrote to the Minister of Education (copy to Yeivin):

1. The allocation of offices and exhibition halls for the IDAM has in recent years been the subject of an exchange of letters between us and the manager of the IDAM. The manager asked for a place within the *Qiryah* because the IDAM is in close contact with various governmental offices found in the *Qiryah*. On the other hand, some say that since the exhibition halls must be open to the public on days and hours not fitting those of the *Qiryah*, they ought to be located outside it. The matter has not been decided yet.

2. The JNF now plans the development of the area of the Mazleva valley [the Monastery of the Cross, in southern Jerusalem] and its vicinity. The plan has a section allocated for public buildings, such as the Bezalel museum, the art school, an academy of music, etc. The *Qiryah* committee thinks that it is appropriate to also locate the IDAM near these buildings. The Department of Planning has accepted this suggestion.

3. If your Excellency approves of this idea, I suggest that he approaches the JNF asking to allocate ground for the IDAM buildings ... About two years ago we received from the manager of the IDAM certain data about the required land for the buildings, but I am not sure that this data is valid at present. It would be better to ask now for details from the manager to verify the size of the required ground.   (GL44783/10 no. 5014a)

In the margins Yeivin noted by hand: "the negotiation with the university was completed". The matter is not discussed more in the file; and the next letters are addressed once more to the American Fund. On 17 September 1954 Yeivin wrote to Ariav (GL44783/10 no. 4712a). The letter explained that the American Fund had agreed to try to help with the financing of the plan; Eliezer Peri, the chair of the Israel committee of the fund (former Director-General of the Ministry of Defence, and also on the Tel Aviv city council), even declared it in public during a lecture in Jerusalem. Perhaps this caused the reinvolvement of the *Qiryah* planners. So far practical acts were impossible because there was no exact location for the museum, but now it was agreed to build it in the Hebrew University area, opposite the *Qiryah* west of Rupin Street. Yeivin asked Ariav to raise the issue again with the American Fund, as the university had requested an immediate investment of about 50,000 Lira to start preparing the grounds, and declare a competition to design the buildings. If the money was delivered to the university, it was ready to put its administrative organization to the services of the IDAM; work had started on reparing the ground. Yeivin even suggested that such an arrangement would save later expense, and asked for a reply.

Yeivin wrote to Norman again on 10 December 1954:

I also heard from Ben-Dor that you are about to establish a public committee for raising funds to build a central museum of antiquities for the State of Israel in Jerusalem. Surely you know that an appropriate location was allocated to it in the area of the buildings of the Hebrew University. I, like Dr Ben-Dor, believe that Dr Rabinowitz would be a perfect person to chair this committee, but the final decision is certainly yours. I hope that you will soon notify me about your first actions in this matter.

(GL44873/10 no. 5240a, English modified)

Another six months elapsed, and Yeivin wrote to the Minister of Education on 6 May 1955:

> Following our conversation of 20 April 1955 I hereby attach the copy of a memorandum sent at the time to the then deputy general manager, Mr Y. Avrech. Apart from the sums of money mentioned in the final paragraph there, nothing has changed and the plan is still good today.
>
> Nevertheless, if your beautiful suggestion to concentrate a group of fine art and humanities museums at one place is accepted, the calculations of the grounds needed should change, and in that case sections 14–16 at the end of the memorandum are to be ignored [referring to the five-page memorandum of January 1952].
>
> At my request, A. Hiram, Keeper of Monuments at the IDAM, prepared a very general sketch of the group of these museums, and also compiled an attached memorandum, giving a very tentative estimate of the areas required for the group of buildings, the number of rooms and halls and the sums needed to execute the plan. Such a general plan is advantageous to a certain extent, for it saves ground; one large garden that can be used by all [the museums, is] smaller in size than the several gardens around each separate museum, if they are distributed at different places [Fig. 23; here is one central garden, so it dates to 1955. The same concept existed in a listed form in April 1953 (see above). I am not sure if the 1953 idea included a drawing of a plan, modified in 1955; or if the drawing was just added in 1955.]
>
> I think further explanations are superfluous; the plan with the memorandum is self-explanatory. In any case, if you wish for more explanations, Hiram and I will be ready to supply them ...   (GL44873/10 no. 6513a)

Again a gap of a few months followed. On 26 December 1955, Ventic of the *Qiryah* appeared with a plan: to allocate land in the *Qiryah* south of the governmental press office (GK.44783/10 no. 20). Why did the *Qiryah* planners suddenly offer a site? It seems that the budget was the key: in 1951–52 the *Qiryah* planners realized that there was no budget available, so they concluded that there was no site. Now that they believed that the budget was forthcoming from the American Fund, it was probably worth finding the space and thus not losing the planning job. Yeivin declined politely. He wrote on 28 December 1955 that he would bring the question before the Minister of Education, but:

> As I notified you formerly in our last talk about it, the problem is not at all simple, and concerns several bodies that are not under the control of the IDAM ... In any case, I would ask you to delay the decision about the final destination of the said area for a while; I hope that I can notify you soon if the IDAM is interested or not in that area.   (GL44783/10 no. 8522a)

Here the file ends (apart from a plan by Hiram from May 1956, probably related to the Hebrew University).

THE MONASTERY OF THE CROSS

Plans to house the IDAM in the Monastery of the Cross were discussed several times in the 1950s. This monastery, partly built during the Crusader period, was occupied by the army in 1948. In late 1951 the IDAM discussed with the army the possibility of obtaining the building. The army left in April 1953. Yeivin wrote urgently to the district authority (*Minhal makhoz*): he knew that another non-governmental public institute wanted the building (GL44869/2 no. 1042a). He pushed the Minister of Education into action; although they would have to make some changes and create a larger entrance (GL44869/2). The idea was contemplated again in 1957, when the Christian Department of the Ministry of Religious Affairs informed the IDAM that the monks were ready to rent out the building. Yeivin wrote on 18 October 1957 that he had been there to check whether it could be used for "three of four years, until a special building is built for the IDAM and its museum" (GL44880/13 no. 6109). The monastery, noted Yeivin, was a registered historical monument. The plan alarmed Greek diplo-mats and Yeivin assured them via the Ministry of Foreign Affairs that he had no intention of confiscating anything. At the end of 1958 Yeivin tried again to confirm a plan to buy this monastery with the GTC (GL44883/12, 4.12.58). These romantic plans never materialized.

STILL WAITING

The IDAM still waits for a building of its own. It is, at the time of writing, a 56-year-old dream. The plan to use the building at the Monastery of the Cross failed. So did the plan of a museum complex in the Hebrew University. On the other hand, the Israel Museum was opened in 1965. Yeivin's contribution, despite Avrech's exuberant prediction in 1952, was forgotten. Ish-Shalom (1989: 317), Mayor of Jerusalem in 1959–65, thought that the idea about the museum came "out of thin air". Tamir credits Narkiss alone (see p. 108, above), and writes: "clearly, neither the idea of a new building nor of uniting the two museums [for art and for antiquities] into one complex had entered the minds of the archaeologists" (Tamir 1990: 7).

Clearly, the many files of the State of Israel Archive were not checked by Tamir, nor was Kollek an objective source on the history of the Israel Museum. We know now that Kollek learned about the Ministry of Education's plan for a complex of museums in Jerusalem from Yeivin, and that only in 1955 (GL44880/13, 4.7.55).

In *The Restaurant at the End of the Universe*, Douglas Adams discusses travels to the past. He writes that becoming one's own father or mother, or changing history, are not problems at all: things sort themselves out in the end. The chaos remains, but the pieces fall into place with or without our interference. For Adams, the real problem with travels to the past is grammatical: how to speak about something that occurred before someone avoided it by going back and changing the causes (Adams 1980: 101).

For forty years the names of the dreamers of the Israel Museum were obscure. Ironically, as part of its 40-year celebrations in 2005 the Israel Museum held an exhibition entitled "In the Beginning: Prehistory and the Origins of Myth". In the journey into the past we have taken in this chapter we discovered that in the beginning there were as yet unrecognized "parents" of the Israel Museum: Avrech and Yeivin. Narkiss deserves praise, but his part mainly concerned turning Bezalel into a central museum (Hirschberg 1961: 1–2). Yeivin was deprived of the possibility to take a part in fulfilling this dream (below) and his vision was forgotten. But I am sure that, as Adams wrote, it will all fit together in the end.

11 A DEAD MAN ON THE COUNCIL: THE STORY OF THE SUPREME ARCHAEOLOGICAL BODY IN ISRAEL

In his tribute to Chamberlain of 12 November 1940, Sir Winston Churchill (1949: 487) suggested that a person is judged not by what he or she does or does not do, but by the sincerity of his or her actions: integrity. Armed with integrity, whatever happens, one marches always "in the ranks of honour". In this chapter I shall follow the tortuous, at times bizarre path of the history of the highest archaeological body in Israel, the "Archaeological Council". This route takes us through a bitter and prolonged conflict between the IDAM and the IES/Hebrew University. So bear with patience the many committees and councils, mercilessly abandoned like bones of Leviathans on the forsaken shores of Israeli archaeology.

THE FIRST ARCHAEOLOGICAL COUNCIL

At first relations between the IDAM, the IES and the Hebrew University were very cordial. Until 1948 Yeivin was a member of the IES managing committee and editor of almost all volumes of the society's bulletin, the *Bulletin of the Israel Exploration Society* (*BIES*) (*BIES* **14** (1947/48): 73). Mazar and Yeivin served together in 1948 as archaeological army officers, and the IES blessed the establishment of the IDAM, "excellent in its choice of workers and strength" (*BIES* **15** (1949/50): 45, cf. 118–19; *BIES* **18** (1953/54): 94, 104).

From 1951 the IDAM had an advisory archaeological council. Yeivin called it *Mutab Archeologi*, but the word "*Mutab*" did not survive the early 1950s. Even then it was rare and Yeivin often had to explain it. The Mutab council sprang directly from the Mandatory period "advisory committee" devised by Professor

John Garstang in 1920 (Garstang 1992a,b, 1923); Garstang (1876–1956) was the first Director of the British School of Archaeology in Jerusalem (1919–26), and the first Director of the Department of Antiquities of Palestine (1920–26). The committee's 25 members were nominated for one year: 17 members represented archaeological bodies and 8 were representatives from the public. This was remarkable, considering that in 1958 the professional archaeologists' union numbered 37 people in the entire country. The members were distinguished; the first Mutab council included Avi-Yonah, Pinkerfeld, Biran, Ben-Zvi (the second President of Israel); Narkiss, Savorai, Kaniuk, Schwabe, Stekelis and Dinur, the Minister of Education.

The history of the Mutab council deserves a separate study. Yeivin was quite dominant in the council. Discussions hovered around conducting a shared, large excavation; mounting exhibitions; giving licences for excavations; archaeo-logical terminology; education of the public and so on. The main contribution came from a very active sub-committee focusing on new antiquities legislation. Otherwise, the Mutab council was generally inactive: it held only one annual meeting and although it had some sub-committees, these were short-lived. One sub-committee for "archaeological matters and giving licences" met for the first – and last – time in June 1955. Another sub-committee for the preservation of monuments met three times in 1955 (GL44870/13; *Alon* 3 (1951): 58; 4 (1953): 15; 5–6 (1957): 56; Yeivin 1955b: 3, 1960: 1–2).

THE SCIENTIFIC COMMITTEE (CAAR)

A new entity appeared in February 1953, the "Scientific Committee for the Advancement of Archaeological Research" (CAAR). I shall summarize its short history. It was inspired by Minister of Education Dinur, who wanted to encour-age the cooperation of archaeological bodies in Israel (and to bask in the high status of archaeology at that period). The CAAR included distinguished people in pairs, like animals entering Noah's ark: chairman Dinur and Avidor, his deputy, from the Ministry of Education; Ben-Dor and Yeivin from the IDAM; and Mazar, Schwabe, Stekelis and Sukenik from the Hebrew University and the IES.

The main aim of the CAAR was "planning archaeological work in Israel" by Israeli institutions. The intention was good: to coordinate and share excava-tions, equipment and publication and to promote a new general survey. Salvage ("trial") excavations were explicitly taken out of the jurisdiction of the CAAR. Cooperation was a laudable idea; obviously one institution could not hope to perform an entire survey of Israel, for example. CAAR members were equal partners. Most discussions took place in an atmosphere of good will among colleagues (GL44889/2).

Another factor contributed to the peaceful atmosphere: the CAAR was dogged by a complete lack of funds. Each body held tightly to its own independent budget, which was already committed to various aims. Naturally, the IES and Hebrew University hoped to use governmental funding for their projects, while the IDAM wanted to see the university and the IES raising funds for the IDAM's projects. Without funds there could not be much shared activity, so little came out of the discussions, but there was no harm in social meetings. There was no reason for conflict. Some minor disagreements arose, for example about shared publication, but were dropped for other reasons. Publication is crucial to any institution that includes researchers, but each participating body did not want to risk its own journal, or give up influential editorial positions. The members of the CAAR often presented ideas for "shared" excavations to the Ministry of Education, but in reality the degree of sharing was minimal.

Yeivin was quite influential in the CAAR and took it seriously, preparing and presenting many plans for action. The sole result was some very small-scale surveys (Fig. 24) (e.g. by Aharoni in the Galilee), which incidentally only the IDAM financed. A petty sum of 4,000 Lira was once promised by Mazar for this aim, but it remained on paper. Then there was the Masada project of the CAAR. This project signalled the start of serious archaeological exploration of Masada, starting with a new survey of the site and culminating with large-scale excavations in the 1960s, followed by restoration and development as a national site.

The CAAR members suggested Masada explicitly as a large project that could generate "noise" and external funding, but were ready to swap it if necessary. A preliminary stage of this project was a survey. The matter was handed to a sub-

Figure 24. Judean Desert (Nahal Hever) survey, 1955. (Photograph by Aharoni, IAA 12,344)

committee consisting of Avi-Yonah (Chair), Avigad and Dothan (GL44889/2 no. 1088a). It took a full 18 months to deliver its conclusions in December 1954. Do not imagine that the conclusions were lengthy: the single-page plan suggested that during the survey the depth of remains in the site should be probed; small dams in nearby dry-rivers should be prepared, to provide water for excavation; and access roads should be improved. The plan called for 20–25 people and about 800 Lira (GL44889/2). The CAAR was resurrected and declared the conclusions worthy. Yeivin suggested nominating Avigad, Avi-Yonah and Aharoni (replacing Dothan, who was not in good health) to undertake this survey. Mazar suggested that Aviram should organize the team and the army promised help, including financial help: "and in any case, the budget is not important" (GL44889/2, minutes of meeting 28.12.54). As for the main phase, the excavation, Mazar named Yadin as leader, if he wanted to take it on (Yadin was abroad at the time). Stekelis objected; the leaders of the survey should also head the excavation. Mayer came up with the compromise that the survey be carried out by Avigad, Aharoni and Avi-Yonah; but they should be told in advance that Yadin might lead the excavation (GL4489/2, minutes of meeting 28.12.54).

Yeivin invited Avigad, Avi-Yonah and Aharoni to head the survey (GL44889/2 no. 5452a, 31.12.54). The letters did not mention the possible transfer of authority to Yadin. (I do not know if Aharoni was told later, but the documents prove that Yadin did not "snatch" Masada from him.) News about the survey was published by *Hazopheh* on 3 January 1955, which stated that the work would be financed equally by the three bodies (cf. *BIES* **19** (1954/55): 137).

On 26 April 1955 the Masada survey team delivered its conclusions. It is a fascinating report. The survey took ten days (18–29 March 1954; cf. Avi-Yonah *et al.* 1957: 10–11). Here we need only note that the team estimated the cost of the first season of excavations at about 70,000 Lira, excluding restoration, "without which excavation should never start" (GL44889/2, 26.4.55). The moment of truth was nearing; the Minister of Education assembled the CAAR. In the invitation letter Yeivin informed Mazar that, perhaps, it was time to nominate a replacement for the long-ill Schwabe. Yeivin intimated to Mazar that the IES would, of course, be free to choose the new nominee, but that he expected to be informed (GL44889/2 no. 6445a). It is ironic that Yeivin took special care here to ensure that most of the representatives on the CAAR came from the IES and the Hebrew University. This is because the CAAR did not threaten him; it was not a place where conflicts were staged. For the same reason, Mazar did not hurry to find a replacement.

The CAAR met on 2 May 1955. There was some disagreement, for example resentment about the 4,000 Lira promised by Mazar, but the minister diverted the discussion. The participants revealed that instead of the hoped-for "shared excavations" they would start major *individual* projects: Yadin at Hazor (with Rothschild's donation) and Yeivin at "Gat" (with a budget from the Ministry of Labour to employ relief workers, so it "must not be refused"; Fig. 25). Aviram

Figure 25. Excavations at "Gat":
installation for removal of debris, 1956.
(Photograph by Porat, IAA 16252)

suggested that it could be a shared project, but Yeivin said quite bluntly that he did "not see any point in a shared project as long as there is no shared financing and sharing in the team of scientific workers" (GL44889/2, minutes of meeting 2.5.55).

The minister changed the subject again: what about Masada? He wanted this project to go ahead and was ready to discuss it with the Ministry of Finance. Aviram said that volunteers and the army wouldn't suffice for an excavation. He suggested promoting the idea at a party, perhaps in the President's house (this was done; *BIES* **19** (1954/55): 140). Maybe the Minister of Education could present the plan to the government, which should finance such a project, estimated at 200,000 Lira. One can imagine the minister turning pale: it must surely be brought to the government's attention, he said, but it would not provide 200,000 Lira.

This was a dead end. Yet Aviram suddenly noted that in order to excavate the following year someone would have to be already in place to plan it (so some funding was needed immediately). Dothan said that he disagreed with Yeivin about "Gat" (referring to a former complaint by Yeivin about the lack of expert archaeologists). He thought that the excavation at "Gat" must be performed by by someone from the IDAM, and "under the existing circumstances" he was the only possibility, and he could also find the staff. This was odd, for Yeivin intended to direct the "Gat" excavation himself. The minister "agreed that a solution must be found" (not clarifying exactly to what problem, but it was probably that of financing the Masada project). He finished with: "I adjourn the meeting, and ask that before the next meeting time is spent on action" (GL44889/2, minutes of 2.5.55: 3).

There would be no more CAAR meetings; the members would have lots of action, although not of the type expected by the minister. It was all peacefull for a while. Excavation managers from the three bodies met on 12 June 1955 and decided on salaries for students participating in excavations. Students today might be interested in their decisions:

A. "Stagers" [student workers taking part in a dig before or during thier compulsory work experience, the equivalent of the current "learning excavation" (*khafira limudit*)] will receive full expenses for food, etc., or the salary of an unprofessional worker.

B. Students who have finished their compulsory work experience but do not yet have a BA (or vice versa) will have expenses, plus half the lowest salary of the IDAM's assistants in excavations (3 Lira per day).

C. Graduates (BA), after completing compulsory work experience, receive expenses plus the salary of grade D assistants in the IDAM (7.1 Lira per day).

D. MA holders are not considered students and are not under the terms of this agreement.   (GL4489/2 no. 8303a)

Students also volunteered on many occasions. In any case, the participants moved to allocate students to excavations, but "the discussion was not completely finished". A committee (Avigad, Dothan, Yadin and Stekelis) was formed to hear the wishes of the students, and certain excavations – on paper the "shared" ones – were assigned for student employment in summer 1956: Caesarea, "Gat", Hazor, Bet She'arim, and two prehistoric excavations of Stekelis's (GL44889/2 no.8303, 18.6.55).

Yeivin later corresponded with Mayer, asking him to acknowledge in writing that students could receive recognition for fieldwork done with bodies other than the university (GL44889/2 no.6844a, 15.6.55). Mayer told him on 19 June that there were no objections to this in the entire Department of Archaeology, but that each excavation would be discussed on its own merit; excavations headed by Yeivin would certainly be recognized (GL44889/2 no. 8344a). On 23 June 1955 Yeivin fully accepted this decision, but asked that the excavations of Dothan at Nahariya and Aharoni at Ramat Rahel, performed "with a beautiful method and with caution and carefulness", also be recognized in this way (GL44889/2 no. 6943a).

There was no conflict here and one good example of cooperation: the IDAM could employ students from the university to assist in excavations. Yet the storm clouds were gathering and in the same month cordiality turned into bitter conflict. The year 1955 marked a watershed for the IDAM. Until 1955, Yeivin was occupied by establishing and expanding the IDAM, but after that he was fighting more and more for maintenance and survival.

TENSION WITH THE MINISTER OF EDUCATION

In February 1955 Yeivin complained to the Minister of Education Ben-Zion Dinur (see Ben-Arieh 2001: 321–6) about the board of trustees of the Dead Sea Scrolls, who were responsible for building the Shrine of the Book (Broshi 1991; Landau & Zalmona 1998; Roitman 2003). He said that the Hebrew University, "the supreme scientific body in the state", as well as other representatives, must be on this board. However:

> I find it hard to understand why, in this case, they have ignored the govern-
> mental body upon which the government places the care and responsibility
> of ancient remains; and not only practically, but also and mainly from the
> points of view of science and research. I think this can still be put right, and
> the representative of the IDAM should be added to the board of trustees …
> I am certain that you will see the justification for the IDAM's position and
> talk with the Honourable Prime Minister in order to amend the composi-
> tion of the board of trustees.   (GL44880/13 no. 5918a)

In November 1955 Zalman Aranne replaced Dinur as Minister of Education. Aranne changed the way his office worked, and Yeivin was no longer in
favour. Yeivin pleaded with the new minister in April 1956, in a letter termed
"confidential", "personal", and "delivery by hand":

> Dear Minister,
> I ask your forgiveness for bothering you with this letter, but I see no other
> way to clarify the situation.
>   Perhaps you were not informed about the special status of the IDAM in
> the Ministry of Education and Culture. Since the Department of Antiquities
> (Antiquities Unit (*makhlaka*) at the time) was transferred to the Ministry
> of Education and Culture in the time of Mr Z. Shazar [Minister of Educa-
> tion March 1949–October 1950], it was placed in direct contact with the
> minister's office [*lishka*], because the special matters handled by the IDAM
> are beyond the regular framework of the educational work of the ministry.
> Thus this placement was clarified in the structural diagram of the ministry,
> a copy of which I hereby attach.
>   In all those years I tried not to bother the ministers of Education and Cul-
> ture with the daily matters of the IDAM; and certainly with regular matters
> … I contacted the Director-General or his deputies. In other problems I
> acted according to my judgement. Yet, quite often significant problems
> arise that I do not see fit to decide on my own; or I consider it sensible to
> consult about them with the Minister of Education and Culture; and then
> the minister's door was always open to me.

As much as I appreciate and respect the way the Director-General of the Ministry of Education and Culture works, the problems about which I need advice or orders usually also transcend his limits of authority. The work processes recently applied make it harder to handle such problems, especially when they are urgent. If I apply to the Director-General and he brings the matter to you, he often cannot answer further questions immediately, as he is not an expert in the concerns of the IDAM; and he must anyway ask me and return to you; and so on.

I would therefore ask you to return to the previous system, and set a time for me now and then (perhaps once every two weeks?) when I can bring you the IDAM's problems and receive the necessary orders.

Hoping that you will accept this wish in the same spirit in which it was written, I sign, with feelings of honour and hearty blessings.

[signed] S. Yeivin   (GL44880/13 no. 577)

This letter was far too long, but it was trifling in comparison with the events that followed, which had already been set in motion in July 1955.

CONFLICT BREAKS OUT

On 24 July 1955, the IES council met in the Israeli President's house in Jerusalem (not unusual in that period). A week later, on 31 July 1955, Yeivin happened to read a section in the daily newspaper *Al ha-Mishmar* about the meeting:

> *A Supreme Archaeological Council will be Established*
> … Professor B. Z. Dinur, the Minister of Education and Culture, congratulated the society on its excellent initiative, on publishing details of its activities in the public domain and on its success in interesting the wider public in its work … [details about publications and the annual conference, declaration of a new journal *Qadmoniyot*, etc.].

There was nothing particularly unusual here, apart from the title, but then the article went on:

> The last part of the meeting discussed the problem of archaeological planning in the land, and Professor Mazar asked that resolutions be decided as worked out in the meeting of the Management Committee [of the IES]. According to this proposal, two bodies should be established. 1) A national and university museum should be built in the *Qiryah* of the university, in which the museum currently in the IDAM, the university collections and

221

other [collections] will be gathered. A constitution [*taqanon*] should be worked out for this institution, which would be run by a special *quratoriyon* [roughly, board of directors]. 2) A supreme body with wide authority called the "Supreme Archaeological Council" should be established in the Prime Minister's Office, along the same lines as the Scientific Council [of the exact sciences]; it should be composed of representatives of the scientific institutions and dignitaries from the public [*ishey zibur*]; and it should plan archaeological research in the country and coordinate activities done in it by various institutions from this country and abroad. It should also coordinate publications. The IES would have a part in both bodies.

According to him, Yeivin was completely surprised by this article. The IES report of the meeting of 24 July 1955 added a third decision, namely:

> 3. The governmental Antiquities Unit [the IDAM] will handle the preservation of antiquities and their supervision, and will work in close cooperation with the [governmental] tourist corporation.
>
> (*BIES* **19** (1954/55): 243)

This makes it clear that Kollek was pulling some strings too. The addition warned the IDAM to work "in close cooperation" with the GTC. This was the period during which the GTC was formed; soon, ironically, Kollek's demand for cooperation would turn into the GTC's refusal to cooperate with the IDAM (see Ch. 12).

The list of members of the IES council is enlightening. Schwabe died in 1956 after a long period of illness (*BIES* **19** (1954/55): 110, 240; **21** (1956–57): 3), but in his absence a new council and management committee were elected in June 1955. Avigad and Yadin were included on the committee; and Kollek, Malamat, Kol and Shazar were on the council (*BIES* **19** (1954/55): 240–43). There was no longer senior IDAM representation: both Aharoni (committee) and Amiran (council) resigned from the IDAM in early July 1955 (GL44880/13 nos. 1069a, 1071a); Avi-Yonah had resigned earlier. We also learn that Minister of Education Dinur was at the meeting, and reputedly said, rather vaguely, "As for the archaeological research, it ought to be combined with the historical research. The archaeological research can add many details ... One should form a special symposium to discuss the problem of planning" (*BIES* **19** (1954/55): 242).

Similar words appeared in the resolutions of the meeting (*ibid.*: 243): "the problem of planning the archaeological work in the country". Where did this problem appear from? The only problem encountered so far (in the CAAR) was in finding funds. What exactly the minister meant remains vague, but we know that the outbreak of conflict was related to the resignation from the IDAM of Amiran and Aharoni. Amiran presented a letter of resignation on 4 July 1955, and Aharoni did the same a day later. Yeivin wrote to both of them on 7 July 1955, accepting their resignations, which, he wrote, were their own choice and had not been forced upon them. He was angry mainly with Amiran, and wrote to her:

> The first duty of each employee in any institution is to the institution's needs and affairs. Nobody forced upon you the path you have chosen to take. It is not at all a matter of the will or lack of will of a governmental institution to help a large or important project. Nobody knows the real situation in the IDAM and understands what the IDAM can or cannot do like the IDAM employees. Of course, I cannot force people to understand what I think is correct, but these people are not permitted to interpret my understanding of the duty of the IDAM as a sign of will or lack of will.
>
> Relatively young scholars who still have many years of work ahead of them cannot judge whether an opportunity will or will not return ...
>
> (GL44880/13 no. 7170a)

There is also a handwritten note by Yeivin, signed "confidential":

> The minister phoned and asked me to reconsider the matter of releasing R.A. [Ruth Amiran] for work in Hazor, for two months only (all the vacation she is entitled to), with a specific note that this is just for this one time and no more. All this is so as not to leave the new minister with an unresolved controversy, for it has already been hinted to him that a question will be brought to Parliament asking why what has been given to foreign teams is not given to Jewish teams. He has not yet reached a decision and asked me to re-think the situation. (GL44889/2, 22.6.55)

So the debate had been triggered on 22 June 1955. The immediate reason was the allocation of assistants for excavations. Although Yeivin had received help from students at the Hebrew University, he refused to allow Amiran and Aharoni to join the first season at Hazor (Yadin 1956: 120). Amiran (as far as we can tell) blamed Yeivin for not wanting to help an important project. Yeivin's intentions are not clear. It was probably not a move against the university, more a lack of desire to "encourage" two promising archaeologists; perhaps he felt that they would later leave the IDAM anyway. It seems that he did not anticipate the nature and force of the retaliation. By 22 June 1955 the conflict was so heated, that a threat of applying to Parliament had been made: what was given to foreign teams, meaning the IDAM's workers, was not given to Jewish teams, meaning Yadin's large-scale excavations at Hazor, made on behalf of the Hebrew University. It is insignificant that the retaliation came from the IES: the senior archaeologists of the IES were professors at the university. For example, for many years Mazar was the rector and/or president of the university, but he excavated Bet She'arim on behalf of the IES, and was chairman of the IES management committee and editor of the *BIES* (see *Israel Exploration Journal* 1995: 210). The meeting of the IES council took place soon after the conflict had broken out, so it was used for retaliatory purposes.

Since the issue of assistants for excavations was never mentioned later, perhaps it was only the spark that ignited a much deeper conflict. We can only guess: maybe the professors felt that the IDAM was taking over "their" privileges. The university and IES prided themselves, with some justice, on being the cream of Israeli archaeology. Their institutions were the oldest, preceding the IDAM by decades, and conducting excavations that caused a stir in the media. Perhaps they felt threatened by Yeivin's proposal for new legislation, which became public knowledge in those years. They did not appreciate rules that were not of their own creation. Perhaps they envied the fast-growing IDAM for its many employees. In 1955 the IDAM had also launched a new professional publication: '*Atiqot*. Yeivin wrote that it filled "a tangible gap" felt by all those "interested in Israeli archaeology" after *QDAP* ceased to exist (Yeivin 1995c: Preface). The IES/university could not be flattered by hearing that their publications left such a gap. The IDAM already had a large museum, scores of excavations each year, authority over licences and preservation of sites, a large fixed budget, close ties with foreign teams, and was leading the survey of the Galilee (as long as Aharoni remained) (*BIES* **19** (1954/55): 136–7). The older professors (Mayer and Schwabe) were on close terms with Yeivin, but Mazar was extremely influential and he spearheaded this conflict, probably with Yadin. The *Al ha-Mishmar* article of 31 July 1955 had reported that "Mazar asked that resolutions be decided as worked out in the meeting of the management committee"; but his name was omitted in the bulletin report (*BIES* **19** (1954/55): 243), while the *Israel Exploration Journal* (1955: 275) passed over the whole matter in silence.

If some of these concerns were factors, conflict was bound to erupt sooner or later. Documents by Mazar and Kollek are missing, and probably the initial phase was expressed in conversations between a few people, and not in written papers. As Mikhail Bulgakov wrote, "manuscripts don't burn" (Curtis 1992: xii), so one can hope that we will know more in the future. The general picture seems clear.

Back to July 1955. The news came as a severe and unexpected blow to Yeivin. He was threatened on several fronts: the central museum; supervision on the IDAM's excavations; licences to be given to all excavations; the question of a new "Supreme Council" when he already had the Mutab council. The blow was more painful since he was not told any of it beforehand by the IES/university. Moreover, the appearance of the Minister of Education created the impression that he supported Mazar. This is not certain: high officials gave speeches in every IES annual conference in the 1950s.

It took Yeivin a month to respond because he was excavating at Caesarea (Fig. 26). He wrote to Aviram, secretary of the IES, on 13 September 1955:

Figure 26. Visit to Caesarea excavations, 1955. Yeivin (left), President Ben-Zvi (second from left), Shalom Levi (right). (Photograph by Schulman, IAA 12,779)

Honourable Aviram,

I knew that in July a meeting of the council of the IES took place in the house of His Excellency the President of Israel at his invitation. In the invitation there was no programme and no announcement was given about the content of the recommendations or decisions brought before the council.

Unfortunately, I could not attend this meeting because, as you know, I was in Zichron [Ya'acov] and directing my excavations in Caesarea. I had been wondering why I had not received a memorandum or some other notice about what had been said and decided at that meeting; and I knew nothing about it until I happened to see … on returning from Caesarea, a newspaper clipping that gives a report about the said meeting.

To my great surprise, I found in that report that the management committee of the society brought before the council proposals for decisions that relate to the principles of archaeological work in Israel and its planning. It is a great wonder to me why the management committee did not find it fit to consult with the IDAM about the principles of those decisions, or at least to notify it that it [IES] was about to propose those things, especially when it is known and obvious that the form of the proposals does not conform to the opinion of the workers of the IDAM in several matters. Furthermore, one of the decisions means going over the same ground again. There is no need to establish supreme new bodies when such bodies already exist, for, in addition to the advisory archaeological *Mutab*, in which all the bodies that relate to matters of archaeology are represented, and whose members include almost all the archaeologists in Israel [!], there is already a scientific committee for the advancement of archaeological research in Israel [CAAR]. The three bodies that deal with matters of archaeology in Israel are represented there in equal numbers, and its President is his Excellency the Minister of Education and Culture. If this committee does not fulfil its role properly, in the view of the IES, then it would have been possible to bring in front of it proposals for amending the situation. The IDAM has taken the trouble to assemble the committee when required and to bring to its ears for approval all its plans for cooperation, whereas the representatives of the university and the IES never saw fit to bring before it any plans, and some [of them] even refrained from participation in its last meeting. The IDAM has always taken the trouble to cooperate out of goodwill and from a strong desire for mutual work with all the archaeological institutions in Israel. However, it has always insisted that cooperation means mutual consultation and reciprocal work between all the bodies as one; and not dictating one will and trying to force it on all the other bodies.

Even today, the IDAM is ready for honest and loyal cooperation, by agreement and mutual consultation; but it seems to me that you will also admit that such decisions, thrown like "bombs" from a public arena, are not going to promote such cooperation. Or perhaps the things in the report that I read in the newspaper (*Al ha-Mishmar* of 31.7.55) were distorted?
[signed] S. Yeivin
(copy Minister of Education)   (GL1430/13 no. 7611a)

The only IES representative missing from the CAAR's last meeting was Mazar (since Schwabe was absent as a result of illness); but we have no evidence that the absence was deliberate. Aviram's response of 23 September 1955 was evasive, but in an explicit way: it used evasiveness to express lack of consideration:

Dear Mr Yeivin,
I acknowledge receipt of your letter of 13 September, this year, but due to my many worries before the conference [at Tiv'on] I will answer it briefly.
1. In addition to the invitation we sent a memorandum to the members of the council in which we informed them that daily matters of the society and general archaeological matters would be discussed at the meeting.
2. We do not customarily send memoranda on what has been discussed and decided at the meetings, but these things are published in *BIES*. Also, the summary of the details of the above-mentioned meeting will be published in Vol. 19, 3–4, which will be issued before the [Tiv'on] conference.

3. I have not read the article in *Al ha-Mishmar*, so I cannot express my opinion about it.
4. To the core of the matter that you mentioned, I will present your comments to the meeting of the management committee of our society, which will take place in November.

With much honour and blessing for the holiday,

[signed] Y. Aviram, on behalf of the Management Committee.

Copy: Minister of Education and Culture   (GL1430/13 no. 9903)

Aviram mentioned a publication in press, but did not bother to attach a copy. He did not comment on the newspaper article because he did not read that newspaper. He would present Yeivin's comments to a meeting, but not invite Yeivin in person. Mazar and the IES management committee probably met the Minister of Education at Tiv'on in early October 1955. They discussed the "Supreme Archaeological Council", but we do not know the details. Yeivin did not respond in public until the conflict erupted again in summer 1956.

THE CONFLICT CONTINUES

On 2 July 1956 Mazar held a press conference in Jerusalem. It presented the activities of the archaeologists of the Hebrew University, so most of the news surrounded various excavations and discoveries. But one sentence in the report in the newspaper *Davar* ran: "The President of the University, Prof. B. Mazar, stressed the need to establish a supreme institution that will coordinate and encourage archaeological excavations in Israel" (*Davar* 2.7.1956). The news reached Yeivin while he was (again) excavating at Caesarea. Yeivin sent a handwritten response to the editor of *Ha'aretz*. He explained that he did not have a typewriter, but hoped that his letter would not be rejected on that account. The handwriting is angular, showing that Yeivin was under stress. The newspaper published his letter on 29 August 1956:

Sh. Yeivin, Director of IDAM
Archaeological planning
For the second time within a year [the first was on 31.7.1955, see above] Professor Binyamin Mazar has broadcast a vibrant call about the need to establish a supreme archaeological authority in the state, in order to plan archaeological activity in Israel.

In these days, where the atmosphere is alive with calls to plan works of all kinds, this call seems as a healthy, true one in order to prevent duplication of activity and duplication of authority. The audience, not knowing the reality behind the situation, might be impressed that what is currently a mess could thus enter the world of science and research, and could think that a quick salvage action is all that is needed to prevent chaos occupying this field.

But the truth is that Professor Mazar covers the same ground again, for a supreme authority already exists. As early as February 1953, a supreme committee for promoting archaeological research was established under the initiative of Professor B. Z. Dinur, the Minister of Education at that time, in which the three bodies that deal with archaeological work in Israel were represented … (Ha'aretz, copy in GL44889/2)

Yeivin gave a short history of the CAAR. He claimed that only the IDAM brought suggestions to it, and that the IDAM had suggested merging publications, but Mazar had asked the IDAM to give up the new journal '*Atiqot* and all the other CAAR members had objected to this idea. Then Yeivin mentioned that the idea about Masada was conceived by Mazar. He reviewed the history of the project and complained that while the IDAM had suggested a shared excavation at Caesarea, the university had required – and received – a licence to excavate a Synagogue there by Avi-Yonah without the IDAM having a share in it. This was a new allegation, but not a very serious one, for the plan for excavating Caesarea had never included shared work, but just a shared site with individual excavation areas. Yeivin continued, saying that Mazar, in the press conference, included excavations of the prehistoric caves without mentioning that the IDAM had a major part in them. Yeivin had expected an apology on this matter, but had not received one. He concluded:

It is completely clear which institutions silenced and caused to fail the work of the CAAR, and who is responsible for this. So why all the pathetic calls to establish a supreme archaeological council? Professor Mazar has only to ask for the scientific committee [CAAR] to be reconvened and bring before it clear plans of his own, or give answers in goodwill to plans brought by the IDAM. (Ha'aretz, 28.8.1956)

Yeivin went abroad in August and returned in September. In the meantime, Mazar had sent an official letter from the Hebrew University to Aranne, the Minister of Education:

Honourable Minister
Following our conversation at Tiv'on on 22 July 1956 according to the attached memorandum, we are honoured to invite your Excellency to establish a supreme archaeological council, whose role will be to plan and coordinate archaeological activities carried out in Israel by the appropriate

institutions (the university, the IDAM and the IES). This body will be a temporary one, until its authorities and composition are defined by the new Law of Antiquities. This council will immediately attend to the preparation of a proposal for the new Law of Antiquities, in which the functions of the three institutions that deal with archaeology in the land will be defined. Until the acceptance of this law in Parliament the council will act under authority given to it by the government. This council will immediately start to plan the archaeological research in all that concerns scientific excavations, a national archaeological museum, publications, libraries, etc. This body will also be responsible for giving excavation licences to various expeditions.

We propose the following composition to the council:

1. Minister of Education: Chairman [Aranne].
2. Director-General of the Ministry of Education and Culture [Avidor].
3. Manager of the Prime Minister's Office [Kollek].
4. Mr Sh. Yeivin: IDAM.
5. Prof. Mazar: University.
6. Dr Yadin: University.
7. Dr Stekelis: University.
8. Prof. Mayer: IES.
9. Mr Avi-Yonah: IES.

With great honour, B. Mazar   (copy, GL44889/2, 3.8.56)

There is a problem with the date of 22 July 1956 that Mazar gives for their meeting in Tiv'on. The Tiv'on conference had been held in early October 1955 (*IEJ* 1956: 129), and the Minister of Education was still Dinur. Perhaps Mazar meant the meeting of the IES council on 24 July 1955, but that was in Jerusalem, not in Tiv'on; maybe Mazar and the minister met privately on 22 July 1956. In any case, on 15 August 1956, while Yeivin was still abroad, Avidor sent him Mazar's letter, at the request of Aranne. Yeivin probably saw it only upon returning to Israel on 5 September 1956. It was New Year's Eve (*Rosh Hashanah*) in the Jewish calendar, so it took him some time to respond. He was usually very polite, but on 28 September 1956 he wrote to Ben-Dor, a close colleague:

Immanuel my Friend

As you see, we finally returned home on New Year's Eve, and, of course, I found here a large pile of letters and urgent matters that require immediate attention. Still I sink in a sea of troubles and worries. Our dear friends at the university and the IES probably have it as their goal to abolish the IDAM and to lay their already overburdened hands on matters of practical archaeology in the land. And they work at it relentlessly [*shokdim*], not only by writing memoranda [*pashkvills*] to the government and by loud publicity in official press conferences; but also by word of mouth, both in the circle of ministers and in the wider public. If this were only a matter of internal disturbance, I should not have paid much attention to it; for this department is already used to worries and troubles. However, this has undesirable echoes in our own community, and it ridicules [*oseh plaster*] our efforts to take hold of the lawlessness [*hefkerut*] by all means. Were I to describe the matters to you in all their details, the page would not have sufficed.

I hope that in the following days, after the Minister of Education and Culture has returned from vacation, it will be possible to end this shameful affair in one way or another; of course, upon that hangs the question of my continuing to work in the department, for I at least will not agree to the department being turned into a sort of puppet [literally thin-haired tail (*zanav meduvlal*)] for those who "pull strings" from the outside, and to the ruin of the entire building, for whose establishment I toiled so much, with the dedicated help of some of my colleagues.

(GL44881/13 no. 2282a, 28.9.56)

Yeivin did not reveal all the details, but they are quite clear from the other documents. He felt that the issue was crucial for the IDAM. Yet, he was not sure how the minister would react. His requests for interviews were not answered, so he pleaded with Aranne on 3 October 1956. He has no option, he wrote, since the issue concerned not just the "supreme council", but "the entire relationship between the IDAM and the archaeological institutions in the land and the position of the IDAM in the framework of other governmental institutions". Yeivin explained the urgency: "certain institutions are not avoiding spreading in public various rumours about the elimination of the IDAM". This made it extremely difficult to continue regular work, and especially to deal with "the community of transgressors of the law" (he didn't specify further). Yeivin stressed again that the IDAM was not a regular department, but was directly tied to the minister. No other person could deal with the issues at hand, and only Yeivin could explain them to the minister. Yeivin reminded the minister of his words in their last interview:

At that time you promised me that "you may not always have money, but you will always have time for me". I therefore ask you to set an urgent meeting for me, so as to discuss all the problems and eliminate them as far as possible; and I thank you for this in advance …
[signed] S. Yeivin   (GL44880/13 no. 2296, "confidential" and "urgent")

The minister and Avidor met with Yeivin on 9 October 1956 and Yeivin wrote a lengthy memorandum about "Resumption of activity of the Supreme Scientific Council for the Advancement of Archaeological Research in Israel" marked "urgent" and "personal". Yeivin opened by stating that he was not at all against the resumption of this council, but on the sole condition that it would be an honest and fair cooperation; and that the decisions would be implemented in good faith through mutual efforts, "without the attempt to distort them by empty rhetoric [*pilpulim*]". The Supreme Scientific Council:

A. Will discuss in general guidelines for archaeological work in the country and proposals for large excavations planned in advance; also coordinate the work of excavations in the country as far as possible with regard to the team of workers and the funding.

B. Will review again the question of shared scientific publications of all the member bodies in it, out of an honest effort to reach an acceptable solution that will not deprive any of the bodies that cooperate in it.

C. Will not handle and not discuss and not be authorized to discuss any administrative matters that relate to one of its cooperating bodies; there-fore also the matter of giving licences to excavations will be taken out of its scope of discussion; whether they are[licences] for foreign bodies, or for Israeli bodies.

D. Will be authorized to make final decisions in the matters under discussion, and the representatives of the various member bodies will not need to bring these matters before the management of these bodies for further approval.

E. Its decisions will maintain the framework of the budgets of the cooperating bodies; and where it is necessary to divert from this framework, the representatives of these bodies will take responsibility for finding the further funding according to the format agreed upon.

F. Its composition will be parithetic, with two representatives from each body that treats archaeological problems in the country. At the head of this council will sit his Excellency the Minister of Education and Culture; next to him will be the Director-General of the Ministry of Education and Culture. In fact I would recommend this composition:

Chair: his Excellency Minister of Education and Culture.
Members: Director-General of the Ministry of Education and Culture

Director IDAM
Deputy Director IDAM } as representatives of the IDAM

Dr Y. Yadin
Prof. L.A. Mayer } as representatives of the IES
Prof. B. Mazar } and the Department of Archaeology
Dr M. Stekelis } of the Hebrew University

I suppose that those concerned will decide which of the four represent the IES and which the university. I would not object if instead of these four representatives, or some of them, they nominate others; but the overall number of representatives from these two institutions will not exceed four.   (GL1430/13 no. 2370-1, also GL44880/13)

Let us make a few observations. First, the title "Supreme Scientific Council" is the one desired by Mazar ("Supreme Archaeological Council"). However, Yeivin talks about the resurrection of the CAAR, while Mazar wanted a very different body. The composition suggested by Yeivin creates an equilibrium of power between the IES/university and the IDAM/Ministry of Education. By this Yeivin avoided the possibility that the first two bodies could force decisions by majority vote, assuming that the minister (and the chair) would be on his side. Secondly, the debate is about supervision of excavations, including giving licences: that is, control over all types of field archaeology. Yeivin did not object to discussing the few large-scale excavations (A). However, he insisted on taking salvage excavations out of the authority of the council. Yeivin returned to the hobby-horse of the merger of publications (B), but on this he was flogging a dead horse. Section E meant that each body would keep its own funding. Yeivin continued:

As you can see I have added two sections (D, E) not mentioned in our verbal agreement; but we talked about section D during the meeting, and in my mind section E derives from section D.

I do not want to bring up forgotten matters and discuss previous problems in a kind of *post mortem* [these last two words were in English, which was most unusual for Yeivin in a Hebrew document]. But I want to return and emphasize what you have already emphasized in your words too, that agreements and treaties are good and proper only if the sides set out to implement them in good faith, and an earnest desire to always find a ready compromise, by way of "you scratch my back and I'll scratch yours". No agreement will hold if each side expects the others only to keep to the agreement and wants to force its opinion on the work, whether by law or by ingenious empty rhetoric [*hitkhakmuyot shel pilpulim*]. On my side I can assure you that for all my life I have been careful to keep to agreements that I have signed or agreed verbally, even when the decisions were against my will or benefit. If the other sides will also attend the resumption of work of the CAAR and the implementation of its decisions in the same spirit, I am certain that the cooperation will be a benefit and a blessing to each one of the cooperating bodies in the council, and to archaeological research in Israel in general.

As I already told you verbally, it is not my nature to raise my voice in loud proclamations about my private efforts or about the public enterprises that I try to lead and guide. I have never done so, and do not intend to in the future. But it does not mean that I do not recognize their value and importance. In the eight years that have passed since the establishment of the state of Israel I have tried here in the IDAM to establish a body fitting its name and role. I had the full and honest help of my friends to work in the IDAM, and without them and their help surely we could never achieve what we have achieved. We began from complete zero; the department had nothing: not an archive, not a museum, not a library, not a laboratory and not even accommodation. Today we have a department that in those years has performed close to 350 archaeological excavations; mostly not large, trial excavations; but also in those there was considerable practical and scientific interest. Apart from these, there have been many seasons of excavation in large and important excavations such as Beth Yerakh, Caesarea, Tiberias, Nahariyah and "Gat" [=Tell el-Areini]. In archaeology one should not speak about more or less important excavations, since all are of equal scientific interest. But regarding interest, finds and scientific importance, these excavations do not fall short in any way of those that are so much hailed [in public] by other bodies. (GL1430/13 no. 2370-10)

Yeivin continued to list the IDAM's achievements: the best archaeological library in Israel; the archive; the permanent exhibition; exchanges with museums; conservation of monuments; popular and scientific publications; the Friends of Antiquities; efforts to spread news and education; and:

> To some degree we have set in order the lawlessness (*hephkerut*) and the mess (*irbuviya*) that was governing ancient sites with the state's establishment. The situation is not pleasing, but forceful efforts are made to increase the authority of the IDAM in these things.
>
> Furthermore, one has to remember that all this was performed by a very limited number of people with a minimal budget. We are always looking to the future, and we all know how much work still remains; but when I review the past for a moment, I believe that I may say that the state of Israel need not be ashamed of its Antiquities Department, and it can serve as a model for what can and should be done. Of course, I observe with heartache any effort to undermine this work and delay its progress.
>
> (GL1430/13 no. 2370-1)

Yeivin fought, but the letter is both a defence and a summary. The debate was not now about the past. Yeivin would not have had to list all these achievements if he had the minister's support. This was no longer assured. Negotiations now took place indirectly, with Avidor as negotiator. On 20 December 1956 Avidor wrote to Yeivin that he had given the minister a suggestion for the "central archaeological council"; it was not the same as Yeivin's suggestion, but included the most important points (GL1430/13 no. 9903-1077). Yeivin and Avidor met for discussions and Yeivin summarized his position:

A. About the nomination, I do not see the point in trying each time to tie the nomination of the council with the problem of approving the new Law of Antiquities. I suggest nominating the council for two years. If in the meantime no proper legal arrangement is achieved, it can be renominated later.

B. About authorities and roles ... I do not object to the council dealing with the problem of archaeological publications in the country. However, from the experience of trials already made in the past in this matter, I do not think that any good will come of it. The same is true regarding archaeological libraries. Although in this case there has been no previous discussion of it, in advance I do not see any benefit in discussing this problem. A professional library is like the air to be breathed for any institution that deals with archaeological fieldwork and research. As long as many institutions that deal with our profession exist, there will be libraries next to each institution.

To section C, I strongly object to discussing the question of a national archaeological museum in this framework, which I do not see as authorized to discuss or even to advise about this problem.

One final note. Formerly this institution was called the Supreme Scientific Committee for the Advancement of Archaeological Research in Israel, not by chance, but because we meant, both Professor Dinur and I, to discuss only scientific problems and nothing more. Furthermore, there exists already an archaeological council running alongside the IDAM, and one need not confuse the two affairs now. As I already told you, my view is that finally this committee will also need to be entered into the framework of the existing archaeological Mutab (archaeological council) ...

(GL44880/12 no. 3227, also GL1430/13)

By now Yeivin had accepted that a new body would be established, and his fight was now about superiority (keeping the Mutab supreme). Also, he was fighting on the main point of control over licences and salvage excavations. The new antiquities legislation would not materialize until 1978, but he did not know that. He refused to let the IES/Hebrew University take over an idea that he had started and developed so far. Yeivin also refused to discuss the museum. He controlled the IDAM museum and hoped that it would become part of a national complex of museums together with a new building for the IDAM (Ch. 10). Yeivin's words about libraries and the list of the IDAM's achievements (see p. 233) was impressive, but Mazar commented coldly on Avidor's suggestion:

The suggestion included in your letter seems to me like a return to the committee [CAAR] established by Professor Dinur [in 1953], with the addition that its discussions should include also the issue of the museum. It no doubt is a complete diversion from the things that were agreed in the meeting held at Tivʻon.

As for myself, I see no use in establishing such a council. Anyway, I will bring the matter for discussion to the appropriate bodies.

[signed] B. Mazar   (GL1430/13 no. 9903, 17.1.57)

The management committee of the IES and the Institute of Archaeology at the Hebrew University met on 18 January 1957. Mazar reported the results to Avidor:

Honourable Dr Avidor,

In continuation of my letter of 17 January 1957 I am honoured to bring to you the suggestions of the management committee of the IES and the Institute of Archaeology at the Hebrew University, as agreed in a joint meeting on 18 January 1957.

A. *Composition of the Supreme Archaeological Council*
1. Mr Z. Aranne, Minister of Education (Chair)
2. Dr M. Avidor (Director-General, Ministry of Education and Culture)
3. Mr T. Kollek (or another senior official in the Prime Minister's Office)
4. Mr S. Yeivin (Director of the IDAM)
5. Prof. B. Mazar (University/IES)
6. Dr Y. Yadin (University/IES)
7. Dr M. Stekelis (University/IES)
8. Mr M. Avi-Yonah (University/IES)
9. Mr Moshe Kol (representative of the public)

B. *Nomination*
   The council will be nominated by the Minister of Education with the approval of the government, and will hold office until the approval of a new antiquities law by Parliament [the members would have to sit for 21 years!] …

C. *Functions and authorities*
1. The council will prepare a proposal for a new antiquities law, to be presented to Parliament for approval.
2. The council will plan, coordinate and decide archaeological activity [*peʻulah*] in Israel (including archaeological excavations, surveys and publications, as well as any matters that relate to archaeology in Israel, which are brought to it by the Minister of Education).

D. *The national museum*
   The university and the society see the matter of the museum as a separate problem, which is not included in the framework of functions of

the above-mentioned council. The national museum is a state institute, which also relates to fields outside antiquities, such as art, natural
science, etc. In a meeting between the Minister of Education and the
Director-General of the Ministry of Education and Culture with the
representatives of the university and society at Tiv'on, it was suggested
that a restricted committee should be established in order to prepare the
plans for realization of the plan, composed of the Director-General of
the Ministry of Education, the Director-General of the Prime Minister's
Office and the representative of the university. An urgent meeting in
this matter must be held with the Prime Minister, the Minister of Education and the president of the university [Mazar], which will bring the
entire affair before the Prime Minister, to hasten the establishment of
that committee.

In order for the activities of the council to be valid immediately after its
nomination … it is necessary to appoint a permanent secretary for the
council.
With much honour, B. Mazar
(unsigned copy, GL1430/13 no. 9903, 22.1.57)

Mazar wanted a supreme council controlled by the Hebrew University/IES.
Six of the nine members would always back him: the four Hebrew University/IES
representatives, Kollek (or an official nominated by Kollek) and Kol (the influential head of the Jewish Agency and, since 1965, the Minister of Tourism; he
was on the IES council from 1955) (BIES **19** (1954/55): 240; **20** (1955/56): 62).
The council would decide about the antiquities legislation and about all excavations, including salvage excavations. Although the issue of the museum was
separate for now, it would be discussed at a committee that did not even include
the IDAM. Aranne was offered the temptation of the chair and responsibility for
nominations; and probably Kollek's influential support if he would support the
museum committee plan. To be honest, Yeivin's chances of coming out on top in
the conflict with the IES and Hebrew University were remote. The IDAM could
not bring to bear such heavy cannons as the President of the only university in
Israel, Kollek and a society with several thousands of members. Yeivin's Mutab
council did not meet at the house of the Israeli President.
On 5 February 1957, on receiving Mazar's letter, Yeivin wrote to Avidor:

It seems that by now matters should be very clear to everyone, although
for me they were totally clear before now. The question is, in my mind,
significant and critical. Should the state be responsible for law and order,
or should one make it possible for any institution that wants [mit'aveh] to
occupy a certain field to fulfil its ambition, and bypass any customs and

laws that exist, *de jure* and *de facto*?

The IDAM wanted and will always want to cooperate with any body that holds matters of archaeology close to its heart. The IDAM itself was also the first to initiate and perform shared works such as these... [mentioning shared excavations with Stekelis and Perrot]. However, I think that cooperation means goodwill from all sides to work through constant and permanent consultation, and not by forcing obedience by one body to another and one body enforcing the cooperation of the others through complete ignorance of their needs and opinions. Out of such goodwill for cooperation the IDAM took part in the preliminary survey at Masada, and positioned itself as a partner both in allocating a scientific team and in allocating funds for the project's expenses. I must say that despite the very interesting and important scientific results, this project was not a success. The representatives of the Hebrew University acted as if all this work were theirs alone. They did not ask for the opinion of the IDAM about matters related to this work, and did not even bother to inform the IDAM about the publication of the report [Avi-Yonah *et al.* 1957], which I discovered just by coincidence.

In the past I have agreed, from the same desire to cooperate, to the suggestion of the former Minister of Education, Professor B. Z. Dinur, to establish a "Scientific Committee for the Advancement of Archaeological Research", to be joined by the IDAM, the Archaeological Department of the Hebrew University, and the IES, chaired by the Minister of Education. The files of the IDAM hold a memorandum about the composition and areas of authority of this committee and on that memorandum the Minister of Education added a handwritten note: "I agree B.D.". I attach a copy of this memorandum for your information. As you can see the following composition was decided upon: Minister of Education and Culture, chairman; two representatives of the IDAM, three of the Hebrew University and two of the IES. The three representatives of the university were to be Professor Mayer, Professor Sukenik and Dr Stekelis.   (GL44880/12 no. 3588)

Yeivin added that Sukenik was already ill, so the Hebrew University had only two representatives on the CAAR. The university never asked for a third representative to be added, and the CAAR members never commented on the nominations. The members never discussed the establishment of a supreme archaeological council (*moa'zah archeologit elyonah*), for:

It was clear that an archaeological council [the Mutab advisory archaeological council] exists and is by law affiliated to the IDAM, according to the regulations of antiquities published in the annals (no. 79 of 28.3.1950). Twenty-five members participate in it, including seven representatives of governmental bodies and 18 representatives of the public [Yeivin added details and a list of members]. I must note that all the members of the above-mentioned scientific committee are also members of the advisory archaeological Mutab (the archaeological council).

I see no reason to change the face of the presently existing archaeological council. Furthermore, it is also impossible legally, unless the minister publishes altered regulations that annul the existing ones. I already told you my opinion that the matter of the said scientific committee for the advancement of archaeological research can be legally arranged like this: it can be regarded as a sub-committee of the archaeological council ... If memory serves me right, I spoke about it with Professor Dinur at the time; and he thought that this could be done also in order to invest the said committee with legal standing. However, on this point I have no written documents. I also see no reason to insult the present members of the archaeological council (the Mutab advisory archaeological council) by dispersing the council, nominating another one, and not including most members in the new one. [Added in handwriting: By law one has to consult with the present council about the amendment of the regulations for appointing a new council.]

You will yourself understand that this attitude seems to me correct and right for the situation, and it completely disqualifies the attitude of Professor Mazar to the whole issue. We are not discussing a supreme archaeological council, but a limited body designed for certain purposes ... So the composition suggested in Professor Mazar's letter is groundless. I do not object to the Director-General of the Ministry of Education and Culture joining the said committee; nor will I object if the Hebrew University demands three representatives and not two; but I see no point in adding to this committee a representative of the Prime Minister's Office who has no relation to the matter. There certainly need not be a representative of the public, for the committee deals with scientific matters, and representatives of the public sit on the existing archaeological council. Incidentally, I wonder why the name of Professor Mayer was dropped from the new list suggested by Professor Mazar, although I can imagine the reasons for this. Professor Mayer is not one of the sworn "boom" speakers [probably meaning "yes-man"].

(cont. GL44880/12 no. 3588)

Yeivin also objected to the idea of decisions being made by the government. Nomination of the Director of the IDAM did not require approval of the government, so one could not "place above his head" an advisory council that would be approved by the government:

unless the Ministry of Education and Culture also thinks that the Director of the IDAM does not fit his position and should be some "petty official" [*pkidon*] who follows the orders of a body of supreme and wise persons that command him. I wonder whether a person of stature [*shi'ur qomah*], even if not a man of science, could be found to take up such a position; in any case, I will not. (cont. GL44880/12 no. 3588)

Yeivin stated that the proposed antiquities legislation was no business of the new committee. It had already been discussed in the Mutab and was almost ready after many hearings and appeals. Those who had worked on this law included Schwabe and Avi-Yonah from the university; Narkiss, Kaniuk, Zerah Wahrhaftig, Nebenzahl and Dr Leo Kadman. There was no reason to reopen the issue. As for the central museum, the government has to decide first if it would include exhibits from the humanities only (art and antiquities, following Dinur's proposal), or also exhibits from the natural sciences. In any case, the committee for the museum must include representatives of the IDAM, art museums and experts about museums in general, but:

> I do not see what business this is of the Hebrew University. The role of the university is to raise men of science and to nurture scientific research ... If the museum people do not meddle in university matters, although many of them have something to say and to comment about the last, I see no reason for the intervention of university people in museum matters.
> (cont. GL44880/12 no. 3588)

Yeivin added that he did not object to the nomination of an "honorary secretary", as long as it was not expensive. The IDAM was ready to continue giving technical support to the council (secretary, etc.). Yeivin insisted on one thing: that the deputy chairman would always be the Director of the IDAM, as it had been before in the Mutab council. Finally, he pointed out that these negotiations through an intermediary were cumbersome. The positions of all the sides were clear by now. It was time for the minister, Mazar and Yeivin to meet in person and "Finish the affair one way or the other; for at the end of the day, his Excellency the Minister will have to decide what he intends to do, and the sooner the better" (GL44880/12 no. 3588).

There is one more memorandum called "Headlines of proposal for discussion in a meeting of the heads of archaeological institutes in Israel". This meeting was scheduled for 2 May 1957, and Yeivin did his homework in advance. He listed four main aspects of archaeology in Israel:

> 1. Registration of the archaeological reserves in the state, supervising them and preserving them from damage. 2. Preservation, restoration and improvement of existing monuments. 3. Field research: survey and excavation; study and work on finds, publication and exhibitions. 4. Education of young students. (GL1430/13)

Yeivin relied here on the recommendations of a UNESCO committee "for archaeological problems", which advised states to maintain legal authority in this field through an antiquities department: in Israel this would be the IDAM. Aspect 4 was the business of universities and institutes of higher education; while aspects 1 and 2 were the sole responsibility of the IDAM. The IDAM could not avoid dealing with aspect 3: "For efficient supervision cannot exist without archaeological exploration and investigations in the field. An institute cannot draw on experts of high stature, without whom it will see no benefit from its work, unless it allows them large-scale archaeological research, with everything it implies" (*ibid.*).

Yeivin went on: in order for the IDAM to succeed with the three aspects (1–3), it would have to maintain close contacts with the public and encourage the public to help with its work. The IDAM could not seek a monopoly on restoration works and research, but had to encourage and promote participation of other Israeli and foreign scientific institutions and individuals in these aspects:

> This is done in Israel. The Hebrew University, in addition to its function in educating young archaeologists, is handling field research and scientific problems. The IES raises public interest in the Israeli past by various means and helps in the study projects of scholars in this field and in publishing the results. The IDAM, for its part, through the Friends of Antiquities, encourages local amateurs to help it in its work and to widen their knowledge in archaeology; and it encourages and helps with the opening of municipal museums and local collections; and tries to attract foreign scientific institutes to the country to work …   (GL1430/13)

Yeivin repeated the opinion that the coordination of archaeological work in Israel could be performed in a committee of the Mutab council, which would consist only of representatives of archaeological bodies. He suggested that the functions of such a committee would be: discussing plans for restoration and conservation; defining priorities; checking plans; looking for funds; and so on.

Yeivin's memorandum was not very clear; perhaps he was too worried about the prospects of the coming meeting. His sentences are often very long, but here they became repetitive and clumsy. The document was also too extensive to act as a guideline; the professors were not coming to hear a lecture about a theoretical case study. It is also unlikely that the IES/Hebrew University wanted to abolish the IDAM. After all, someone was needed to do the work of salvage, supervision and conservation. They just did not want a strong and independent IDAM.

Yeivin added a crucial point: without excavation there was no future for the IDAM. Here again his academic merit is evident. He felt on equal terms with the other bodies, and was not ready to have the scientific prospects of the IDAM dwarfed by them. Yeivin offered one concession: the new council should be involved with the planning of restoration and conservation. This was insignificant, since by that time the GTC was the dominant power in that field. Yeivin was offering something that he no longer controlled. He also tried to appeal to the emotions:

> The first condition for such cooperation is the goodwill of all the bodies that need to cooperate in this enterprise. It must be stressed beforehand that cooperation means shared and free discussion between all the partners ... and honest action together ... not occupation and imposition of the will and methods of one partner over the others. The second is a clear definition of the special roles of each partner in such a cooperation, and a lack of interference from the others in the fields of activity that are specific to each and every partner ... A third condition to such efficient working together is that each partner performs the shared tasks with honesty and loyalty, both scientific and economic ...
>
> It seems to me that without consideration and acknowledgement of these principles there will be no value in any agreement in the said matter. A sense of contempt and the lowering of the value of one partner by another will muddle the cooperative work from the start.   (GL1430/13, cont.)

The meeting of 2 May 1957 took place, as a short handwritten note by Yeivin proves. The note is confused (maybe written during the meeting). For example: "Authority. Sections 2, 3 of my memorandum. Answering Mazar: power of decision and authority. Where does the IDAM decide? How can a council enforce? Why is archaeological policy needed? ..." (GL44889/2).

When he retired in 1959, Yeivin referred to the debate in the press: "the issue was whether the department should merely act as an inspector of the Antiquities Law, or be a scientific body with a scientific archaeological programme" (*Jerusalem Post*, 10.7.1959, copy in GL44868/7). The newspaper *Haboqer* portrayed the debate thus:

> *A Mandatory Period Tradition.* Our institutions that handle archaeology find it difficult to adapt to state conditions. The University and the IES claim that they have carried Hebrew archaeology on their backs; that they indeed have acted for the benefit of Hebrew archaeology for dozens of years, standing against the narrow-mindedness of the Mandatory Authority, which wanted to suppress the Jewish side of the science of archaeology in the country. In their view, their past rights necessitate their consideration now. The governmental antiquities department, on the other hand, claims that by giving up the right to be responsible for supervision and in initiating activities, and without making excavations, the department is to deteriorate.

For the time being one does not see the way to achieve compromise, and
Mr Kahane, one of the veteran workers at the department, remains as a
replacement deputy manager; and everybody is pleased.

(*Haboqer*, 17.10.1959)

THE CASE OF RITA R

Enter Rita R, whose case demonstrates how far the IES was prepared to go in order
to avoid recognizing the authority of the IDAM. One fine morning Mrs Rita R, a
US citizen, was injured in an accidental fall at Bet She'arim. She issued a lawsuit at
the Tel Aviv court against the Ministry of Education (the IDAM), the IES, and the
taxi company that took her to the site. The IDAM was not sued directly because
it was not an independent unit but part of the Ministry of Education. Aviram
of the IES approached Yeivin, who had known nothing about the case, and told
him that there was a first hearing at court. The defendants were a lawyer representing the Ministry of Education and a lawyer for the IES. Aviram claimed that
the ministry's lawyer could not answer the allegations, and that the IES lawyer
had tried "to save" the situation. Yeivin wrote to Staner, the legal advisor of the
Ministry of Education, on 12 September 1957, asking why he or Staner had not
been notified of the lawsuit sooner. Most of his letter discussed insurance to the
general public in historical sites. As for the present case, he wrote:

> Usually all ancient sites are supervised by the IDAM. But I think that one
> should understand that this supervision is only from the scientific side. The
> state just supervises to ensure that the remains of the past do not collapse
> or suffer damage, but is not responsible for damage that may be caused to
> people through lack of caution, when they enter such areas …

Yeivin admitted that the IDAM had a guard at Beth She'arim, but only to keep the
antiquities safe. If the guard also acted as a guide, this was through some private
agreement with the IES, unrelated to the IDAM. The IDAM had not published
any notices or invitations to the public to visit this site. Hence, wrote Yeivin,
the section of Rita's suit saying "and the prosecutor was present in those rooms
as invited for some interest mutual to her and to the prosecuted" was not true;
nor did it concern the government (GL44883/7 no. 5842). Much later (27.10.57)
the lawyer for the Ministry of Education complained that the court had taken
preliminary evidence only because Rita R was returning to the US. The lawyers
agreed that the IES lawyer would question her first; at this stage they did not
answer any claims and the story of "saving" the situation is farcical (GL44873/7
no. 3512a/57). Yeivin issued an apology of a kind to the lawyer representing the

Ministry of Education, who had received Yeivin's letter asking why they had not been informed of the case sooner (GL44873/7 no. 4242). Staner used Yeivin's arguments in a letter to the district attorney of Tel Aviv, writing that the IDAM was not involved as its supervision on sites was only scientific, similar to the supervision of the Ministry of Education over private schools; the owners of private schools were responsible for any damage. Staner added:

> I tried to find the legal nature of defendant No. 2 [=IES]. I am told it is an "Ottoman" association [not for profit], but the supervisor of the Jerusalem district did not find its name in his list. I also talked to lawyer Yehudah Lumbroso on behalf of defendant No. 2, who told me that he presented a defence paper in this case and his general claim is that all the responsibility falls on the IDAM, since the society [IES] does not operate the concession [*zikayon*]. I am sending a copy of his letter to the Director of the IDAM, who will surely respond to this claim.   (GL44883/7 no. 3804)

What the IES lawyer meant was explained by Yeivin in his answer:

> From a strictly legal position it is true that this year the IES did not renew its request to excavate at Bet She'arim; and from this perhaps a "keen" (*meful-pal*) lawyer may free it from any responsibility for what is done there. But now it was evident that it [IES] also did not ask to renew its licence last year, yet still excavated there. Indeed, the supervision of the IDAM is to blame here; it did not see this flaw in the proper administrative procedure. How-ever, even if the IES has no legal connection to the Bet She'arim excavation, in all its acts, publicity and propaganda it declares day and night its rela-tion to the site and its intention to continue excavating there. Also about restoring the site and making it an attraction for visitors ... This fact it cannot deny and the GTC will also testify that all the negotiations about the improvement and restoration of the ancient site of Bet She'arim were made directly between the IES and the GTC ...   (GL44883/7 no. 5925)

Yeivin added that in archaeology the custom was always that excavators were responsible for the safety of their areas of excavation; this is also true today. Staner therefore wrote to the Tel Aviv district attorney that the prosecutor was a licensee only, not an invitee; giving legal precedents that, in her view, proved that if a public authority did not fulfil a statutory obligation, the procedure was not to sue it for damages but to appeal to the highest court (GL44883/7 no. 3880). Still, she asked for a copy of the IES's excavation licence. Yeivin sent her the licence of 1955, explaining that in 1956 as well as in 1957 the IES had excavated without asking to renew its licence. It had been "revealed just now on account of a regular review (*bdikat shigra*)" (GL44883/7 no. 5977).

According to the ethic of the period, excavators acquired long-term rights on sites. If someone excavated a site, it was "his" until he died or announced that it was available for others. The problem was not the rights of excavators, though. The IES saw Bet She'arim as private property. For two years it had not bothered to ask for a licence, although it only needed to send a request to the IDAM. Yeivin's words about supervision of the IDAM being to blame, or "regular reviews" were clumsy excuses. If the IDAM had bothered to carry out any checks before the case of Rita R forced itself upon it, the lack of a licence would have been discovered. The excuses miss the point: nobody in Israel could fail to notice that Bet She'arim was being excavated. After all, as Yeivin plainly said, everybody knew about it.

The real problems were twofold. First, the IES defied the authority of the IDAM to such an extent that it preferred to disregard the regulations rather than seek a legal licence from the IDAM. Secondly, the IDAM displayed a complete lack of response, preferring to play ostrich. Probably Bet She'arim was not the only example. As the Mutab council ceased to exist in late 1956, there was no procedure for consultation and approval of requests for licences. Licences in this period were given by the IDAM alone, if at all.

As for Rita R, we do not know how her case ended, but later, a line item for insurance to visitors in archaeological sites was added to the IDAM's budget (GL44884/7, 1963–64).

BORN OUT OF TORMENT: THE SECOND ARCHAEOLOGICAL COUNCIL

In 1959, Mazar spoke at the IES council meeting, and "stressed the need to establish a supreme archaeological council … With the retirement of Mr Sh. Yeivin, the Director of IDAM, the matter became much more urgent" (*BIES* **24** (1959/60): 68). A year later, a description of a meeting of the IES general assembly of 16 March 1960 expressed again "the urgent need to establish the supreme archaeological council" (*ibid.*: 283).

Yeivin's retirement removed a major obstacle to making reality the professors' fantasy: a supreme archaeological council. This was the meaning of the "urgency": now was the time to act because Kahane (Yeivin's replacement at the IDAM) lacked his status. However, the urgency also had other reasons, not explained by Mazar: it is the peculiar history of the origin of the second archaeological council, which still functions as Israel's highest archaeological body.

Until 1959 the debate was at stalemate. We can guess why: the decision could be made only by the Minister of Education. There was no middle ground; one had to choose a side. It was bound to be difficult, so Aranne decided not to decide. An outside semblance of business as usual was kept up. For example,

Yeivin spoke at the IES annual conferences and was elected to its council (*BIES* 22 (1957/58): 102–3). But the IES/Hebrew University increased in power: in 1957 the former Minister of Education, Dinur, received an honorary professorship from the university (*IEJ* 1957: 129). This was fine in itself, but it could influence the current minister, particularly when you add the large coalition of Mazar, Yadin (now with the prestige of Hazor), Kollek and Dayan. There were also influential awards and gifts. In 1960–61, the GTC issued silver "Bar Kochba" medallions, delivered to the President of Israel, Dayan and Mazar (*BIES* 25 (1960/61): 108), and in September 1961 the GTC gave a gift to the participants of the IES annual conference (*ibid.*: 261). Mazar had family connections with President Ben-Zvi and the two families lived close to one another in the Jerusalem neighbourhood of Rehavyah (Ben-Arieh 2001: 333). What could the IDAM offer in return? That Aranne did not decide against Yeivin earlier is praiseworthy in terms of what we hear about present-day "realpolitik" in Israel.

While the idea of the "Supreme Scientific Committee" was postponed, the Mutab council effectively ceased to exist. After 1956 the nominations were not renewed. Yeivin wrote to the Minister of Education on 16 March 1959:

> According to the law the Minister of Education must set up an archaeological council (section 23, 1). One of the duties of the council is to review requests for excavation licences and give an opinion on them, so I fear the IDAM may be mixed up in legal difficulties in relation to issuing excavation licences to foreign expeditions if any legal fault is found in the legality of the membership of the council members ... I therefore ask you to renominate the members of the council ...   (GL44865/9 no. 1122)

Yeivin also offered a list of nominations, a fair one, with seven representatives from the Hebrew University/IES: Mazar, Yadin, Avigad, Avi-Yonah, Prawer, Mayer and Stekelis. However, the council was not reestablished, and on 1 August 1959 Yeivin retired. The Ministry of Education and Culture seemed unperturbed until a very peculiar thing happened, signalling the start of a new archaeological council.

It so happened that the advisory archaeological Mutab council had a representative on another council in Israel, the Supreme Council of Archives, which was trying to find a replacement. Sh. Rosenthal (almost certainly Eliezer Shimshon Rosenthal (1915–80), a noted linguist and Talmud scholar, and professor at the Hebrew University) described what happened next:

> To: Manager of the State Archive
> From: Sh. Rosenthal, member of the Supreme Council of Archives
> *Subject: Representation of the Advisory Archaeological Council in the Supreme Council of Archives*

In the last meeting of the Supreme Council of Archives of 9 June 1960, it was suggested that the recommendation is put to the government to add a representative of another institution instead of that of the advisory archaeological council; since the last has ceased to exist. I noted immediately that this is impossible. Although the council can, under section 3 paragraph (4) of the law of archives recommend that representatives of other bodies are added, it is impossible that they replace the one of the advisory archaeological council. I wish to explain it in more detail.

The advisory archaeological council is represented in the archives council by law, in accordance to section 3 paragraph 3 of the law. Nobody has the right, not even the government, to abolish this representation. It is possible only by changing the law [on 21.7.60 Staner added next to this line: "he is right"].

If this representation is cancelled, or even if one avoids inviting the representative of the advisory archaeological council for the discussions of [our] council, it could have severe legal consequences. One might claim, with a high possibility of accuracy, that resolutions accepted in council without such an invitation have no legal validity.

The advisory archaeological council exists under the authority of paragraph 23 of the Law of Antiquities. Its composition and duties (and they are very distinguished) were set up in the regulations of antiquities of 21 January 1930 ... Therefore the claim that allegedly this council does not exist is strange [tmuhah]. It lives and exists under the force of the said legislation.

If one wants to abolish it, there is no other way to do so except by changing the legislation. As long as that is not done, the advisory archaeological council exists by any means ...   (GL1430/13 no. 1/4/357, 20.6.60)

It was even stranger than that because the last legally nominated representative, Professor Avi-Yonah, had died in the meantime. Staner, the legal advisor at the Ministry of Education, wrote immediately to the deputy minister. She explained the law about representation in the Supreme Council of Archives, then wrote:

So far, all is fine. From here on, the mess begins:
3. Attached is ... the letter of Sh. Rosenthal of 20 June 1960. I fully endorse the attitude and explanations of Mr Rosenthal. The trouble comes from not listening to the demands of the former Director of the IDAM, Mr Yeivin. Explanation follows:
4. On 16 March 1959 Mr Yeivin sent a letter to the then Minister of Education, Mr Zalman Aranne [reference]. In it Mr Yeivin explained the legal situation and suggested that new members should be nominated

for the advisory archaeological council. As you can see in the file, no action was taken.

5. One of the consequences of the lack of action mentioned in the last paragraph is that the "representational status" of Mr Avi-Yonah is placed in doubt (since his "employer", the council, expired). And in addition to that, the mere attendance or existence of a deceased (*bar-minan*) representative raises doubts, as explained in Rosenthal's letter. All this, without mentioning the just fears and legal requests of the former Director of the IDAM, Mr Yeivin ...   (GL1430/13 no. 9903, 22.6.60)

Staner explained that nominating someone else, even with the approval of the government, did not solve the entanglement: it would take a lot of time and did not solve the problem of the inexistence of the archaeological advisory council. She advised that members should immediately be nominated to the archaeological advisory council following Yeivin's suggestion; then the council itself could nominate someone to the Supreme Council of Archives.

So thanks to the Supreme Council of Archives, the Minister of Education had to renew the archaeological council. Biran, then Director of the IDAM, was in close contact with Mazar and the IES. Biran was not going to quarrel with them and his suggestion for the renewal of the archaeological council abandoned all the points made by Yeivin. Biran suggested at first having eight representatives on the council: four from the university and IES and one from the Committee for the Improvement of the Landscape and Historical Sites of the GTC (it is no surprise that this was Kollek). The IDAM and the Ministry of Education and Culture together would have only two representatives. Furthermore, the new council would "discuss the planning of archaeological activity in the country, coordinating archaeological excavations, etc."; and the Director of the IDAM would bring to it all requests for excavation licences. Biran also dropped the word "advisory" from the title and suggested that the council itself would choose its chairman and deputy chairman (GL1430/13, 22.8.61).

Staner (GL1430/13 no. 9903, 22.8.61) tried to warn against these changes. The removal of "advisory" might cause misunderstandings, as the council might believe in the future that it was responsible for making decisions pertaining to, and not just advising, the IDAM. Biran (GL1430/13 no. 9278) replied that the former council had not worked, whereas his suggestion could work. Staner was only a professional official, tackling legal aspects. This is what she wrote to Biran on 22 September 1961:

Attached is the suggestion for regulations. If it seems fine to you (more or less), please return it to me (with or without amendments), so that I can pass it to the Ministry of Justice, before suggesting that the Minister [of Education] sign it.

> I have tried as far as possible to draft the regulations following your instructions, but you will understand that in those cases where the law itself does not permit it, I was forced to submit to its demands.
>
> (GL1430/13 no. 9903, 22.9.61)

The new archaeological council, based on regulations published on 28 June 1962, included Mazar as chairman and Biran as deputy chairman. The Hebrew University and IES were the only archaeological bodies represented except the IDAM, and they had a guaranteed majority. Yeivin was given an honorary position, but retired after the first meeting (GL1430/13, 7.11.62). The celebratory first meeting of the council was held at the home of the President of Israel on 24 July 1962. Mazar chaired it, opening with a long digression on the history of the IES. Biran replied with blessings:

> Dear President, if you allow it, I would also like to bless what has been done, and bless the Minister of Education and ourselves, for we have a council that includes the best people, who hold the exploration of the history of the country close to their hearts. Especially I would like to bless the council for placing at its head the man [Mazar] who symbolizes the progress of archaeology in the country and the study of the knowledge of the country by the Hebrew University and the IES. These institutions, together with the IDAM, carried the burden of research with love, endurance and consistency. (GL1430/13, minutes of meeting 24.7.62: p. 6)

The change in atmosphere finds expression in many other documents, but it was a serpent's kiss; the IDAM was subjugated and placed in a subordinate position. For example, see Biran's blessing for the IES: "The IDAM, which is a branch of the solid trunk [*geza*], with many branches, of the IES" (in Aviram 1965: xii). Never mind the tortuous metaphor, this was not the truth. The truth was that the IDAM sprang from the Mandatory period Department of Archaeology, and thus was based on the British tradition.

The new archaeological council started to function, although Mazar immediately left Israel for seven months. He remained as chair until 1992 (*IEJ* 1995: 210). The council's troubled origins were not mentioned in its first meeting, apart from a few words by Biran, who said that the council was "born in torment" [*yisurim*] (GL1430/13, minutes of meeting 24.7.62).

Capitulation is evident in a letter from Katzenstein to Biran (who was abroad) of 6 March 1962, even before the new council began functioning:

> Yesterday was Yeivin's lecture on the last season at Gat. There were few people attending compared to other lectures, with nobody from the university (Yohanan Aharoni and Ruth Amiran are, of course, out of town,

but it was mentioned to others). Maybe it is good that they did not come. If you allow me to say so, it would be better if Rome did not continue its participation in [the excavations at] Gat. Excavation activity in the country is too large. I had a long talk with Mazar yesterday and he also stressed this; also Avigad told me so a short while ago, and also Aviram. True, they do not think to scale down their excavations. Indeed, they went to [excavate at] Arad, next week they will go to En-Gedi, later Bet She'arim, but if we want to work in Korazim … and Ashdod and Tell Nagilah will demand workforce, then this is enough. Mazar wanted somebody from the IDAM to join in at En-Gedi, and also at Arad, in his words because it is a unique opportunity for the young among our workers to learn something in the field. Others say it is because he needs workers. I do not know. But nobody from those who are capable want to go (Ram [Gophna], whom Mazar very much wanted for En-Gedi, is preparing for MA examinations and asked especially not to have to go on a long excavation over these months). I do not think it is possible to force them …

There are many other matters, but I do not want to confuse you. Several requests for excavation [licences] were handed in (Mazar at En-Gedi, Stekelis and his friends at Ubediyah, now Avigad told me also that he wants to go [excavate] in the university vacation, i.e. in two weeks, to a cave in En-Gedi). In all cases I just ask if all agree, and say that they will receive formal approval only when you have returned, for nobody else has the authority.   (GL44888/6, 6.3.62)

This is what the demand for coordination was all about: having the freedom to perform excavations and the power to stop others, because it was well known that there were "too many excavations". Excavation licences became documented proof of IDAM authority. The IDAM turned to makeshift procedures, following the best traditions of the days of the Yishuv, before the state of Israel was established, when resources were scanty and there was not an established "way to run things". Around 1963, after 15 years of Israeli independence, the IDAM produced a licence called "Permission" (*Harsha'ah*), not mentioned in the law. It was given to all salvage excavations, bypassing the new archaeological council. The entire legal position of salvage archaeology in Israel was thus placed in doubt, although perhaps the IDAM had no other choices remaining. However, the history of the second archaeological council is still hidden in the archives, and its decisions were never made public.

12 "BUT TRUST COMES FROM THE HEART": TRAVELS WITH THE GOVERNMENT TOURIST CORPORATION

There is nothing so contaminated with fiction as the
history of the Company.   Borges (1970: 60)

Two short letters summarize relations between the GTC and the IDAM. Dothan wrote the first letter on 27 October 1955:

> Mr D. Levinson and his entourage from the GTC, as well as his car, are permitted to enter any area of antiquities found under the protection of the IDAM. We ask all antiquities guards and employees of the IDAM to help him and to guide him if so required.   (GL44882/9 no. 9981)

Biran, Director of the IDAM, wrote the second letter on 21 December 1961:

> [To] Mr D. Levinson, the GTC
> In the current situation, it seems desirable to us for the employees of the IDAM to have a certificate from you, allowing [them] access at any time – without payment – to ancient sites held in your hands, such as Avdat and Beth-Alpha. Our workers who ought to be given such certificates are [list of 23 employees] … In fact, problems have arisen lately in two cases: A. When an employee of yours at Caesarea did not let Dr Biran and his entourage see the statue of the "City Goddess". B. When someone guarding Beth-Alpha demanded entrance fees from Mr Zori [inspector of the IDAM].
> …   (GL44882/9 no. 160)

In between these letters lay the direct cause of Yeivin's retirement and an ugly conflict. To understand it we cannot escape exploring the histories of several more councils and committees. There were minor changes in their names, and people referred to them using various unofficial names or short titles, so a concise guide to the major bodies discussed in this chapter is given in Table 4. The

Table 4. A guide to pre-GTC and GTC councils and committees.

Council/Committee	Functions	Established [disbanded]	No. of members	Significant members
Pre-GTC				
Advisory archaeological council [Mutab Archeologi Yóez], *Supreme council of the IDAM* (see Ch. 11, pp. 214–15)	• Advising the IDAM • Discussing excavation licences and policies	1951 [1956]	25	Chair: Minister of Education (Dinur). Yeivin; Kaniuk; Narkiss; Ben-Zvi; Schwabe; Stekelis; Savorai
Committee for the Preservation of Monuments [Va'ada le-Shimur Munumentim]. *Sub-committee of the Mutab* (see Ch. 11, p. 215)	• Discussing preservation and improvement of sites	1955 [1955]	c. 7	Yadin; Warhaftig; Prawer; Yeivin
Committee for the Improvement of Historical Sites and Holy Places [Va'ada le-Shipurim be-Meqomot Historiyim ve-Datiyim] (see Ch. 2, pp. 80–81)	• Implementing the conclusions of the inter-departmental committee • Preservation and improvement of sites	1954 [1955]	c. 7	Chair: Eilam. Yeivin; Arazi; Hiram
GTC period				
GTC, limited management [hanhala mezumzemet]	• Seat of power, running the GTC	1955	5–6	Chair: Kollek. Managers: Beham; Iron; Kol
GTC General Council [Móazah- or Asefah Klalit], *Equivalent to a shareholder's meeting, and devoid of power*	• Annual meeting to fulfil requirements of legal regulations for private companies	1955		
Council of the GTC [Móezet ha-Hanhala] *Yeivin variously called it moézet menahalim [council of managers], va'ad menahalim [committee of managers] and Board of Managers.* Term used here: **Board of Directors**	• A general council (not the seat of power) to advise the GTC management • No decision-making powers	December 1955	21	Chair: Kollek. Yannay; Levinson; Tannai; Kahana; representatives of government ministries, El-Al, tourist agencies, etc.
Professional Committee for the Improvement of Historical and Other Places [Va'adah Miqzó'it le-Shipur Meqomot Historiyim ve-Aherim] (with minor variations). Term used here: **expert committee [under Yannay]**	• Discussion of details of work at sites	December 1955	8–9	Chair: Yannay. Dothan; Kahana; Levinson; Tannai; representatives of government ministries
Advisory Committee for Improvement of the Landscape of the Land and for the Development of Historical Sites and Sites Related to the 1948 War [Va'ada le-Shipur Nof ha-Aretz, ha-Meqomot ha-Historiyim ve ha-Qdoshim ve ha-Meqomot ha-Qshurim le-Milhemet ha-Asma'ut] (usually abbreviated, with several variations). *Yeivin called it va'adah meya'ezet (advisory committee), va'adah ziburit (public committee) and mó'azah ziburit (public council).* Term used here: **advisory committee [under Yadin]**	• Replaced pre-GTC Committee for the Improvement of Historical Sites and Holy Places • Deciding general policy about sites (choice of site, how to improve it, etc.)	December 1955	7–8	Chair: Yadin. Members nominated by the Prime Minister, including: Yadin; Kollek; Yannay (secretary); Eilam; Carlebach; Sharon

conflict lasted from the inception of the GTC in 1955 until 1959, with two major components. The first started in 1955 and concerned the status of the IDAM; the second started in late 1957, and concerned work at sites. Bitter complaints (practically all from one side – Yeivin) often come up in letters discussing minor details of works. The facts are quite clear, but intentions are not; they need careful reconstruction, as far as possible.

THE "ORIGINAL SIN"

The conflict broke out as an immediate reaction to the establishment of the GTC. The GTC replaced the former "Tourist Centre" from 1 October 1955, following a governmental decision of 21 August 1955. The GTC announced to governmental bodies on 1 October that Kollek had been nominated as chairman of the corporation. The explicit aim of the GTC was described to be to strengthen and promote all activities related to the development of tourism. Although it would be a corporation, it would be owned by the government and would not "deal with commercial activities" nor "compete with existing bodies" (GL44892/9 no. 2535a). Two managers had already been nominated: Amos Ir'on to manage the promotion of foreign tourism (offices abroad, contacts with foreign tourist agencies, etc.) and Yohanan Beham to manage activities in Israel (hotels, tourist agencies, entertainment and "improving historical sites"). Following an objection from the IDAM and Minister of Education Dinur, the government amended its decision no. 556 of 21 August 1955:

> We decide: a) to set up a governmental corporation for developing tourism and maintaining antiquities of interest to tourists, their preservation and improvement, *with the consent and supervision of the Antiquities Department* …   (emphasis added; copy with hand-marked correction in
> G-7/5451, 22.8.55; cf. GL44882/9 letter by Z. Sheref, 12.9.1955)

What was meant by "consent and supervision"? On the surface, it seems related to the part of the sentence about antiquities, and not other aspects of tourism such as dealing with hotels or with foreign travel agencies.

The GTC was a very large undertaking from the start, and Kollek had been ready to sacrifice a lot to be the one to run it:

> To: the Prime Minister [Sharett, in office January–November 1955]
> From: Tedi Kollek
> I fly tomorrow morning to London without being certain whether I will succeed in the operation at all.

Until my return I would like to remind you again of the matter of tourism, on which we have already talked. When I first talked with you about it you were of the opinion that we ought to accept the government's decision to transfer the Ministry of Tourism to our [Prime Minister's] office even before the elections. Now, when there is only one more government meeting before that date, I would like to add that I talked about it with [Peretz] Naftali [Minister of Agriculture, 1952–55] and I think he would not oppose it on his side. Also talking to Ziameh [= Aranne] I raised the matter, and he also supports the transfer.

Ben-Gurion also supports it and I think Eshkol will not object to the transfer, although he thinks it is totally unreasonable that the Ministry of Tourism will be within the framework of the Prime Minister's Office [!].

It is difficult for me to write this last sentence, but I wish to point out that I do not see for myself at the moment a role in the Prime Minister's Office, unless the matter of tourism is added to us.

With blessing, T. Kollek

(G-2/5456, unsigned copy, no. 220/13, July 1955)

For the IDAM, an "original sin" lurked behind government decision no. 566, which marred relations with the GTC for four years. Yeivin mentioned that a verbal agreement had been made before decision no. 556 was taken: the IDAM was promised representation in the management of the GTC, so as to be a "partner to discussions and decisions about conservation and restoration of historical sites" (GL44881/13, 13.1.59). Yeivin saw the amendment to decision no. 556 as a legal basis for his claims against the GTC, so he often mentioned it.

A second announcement of the GTC stated that the management would be "activated by a council" [mo'azah] composed of representatives of government offices, tourist agents, El-Al airline, etc. (GL44882/9 no. 2535a, 6.10.55). After seeing this announcement, Yeivin wrote to Kollek on 14 October 1955:

I received the memorandum of the GTC [of 6 October] …, and to be honest I must say I found room for doubt over some parts of it. When we discussed it you indeed told me that two executive managers would be appointed to deal with administration and execution of the decisions of the corporation, but that there would be a board of directors [written twice, in English and Hebrew, although Yeivin used the English term "board of governors"], as you said, which would rule on the corporation's activities. And that there would be a representative of the IDAM on the board … So the IDAM would also have a legal status in the corporation's management; so that no action can be taken with regard to historical sites without its knowledge.

From the memorandum I learn that there is no intention to set up such a board of directors … The corporation will have only a council [mo'azah], surely with the representation of the IDAM – although this was not explicitly mentioned … As we know, a council is very different from a board of directors: it can only advise and does not make decisions; it meets occasionally … and has no hold over the corporation's activities like a board of directors.

I must say that despite the promise given in writing that nothing would be done in relation to historical sites without the approval and guidance of the IDAM, I have some concerns about the legal position of the matter. As long as the corporation is headed by the same people with whom I have negotiated, I believe that there will be no conflicts and lack of agreement on that matter, and I hope for full cooperation … But who knows who will have control after a while? As long as the IDAM has no legal position in the management of the GTC, the IDAM cannot be certain that something is not done without its consent and guidance, as far as historical sites are concerned.   (GL44882/9 no. 7864a)

What a peculiar letter. Why cast doubt in advance over nominations not yet made? The only explanation is that Yeivin expected to be one of the GTC's managers, or at least a full member of its "board of directors". This was the nature of the promise – the verbal agreement – the "original sin". The question was not just one of personal status, but mainly who would decide which sites to improve, how much budget to allocate to each site, how to plan the work and so on. The GTC did not want Yeivin involved in its management. It was ready to acknowledge the IDAM as far as ancient sites were concerned, but only as an advisor from the outside, or maybe a contractor for some works (e.g. GL44892/9, 25.10.55).

Kollek never answered Yeivin's letter. Furthermore, throughout the conflict the two almost never exchanged letters directly. Yeivin's anger (see below) was aimed directly at Kollek. All this proves that Kollek had made the verbal promise: the "original sin". As to the exact nature of the promise, we can only read between the lines and follow the "integrity" yardstick suggested by Churchill.

At this stage, Yeivin and the Minister of Education were still in the dark about the situation of Yeivin and the IDAM in relation to the GTC. When, on 16 November 1955, the GTC invited a representative of the Minister of Education to the first meeting of the GTC council (GL44882/9 no. 210/13), they hesitated. I can see no other reason for their hesitation apart from the "promise": they were not certain about the status of the council. Was this the all-important board of directors? If that was the case, Yeivin should be nominated as the representative. Or was it just some secondary committee? Until the fog cleared, the minister temporarily nominated Dothan, Yeivin's deputy.

On 18 November 1955 Shlomoh Arazi from the Ministry of Finance sent a letter to Yeivin, asking what had happened to the former "Committee for the Improvement of Historical Sites and Holy Places" (see Ch. 2). Had all the work that had started now been halted in the middle (GL44882/9 no. 23/28/10)? Yeivin answered that the committee had not ceased on its own account, but had been disbanded by the GTC. New management related to the GTC would shortly be in place, and then the committee would surely be reconvened. Yeivin even referred Arazi to Kollek (GL44882/9 no. 8299a,1.12.55). It seems that Yeivin was waiting for an invitation; followed by the renewal of the former body (cf. *Alon* **5–6** (1957): 4, written 2.11.56). Formerly, Yeivin had been emphatic on the issue of improving historical sites. He did not yet realize that Arazi's letter was the last gasp of a dying order: the new era of the GTC had begun. Indeed, a similar committee was soon renewed by the GTC under a different name, and without the involvement of the IDAM.

The first meeting of the GTC council was celebratory, held on 16 November 1955 at the Prime Minister's Office. On 1 December 1955 the GTC invited Dothan for a meeting of the Management Board (Mo'ezet ha-Hanhala; literally Management Council). Either Yeivin or Dothan marked in pencil on the invitation "Directors" above "Management", as if correcting the title of the board (GL44882/9 no. 171). This quite absurd correction reveals that the IDAM expected another body to appear – one for Yeivin to join – but an invitation was not forthcoming. To the invitation that came for Dothan was attached a list of members of the Management Board, a budget proposal, a structural diagram and the articles of the corporation (*takanon*). The structure revealed a position called "Overseer [*memuneh*] over Improvement of the Landscape in Israel and Development of Historical Sites related to the War of 1948" and also a "Unit of Sites" to work in Israel "with cooperation with various governmental and other bodies". Nominations were not yet declared for the "Overseer", so perhaps Yeivin hoped that he would be appointed. The first budget proposal for 1955/56 made no mention of historical sites. Soon the nominations were made and Yannay became the "Overseer". The articles of the GTC announced its aims in no fewer than 16 sections. Only one section was directly related to historical sites:

> 4. To preserve, develop and maintain antiquities and ancient sites, holy places and places of national interest, among other things by paving access roads … establishing and assisting museums, assisting in the performance of excavations and studies related to finding antiquities and monetary help for the said aims by any means.
>
> (G-7/5451, copy in GL44882/9)

Yeivin received the articles (through Dothan) and made a handwritten note next to section 4: "as written in the government decision – only by consent of the IDAM!" Beside section 6, which allowed the GTC to sell, exchange or rent any property, Yeivin wrote: "limitation in case of ancient sites". He sent the articles with his notes to Staner, but she answered on 4 December 1955:

> I do not think that we need suggest any changes. I do not approve the ink-marked notes on the side, since clearly a memorandum and the articles of a corporation do not give it any rights that stand against the law or the regulations. Therefore, the status of the corporation in relation to the Law of Antiquities and the IDAM is like the status of any person or body interested in antiquities. There is no need to "hammer home" limits (*li-qbo'ah be-masmerot hagbalot*) that the law has already declared.
>
> (GL44882/9 no. 540/9/2-397)

Yeivin had no legal justification for his demand to be a manager in the GTC. It was not mentioned in decision no. 566 or in the legislation. He lacked the power to change the constitution of the GTC. Kollek, Beham and Ir'on had a powerful base in the Management Board, probably a secured majority. Adding Yeivin to this body would not give him real power. The GTC also had a general council, but it was a rubber-stamping body, which met once a year only because it was necessary under the regulations for private corporations (G-6/5450, G-1/6878). According to the articles, all power was vested in the hands of Kollek, Ir'on and Beham. The body actually ruling the GTC was a limited management team of not more than five or six people, dominated by the same triumvirate, with the addition of Kol. What power could Yeivin wield there? To make matters worse for Yeivin, Minister of Education Dinur was replaced by Aranne in November 1955. Aranne was not a witness to the verbal promise and had now to back the small IDAM against the Goliath, the GTC. Perhaps Yeivin did not understand the GTC circles of power for a while; of course, he did not have all the documents at hand. Even at this stage he was fighting for justice; power was out of his reach.

Soon the GTC appointed an expert committee (*va'ada miqzo'it*) under Yannay, who was now called the "Supervisor of Development of Historic Sites and Landscape Preservation" (this title replacing the previously mentioned "Overseer" of the "Sites Unit"). It was meant to discuss matters of planning and execution, and the Minister of Education would have a representative on that committee. Again Dothan was nominated (GL44882/9 no. 891, 13.12.55) to sit on this committee.

Yeivin's hopes of involvement were finally shattered when the media ran the following story:

> *Historical Sites Committee Meets*
> The first meeting of the committee recently appointed by Prime Minister David Ben-Gurion to advise on the preservation of the country's landscape and also of its many historical sites and places associated with the war of independence was held yesterday. The committee is composed of *Rav-Aluf* Yigael Yadin (Chairman), *Aluf-Mishne* N. Z. Aharoni, Mr Y. Eilam, Mr Y. Yannay, Mr T. Kollek, Dr A. [Azriel] Carlebach, editor of *Ma'ariv*, and the

architect Mr A. [Arieh] Sharon. Mr Yannay, who will work jointly with the
PM's Office and the GTC, will be in charge of planning.

(Jerusalem Post, 27.12.1955)

Yeivin realized that, unlike Yadin, he was not an invited guest to the feast of the
GTC, but the meat. He erupted in an angry "confidential" letter to Avidor on
28 December 1955:

> At the time his Excellency the Minister of Education agreed to include the
> handling of restoration and maintenance projects at historical sites as one
> of the roles of the GTC ... on the explicit condition that nothing would be
> done without former consultation with the IDAM about planned projects
> as well as about their practical execution ... This condition was placed in
> the amended government decision about this matter.
>
> As you know, an advisory archaeological council (Mutab) exists related
> to the IDAM, whose members are nominated by the Minister of Educa-
> tion. It exists by law ... and it has a sub-committee for the preservation
> of ancient sites, their restoration and maintenance ... I have read in the
> newspaper that an advisory committee [under Yadin] *(va'adah meya'ezet)*
> has been nominated by the Prime Minister's Office, and included in its
> plan of activities is the preservation of historical sites ...
>
> I do not know who needs this duplication and why. On the one hand
> we have the IDAM's Mutab with seven official members (state employees)
> and 18 representatives of the public, mostly archaeologists; and on the
> other hand suddenly we have a second committee in the PM's Office with,
> according to the newspaper, four official members and three representatives
> of the public ... Furthermore, the real man in charge himself, that is, the
> representative of the IDAM, was not added at all [to the new advisory com-
> mittee under Yadin]. It [IDAM] is the only body with expertise in matters of
> ancient sites and their preservation. With all the respect and friendship I
> feel for Dr Y. Yadin as [someone of] great knowledge and very great talent,
> his experience in matters of preservation of ancient sites and in matters of
> archaeological work cannot be very great ...
>
> (GL4480/13 no. 8530a; copy in GL44881/13)

Yeivin continued: he had tried to arrange an interview with the Minister of
Education, who had been too busy; but the matter could not be passed over in
silence. The IDAM gave its consent to the GTC being involved in the development
of historical sites, wishing to cooperate and prevent duplication, but "efficiency
necessitates efficiency in all matters, including advisory committees". If two
committees remained, but the "the representative of the IDAM" had "a decisive
opinion" on the GTC's committee, the latter would be redundant: "what value

will its decisions have if they divert from or oppose the courses of action that follow the IDAM guidelines?" Yeivin expressed fears that the GTC did not intend to cooperate with the IDAM. To avoid difficulties and duplication, the Prime Minister's Office should be asked to remove the matter of historical sites from the activities of the new advisory committee under Yadin. However: "If it is not achievable and only as a second line of defence ... one must require that representatives of the IDAM are added to it – a director or a deputy director and a conservator of monuments" (GL44880/13 no. 8530a, copy in GL44881/13).

On 5 January 1957 Kollek wrote to Yeivin directly (it is unclear whether he was aware of Yeivin's letter of 28 December):

> Two weeks ago the PM nominated a public committee [the advisory committee under Yadin] whose role is to advise the PM's Office and the GTC how to handle preservation of the landscape and how to develop the historical sites and the sites related to the war of independence. This means that the committee will have to consult in the area that belongs to you, which places to represent and how to represent them.
>
> We want to dedicate the second meeting of the committee to discussing archaeological sites along these lines. Therefore, I would be grateful if you could notify me as soon as possible who you will nominate to participate in this meeting so that he can explain the entire problem and give us a picture about what is being done; also bring to the committee a list of places that the IDAM think should be improved and restored for visits by tourists.
>
> (GL44882/9 no. 7020; Kollek gave all letters in this file the same number, and often his letters were dated only by months)

This was not a letter of appeasement; it spoke only about an invitation to one specific meeting of a committee (under Yadin), and not to the Management Board. Much later, on 13 January 1959, Yeivin noted that despite Kollek's words about the "area that belongs to the IDAM", no IDAM representative had been invited to the more important committee (he called it the "public committee" (*va'adah ziburit*), meaning the advisory committee chaired by Yadin). Yeivin explained: "This meant that the decision of how and what to do in improving ancient sites was completely taken out of the hands of the IDAM, in complete opposition to the government's decision and to what was agreed [verbally] before this decision was made" (GL44881/13, 13.1.59).

While speaking in the name of legality, in his letter to Avidor of 28 December, Yeivin had made it clear that he would agree to the new committee under Yadin, at the price of two IDAM representatives (although this was not the all-powerful Management Board, but a secondary committee). Still, the issue was critical for his honour and the status of the IDAM. He asked Avidor to approach Kollek, and Avidor sent Kollek a letter on 8 January 1957. Avidor was faithful to Yeivin.

He started by noting that they had learned from the newspapers about the new advisory committee (chaired by Yadin), and that it duplicated the Mutab council's sub-committee for preservation:

> Why this duplication? What is the connection between the said committee at your office and the IDAM? It seems to me that the problem must be amended by one of two possibilities: A. Take out from the frame of discussion of the said advisory committee [under Yadin] the matter of historical sites; or B. Add to the committee two IDAM representatives – the Director or his deputy and the conservator of monuments.
>
> (GL44882/9 no. 9931-18)

We also know that Yeivin went to meet Kollek personally in his office, most probably after making an appointment, but Kollek wrote to him later to explain that he had had to appear in Parliament and could not even phone his office to let Yeivin know that he would be unable to meet him (GL44882/9, 9.1.56). Kollek answered Avidor on 10 January 1958:

> The committee [va'adah] for advice on improvement of the landscape of the country, historical places and places related to the war of independence [Yadin's advisory committee], established by the PM's Office, handles only matters that relate to what and how to show to tourists. As for the area of antiquities, the committee members will be glad to hear the opinion of the IDAM, which will always be the body to decide the form of the preservation and restoration of the antiquities. The members of the committee will be free to decide about priorities in regard to the presentation of the sites.
>
> From this you will understand that there is no duplication between the committee at the PM's office and the [Mutab council's] sub-committee for preservation of ancient sites in the IDAM. Also I see no need to add a representative of the IDAM as a permanent member to the advisory committee, since Mr Dothan of the IDAM is a member of the expert committee [under Yannay], whose role is to advise about each and every plan. This expert committee will decide about restorations, etc.
>
> With blessings, T. Kollek   (GL44882/9, no. 7020)

The Management Board and the expert committee [under Yannay] that Dothan sat on met several times. Yeivin was even present at two meetings of the expert committee (on 22.4.56 and 10.2.57) and was treated with respect. As for the advisory committee chaired by Yadin, it did not enter the sphere of knowledge of the IDAM. On 1 May 1956, after a meeting with Minister of Education Aranne on 25 February 1956, Yeivin sent him a letter about "the advisory committee of the GTC, whose authority includes also advice in matters of ancient sites [under Yadin]" (GL44882/9 no. 795). It was a draft that Yeivin intended to send later to the Prime Minister, but it never reached its destination. In it, Yeivin again explained about the overlap of the GTC and Mutab council committees. The document is important in understanding the Mutab council, although its sub-committee for preservation was not itself required by law, but was an internal body. Yeivin stressed the issue of duplication. He suggested that apart from the Hebrew University representatives, the composition of the new GTC advisory committee under Yadin was not archaeological and lacked expertise. He quoted the amendment to decision no. 556 and noted that "of course, there can be no agreement or supervision of the IDAM over a council that the IDAM did not nominate and is not part of". He again offered two alternatives. The first was to take out historical sites from the authority of the new advisory committee. Then the GTC would have to consider the opinion of the sub-committee of the Mutab council, reaching final decisions only with the consent of IDAM representatives "in the executive management of the GTC" (of which there were none). The second (strange) option was "a merger" of the two committees into one that would advise the two bodies. Still, the IDAM would retain its rights according to decision no. 556. Finally, Yeivin mentioned that it was not a theoretical problem; the new advisory committee had already accepted plans of its own, ignoring existing IDAM plans (GL44882/9).

A few months passed and on 17 March 1957 Yeivin sent Avidor another long letter, reopening the issue (GL44880/12 no. 3950, copy in GL44882/9). It was headed "Relations between the IDAM and the GTC". Yeivin wrote that he had several times drawn attention to the problem of "undesired relations" because of the unilateral action by the GTC that had broken the verbal agreement. The GTC should have invited the IDAM to sit on its Management Board (*hanhala*), and this was the meaning of the amendment to decision no. 556. But the GTC Management Board included Kollek, Beham and Ir'on. When Yeivin had asked, he was told this was just the "practical management" and that Beham and Ir'on were just "officials that receive salary" (meaning not real managers; probably said ironically, directed towards Yeivin!). Yeivin was told that there would be a council (*moa'zah*) to run the corporation. A council of sorts was formed and Dothan was nominated to it, which Yeivin had agreed to, hoping that this was the important body. However:

> My understanding was mistaken. Suddenly the IDAM was surprised by an announcement in the press about the nomination of a public committee [the advisory committee under Yadin] for those same functions that were relegated – in the first place by the articles of the corporation and by the [verbal] agreement – to the council I mentioned earlier. In this new committee the IDAM has no representation, although several other government offices have ... I protested immediately, and you [Avidor] wrote about it to

the Director General of the Prime Minister's Office [Kollek]. Although his answer was not sufficient, no action has since been taken by the Ministry of Education.

Now we have been confronted by a new fact. Slowly and without a word the former GTC Council [with Dothan] has been "buried", and instead a new and strange body has come to light, an "expert committee" [under Yannay] (*va'adah miqzo'it*), although indeed a representative of the IDAM is in place on it.   (GL44882/9 cont.)

This is the history – now for the core of the conflict:

The IDAM does not see itself as just as a professional advisor in the matter of preserving and improving ancient sites, but as a full partner in this task, and the senior and decisive partner. Since the expenses for these needs are provided by the GTC, it might have its own considerations in setting the projects. The IDAM would be ready to listen to its arguments and to consider them, reaching some agreed order of work through a concentrated discussion between equal partners. But the IDAM is not ready to be a professional advisor in decisions thrown on it from above by a foreign body that rules things, without knowing the special conditions and needs for the restoration and improvement works. This was not the agreement before the corporation was established, when the IDAM counted on the [verbal] agreement and the position of his Excellency the [former] Minister of Education and Culture, Professor B. Z. Dinur.

Recently, I received a letter from the GTC with a report of a meeting that I attended discussing improvement and restoration for the next year. The GTC council [with Dothan] was one matter, and now suddenly an expert committee [under Yannay] has been revealed. Had I known of it, I would never have bothered to attend its meeting, nor let the representative of the IDAM do so.

From the point of view of the GTC matters are clear. One cannot hold two councils with conflicting authorities, and one has no need to. So the first GTC council was taken down to the level of an expert committee [under Yannay] after the advisory committee [under Yadin] was nominated. But this was not the agreement.

Incidentally, I must note that the whole matter was a bad deal. I do not know, nor care to know, what the GTC does in its many areas of interest. But in the matter of preserving and restoring sites it does almost nothing above what was done already by the shared [former] committee of the Tourist Centre and other government offices, including the IDAM [i.e. the Committee for the Improvement of Historical Sites and Holy Places, with Yeivin, Levinson etc.]. Even in matters for which money was set aside for preservation, such as the old quarter in Jaffa, the money has not reached its target … The IDAM, with its tiny budget for restoration, has a few times done more.

I therefore ask that this matter is brought to a conclusion once and for all: either give the IDAM proper representation on the council that determines the activities of the GTC, or take this matter out of the hands of the GTC.

(GL44882/9 no. 3950)

The claim that the IDAM did much was perhaps true (the tempo of GTC work on sites grew only in 1958), but it was a mistake to use it to argue his case. Yannay used it sharply after Yeivin pleaded for the budget to save Accho:

The matter is a bit strange in my eyes. In all your latest letters you point out that you are the "boss" (ba'al bayit) over all sites, and rely on governmental decisions and on various sections of law, etc. If this is so, why do you keep demanding that we take action to prevent collapses, etc.? I think the IDAM should take care of it … We know our own field exactly, which is improvement and restoration related to, and aimed at, easing visits by tourists. This is not personal, as in fact we want to help in such cases …

(23.2.58 no. 5700; cf. no. 6035; G13-5451, 1.11.59)

One rarely wins by caring more about something when the opposing side has the power and the budget. Yeivin's words about his willingness to hear the considerations of the GTC were the exact opposite of the real situation: would the GTC be ready to listen to the considerations of the IDAM? As for lack of competence, Yeivin presented no evidence; work on sites had so far continued without serious protest. Avidor did not save Yeivin this time, but delivered his letter to the GTC. Yannay (not Kollek!) answered on 8 April 1957:

1. I was very sorry, but I had to read the said letter a few times to be convinced that it was indeed written by Mr Yeivin.
2. Throughout the period I have worked in preservation of sites (a year and half or so), it is the first time I have seen such claims by Mr Yeivin. So far I was under the impression that we work in full understanding with the IDAM. There was no case where we did not share in some work with the IDAM, or reject its decision in matters under its supervision.
3. As for representation of the IDAM, Mr Dothan, Deputy Director of the IDAM is attending as a member of the GTC council and also as a member of the expert committee [under Yannay], which among other things deals with historical sites. When Mr Yeivin speaks about the public council, he probably means the Committee for Improvement of the Landscape of the Land [the advisory committee under Yadin]. As

we have already answered him, representatives of governmental offices were not nominated to this committee. Nomination was certainly personal and made by the PM [true, except perhaps Eilam; but there was no reason not to nominate Yeivin]. It is not true that the Committee for Improvement of the Landscape of the Land was "slowly buried without a word" and replaced by the "expert committee"... The Committee for Improvement of the Landscape of the Land exists and acts, and will continue to. [Yannay confuses the committees and councils here, because Yeivin's letter was confusing in its mention of the "council" of management. Yeivin claimed that the first GTC council, with Dothan, which was supposed to be the seat of real power (the Board of Directors) had been replaced by the committee under Yadin, and hence restructured into a secondary "expert committee" under Yannay.]

It is true that the expert committee [under Yannay] was established in the same month as the Committee for Improvement of the Landscape of the Land [under Yadin] was ... Mr Dothan, Yeivin's representative, participates permanently in [the former] ...

4. I do not accept Mr Yeivin's extreme view that he is ready to hear the corporation's opinion about sites since it holds the budget. In the field of improving the beauty of the landscape as a whole the GTC has interests of its own, which it must first and foremost consider. For historical sites, the IDAM is a factor and I will always be glad to work with it in cooperation, and in certain cases, purely professionally, even accept its direction [*marut*] ... (GL44880/12 no. 471; copy in GL44882/9)

Yannay asked why, since Yeivin and Dothan had both attended the expert committee, did they complain about it only now? He refuted the idea of duplication between two GTC committees and continued:

7. I am not ready to accept Mr Yeivin's assessment of our acts, since I believe that his letter was written out of a certain predisposition. I am also not ready, for the same reason, to enter into any debate with Mr Yeivin [as if there were no debate already].

8. I will not comment about the sentence in Mr Yeivin's letter saying "the IDAM has a few times done more" ... I still want to believe that his letter is nothing but the fruit of an unfortunate misunderstanding.

9. As for the last sentence in Mr Yeivin's letter, the GTC – with the help of the advisory committee [under Yadin] for the preservation [improvement] of the landscape, whose function is to define a general policy about improving the landscape; and with the help of the expert committee [under Yannay], whose function is to check any plan, not necessarily of improvement and conservation of ancient sites – does not enter the field

of activity of the IDAM, but is helped by its advice and even accepts its authority [*marut*] in all areas under its jurisdiction. There is, therefore, no need for a decision, since there is, in my mind, no overlap of areas here.   (GL44880/12 no. 471)

We must agree with some of his points. The unwritten agreement was made and broken by Kollek before the arrival of Yannay on the scene. So far Yeivin had not complained about the work of the GTC, but had cooperated with it. He had no legal basis in decision no. 566 or in the laws. Debating about the names of committees or councils was pointless. The notion that committees were changed just in order to mislead the IDAM was over-sensitivity; it was more probably a result of carelessness. If there was duplication, the GTC couldn't care less about it. Other problems originated from the whole concept of a private governmental corporation, and the secrecy necessary when using "frozen funds".

Why did Yeivin insist on carrying on the debate against such heavy odds? The answer can be found before the creation of the GTC. The IDAM and Yeivin had a very high status in the matter of historical sites, not through legal regulation, but through hard work and Yeivin's organization of the interdepartmental committee (for the improvement of historical sites and holy places; see Ch. 2). But this special status was temporary. It was neither assured by law, nor backed by permanently large funding. The GTC changed the order of things. It now had both the funding and the support of the Prime Minister; so what if they promised Yeivin something and then denied it? The decision Yeivin had wanted to be a part of had been made right at the start, with the transfer of responsibility over tourism to Kollek and the nomination of Beham and Ir'on as managers of the GTC late in 1955. The addition of Yeivin to any committee or council now could be only symbolic.

A wise politician would have blunted the force of Yeivin's arguments by adding him to one of the committees, but Kollek failed to do so. Perhaps his contempt was so strong that Kollek did not want to see Yeivin on his committees and risk being reminded about the "original sin" in face-to-face meetings. Yeivin's insistence is telling: he was wronged. Avidor gave Yannay's letter to Yeivin, who responded on 9 May 1957. He admitted that working with Yannay was fine, but this was not the issue: "In my last letter I raised again the problem of the relations between the IDAM and the GTC at a high level; and I do not understand why Mr Kollek ignored it. On this Mr Yannay cannot give me an answer …". Note how Kollek stands at the heart of the matter. Yeivin reiterated the history of the verbal agreement, writing that it had given the IDAM the right to choose the sites and the preferred plans for restoration, and that the GTC had broken it by setting up the new advisory committee under Yadin (Yeivin calling it a "council" – *moa'zah*). Of course, he wrote, the Prime Minister had nominated it, but the proposal came from someone "and that someone [i.e. Kollek] did not keep the agreement". Yeivin repeated his two solutions, only this time his "price" went down to only one representative on the committee under Yadin. He added:

> I admit that this problem is just part of the general problem of the position of the Ministry of Education and Culture regarding the relations between the IDAM and other bodies who are active in the field of archaeology and preservation [a hint about the conflict with the IES and the Hebrew University]. You know well my position in this case and I need not add anything here. Correspondence with Kollek will not help. The core of the problem must be decided and [one should] act according to this decision; then I can decide what my personal position will be once the decision has been made. (GL44880/12 no. 4401, copy in GL44882/9)

The hint of resignation appears here for the first time, but resignation would be a dramatic but futile gesture. Tension crept into the letters about work on sites exchanged between Yeivin and Yannay from 1956. An example appeared when Yeivin wrote that the GTC should wait patiently for the IDAM, for the IDAM had patience for "many works that the GTC has promised but has not yet performed" (GL44882/9 no. 4529, 21.5.57). Yannay was offended:

> I was sorry to read the biting section in your said letter, and ask you, for the aim of fair work relations between us, to avoid such words … The corporation did not promise anything to the IDAM and does not owe it anything. The corporation does not work to the IDAM's plan, but the IDAM is partner in the planning of the works [of the GTC] (GL44882/9 no.3247, 4.6.57)

It brings to mind Kafka: "The court ask nothing of you. It receives you when you come and it releases you when you go" (1974 [1925]: 173). However, one must notice the possibly subconscious use of the word "promise" in Yannay's letter. True, the GTC had not promised anything to Yeivin before decision no. 566, because at that time the GTC did not exist; but someone made this promise, and broke it.

Yeivin returned to the issue on 9 January 1958, sending a complaint to Avidor about the "sudden discovery of a supervisor for the conservation of historic sites in the regular workforce [teken] of the Prime Minister's Office". This, he wrote, was a useless duplication, that was in opposition to the law (GL44880/13 no. 6903, copy in GL44892/9). Furthermore, "this position is held by a man with no idea about archaeology or about conservation of ancient sites" (meaning Yannay). But "I do not mean him in particular. Indeed, he is a man of considerable vitality, and work with him is undertaken in cooperation and friendship". Luckily this letter did not reach the GTC, but nor did it bring about any change.

CONFLICTS OVER THE WORK OF THE GTC

In another letter to Yannay of 28 January 1958 Yeivin wrote: "I must warn you clearly and unequivocally that the conservation and restoration of monuments in Israel is by law the responsibility of one and only one governmental institution: the IDAM" (GL44882/9 no. 7097). This was the first letter strongly complaining directly about work on sites, although the correspondence between Yeivin and Yannay remained more or less reasonable until March 1958. Tragically, by this stage Yeivin was isolated; his arguments and complaints were now met with apathy. Naturally, most conflicts concerned sites of major works of improvement by the GTC, and there is no room here to describe them all. They included complaints about Megiddo, Hefzibah, Athlit, Ashkelon, Avdat, Shivta, matters of publication, and so on. I will present three examples.

Licences for dealers and the sale of mementos

The GTC interfered in IDAM decisions about giving licences to antiquities dealers. It asked the IDAM to recommend some dealers, which could have resulted in lawsuits against the IDAM. It also gave some dealers data and letters from the IDAM that discussed the policy relating to dealers (GL44882/9 no. 8061, 20.4.58; no. 581, 29.4.58). According to Yeivin (letter of 13.1.1959), Kollek tried to interfere in the granting of export licences in favour of a dealer or collector called Moshe Phillips. On the positive side, the IDAM relinquished its interest in the sale of antiquities (Kletter & Kersel, forthcoming). The GTC also noticed the problem of replicas being sold as originals (GL44882/9 no. 6657, 14.5.58).

Kollek was on the side of the dealers. A state auditor's report about the first year of activity of the Company for Developing Tourism (a lending bank and sister company of the GTC) in 1957/58 reveals that it gave about 2 million Lira in loans, mostly to develop and improve hotels. It also gave no fewer than 26 loans to shops selling mementos to tourists; not for development but for "returning capital" (*hon khozer*) (G13-5451). Kollek determined everything, even the smallest details:

> In fact I do not care who will manufacture it in Israel. What I would like is for one to be able to buy cheaply, somewhere in Israel, one or two kinds of ancient lamps. This has not yet been done. I also wish that at Megiddo and also at Hazor they would sell a model of a chariot and at Bet She'arim a model of a small sarcophagus with the lions. These products could be manufactured in a certain shape suitable to use as ashtrays …
>
> (G12-5451, February 1959)

Alfasi Street 10, Jerusalem

In February 1956 a Friend of Antiquities informed the IDAM that a tomb had been discovered while digging foundations for a private building. The IDAM arrived immediately and excavated the tomb (Fig. 27). The mainly Hellenistic period remains included drawings and inscriptions, one with the name "Jason" (Rahmani 1964: 1, 7).

Yannay expressed the desire to turn this site into a tourist attraction, either by buying the plot or by arranging access to the tomb. At this time, the Old City of Jerusalem, with most of the tourist attractions, was held by Jordan, so Israel was keen to develop sites that would attract tourists to western Jerusalem. At a meeting on 8 March 1956 it was decided to confiscate the plot and build a structure to protect the tomb, at an estimated cost of 50,000 Lira shared between the GTC and the Ministry of Religious Affairs.

However, after the site had been confiscated, Kollek sent a letter (not found) to Avidor, presumably demanding that the Ministry of Education and Culture pay for it. On 5 October 1956 Yeivin wrote to Avidor. He told him that the IDAM had explained many times to Kollek and to Yannay that it had no budget to cover confiscation after a contractor had started building. The site was important, but scientifically the IDAM was satisfied (it had finished excavation, photography, etc.). The IDAM could remove the plaster bearing the drawings, but they were already much faded and it could be a pointless activity. The GTC had confirmed that it was responsible for financing the confiscation. Yeivin continued:

Figure 27. Yeivin (right) and Dothan leaving the Alfasi Street tomb, February 1956. (Photograph by Shor, IAA 14030)

267

As all these matters were discussed verbally, I cannot prove the facts, but can only give my word [*divrati*] … The corporation also handled the entire affair with the JNF with the intention to exchange plots. Only then did the GTC ask the IDAM for an official letter about the confiscation of the plot, and I refused to send it until the GTC had confirmed in writing that it would cover the [costs of] confiscation and its results. Kollek signed this letter (no. 7020, 12.6.56) and I attach a copy … Only on the basis of this letter was a request sent to confiscate the plot …

A few days later I received a letter from the legal advisor of the Prime Minister's Office, not in the kindest words, since he had just woken up to the problem, trying to blame it on the IDAM. If Mr Kollek promised what he promised without first consulting his legal advisor, the IDAM should not be blamed … I immediately phoned the legal advisor and demanded an apology, for the facts he said had been "denied" are true, as proved by Kollek's letter … Indeed, the legal advisor apologized in a second letter (no. 220/13, 29.6.56) … The negotiation [with the owner] was not stopped by the IDAM, but by the GTC. Although their position was clear, it stood in complete opposition to the promise they gave in writing.

(GL44882/9 no. 2326, copy in GL44880/12)

Kollek wrote another letter (not found) and in response Yeivin sent the whole file to Avidor. Kollek's letter, said Yeivin, "to put it gently, deviated from the common procedures of correspondence" and "also a few of the facts mentioned in it are not exact"; Yeivin was implying that Kollek was lying. He also said that Kollek had made decisions about matters outside his area of expertise (GL44880/13 no. 6903). On 19 September 1958 Yannay wrote to Avidor explaining that a committee was in place to settle the case, but nothing had been done (G11-5451). On 16 October 1958 Kollek wrote to Meir Ben-Uri, an architect who worked for the GTC:

The Committee for the Improvement of the Landscape of the Land [under Yannay] expressed at the time its consent to allow us to build, on the Alfasi plot, a residential building, on the condition that we keep the entrance to the site from Alfasi Street, the courtyard [of the cave] and the cave. I would therefore be grateful if you could find a contractor ready to build a residential building at this place on these conditions. Possibly, to enlarge the area, the plot could be joined with the Ramban Street plot. If during my absence [abroad] you find such a contractor, you will be blessed.

(G11-5451 no. 220/13/3652)

Notice how Yannay's committee – a body of the GTC – gave permission to the GTC, without any consideration for the IDAM. At the same time Kollek wrote to Avidor: "Following your offer as a solution to the Alfasi Street [problem], to build a building without damaging the cave and the courtyard, I asked for a contractor to be found ..." (G11-5451, October 1958). Whether the idea originated with Avidor, Kollek, or Yannay, it was discovered in time by Yeivin, who wrote to Avidor:

> As I notified you verbally, on the 5th of this month an official of the Department of Properties [Agaf ha-Nekhasim] at the Ministry of Finance telephoned me and told me that the representative of the Director-General of the Prime Minister's Office had come to him on the instruction of the Director-General [Kollek] and demanded to put up for sale the said plot, on condition that the entrance to the tomb would remain open [to visitors].
>
> Fortunately for the IDAM ... the said official phoned me to ask if this was being done with the agreement of the IDAM. Of course, I told him that the Director-General of the Prime Minister's Office has no authority to give orders about what should be done with ancient sites. Since the plot has been proclaimed an ancient site, no action can be taken without the agreement of the Director of the IDAM; and I am not ready to permit its removal from governmental to private hands.
>
> I believe matters have reached a point that cannot be borne any longer. There is an immediate need for discussion with the Prime Minister about the way the manager of the GTC [Kollek, actually GTC Chairman] acts and about his recurring deviation from the limits of his authority. I ask you to ensure that, as soon as Mr Kollek returns from abroad, there will be an inquiry with the Prime Minister ... I also insist that I am present at every inquiry of this sort, for no one else knows the facts and all the related details. To my regret, many of the people concerned have hidden major evidence and distorted details that only I can clarify.   (GL44882/9 no. 126)

Yeivin added later:

> I would never have a hand in making the IDAM and the government of Israel a laughing-stock for the entire public through the public sale of a plot that had been confiscated from private owners as a historical site. And after thousands of Lira have been invested in it over the past two years to reconstruct the monument and to improve the look of the plot.
>   (GL44881/13, 13.1.59 #7)

Yannay later claimed the same thing: the IDAM had continued to invest "tens of thousands of Lira" in the Alfasi site just because the GTC had objected to it (G13-5451, 9.6.59). Maybe this was the case, but the way the GTC had handled the affair had been unfortunate (cf. GL44884/3, 15.5.60; GL44889/2 no. 8513).

Avdat and Shivta

The "restoration" works at Avdat and Shivta were planned using the American frozen funds. Yadin, in his role as chair of the GTC advisory Committee for the Improvement of the Landscape and Historical Sites, applied to Yeivin for approval, mentioning only restoration work (G11-5451, 4.3.58). Yeivin agreed under certain conditions, but received no acknowledgement of those conditions, and in the meantime, he complained in a letter to Yadin, "certain people" arrived at the IDAM saying that they had been hired to work at Avdat or Shivta and asking for instructions: "This is not the right way to cooperate" (GL44882/9 no. 8505, 2.6.58). Nevertheless, the IDAM agreed to Yadin's suggestion that Avi-Yonah supervise the works (Yeivin no. 8789, 6.7.58). Yeivin discovered the truth only after visiting Avdat:

> To my surprise I found that a large-scale excavation is being carried out there, something that was never requested and for which a licence was never given. Moreover, the excavation is not being carried out … scientifically. Mr K. is not expert enough to be responsible even for the removal of debris; and certainly not for a large-scale excavation exposing [remains], such as the unnecessary one surrounding the bathhouse …
>
> Now for details. In large parts of the buildings on top of the mound, already cleared, and in those that (according to Mr K.) are going to be cleared, the position of architectonic items, now collapsed, may surely teach us something about the plan of the buildings – for their restoration. Such clearance work should be done only under the constant supervision of an expert archaeologist or an architect with knowledge of the history of ancient architecture. Mr K is neither of the two.
>
> Also, you did not attach to your letter a detailed plan for strengthening and restoring the buildings to prevent their recollapse after they have been cleared from the debris that holds them together. It is evident to anybody that at many places any small movement or rainfall will cause the complete destruction of the buildings … unless action is immediately taken to support the buildings … Such actions were not mentioned in your letter. In this case I want to see not only words, but detailed engineering plans …
>
> B. Shivta. I have not yet visited and do not know if and how [work] is being done there; but I fear it is no different from Avdat. Textual description cannot replace detailed plans of action with real engineering drawings.
>
> C. A general note. I was told at Avdat that all the finds were being sent to Mr Yannay in Tel Aviv. Then you said to me that they would finally end up in the Hebrew University. I do not know why they should reach Mr Yannay at all and I do not understand what business this is of the

university's. If there is no possibility to keep the finds in a safe place near the site until the end of restoration and improvement, they must be immediately transferred to the offices of the IDAM in Jerusalem, where you can handle them for publication ...

D. Because of the great interest that the IDAM has in the restoration of all the said sites, and because the IDAM wants to avoid unnecessary quarrels, I did not immediately stop the work during my visit to Avdat, preferring to discuss it with you and with Dr Yadin. But I think that it is clear to you too that matters cannot continue like this ... [Yeivin also asked whether remains were being photographed before work, to enable comparison with their condition after work; if not, it should be done from then on.] (GL44882/9 no. 9228, 22.8.58; sent to Avi-Yonah, Yadin and Avidor)

People who saw the sites were horrified and complained in writing. One such letter was sent on 16 October 1958 by Asher Schlein in Tel Aviv to Aviram of the IES, who passed it on to the IDAM:

Recently I received news from several sources, including a graduate archaeologist, about an affair I will detail below. I am not sure about the facts of the affair, and I hope your honour will clarify this, but I believe it is along these general lines; although I would be happy to find out that it is all lie from beginning to end.

The matter is restoration works at Avdat. These digs are being carried out under the responsibility, or in any case at the expense of, the GTC. Only one archaeologist (to the best of my knowledge Professor M. Avi-Yonah) supervises the work scientifically. As is known, he is not present all the time there, so work runs without enough professional supervision: this is wrong (*pasul*) in itself.

To the best of my knowledge, this and perhaps other matters have affected the work. Items of archaeological/scientific value are rudely destroyed. I have heard that the sorting of sherds is very inadequate and perhaps completely lacking; that there is even no sorting of layers; that the restoration of a church was done by moving stones from one place to another without professional supervision and, as a result, badly.

I myself have no connection with archaeology, but I am interested in it as would be any normal cultural person interested in the antiquities of his land, which have for him a significant sentimental value. Therefore I was quite shocked when I heard about this affair, which I regard as more than an ounce of vandalism.

I was told that the "society for the protection of nature" finds itself from time to time in dispute with the GTC on protecting nature in the country

271

against GTC projects. Is it not the duty of the … [IES] to protect archaeological values? … I hope that the society, out of real concern for eternal values, will not let personal considerations [*maso panim*] prevent it from fulfilling this role. Because of the urgency of this matter, I have delivered copies of my letter to some members of parliament, fearing that the IES will delay its action for reasons out of its control …
Please acknowledge receipt of this letter.

(GL44882/9 no. 9849, received 7.11.58)

How convenient it was for the IES to deliver this "hot potato" into the hands of Yeivin! There is evidence of the nature of the "archaeological" work at Avdat and Shivta in documents from the Committee for the Improvement of the Landscape and Historical Sites. For example, a report by Ofer of 18 July 1958 refers to his visit to Shivta, where 60 relief workers worked in two groups: "It was decided to clean [*sic.*] streets, including house entrances, not to clean courtyards, to clean churches, to clean and restore one building; this is in the present phase" (G11-5451). This report went straight to Kollek; Avi-Yonah is not mentioned as a factor in making decisions. In a meeting of 26 September 1958 Yannay dictated orders for Avdat:

Section 7. The fortress. A. demolish any plot that endangers the visitors. B. clean the area and remove the stones with railway carts; C. work shall be done in the main entrance; D. inner southern tower. E. behind the said tower – to destroy and rebuild. F. outer southern tower. G. external towers. Y. [one of the Kibbutzniks' supervisors] will work out a plan with a budget of 20,000–25,000 Lira and bring it for approval.   (G11-5451)

So the plans would be made by someone who was neither an architect nor an archaeologist. On 22 September 1958 Kollek wrote to Avi-Yonah: "Since all the 'goodies' [*mezi'ot*] discovered at Avdat have been collected by you, I am sending you an inscription that I received on one of my visits there" (G11-5451). Avi-Yonah had not been present, but the workers had given Kollek a gift – an inscription – which he had taken to Jerusalem. How was Avi-Yonah supposed to determine the context of this inscription? In response to the complaints the GTC asked the American archaeologist Nelson Glueck to write a supporting letter to the *Jerusalem Post*. He did, speaking "solely of approval and praise", and of the "magnificent work being undertaken of cleaning up and restoring these remarkable ruins", calling the two sites "great national treasures" (G12-5451, 15.8.58).

On 21 October Yeivin wrote to Avi-Yonah again (GL44882/9 no. 9679, copy to Avidor) to say that he had not recived any information about what was required to be done before the winter, and that Yadin had said that Avi-Yonah was responsible for all the work in Shivta and Avdat. Unless Avi-Yonah immediately delivered all finds to the IDAM, Yeivin threatened "unpleasant complications for both sides". On 22 October Yeivin wrote an "urgent" letter to the "Manager of the GTC" [not naming Kollek in person]:

> Since the IDAM recognized the value and importance of the said projects for the preservation of historical monuments in Israel, it has been very patient about the way these projects have been handled, which has mostly been without agreement about many important details of the work. However, recently these un-agreed details have known no bounds. Furthermore, the experience of recent times has shown that ignorance of the requirements of the IDAM in completing improvements at certain places might make the IDAM responsible for damage that it has not caused; it [the IDAM] demanded that precautions against damage were taken, but they have not been.
>
> In the course of GTC projects at Megiddo, Ashkelon and Avdat, time and again in letters to Mr Yannay and others, I requested several necessary repairs ... and asked that unauthorized works be avoided. I was promised these things in conversations and in writing several times, but so far nothing has been done ... [Among the things Yeivin demanded was] removing the armband reading "antiquities guard" from the guard that you have placed at Avdat, for he was not chosen and placed there by the IDAM, and the IDAM cannot be responsible for his actions.   (GL44882/9 no. 9685)

Yannay (not Kollek) answered on 4 November 1958 that he could see no reason for the tone of the letter and was not prepared to be threatened (GL44882/9 no. 9807). Still Yeivin retained some loyalty by not going to the media (which knew about Avdat and Shivta, but not about relations between Yeivin and Kollek). For example, Avinoam Haimi of *Ha'aretz* newspaper addressed the IDAM, but was told to approach the GTC. He did not give up easily:

> Dear Ina [Pomerantz, secretary at the IDAM]
> ... Regretfully I must tell you that your reply about the restoration works in Shivta and Avdat is not an answer. Meanwhile we have received another complaint about it and I was asked to handle it and if necessary write about it. You refer me to the answer of the GTC in the *Jerusalem Post* of 20 October. Well:
> a) The GTC is not an archaeological institute. Does this mean that you relinquish responsibility for the entire business and is it the responsibility of the GTC alone?
> b) The GTC answer is not acceptable. It says that works at Shivta and Avdat are not an excavation, but only restoration work, but you understand this is just an excuse for the lack of scientific supervision. Then it claims that Avi-Yonah is responsible for such supervision, but he is there only

occasionally. Daily supervision is, according to the GTC, given to two Kibbutz members whom I do not know: K. of Sede Boqer and F. of Revivim. Can they be trusted? Also, the GTC claims that you receive a constant flow of information on progress of work. What can you say based on this information?

I ask you not to evade me by referring me to the GTC. This time I need your detailed answer as soon as possible, even urgently. I also very much ask you to add one or two photographs to publish in my section. An edict [*gzerah*] was issued that the section must always be accompanied by some pictures ... meanwhile give my regards [to workers] in the IDAM ...

(GL44882/9 no. 9853, annotated "Haimi phoned Yeivin")

On 2 December 1958 Yeivin and Yannay agreed that Avi-Yonah must send the plans, finish registering the finds and deliver them to the IDAM. Yeivin wrote more gently to Yadin on 29 December 1958: matters at Avdat were not "completely satisfactory", but were "more reasonable" at Shivta. He asked that the IDAM be consulted over plans for action at Shivta, "so that they will not be made with the same lack of efficiency and lack of planning as at Avdat". He added:

I was also told that there were negative reactions in the press last Friday and yesterday. Understand my situation, for I do not want to broadcast the unsatisfactory relationship between governmental and half-governmental [= GTC] bodies. I wanted to keep [written *li-shmoa*, meaning "hear", instead of *li-shmor*, "keep", but I am assuming this was an error] cordial relations in this regard. On the other hand, I cannot assist by creating the notion in public that the IDAM covers up improper actions.

Moreover, I have several times demanded the delivery to us of all the finds discovered during the conservation projects, which in fact turned into illegal excavations. So far nothing has been done ... I want to avoid any drastic action in relation to the conservation projects, since I very much appreciate the need for them. Still, I think that those who perform them must help me to avoid such acts [meaning that he wanted them to help him so that he would not be forced to declare the works illegal and initiate legal proceedings]. (GL44882/9 no. 294)

Yeivin's avoidance of using the media or his legal authority to declare the illegality of the work did not serve his cause. It was his only chance now to reach the attention of the Prime Minister. His loyalty was related to his personality and especially to the "frozen funds" origin of the finance: declaring the activities illegal might cause serious complications with the US (see Ch. 4).

The facts were still being denied by the GTC. For example, Yannay wrote to Yeivin on 2 January 1959:

Regarding our phone conversation of last Monday, in which you complained that there are excavations at five sites in Avdat and that the archaeologist – the supervisor there – had told Mr Prausnitz [of the IDAM] that he could not supervise all the works, I went there yesterday and found that: (1) there are works only at one site; (2) work at this site will finish within one week; (3) we shall not start any other projects there; (4) Mr Avraham Negev claims that he does not know where Mr Prausnitz got his allegations …

Dear Mr Yeivin, things like this just spoil the atmosphere between us … I suggest making a detailed inquiry in this case in order to see whose claims are untrue and who is willing to set us one against the other …

(GL44882/9 no. IDAM 635, copy to Yadin)

Yannay maintained his innocence here, but pleaded for reconciliation. Yeivin summarized:

I do not want to speak in detail about the activity at Avdat. It caused many scandals in the press and severe complaints against the IDAM, which tried countless times to explain to those who performed [the work] their mistakes, without significant results. I will only say that the agreement for the work in Shivta and Avdat was given under very special conditions. No response came to the letter of agreement, and the conditions were not met. The IDAM discovered that the work had started only by chance, from the press. The IDAM did not give permission for extensive excavations there, and they are in fact illegal. The GTC has taken advantage of the IDAM's lack of will to cause a public scandal by calling a halt to the work, which is the [IDAM's] right …   (GL44881/13, 13.1.59, #6)

On 1 April 1959 Yannay "returned" Avdat to the GTC for maintenance, although development of the sites still continued (G12-5451, 4.5.59). Work finally stopped and a celebration was held on 18 August 1959. Dothan was invited; Yadin, Chair of the Committee for the Improvement of the Landscape, delivered blessings; Avi-Yonah directed a tour of the site. Yeivin had just retired.

UNSEEN BY THE GTC

The conflict with Yeivin never appeared in minutes of the GTC management meetings (G-1/6878; G-6/5450); for them the "original sin" was a non-issue.

Files G11/5451–G13/5451 of the Prime Minister's Office relate to the Committee for the Improvement of the Landscape and Historical Sites: that is, Yadin (chairman), Kollek (member), Yannay (secretary) and a few other, secondary members (architects Dan Tannai and Arieh Sharon, and Director-General at the Ministry of Labour Yitzhak Eilam). The triumvurate of Yadin, Kollek and Yannay alone was registered as the Israel–America Archaeological Foundation in late 1957, in relation to the American frozen funds (Ch. 4). Unknown to archaeologists in Israel (except Yadin), section 4c of the articles of this foundation stated explicitly the aim to "organize archaeological excavations" (G11-5451, articles *c*. 10.11.57). The conflict with Yeivin found some expression there. Thus Yannay wrote to Yeivin on 20 April 1958:

> I refuse to enter into debate with you about the function of the Committee for the Improvement of the Landscape. It is an official institution nominated by the Prime Minister, and if it requires a law in Parliament it should be created. But in any case I do not think that this institution should be at the mercy of the IDAM. Even when Parliament approves this institution, I will be in favour of cooperation with the IDAM ...   (G11-5451)

On 29 April 1959, Kollek wrote to Avidor:

> ...Unfortunately, I have no alternative but to bring the affair of our relations with Dr Yeivin to your attention so that you can handle the case. Allow me just a few notes: the said unit [*mahlaka*] and the advisory committee for it [= for the improvement of the landscape, under Yadin] were established in the past – with the knowledge of the Prime Minister – in order to improve and develop the landscape of the land and various sites with historic and archaeological merit. Everybody has agreed that so far the unit has done good work in fulfilling these goals ... So far we have encountered quite formidable difficulties with Mr Yeivin. Many of our efforts have been dedicated to persuading Mr Yeivin about the necessity of our acts. I do not think these difficulties had good justification. We would be glad if you could solve the problems for us, but if you think it necessary to bring the entire matter before the Minister of Education, please do so.
> With blessing, T. Kollek   (G12-5451)

When Yeivin complained, it could be ignored; it was a different story when Kollek complained.

A few words about funding are appropriate. The first regular GTC budget for 1955/56 was 1,121,850 Lira. In 1956/57 the budget was 1,188,700 Lira (with 652,000 for expenses in Israel). It grew to 1.7 million Lira in 1959/60, 2.05 million in 1960/61 and 2.7 million in 1961/62. The publication budget alone in 1957/58 was about 150,000 Lira. Apart from that, there was a development budget and the American "frozen funds". The scope of activities was endless: examples include trying to amend the law concerning noise prevention in order to help a hotel in Jerusalem; changing citizenship laws to prevent tourists having to wait while new immigrants were checked (G7-5451, 2.11.55); discussing in October 1958 a plan to build a casino (the issue is still being debated in Israel today); presenting tourists with glasses of orange juice upon landing; preparing propaganda films; maintaining offices in Europe and the US; giving licences to tourist shops and to guides; and so on (G-1/6878; G-6/5450).

Katz (2004: 179) gives very few details about the budget for improving sites. We might add that the first budget item mentioned in this regard in July 1956 was 150,000 Lira (G-1/6878, minutes 2.7.56). For the first two years, Yannay's committee had "only" 225,000 Lira in 1956/57 and 200,000 in 1957/58. In 1958/59 this was augmented by 600,000 Lira from the "frozen funds", while the Ministry of Finance added 175,000 in 1958/59 and at least 125,000 in 1959/60. For a five-year plan for 1959–64, Yannay asked for 3.65 million Lira just for relief workers and another 4.65 million Lira for activities (G11-5451, 24.12.58). In contrast, in 1954/55 the IDAM had 22,000 Lira for preservation of antiquities and 7,850 Lira for the wages of workers for that aim; in 1957/58 it was 22,500 Lira for preservation and 8,900 Lira for workers.

In July 1959 the State Comptroller discovered the Committee for the Improvement of the Landscape. He could not understand whether it was a private company or a government entity. It was run from the Prime Minister's Office, but financially organized by the GTC. Who supervised it (G13-5451, 10.7.59; 15.7.59)? Yannay claimed that it belonged to the Prime Minister's Office (G13-5451, 26.6.59). In fact, the various bodies and companies were entangled. Yannay often wrote letters from the Committee for the Improvement of the Landscape on official GTC stationery, and even sometimes on official Prime Minister's Office stationery. In 1960 Yannay's committee was removed to the Prime Minister's Office (G13-5451, 2.8.59); the Israel–America Archaeological Foundation was now inactive, since the "frozen funds" had been spent.

The Committee for the Improvement of the Landscape functioned until 1963, when the national gardens and parks authorities were established (Katz 2004: 112–25). Katz praises the committee and lists the improved sites (*ibid.*: 77–92), ignoring the IDAM even in archaeological works (such as the restoration of the Beth-Alpha mosaic). Katz follows the GTC's line on the events; for example, in Avdat they only "cleaned" the streets. He barely mentions the debate with the IDAM, referring only to one letter from Yeivin to "Dr Avitzur" (Katz 2004: 92, read Avidor). Katz concludes:

> The Ministry of the Interior (the Planning Department) and the Prime Minister (the unit for improving the landscape of the land) were leading the process of creating state tools for supervising and preserving the values of landscape, nature and historical tradition. The parts played by the Ministry

of Education (the IDAM) and the Ministry of Religious Affairs (the unit for
Holy Sites) were less central ...   (Katz 2004: 126)

FROM RESIGNATION TO RETIREMENT

Yeivin's letter of resignation of 28 December 1958, was dry:

> Dear Minister,
> On the 17th of this month I wrote you a detailed letter about my position as
> Director of the IDAM in the Ministry of Education and Culture, and asked
> an urgent interview to be arranged to discuss this question, especially in
> relation to the proposals for the budget year 1959/60. To my great sorrow I
> have received no answer to my letter; nevertheless I phoned your secretary
> last Thursday and asked to know whether we could arrange such an inter-
> view. Your secretary promised to remind you of the matter of the interview
> and to let me know the very same day whether you would arrange it. So far
> I have received no notification.
>   In accordance with the last paragraph in my aforementioned letter, I do
> not see, therefore, any other alternative but to reach the clear conclusions
> that result from this matter. I therefore attach for your information a copy of
> my letter to Mr D. Rosolio, in which I asked him to approve my resignation
> from the service of the State and my retirement from 1 August 1959.
> With feelings of honour, [signed] S. Yeivin
>   (GL44880/13 no. 281, copy to Avidor)

The letter of the same day to David Rosolio, the Civil Service Commissioner,
was also dry:

> Honourable Rosolio
> To my sorrow, work conditions and other circumstances have recently
> arisen that do not allow me to continue to fulfil my role as Director of the
> IDAM in the Ministry of Education and Culture. I have therefore come to the
> conclusion that I have no alternative but to ask you to approve my resigna-
> tion from the service of the State and my retirement under sections 15(2)
> and 16 of the Civil Service (Pensions) Law, 1955. Since I was 60 years old
> on 24 Elul 1956, it seems to me that I am permitted to ask for this approval
> ...   (GL44880/13 no. 282)

The minister did not approve the resignation and the two talked on 5 January
1959. Yeivin was ready to withdraw his resignation on certain conditions, which

he set down to write, first preparing handwritten notes (GL44881/13, 7.1.59), and then a detailed three-page list of complaints against the GTC, headed "Review of Affairs between the IDAM and the GTC" (GL44881/13, 13.1.59). I have already referred to sections of this document, which he sent to the minister with a letter marked "confidential and personal" on 14 January 1959:

Dear Minister

As agreed in our last conversation on the 5th of this month, I hereby submit to you the list of illegal actions, or unagreed actions, of the GTC and its management. As you can understand, the problems began immediately with the establishment of the corporation. Although the IDAM informed the corporation about these matters shortly after they started, the corporation avoided fixing the wrongs, either offering irrelevant excuses or wearing us down [*shkhika*]. Surely you can also see that there is no possibility of continuing to work like this and the matter needs to be addressed immediately, [to come up with] an arrangement that will be followed in goodwill by both sides and in honest cooperation ... I need not promise you that the IDAM has this will, and it has no intention of completely taking over matters related to both bodies ... but the IDAM cannot and is not allowed to give up its authority to make decisions, together with the GTC, about activities and their execution, based on prior negotiations [between the two bodies].

I also have concrete and practical solutions to the problem, whether in the frame of the ... advisory archaeological council (Mutab), or in a new body established by combining the two related bodies (the IDAM and the GTC), or by altering the composition of the structure of the GTC, which in my view breaks the agreement. Moreover, mending the relations between the IDAM and the GTC also depends to a great extent, so it seems to me, on mending the attitude of the Ministry of Education towards the IDAM. It seems to me that the Ministry [of Education] must insist that its expert for matters of archaeology and antiquities is first and foremost the IDAM. Of course, it does not prevent consultation with other archaeological bodies, but it does prevent consultation only with other archaeological bodies ...

I was glad to hear you promise that in budget year 1960/61 you are considering addressing seriously and forcefully the bias in the budget and the number of workers at the IDAM. I am ready to count on that promise. If within a reasonable time relations with the GTC have improved, and also the Ministry of Education and Culture has accorded the correct status to the IDAM as a body of research and science in the field of archaeology in the country, I will be ready to notify the Civil Service Commissioner that I would like to ask him to postpone my resignation until the legal date [i.e. 1961, when Yeivin would be 65 years old].

(GL44880/13 no. 472, copy in 44881/13)

As we can see, Yeivin insisted not only on the legal authority of the IDAM (antiquities licences, excavations, supervision of restoration works), but also on sharing authority with the GTC over planning and setting priorities. By this time, relations with the minister were strained and Yeivin was also complaining about the status of the IDAM. The minister trusted the "other archaeological bodies" (Hebrew University and IES). Even he probably lacked the power to make changes in the GTC structure, yet he did not want Yeivin's resignation. Instead he offered temptations in the form of an increased budget and more workers. Yeivin could have accepted it and called it a partial victory – these inducements were desperately needed – but he chose not to. It seems that the minister did not respond in writing to the letter of 14 January 1959. Finally, Yeivin wrote to him again on 28 April 1959:

> Dear Minister,
> Subject: My retirement
> Following our last conversation on this subject, I wrote to you at your request a detailed letter about the working relations that have been formed over time between the IDAM and the GTC; relations that need to be worked out in order to allow proper work and the IDAM to carry out its responsibilities.
>
> Meanwhile I have been offered a few suggestions related to possible projects for 1960 and I must respond to these people. You know my intention and my desire, but since I promised you to consider delaying my retirement – in view of the problems being addressed, which would have permitted such a delay – I cannot give final answers to the people who have approached me with new suggestions.
>
> I therefore ask you to notify me within the next few days whether the matter can be addressed following my suggestion or not. If a desirable solution is impossible, I ask you to send the State Civil Service a good enough recommendation [for pension of a "reasonable sum"].
>
> (GL44880/13 no. 1551, "personal" and "confidential")

The *Jerusalem Post* interviewed Yeivin just before his retirement: "The antiquities department is not being allowed to develop as it should, and 'certain quarters' are intent on curtailing its activities', Mr Yeivin, outgoing director, told the *Jerusalem Post*". Yeivin said that he had retired because of a failure to agree with the Ministry of Education about the activities of the IDAM. The IDAM had allowed the GTC to "preserve" sites for tourists, but the GTC had started to conduct excavations without "proper scientific supervision". The IDAM had not been able to condone this: these works must be "demarcated and coordinated with the IDAM". The Minister of Education had formed a committee for the national museum without the IDAM being represented: "I cannot agree ... the IDAM cannot exist without its museum; or the museum without the IDAM."

Yeivin added: "the department cannot mark time; it must either develop or die". He said that the question was not one of money, but of attitude. As long as the minister had "the right attitude" he could stay (Cohen 1959; copy in GL44868/7).

Yeivin retired on 1 August 1959. Professor John Bowman from Melbourne wrote to him on 23 October 1959, not knowing the background and exact date of his retirement:

> I am sorry about this because you have done so much for the Depart-
> ment of Antiquities in Israel ... I never thought that you were anywhere
> near retirement age because you look so youthful. Undoubtedly it is your
> enthusiasm for archaeology that makes and keeps you so young.
>
> (GL44881/13 no. 4499)

It was not new for Yeivin to receive offers of other positions; he almost went to teach in Los Angeles for two years. Yeivin described his work at that time: regular work in the IDAM; member of the Biblical Encyclopedia; involvement with the Academy for Hebrew Language (chair of the organizational committee, member of management, terminology committee, etc.), and research in the time that was left (GL44881/13 no. 5934a).

In 1955 Yeivin had met with Haim Levanon, Mayor of Tel Aviv, to discuss establishing an archaeological institute there. Yeivin asked him to keep it confidential (GL44881/13, 16.12.1955; GL44881/13, 19.12.55). By February 1957 it was no longer a secret and Yeivin was teaching at the new Tel Aviv University. He explained it in a moving letter to the Ministry of Education:

Subject: Teaching at the Tel Aviv University
In relation to the said letter of the Civil Service, which you showed me during our last conversation, I have to note that:
A. I do not see at all the need to go round and round [*skhor-skhor*] and cover the naked lack of trust disguised in concern about my health. If the Civil Service does not trust that I see to it that no harm comes to my work in the Department by giving courses at Tel Aviv, I can only feel regret about it. After such a number of years, they should already know that, despite my many and varied occupations in matters of science and the public, I have never allowed such external things to detract [from] ... the regular work of the Department.

  I have never left the office even a minute early and I have always returned on the same day [from Tel Aviv] to Jerusalem, so that I will not have to be late to work the next morning. But trust comes from the heart; and if there is none, of course I cannot plant it in the heart of the officials of the Civil Service by force.

B. In any case, this year it is a little too late to stop giving the classes. As for the next academic year (from November 1957), I will always have enough time on my hands to decide if I prefer retiring [from the IDAM] and continuing to teach at Tel Aviv, or stopping teaching at Tel Aviv and continuing my work in the Antiquities Department. According to the situation created recently, I am not at all certain what I will finally choose … (GL44880/13 no. 8553, 3.2.57)

In truth the strain affected Yeivin and it shows in his handwriting; it becomes angular (e.g. GL1430/13 no. 9903, 7.11.62). The Tel Aviv Department of Archaeology was established in 1962 and Yeivin headed it. The first excavations on behalf of Tel Aviv University were made in 1968. An Institute for Archaeology was established in 1969, but Aharoni took the lead in it (Aharoni 1973a: Preface). Yeivin published vigorously, especially in his later years (Avramski 1970; Yeivin 1957, 1960). His list of publications in 1973 ran to 519 items (in Aharoni 1973a). He died, aged 86, in 1982.

LATER RELATIONS WITH THE GTC

Now that Yeivin had retired, relations with the GTC could improve. For about two years the IDAM had only a temporary director in Kahane. Then Biran was appointed. Biran was very close to the IES and to the Hebrew University, and as a politician knew better how to bow to the GTC. In 1961 the GTC started to perform archaeological excavations (GL44882/9 no. 3460). These were first made at Beth Shean by the Department of Public Works (Ma'az), which won a contract from the GTC. Yannay had already decided, and also explained, that the contractor would provide the workers and the equipment, and even the engineer; only the architect remained a problem. The GTC did the archaeologists a favour though, by considering financing the publication of this excavation since, after all, the GTC was only interested in tourism: "The printing (*hadpasah*) of the report: Mr Yannay notifies us that although he is not interested in publication, they still published details of the excavations at Avdat. No doubt a way will be found also in the matter of publication [at Beth Shean] in due course" (Yannay, GL44882/9, meeting 15.2.1960).

The IDAM lost control of all the sites improved by the GTC. We saw an indication of this process when the GTC placed a man with an armband reading "antiquities guard" at Avdat. At Megiddo they placed a guard of their own in addition to that of the IDAM in late 1959 (44882/9 no. 1). After improvement, the sites were "returned" from Yannay's committee to the GTC (G12-5451, May 1959). Katzenstein asked Avidor on 19 November 1959:

Is it desirable that after historical sites have been improved (and museums opened at them) by the GTC, a site is guarded and maintained by that company, while the IDAM [should be] recognized as the authorized body [for these matters] according to the Law of Antiquities? The GTC wants to place its own guard at Megiddo from 1 December 1959. Since experience has taught us that the corporation does not tend to consider the requirements of the IDAM, I will be very grateful to you if you could advise us in principle about questions related to this matter as soon as possible.

(GL44882/9 no. 3389)

From the point of view of the GTC, maintaining sites once they had been improved required funding, a fact not considered in advance. This problem first surfaced in a meeting of 7 October 1957 (G-1/6878). The GTC decided to demand that local municipalities and regional councils maintain improved sites, or try to establish an association with that aim. On 2 June 1958 Kollek suggested legislation forcing municipalities and regional councils to maintain improved sites; but it was postponed (G-1/6787). On 2 July 1959 the GTC decided to establish an authority for preserving historical sites, and to take entrance fees to support this new body (G-1/6787). In 1961 all the sites were transferred back to the Committee for the Improvement of the Landscape (G-1/6787, 17.8.61; 23.10.61). In 1963 this became part of the Nature and Parks Authority of Israel.

Finally, in 1965 the government decided to establish a Ministry of Tourism under Moshe Kol, whom we met earlier. The GTC had a facelift, being incorporated in the new ministry as a company responsible for a whole host of subsidiary companies and institutions (G-1/6787, minutes 12.6.65; 13.12.65). In the same year Kollek left the GTC and the Prime Minister's Office to become Mayor of Jerusalem.

13 "WHETHER IN A COURTYARD OF A SYNAGOGUE, IN A COURTYARD ADJACENT TO A SYNAGOGUE, OR UNDER A SYNAGOGUE": THE SAFAD AFFAIR

Everything discovered so far is but the mere beginning from the hidden [genuzim] treasures, in which the scroll of lineage and sovereignty of Israel over its land is folded.
Aranne (1957: 100)

There is evidence, however, that at that time the question whether the presence of such an animal might be tolerated in the house of God was investigated from the point of view of the Law and the Commandments.
Kafka (1935: 57)

A series of letters reveals an affair that was never published. It concerns a plan by Dr John Bowman of the Department of Semitic Languages and Literature at the University of Leeds, together with a converted Jew from Edinburgh, the Reverend Nahum Levison, to excavate *"genizot"* of Synagogues in Safad and near the famous tomb of Shimeon Bar Yochai at Mount Meiron. The Hebrew word *genizah* is roughly equivalent to the Latin *favissa*: an underground or closed treasury of religious objects, such as Torah scrolls that were damaged or worn and could no longer be used. The plan involved not only Yeivin, but also the second President of Israel, Itzhak Ben-Zvi.

The correspondence mainly consists of letters by Bowman and Yeivin, kept in GL44881/13, with some additions in GL44880/13. The University of Leeds was one of the first foreign institutions to excavate in Israel (in Jaffa in 1952; Bowman & Isserlin 1955). On 11 February 1957 Bowman sent Yeivin an aerogramme:

Dear Dr Yeivin,

… Last September when I was in Edinburgh to give a lecture at a conference a Church of Scotland minister, the Rev. Nahum Levison, spoke to me after the lecture and told me of three genizot in Safad. Mr Levison was born in Safad and lived there until his late teens. One of the genizah he himself, as a boy some sixty years ago, had seen being shut up. The opening to it apparently lies between two Synagogues and runs under one of them. He is convinced that this genizah is fairly accessible and that there should be in it material going back for many centuries. The other two genizot of which he knows are in the circle of Simeon Ben Yokhai. Mr Levison told me that he would be willing to supply details of the whereabouts of all three genizot provided the Israeli authorities allowed that both he and myself be granted permission to work on any of the material found there.

I spoke to Mr Levison of your great helpfulness to us at the University of Leeds in connection with our little dig at Jaffa in 1952, and he was agreeable that I write to you about the matter. He is aware that there might be some difficulty about the two genizot in the circle of Simeon Ben Yokhai, but he is convinced that in the case of the one that he saw shut up sixty years ago we would not be confronted with such difficulties. Mr Levison says that his cousin Senator Javits of New York knows the Israeli Prime Minister and most of the members of your government, and if need be he would ask Senator Javits to speak to the Prime Minister and members of the government for any help that may be required for permission to open this genizah. [Senator Jacob Javits (1912–1986) began his phenomenal career in 1932 and served under seven presidents. He was elected to the senate in 1946 and re-elected three times. His papers are now kept at Stony Brook University, New York: www.sunysb.edu/library/javits.htm]

I wonder if you would be so good as to give me an assurance that if permission was given to open this genizah the material found would be available for Mr Levison and myself to study. If I am given this assurance I will pass it on to Mr Levison and he will then give me exact details about the genizah, which I in turn will forward to you. I hope that I do not seem to put the cart before the horse. Obviously no one can open the genizah or start to make investigations as to its whereabouts without your permission as the Director of the Department of Antiquities for the State of Israel, but Mr Levison will only give information as to its whereabouts when he is assured that if the material is found it will be made available for him to study. I am aware from what Dr Isserlin has told me that just now may not be a very auspicious moment to seek permission to open a genizah near one of the Synagogues in Safad as some religious people might think this is bordering on sacrilege. On the other hand, Mr Levison has the secret of the genizah and he is an old gentleman; it would be well if we have this information while he is still with us. I am sure that you with your great standing in all matters affecting archaeology and antiquities in Israel would in any case be able to obtain the necessary permission for us to open the genizah, and Mr Levison's contacts through his cousin, Senator Javits, will be quite unnecessary …

> Kindest regards and best wishes to you and Mrs. Yeivin, and congratula-
> tions to you on all your magnificent achievements in the field of Israeli
> archaeology,
> Yours sincerely,
> [signed] John Bowman   (GL44881/13 no. 3750)

Dr Isserlin's judgement was sound, but not heeded; he was not further involved with the affair and did not know Levison in person (email correspondence, August 2004). Yeivin answered on 20 February 1957 to say that the matter of the *genizot* in Safad ought to be handled with great delicacy. He had discussed it with the Director-General of the Ministry of Education and Culture and was making discreet enquiries. It might be necessary to enlist "certain scientific institutions" and "I take it that Rabbi [*sic*.] Levison and you will not object to such possible cooperation" (copy in GL44881/13 no. 3756). Bowman was late responding, owing to research and departmental commitments (GL44881/13 no. 1794, 14.3.57). Levison had not yet supplied any new information, but Bowman did not object to the cooperation Yeivin had mentioned. Yeivin's next letter to Bowman (no. 3983, dated 22.3.57) stressed again the need for "delicate handling and negotiations", not all of which could be "put in writing". He was going to be in London in June and suggested meeting there to discuss details. Bowman agreed, but Levison would not be able to come to London (GL44881/3 no. 4147). Yeivin wrote to finalize the details of the London meeting (GL44881/3 no. 4571). Apparently it was successful and on 18 June 1957 Bowman informed Yeivin (then on a visit to Brandeis University in Massachusetts) that Levison had agreed to the terms set in London and gave "complete information as to the whereabouts of the geni-zah". Bowman had secured a promise of £270 in funding from the bursar of the university. Levison was hopeful that more money could be raised, if necessary through his cousin, US Senator Javits. They planned to excavate in the summer of 1958 (GL44881/13, 18.6.57). There was no further progress for a few months, until Bowman visited Israel in the summer, saw the sites and wrote to Yeivin on 19 November 1957:

> While in Israel I had the privilege of an audience with the President. I
> discussed the dig with him and he seems favourable. He told me that I
> should contact you in London ... but I am sorry I missed you. I hope that
> you will give my university the licence to dig at the site which I discussed
> with you in June ...   (GL44881/13 no. 4545)

Bowman added that he now had some £300 available. A few days earlier, unknown to Bowman, Yeivin had written to Yitzhak Almog of the President's Office in Jerusalem. For the first time the title "confidential" appeared in the correspondence:

My Honourable Almog,
I attach hereby a draft of a letter to Dr Bowman, which I prepared as a result of my conversation with H.E. the President [Ben-Zvi] on the 1st inst. I would ask you to show this draft to H.E. the President, and I would be very grateful to him if he would be kind enough to initial any changes he wants, if he sees the need for any. Afterwards, please return the draft to me so that I can send the letter to Dr Bowman ...
[signed] S. Yeivin   (GL44881/13 no. 6287, 10.11.57)

Almog confirmed that the President had read and signed the attached letter (GL44881/13 no. 4440). The files contain a draft dated 11 November 1957 (copy in Fig. 28), marked "confidential" and annotated with the President's initials (YBZ) on the left:

Dear Dr Bowman,
Though I have not heard from you since your last visit to Israel to attend the Second World Congress of Jewish Studies, I have been in touch with H.E. the President concerning the possibilities of the suggested fieldwork in Safad. His Excellency thought that Rev. Levinson [*sic.*] should now give some more pertinent information concerning the genizah in question, whether it is in a courtyard of a synagogue, in a courtyard adjacent to a synagogue, or under a synagogue [added by the President: or in the cemetery], whether it is in a cave, a hole in the ground, or a burial in jars, etc.
    Secondly, seeing the circumstances of the case, all parties concerned have thought that it would be advisable for Rev. Levison to arrive incognito in Safad and point out the place preferably with a sketch plan; but it would be inadvisable for him to be present at Safad during actual fieldwork. Of course, no one would prevent him from staying somewhere else in the country during that period.
    Thirdly, I should very much like to know what financial resources would be at your disposal to carry out the work in the field, and participate in the publication of the material, if any is found.
    I on my part, with the full consent of H.E. the President, can promise you that there will be a fair division of finds if any are made; there will be a fair division of material for publication purposes; and that photographs of any material either retained by this department on behalf of the State, or divided for publication by the expedition and the Ben-Zvi Institute for Research on Jewish Communities in the East, will be supplied to you ...
With best regards, yours sincerely,
[signed] S. Yeivin   (GL44881/13 no. 6295; copy GL44880/13 no. 6355)

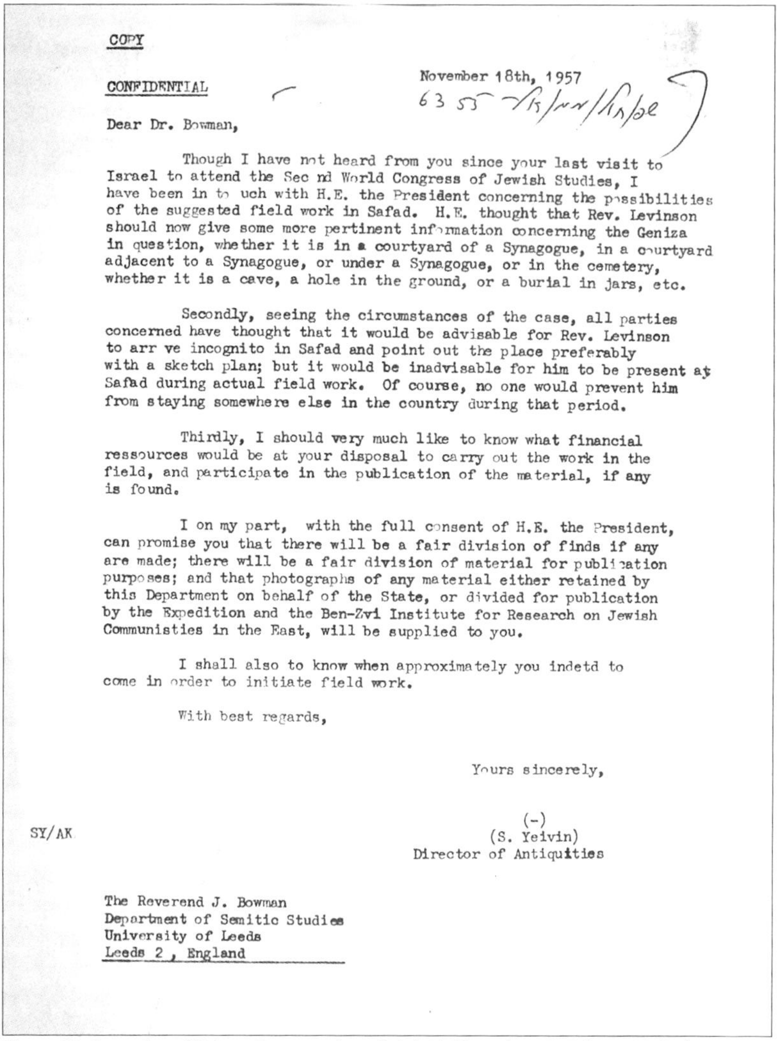

COPY

CONFIDENTIAL

November 18th, 1957

63 55 ~/ s/אٜx/אٜx/ʃ

Dear Dr. Bowman,

Though I have not heard from you since your last visit to Israel to attend the Second World Congress of Jewish Studies, I have been in touch with H.E. the President concerning the possibilities of the suggested field work in Safad. H.E. thought that Rev. Levinson should now give some more pertinent information concerning the Geniza in question, whether it is in a courtyard of a Synagogue, in a courtyard adjacent to a Synagogue, or under a Synagogue, or in the cemetery, whether it is a cave, a hole in the ground, or a burial in jars, etc.

Secondly, seeing the circumstances of the case, all parties concerned have thought that it would be advisable for Rev. Levinson to arrive incognito in Safad and point out the place preferably with a sketch plan; but it would be inadvisable for him to be present at Safad during actual field work. Of course, no one would prevent him from staying somewhere else in the country during that period.

Thirdly, I should very much like to know what financial ressources would be at your disposal to carry out the work in the field, and participate in the publication of the material, if any is found.

I on my part, with the full consent of H.E. the President, can promise you that there will be a fair division of finds if any are made; there will be a fair division of material for publication purposes; and that photographs of any material either retained by this Department on behalf of the State, or divided for publication by the Expedition and the Ben-Zvi Institute for Research on Jewish Communities in the East, will be supplied to you.

I shall also to know when approximately you indetd to come in order to initiate field work.

With best regards,

Yours sincerely,

(-)
(S. Yeivin)
Director of Antiquities

SY/AK

The Reverend J. Bowman
Department of Semitic Studies
University of Leeds
Leeds 2 , England

Figure 28. Letter from Yeivin to Bowman about Safad, 18 November 1957. (GL44880/13)

At this stage, the plans seemed to be progressing nicely and Yeivin and Ben-Zvi were asking for specific details to make the necessary arrangements. They even made an explicit promise about a fair division of finds. Bowman seemed very impressed by the promises and repeated them fully in his next letter of 17 December 1957, as if for reconfirmation. He then added:

> I sent your letter to the Rev. N. Levison. He is going out to Israel in January. I have just received back your letter from him and he seems to be perplexed

as to how he can arrive incognito in Safad as he is known in every town and village in Israel. Nevertheless I expect you will see him in January …

As to financial resources at my disposal. As I told you in an earlier letter we have somewhat over £300 in the Leeds University Semitics Department Research fund to begin with. To this can be added probably another £200 from the Departmental Research Grant. I have also made application for a Leverhulme Research Grant. Mr Levison earlier told me that he knows where money could be raised … I do not think we need worry about the financial resources … (GL44881/13, no. 4842)

The exact spots for excavation had not yet been revealed to Yeivin, but now a rather comic interlude took place. Levison assumed that he needed to arrive in Israel incognito, but did not know how. He did not wait for further instructions, but approached Dr Eliyahu Elath, the Israeli ambassador in the United Kingdom:

Your Excellency,
You may remember my calling upon you some years ago, or that my cousin Senator J.K. Javits spoke to you about me. The enclosed letter from Dr S. Yeivin to Dr John Bowman … has faced me with a problem that I cannot resolve, and I would be most grateful if you could help me.

Dr Bowman saw H.E. Ben-Zvi when he was in Israel, and talked the matter of excavating the genizah in Safad over with him. H.E. made it clear to Dr Bowman that a special order from him would have to be issued for the work, and it would have to be applied for by Leeds University, as there might be grave objections by the orthodox elements in Israel to the excavation, since the genizah is near a synagogue, and since it would raise protests from the orthodox community in disturbing sacred materials. H.E. warned Dr Bowman that the term "genizah" must not be used or implied in the dig. It must be given out that the dig is for information about Palestinian history.

Dr Yeivin now suggests that I should come to Israel "incognito" and I would like to do that, for I am interested not only in the Safad place but also in a place in the vicinity of Mairoun [= Meiron]. In 1891 I was taken to Mairoun to the grave of Rabbi Simon Bar Yochai to have my first hair cut during Lag B'Omer [feast] and there stuck in my memory the fact that I saw my two brothers Moses and Sir Leon carrying sacks. A year or so before my brother Sir Leon died, I mentioned the matter to him, and he told me that my memory was not playing tricks with me, for in fact he and my brother Moses and others did do so. The genizah at Mairoun had become too full, and [when] the authorities decided to empty it, they found a cave into which the material was hidden, and they obtained the services of some of the young people to carry the material, taking great precaution that the

Arabs of the village should not become aware of the fact. As you will know, Rabbi Simon Bar Yochai was a student of Rabbi Akivah and both lived in the 2nd century CE. It is possible that some of the material that was taken to that cave or other caves might go back to that period, and would be of inestimable value.

I do not know the location of the cave or caves, but only the direction from the court of Meiroun. I am anxious to have this matter explored and I would take the subject up with Dr Yeivin too. Again I think that it would be best if I could be incognito ...

I am at present working on a book of Biblical and Intertestamental Sects and Parties [mentioning a very long list of various sects, etc.] ...

My wife and I plan to sail to Israel on the *Jerusalem* on 25 January and stay until the end of March. My wife's maiden name was Nichol. Would it be possible for us to travel under her name?

I make the foregoing suggestion because I can think of no better, but I am sure Your Excellency can help us resolve this very difficult problem ...
Faithfully yours, N. Levison   (GL44881/3)

Mr Elath contacted Yeivin (GL44881/13 no. 4784, 5.12.57), describing Levison as a "converted Jew". If Elath had doubts, he kept them to himself and asked Yeivin to let him know how to proceed. Yeivin had to write to Elath to explain that the idea was not incognito arrival in Israel, but just in Safad, as a precaution from "stormy public opinion". Levison's conversion to Christianity was probably well known, although people at Safad and Meiron would hardly recognize him after so many years. "Of course, care must be taken that the press will not publicize his coming to Israel at all" (GL44881/13 no. 5687, 23.12.57).

Mr Levison arrived and visited the two sites. At last Yeivin received the information about the exact spots. From his following memorandum (marked "confidential") we understand that at least the *genizah* in Safad was right under the Ari Synagogue, with the opening in the courtyard:

On Sunday 23 March 1958 I visited H.E. the President (11–11.35 am) and gave him a report of my visit to Safad and Meiron together with Mr Levison ... It was agreed that we should try something with the Mayor of Safad, as perhaps we might establish in the alley a dig for the needs of sanitation or the like, and "stumble" upon the genizah. Then there will be a possibility to check [it], even with the knowledge of the Ministry of Religious Affairs (Dr Z. Warhaftig) ... If not, there will be no possibility to carry out such an exploration.

As for Meiron, one may carry out the exploration of the caves by Leeds University, which need not be involved at all in the Safad examination.

(GL44881/13, 25.2.58)

The last sentence probably meant the fieldwork, because of fears from public reaction. Bowman met Levison after his return from Israel, and wrote to Yeivin on 23 April 1958 to tell him that Levison was very pleased and that Bowman would receive the Leverhulme grant. They had £650, which would possibly be augmented by £200 the following year from the department's Apparatus and Research Grant. However, "My wife is having another baby in July, and it would not be fair of me to go this summer to the Middle East, and leave her to cope with the family", so Bowman asked for the operation to be postponed. He also enquired about the legal position regarding ownership of the finds:

> In a previous letter you said that there would be a fifty-fifty share of the material between your Department and the University of Leeds, but it is not this that I am thinking of. I mean can the local [orthodox] authorities of the buildings adjacent to the sites which I will be working, claim that the material is theirs, and prevent me from working on the sites? What is the legal position? (GL44881/13 no. 8289)

In a postscript, Bowman added that Levison had agreed to dig the following spring. Bowman understood from him that permission would have to be given by the Safad municipality beforehand, and asked Yeivin to help. Yeivin answered on 12 May 1958, accepting the postponement but asking for final confirmation of the new date. He suggested separating the two sites. The search for the *genizah* at Meiron could be undertaken, but Yeivin was not sure about procedures once the cave was found, although "bridges should not be crossed before one reaches them". An examination of the *genizah* of the Ari Synagogue in Safad was definitely beyond the reach of the University of Leeds, and even of the IDAM:

> I am trying to arrange for an "accidental" find by repair workers of the municipality. I do not yet know whether these efforts will be crowned with success; but let us always hope for the best. If and when this genizah is revealed, again we shall have to consider the best way to proceed with a possible examination of contents. I am sure we shall have the support of certain high placed personalities in the State.
>
> Now a remark concerning the material which may be discovered. In none of my letters have I spoken of a fifty-fifty share, for the simple reason that I do not think that anybody would be allowed to retain the material indefinitely. As I see the matter at present, the best we could hope for is the possibility to examine the material, copy it and publish it, before it is re-interred again. It is not a question of ownership; it is a question of religious customs. Of course, I did speak of a fair division of finds (nowhere mentioning a fifty-fifty basis) before I knew the exact position of the genizah, when I thought that it would be possible to dig in the neighbourhood

without the full knowledge of the public. The position revealed now shows that the genizah lies partly under the synagogue (a study room adjoining the main prayer hall) and partly under a public street, from which it will be impossible to exclude the public. In my letter of November 11, 1957, I did promise a fair division of material for publication purposes, and the supply of photographs of that part which would be retained by the Ben-Zvi Institute for publication purposes. By that promise I do stand.

I am sure you will appreciate the delicacy of the situation and the problem involved, and the new conditions obtaining now after Dr Levison has revealed the supposed place of the genizah in the town.

I should think it only correct to tell you that personally I do not believe that material of any interest is likely to be found in either genizah. The Synagogue of Safad has been rebuilt after the big earthquake of the 1830s and is not likely to contain any material antedating this reconstruction. On the other hand, the climate of Safad and the humidity of the ground have most probably caused full decay of any paper or parchment objects. However, there is nothing like trying to find out, if circumstances permit.

With best wishes, yours sincerely,

[signed] S. Yeivin, Director of Antiquities   (GL44880/13 no. 8289)

The Ari Synagogue of the Eastern Jews, probably built in the late fifteenth century, was very famous. There was also an Ashkenazi Ari Synagogue in Safad, established in the sixteenth century. The Eastern Ari Synagogue was destroyed in the earthquake of 1837 and rebuilt in 1852. I am not completely sure which synagogue was being referred to, although it was more probably the "Eastern" one, which was located in the lower part of the city, near the Jewish cemetery (which explains the President's addition about the cemetery in his letter to Bowman; see p. 287). For the Ari synagogues in Safad see Yizrael (1996) and Damati (2002: 151–55). Ben-Zvi was interested in the history of Eastern Jews and in Jews in the Galilee in particular (Ben-Zvi 1955; Aviram 1965: 137–40; Ben-Arieh 2001: 334). Bowman answered on 4 June 1958; Yeivin marked on the bottom of this letter that it had also been sent to the President. Bowman expressed sorrow that they would not be able to "actually dig in the Synagogue court-yard", but said that the method devised by Yeivin sounded hopeful. He agreed about the material and understood that it must be returned to the owners after study and publication. He confirmed coming to Israel in March or April 1959 for approximately five weeks, accompanied by Levison; a research student who had run a dig in North Yorkshire that year, and perhaps the curator of the Leeds City Museum, who had "several years of experience digging at Kirkstall Abbey". Bowman wrote again on 3 October 1958 (GL44881/13 no. 9450), confirming the date. He suggested coming in the middle of March for three weeks, returning with a larger team the following year. Levison would arrange accommodation with a niece of his in Israel. Bowman added:

> I understood from Mr Levison that we shall require electric lights. He was under the impression that your Department would arrange with the nearby Yeshiba [orthodox school] for electric power to be laid on for us, provided we brought cable. Is this possible? If not, what is your advice?
>
> (GL44881/13 no. 7033, 4.6.58)

Yeivin marked that this letter was also sent to the President. He answered on 12 October 1958, in a letter marked "personal and confidential". He accepted the date and explained that all licences expired at the end of each year. There was therefore no sense in issuing a licence in 1958 for a dig planned for 1959. Bowman should apply around February 1959, and his licence would be awaiting his arrival, or sent to his address at Leeds. However:

> At the same time I must say that your letter caused me some surprise. In all our correspondence it was stressed both by you as well as by me that the matter is to be handled very delicately. Moreover, in my conversation with you in London on June 5, last year, as well as in my conversation with Dr Levison, both here and on the occasion of our visit to Zefat [Safad], I took great pains to explain that a direct excavation of the genizah near the synagogue is out of question, more especially so after we saw the actual position of the genizah *under* the synagogue. It had been suggested, and the suggestion was communicated to you and to Dr Levison that I approach the Mayor of Zefat, and try to arrange with him that the municipality start some draining or similar project in the streets, where the opening of the genizah is located, and when this is "accidentally" discovered, the Department will be notified and will have the opportunity to examine its contents. In my conversation with Dr Levison on my way back from Zefat I very explicitly stressed the possibility that we may even be prevented from removing any material from the genizah, and will have to content ourselves with photographs or perhaps even handcopies.
>
> Because of the secrecy forced on us by the circumstances, I have not approached the Mayor of Zefat. I intend to do so some time in December or January so as to leave as short an interval as possible between my conversation with him and your arrival, for fear of possible peakages [= leakages] in Zefat, which may rouse premature and unwanted opposition on the part of certain religious circles.
>
> Consequently, nobody should know of the connection of your expedition with the projected excavation of the genizah in the city.

> Your licence will be issued for the investigation of caves in Nahal Mey-
> ron west of Meyron [= Meiron], in which Dr Levison expressed interest
> during our above-mentioned visit. Here again, I would advise not to stress
> the genizot aspect, but speak generally about investigation of caves to find
> possible ancient remains …   (GL44880/13 no. 4617)

Dr Bowman wrote on 10 November 1958 saying that he understood about the licence and would apply for it the following February; he promised to avoid "talking unguardedly" about the expedition, but asked: "If however, you manage to uncover 'accidentally' the other place [Safad], we would very much like the chance to examine its material" (GL44881/13 no. 9948).

Fate decreed otherwise. Yeivin was on the brink of retirement, and he mentioned this casually in a private letter to Bowman's wife in summer 1959. Bowman wrote to Yeivin on 23 October 1959, expressing his sorrow (by then Yeivin was already retired). Bowman himself became in the meantime a professor in the Department of Semitic Studies at the University of Melbourne, Australia. He still hoped to come to Israel in February 1960, asking for any news of "developments up at Safad near the Lurian Synagogue" and adding that he would apply later for a licence. He hoped that Yeivin could visit and lecture in Melbourne (GL44881/13 no. 4499, 23.10.59). Yeivin answered on 8 November 1959. He expressed his thanks and his interest in Bowman's plans for Melbourne. He added:

> As to your project, I don't think there will be any difficulty and I am sure
> the IDAM will continue the liberal policy towards foreign expeditions initi-
> ated by me with the full consent of the government. You should, however,
> inform the acting head of the IDAM about a couple of months ahead of
> your arrival, so that he may have sufficient time to sound out possibili-
> ties in Safad. As to that no one can say what the outcome will be until the
> mayor is approached on the subject; and I think it is wise not to approach
> the mayor a long time beforehand, so as to avoid possible complications if
> the information leaks out …   (GL44881/13, 8.11.59)

In the 1960s, Isserlin (also of the University of Leeds) excavated in Israel, but not in relation to this affair. Meiron was excavated by several scholars, especially Eric Meyers in the 1970s, and caves were also excavated but found looted (Feig 2002: 103–4). Bowman currently lives in Melbourne. In a letter of 6 September 2004 he writes that he has no more records, and only vague memories of the entire affair. Isserlin told me (by email, July 2004) that he was not involved in the plan, and the documents support this. I wish to thank both scholars for their kindness.

The elusive *genizot* of Safad and Meiron are still waiting, perhaps, but conditions at present do not favour the renewal of the project, even with the help of the Mayor of Safad.

14 THE POLICY OF SALVAGE
AND EARLY ISRAELI EXCAVATIONS

Iron are our lives
Molten right through our youth.
A burnt space through ripe fields
A fair mouth's broken tooth.

Isaac Rosenberg, "August 1914" (1949: 70)

THE DARK SIDE

The British Mandatory period is "generally regarded as the formative 'Golden Age' of Archaeology in Palestine" (Gibson 1999: 115, with references). True, the period signalled unprecedented progress, but it was not very difficult to improve Ottoman Palestine. There remained many dark spots: ethnic groups were segregated; the bulk of archaeological research was carried out by foreigners; the Law of Antiquities was accomplished at the price of creating legal trade in antiquities (Kletter & Kersel, forthcoming) and each separate group was interested in "our past" (Jews in synagogues; Arabs in Islamic periods and so on) (Broshi 1986: 25–6; Gibson 1999; Ben-Arieh 1999a,b, 2001; Abu el-Haj 2002).

Early Israeli archaeology was very popular (Fig. 29).By 1958 the IES had 1,500 local members and 200 members abroad (*BIES* **16** (1951/52): 76). Hundreds were attending annual conferences: 300 in 1948, 500 in 1949, 800 in 1957 (*BIES* **15** (1949/50): 124, **19** (1960–61): 87; *Alon* **3** (1951): 57). The young were also interested (Yeivin 1960: 2; cf. Dever 1985: 43; Elon 1997: 41–3; Rosen, in press). IES members came, as a whole, from the upper classes. State leaders were enthusiastic about archaeology: President Ben-Zvi was a keen scholar and David Ben-Gurion chaired a Bible study circle. The IES council in 1952 included the Minister of Education, the mayors of Tel Aviv and Haifa, Yosef Weitz of the JNF, Chief of Staff Yadin and American archaeologist Nelson Glueck, and the IES dealt not just with archaeology but also with nature and the recent history of Israel. Was this, then, the Golden Age of Israeli archaeology?

The files and newspaper clippings are filled with the darker side of public interest in archaeology: vandalism and damage to antiquities and sites through carelessness or malice. Contractors, drivers and even official institutions ignored

Figure 29. School visit to Zori's excavations at Beth Shean. (Photograph by Zori, IAA 1337)

and destroyed antiquities without letting anyone know (*Alon* **5–6** (1957): 5). People stole antiquities of all sorts, as well as equipment and materials from restored sites (*Alon* **4** (1953): 1–2). This was facilitated by the lack of an updated Law of Antiquities and effective supervision of sites.

One common custom was the writing of new inscriptions on ancient monuments. This stubborn and stupid habit still exists, but is hardly recent. Even the "holy" site of Masada was not protected from abuse by youth groups and other travellers (*Ma'ariv*, 10.4.1955, copy in GL44875/10 no. 7465). It became a plague:

> The walls become black or white from all the names. A new history was glued to them: Izhak from Kiryat Motzkin decided to love Rina of Migdal Ashkelon, especially on the tomb of one of the followers of Rabbi Yehuda ha-Nasi. Plainly, white on black, inscribed with a broken heart and dripping drops of blood … (Lavie 1956)

Damage and destruction of remains during development was a serious problem. Remains found during the erection of the Binayaney ha-'Ummah buildings in Jerusalem were destroyed on purpose by the entrepreneurs (*Ma'ariv*, 10.4.1955). On 2 December 1953 the newspaper *Masa* published details of some shocking instances: during works in the Negev ancient tombstones were used as filling material for a modern road; near Yeruham an entire site was destroyed.

Whereas some of the news stories were based on rumours that the IDAM denied, Yeivin admitted some cases (GL44875/10, 9.12.53). The journalist Zvi Lavie wrote more stories:

> Two weeks ago young inhabitants near Shivta – from the new settlement opposite it – were amazed … Old Shivta began to be methodically stolen, hastily taken upon lorries and carried away. It was one of the strangest discoveries of ignorance, stupidity and lack of logic by one contractor for building, who found no other way to save expenses on buying building materials … Those who directed the operation of theft were not satisfied with the thousands of stones strewn over the huge area. A direct order was given to bulldozer drivers … The steel arms went down on some buildings that stood hundreds of years against the power of nature.   (Lavie 1956)

Contractors of the new road to Eilat built a toilet right inside a Byzantine bathhouse and then when the nearby section of the road was finished, they destroyed the whole site rather than just dismantle the toilet. There is a story that Yadin forced them to rebuild the bathhouse. At Ozem in the Negev, a Tell was saved by the IDAM by moving a new settlement, but the road to the settlement was not moved and it damaged the Tell (Lavie 1956).

Trespassers were rarely brought to court. Until 1955 no cases came to trial (Amir 1955). Once they reached court, allegations often could not be verified and punishments were ridiculous. Here are a few examples of cases that did not reach court:

- An agricultural company planted "various vegetables, such as watermelons and zucchinis", on the Tell of Ashdod (Dothan, GL44886/4, 14.5.59).
- On 18 October 1958 a group of respectable people from the Kaiser-Frizer Company took "four pillars and four capitals" from Ashkelon for a private house one of them wanted to build. The items were damaged during transport. The commander of the local police station tried to avoid registering a complaint, suggesting that the group acted in innocence (*betom lev*) (GL44886/4, 16.4.59). The Minister of Education ordered Yeivin to ask the police to close this file (GL44880/13, 11.2.59).
- The Safad municipality gave a licence for building in the fortress area, despite knowing it was an ancient site. The police refused to act and once foundations were laid it was too late (GL44886/4, 21.1.59).
- A church inside Caesarea was ruined by a driver (GL44886/4, 11.1.59).
- A supervisor of the JNF robbed a Roman period tomb near Bir es-Safsaf. The police forgot to summon to court the two workers who were digging on the man's orders, so he was just warned (GL44886/4 no. 4566, letters 26.11.57, 4.12.57).

However, the authorities were particularly sensitive in cases involving foreigners. Rabbani, an antiquities guard, reported on 28 May 1950 (GL44886/4) that HL and OV – two Finnish tourists and students of the Biblical archaeologist Aapeli Saarisalo – visited Guy (without Saarisalo's knowledge) and showed him a drawing of a juglet they had "found". Rabbani went to the site and discovered that the two had dug a deep pit and did not find the juglet "by chance", as they said. Yeivin complained to the Director-General of the Ministry of Foreign Affairs (GL44886/4 no. 3380, 25.7.50), since in the meantime the two had left Israel. Yeivin's letter was translated and sent through the consular department to the Finnish consul in Israel (GL44886/4 no. 3080, 7.8.50). The two finally returned the juglet to the Consul of Israel in Helsinki (GL44886/4 no. 4029, 13.10.50).

In another strange case the IDAM reached the conclusion that tourists and diplomats were engaged in robbing sites along the coast. It asked the police to make sudden inspection tours on Fridays in Ashkelon, Yavne-Yam, Caesarea and so on, having previously placed warning signs at all these sites. There were traces of more robbery, but the robbers were not apprehended. In one tour in Caesarea, Prausnitz was showing the police sites that had been robbed when the British consular car arrived. Of course, when the travellers saw the police they refrained from committing an illicit act – even if this had been their intention (GL44886/4, "first report on police and IDAM acts"). Still, Prausnitz was confident that diplomats had stolen antiquities and notified the Ministry of Foreign Affairs. Soon he reported robbery by diplomats and UN personnel at Minat Rubin south of Tel Aviv (GL44886/4 no. 2197, 21.9.56). A picture of the "evidence" was sent by the IDAM to the Ministry of Foreign Affairs, showing "preserve tins [i.e. cans of food] used by illicit diggers" (GL44886/4 no. 2795, 5.11.56). This photograph (IAA 15,505) was delivered on 18 November 1956 to embassies and UN bodies in Israel, together with a letter from the Ministry of Foreign Affairs:

> The IDAM now communicates that, unfortunately, illegal digging still continues and I am enclosing a photograph supplied by the IDAM of a beer can, an empty cigarette pack, a Super Coola can and some Dixie cups found at Yavne. If any member of your mission was involved in this quest for ancient objects, an appeal from you to desist from such diggings would be very much appreciated … (GL44886/4 no. 4009)

We do not know whether W. Murray Anderson, administrative officer of the headquarters of the UN Truce Supervision Organization, was impressed with this sort of evidence, but he politely replied: "None of the UNTSO staff was in the area of Yavne and none of our staff is working in the discovery of antiquities. The items appearing in the photograph are, in the main, not stocked by the Truce Organization" (GL44886/4, 23.11.56).

One cannot avoid the conclusion that the IDAM was ready to go to great lengths when damage was caused by foreigners, even if it amounte to only one small juglet. The matter was treated as a national insult. On the other hand, Israelis like Dayan managed to rob dozens of sites and steal thousands of objects.

Similar problems arise everywhere, and are ongoing in Israel. Measuring their extent is difficult. The letters and newspapers of the 1950s create the impression that this was something new. However, it was known earlier in the Mandatory period, but not to such an extent, mainly because development was much more limited. It is also likely that public attitudes towards antiquities in the early 1950s were influenced by the policy towards abandoned refugee property. With so many abandoned places and looting during the war, and systematic destruction later, people were bound to treat anything as abandoned until proved otherwise. To "save" antiquities, in the few cases where something could be saved, often meant to tear them out of walls of houses before demolition, then remove them to some nondescript storage site, inaccessible to the public. What could laymen deduce from such acts? Add to that the harsh economic conditions and the contempt towards everything old. It was a "new" period; the ideal was to build new settlements, new roads, a new society and a new citizen. Why should old ruins have value? The educated could separate between "our" ancient sites, to be admired and cherished, and more recent sites identified with foreigners and with enemies. The "common man" was not likely to follow such subtleties.

The IDAM realized that the solution to vandalism, robbery and destruction of antiquities was general education of the public (*Alon* **4** (1953): 1–2). The wide media coverage of the phenomenon started in earnest around 1952/53; those who damaged the past were much more strongly criticized, regardless of political positions. The newspapers actually took it upon themselves to educate the Israeli public, mainly about their "past". The common claim was that it was not just the land that was theirs now, but also its past. This past gave Israelis legitimization, so they must keep the remains and nurture their study. In the long run, it was a crucial contribution.

After 1967, "imported" antiquities stolen in the occupied territories became a major problem again. The robbers who looted the sites were motivated by the dire economic situation in these areas. The spoils were mainly enjoyed by Western/Israeli dealers and connoisseurs. However, this is beyond the scope of this book.

Thus it seems that the 1950s were not the "Golden Age" of Israeli archaeology, but maybe the concept of a Golden Age is a myth. When we look for a Golden Age we can never hope to make it real because it is always related to the past. Perhaps the only possible Golden Age is the present. Now is the only time when options are still open, actions possible, and Walter Benjamin's angel of history has not yet seen us (cf. Grunfeld 1988: 240).

THE POLICY OF SALVAGE EXCAVATIONS

The IDAM had an advantage in comparison with the former period: it had more workers and a bigger budget but a smaller area to supervise. However, the pace of development was chaotic (*Alon* **5–6** (1957): 2–3), calling for fast solutions to numerous problems. A policy towards salvage excavations was essential, although the term "salvage excavations" was only coined later.

Such a policy was formulated early. An expression is found in a memorandum by Yeivin of 31 December 1950, of a meeting between the IDAM, the Planning Unit (Makhlaka le-Tikhnun) of the Housing Department in the Ministry of Labour, the Planning Department of the Prime Minister's Office and the Property Department of the Ministry of Finance. This considerable team met to discuss building new neighbourhoods near Ashkelon. Some of the plans included areas of antiquities:

> Mr Yeivin explained in detail the policy of the IDAM concerning develop-
> ment projects that include parts of historical sites; in this case the IDAM
> distinguishes three types:
>
> (i)   The first type [A], important sites where no development projects will be
>   permitted under any condition, for example, the area of ancient Ashkelon
>   within the Crusader walls that are seen today above ground.
>
> (ii) The third type [C], sites whose importance is lesser, according to the
>   information known to the IDAM. The IDAM will permit development
>   projects immediately, provided that during the works (digging founda-
>   tions, levelling areas, etc.) a representative of the IDAM will be present.
>   He will supervise the work and be allowed to stop it if remains are found
>   that, according to his judgement, necessitate further archaeological
>   examination [meaning excavation, although not written explicitly].
>
> (iii) Between the two former types there is type B, where the IDAM will
>   be ready to permit development projects after an initial archaeologi-
>   cal examination. In case such an examination discovers monumental
>   remains that require restoration and exposure for exhibition, these
>   remains will be removed from all the areas where development work
>   will be permitted. The examinations made in relation to types B and C
>   must be budgeted according to the following division: the IDAM pays
>   the expenses of the scientific work (manager of examination, survey,
>   photographs, treatment of finds, final publication, etc.); while the body
>   that performs the development project pays the full expenses of the
>   work salary …   (GL44875/9)

Yeivin asked that developers also supply the services of an engineer or surveyor, which the IDAM lacked; the IDAM would pay the cost. Then, when discussing the specific case of Ashkelon, Yeivin mentioned a fourth type of site (but not explicitly) – previously unknown or "new" sites:

> As for area X in the eastern part of the suggested neighbourhood, it does not interest the IDAM at all, since as far as is known it is found outside the area of the ancient site. However, the rule that is valid for the entire country is also valid in this area. If during works there ancient remains should be found, the developers must notify the IDAM and stop work until the IDAM permits its continuation. The conclusions of the examination of the remains [will be decided] as above.
>
> As for area Y, its western part belongs to type B and its eastern part to C; but setting the exact borders between the B and C type areas is impossible by sight … Excavation of a few trial trenches is needed and hopefully their results will allow setting the borders between these two areas … Mr Levison explained that a contract will be signed on building these neighbourhoods … on sums that will exceed a million Lira and more. Mr Yeivin demanded that in this case, 1% to 2% of the entire sum be dedicated to the expenses of the initial archaeological examination of the planned neighbourhoods.
>
> (GL44875/9)

It is a remarkable document, although it could be better arranged. Actually, archaeological salvage in Israel is based today on similar principles. Development of major sites (Tells) is forbidden (with few exceptions, often due to legal problems). All other sites (Yeivin's types B and C), if registered officially (*mukhrazim*), require preliminary examinations and, if needed, excavations. So do "new sites", but financing their excavation is more difficult. Yeivin probably underestimated the number and significance of "new sites". The decisions had to be made in advance, that is, before projects were started. In many cases, the nature of a site was not well known, especially in the case of "new" sites. Often, sites or areas hold unforeseen surprises. Yeivin also suggested three possibilities following a salvage excavation: releasing the area for development; releasing the area after removal of important remains; and refusing development if very important remains were found. Even more remarkable was the estimation of 1–2 percent of the development budget that Yeivin demanded for archaeology. It was common knowledge, used in many cases in later years.

This policy of salvage excavations was good – on paper. The problem was its enforcement over developers, including the state's various developing bodies. Perhaps the gravest problem was financing excavations. In a lecture delivered in 1951 Yeivin followed a similar typology of sites:

A. Important, where no development is allowed (most of the Tells, about 200 in all).

B. Second in importance, where the IDAM will require trial excavations to decide whether to allow development (but he added that sites of this type were "few and not well defined", e.g. "near Caesarea", "near Ramla's white mosque").

C. Suspected sites, where supervision or small-scale probes are enough, e.g. some parts of Tiberias, the new town of Beth Shean, areas further away from Ashkelon's walls (*Alon* **4** (1953): 9).

The 1951 lecture marked a deterioration in standards of protection. Yeivin did not mention "new" sites. He took it for granted that the importance of an area was directly related to its proximity to the centre of a site. There were no criteria as to how much must be excavated in sites of types B and C before release for development. Yeivin even agreed to excavate large Tells in certain circumstances:

> The prohibition on touching historical sites even of type A is not eternal. It is temporary, as long as the site is unexplored. Even an important Tell, once completely excavated, if it yields no outstanding monuments, [then] its right for preservation is annulled and it should be treated like any other land in the state.   (*Alon* **4** (1953): 9–10)

Yeivin wrote similarly to the Planning Department on 5 August 1951:

> Usually the IDAM will object to including Tells such as Zippori, Megiddo or Wadi 'Ara [Ar'ara] in any plans of building or development. These extensive Tells require detailed archaeological investigation and, owing to their size and depth, such an investigation will take many years and very large investment, impossible in current conditions – also for lack of experts (archaeologists, surveyors, photographers, etc.).
>
>   In some other places, it may be possible to release sites after checking, on certain conditions. But even here one cannot make general rules, each place necessitates special visits …   (GL44875/9 no. 6298)

With these words Yeivin signified that the IDAM would not automatically stop any plan: matters of the living come before those of the dead. In small Tells or *khirbeh*s, from "periods for which our knowledge is plentiful", it would be sufficient to carry out just a small trial excavation. Sometimes, even this could be avoided, if developers agreed to leave the centre of the site empty, for example, as a garden (*Alon* **2** (1950): 5–6). A typology of sites is a difficult and much debated matter even today (why classify? how? what is "important"?). Yeivin could and would not object to the dream of development as an ultimate ideal: Israel clothed "in a robe of cement and concrete" (from Natan Alterman's famous poem "A

Song to Moledet"). Rather than speaking about an archaeology of protection, Yeivin's concern was to fit archaeology into the vision of development. In this he was only typical of his period. Similar views are common today (even the present IAA mission statement speaks about maintaining a balance between development and archaeology); that sites are a sort of "endangered species" is still a minority view (Gal 1996; Kletter and de-Groot 2001).

Policy was one thing: practice another. Developers – public or private – paid for work in the field, usually by cheap relief workers. The IDAM paid the salary of the professional team. The transportation of excavation workers was a grey area. During the 1950s a team in a typical salvage excavation was very small, led by one manager and perhaps an assistant or two (Fig. 30). The manager took the photographs and made interim plans; only the final plans required a professional surveyor. The team consisted of IDAM workers covered by the regular budget. The shortfall in professional excavators was filled with guards, Friends of Antiquities and students. The IDAM paid for post-excavation expenses until final publication. Excavations were almost never undertaken in the "dead" winter (unlike today). There was little understanding of how expensive and complex is the road to final publication (compare Delougaz, in Ch. 4, pp. 92–5).

While supervision was improved and procedures for checking development plans and coordinating the work were arranged with most developing bodies, funding for salvage excavations remained a stumbling block. Yeivin defined the payment for workers as "help" from developers, including private individuals "on whose premises remains requiring examination were found" (Yeivin 1960: 3; see also Yeivin 1955b: 3). However, the regulations did not legalize this procedure and some developers refused to "help", or even avoided the problem by destroying antiquities. In 1957 Yeivin wrote:

> The problem of financing the IDAM investigations, required because of development works, is becoming grave, especially now when the Ministry of Employment has cut the allocation of relief workers for archaeological works. It is not always possible, and it is always difficult, to demand finance for the investigations from the developers.   (GL44883/12, 4.12.57)

Yeivin's pleas for special governmental funding to finance investigations were ignored, although he warned that without it he would have to forbid development even in sites of "secondary importance" (*ibid.*). In a report about the use of the 1955/56 budget Yeivin wrote:

> In all, we made 28 excavations this year. It would not be possible ... unless other institutions paid the salary of the workers. Most of the works were done with the kind help of the employment department of the Ministry of

> Labour, who put at our disposal 8,926 work-days. But in most places the
> IDAM paid for the transportation of the workers ... and in some places also
> social insurance. (GL44880/12)

When the Nirim Synagogue in the Negev was discovered in 1957, the IDAM did not have the budget to handle it. Yeivin hoped that relief workers would be found, but was not sure if there was unemployment in the region. He begged for funding, playing on the fact that it was a synagogue with "political importance in relation to the discussions over the Gaza strip", which was completely untrue. The site had been discovered during roadbuilding; once the road had been shifted slightly the IDAM was not able to demand that the developer pay for an excavation (GL448880/12 no. 3842, 1.3.57).

This situation was no better in the 1960s, when Biran replaced Yeivin as Director of the IDAM. Biran took it naturally that "supremacy" was given to excavations, not publications (IAA 1962). Allegedly, the bulldozer was the friend of the archaeologist: "Thus, under vigilance, the bulldozer and the plough safely lay bare the groundwork for scientific quests" (Biran 1962: 175).

The problem of financing salvage excavations was never properly solved. The use of relief workers, and later the unemployed, was taken for granted. Tragically, even the 1978 Antiquities Law took it for granted, thus failing to acknowledge salvage excavations. The 1978 Antiquities Law did not define what salvage excavations are, who performs them, when they are performed and who funds them. The results of the gaps in the legislation were discovered only in the 1990s. The price Israeli archaeology paid, and will pay, for them is immense (financially, as well as ethically).

EARLY ISRAELI EXCAVATIONS

A dichotomy existed between Jordan and Israel in the 1950s and 1960s (Wright 1970: 35–6). British archaeologists in Jordan had adopted the revolutionary Wheeler–Kenyon method of excavation (Kenyon 1952; Moorey 1979, 1992; Dever 1985: 37; Prag 1992; for criticism see Dever 1973; Barkay 1992; Prag 1992: 115; Reich 1995: 142–7). Local archaeologists on both sides of the Jordan were later to use this method. Israeli archaeologists, writing in the 1960s and 1970s hailed a different "Israeli method of excavation", invented in the 1950s. Allegedly, it was also stratigraphically precise, but avoided the drawbacks of the Wheeler–Kenyon method by excavating large areas and stressing pottery restoration (Aharoni 1973b; Bar-Yosef & Mazar 1982: 314). Today we know that this picture was idealized (Bar-Yosef & Mazar 1982: 314; Dever 1985: 35; Ussishkin 1982: 94–5). Final reports and later excavations at the same sites show that sections were not used; with the exception of prehistorians, archaeologists worked in the "architectonic" or "locus to stratum" method of the Mandatory period (for which see G. R. H. Wright 1966; G. E. Wright 1969: 129–32). Shortage of professionals (*Alon* 4 (1953): 3, GL44883/11), intense pressures of development and inexperienced relief workers aggravated the situation. Standards of excavation in early Israeli archaeology were not good (Figs 31–2, cf. also Figs 16, 30).

Registration of finds was often crude. There was no obligatory system and no specific numbers for each excavation. Sometimes, Hebrew initials were used ("A.H." signified "Ayyelet ha-Shahar"), which was hardly satisfying if more than one excavation was held at a site (Fig. 33). The State Comptroller noticed the faulty registration in 1954: finds were registered neither in the field, nor when reaching Jerusalem (GL44868/7 no. 1/9/1-90, 30.9.54). Yeivin claimed that most finds were sherds that did not require registration; and that the IDAM lacked the manpower to handle the problem (GL44868/7 no. 5031a).

Despite all the difficulties, the IDAM alone performed about 30 salvage excavations per year during the first decade of Israel's existence (Table 5; *Alon* 4 (1953): 1; Yeivin 1955a: 163–7, 1955b: 4, 1960: 3–47). The growth in comparison with the Mandatory period was huge and directly related to the frenzy of development. The IES and the Hebrew University made relatively few excavations, but these were larger and usually longer. The Hazor excavations, led by Yadin with a large team, were especially important. Many later prominent archaeologists in Israel started there. The findings of the excavation were published fast (Yadin *et al.* (eds) 1959, 1960, 1961; cf. Yadin 1972) except the final volume (Ben-Tor

Figure 30. Afulah (Jezreel valley), 1951. Excavation by Dothan. Note the lack of sections. The excavation follows the architecture. (IAA 3412)

Figure 31. Tel Dor, 1950. Excavation by Leibowitz. Workers follow the remains along narrow trenches. (Photograph by Leibowitz, IAA 2729)

Figure 32. Ramat Rahel, excavations of Aharoni, 1955. Note the "office" with the tools. (Photograph by Biberkraut, IAA 11,016)

306

Table 5. Excavation in Israel, 1948–67.

Year	Foreign research institutions	Universities, museums, IES, GTC	IDAM salvage work (estimated)	IDAM initiated excavations	General number	Notes
1948		1	3	1	5	War of independence
1949		2	22		24	
1950	1	3	55		59	
1951		1	46		47	
1952	3	1	28		32	
1953	3	4	36		43	
1954	2	2	28		32	
1955	4	3	41		48	
1956	1	3	43	1 ("Gat")	48	Sinai War
1957	1	4	28	1	34	
1958	1	6	32	1	40	First GTC excavation at Avdat (Avi-Yonah)
1959	7	2	21	1	31	
1960	9	5	26	1	41	
1961	10	2	26	1	39	
1962	7	4	35	1 (Dan)	47	
1963	6	10	23	1	40	
1964	10	10	32	1	53	
1965	6	15	40	1	62	First local underwater excavation (Linder)
1966	9	11	48	1	69	
1967	10	7	28	1	46	Six Days War
Total	90	96	641	13	840	

Notes: IDAM reports usually follow budget years (measured from April to March at that period). Since winter was a dead season, not used for excavations, I have assumed that all excavations within a certain budget year were performed in spring/summer of that year. For example, excavations in budget year 1956–57 were performed in 1956.

Figure 33. Claire Epstein sorting pottery at Susita, *c*.1954. (IAA 10177)

& Bonfil 1997). It proved the ability of Israeli archaeologists to carry out large projects with success (Albright 1970: 62; Bar-Yosef & Mazar 1982: 314).

Local volunteers were used in the 1950s, for example, in Aharoni's 1953 excavation at Kedesh (Galilee); mostly IES members (*BIES* **17** (1952/53): 158). The idea of using foreign volunteers was raised by the GTC. In 1955, Pierre d'Harcout, travel editor of the London-based *Observer* Sunday newspaper, asked about "excavation parties which amateurs of British nationality could join", but the matter was not taken up in earnest (GL44882/9, 17.11.55; cf. nos. 8428a, 422). On 18 March 1957, Aharon Zvi Propes, manager of the Special Events Department of the GTC, suggested that the IDAM should use foreign volunteers and promised to help with publicity (GL44882/9 nos. 1801, 1911). Yeivin failed to realize the potential (GL44882/9 no. 3957). In 1961 the IDAM turned down similar expressions of interest. Yadin started to use volunteers in Masada in the 1960s. The lack of interest during the 1950s was also due to the availability of cheap relief work: there was no need to look elsewhere.

THE FIRST EXCAVATIONS IN ISRAEL: A CORRECTION

It is commonly believed that the first excavation in Israel was that by Mazar at Tell Qasileh near Tel Aviv. It received licence no. 1, issued on 21 October 1948, signed by the Minister of Labour on behalf of the still temporary government. The licence stipulated that the excavation would be performed using "new scientific methods"; the manager would have "a team of experts sufficient for the work" and enough funding to "achieve reasonable scientific results and their publication" (*Qadmoniyot* **117** (1999): 58). The licence was announced in the press (*Ha'aretz* 1948), and the excavation started on 27 October 1948 (*BIES* **15** (1948/49): 8). But this was not the first excavation in Israel.

Two salvage excavations preceded it. They were small ones and did not receive a licence, because licences for salvage excavations were given only from 1963. The first excavation was that of a Roman period tomb at Natanya, north of Tel Aviv, and the first excavator was Yaacov Ory. The tomb was found when a sewage pit was dug for a house. Dr Y. Rosenbusch notified the IDAM about it in early September. There were many finds, and the excavation was finished before the one at Tell Qasile even started (*Ha'aretz* 1948; cf. GL44864/14, 7.10.48). On 27 September 1948 the manager of the Public Works Department suggested mounting an exhibition of the finds at Natanya (GL44864/14). Ory reported the results (GL44864/14, report 31.12.48), and the findings were published in detail later by Reich (1978).

The second salvage excavation was made by Amiran at Tiv'on: a large tomb with clay coffins, damaged during development by the Keret Company and dated to the Roman period. Entrance to another, nearby tomb was blocked by cement to prevent damage. Amiran probably started to excavate on 29 September 1948 (GL44864/14, report 31.12.48; GI.44875/9, report 15.11.48; preliminary publication in *Alon* **1** (1949): 9).

Finally, a third excavation started just a few days after that of Tell Qasile; this was not a salvage excavation but an "initiated" one. It was carried out by Guy in Jaffa in 1948 (see Fig. 7, p. 54). A letter from Yeivin of 9 September 1948 asked the Minister of Education to provide the budget for this excavation from item 41 of the IDAM's budget, relating to excavations and surveys (GL44883/8 no. 958). Guy chose two areas clear of buildings (for Jaffa in 1948 see Ch. 2). One area was near the British Customs House north of the port, the other near the top of the Tell, close to the Latin Church. Excavation was scheduled to begin on 10 October 1948 (GL44864/14; GL44864/14, report 31.12.48) but was delayed because of the conditions at the site until 1 November 1948 (from data based on the IAA excavation file studied by Martin Peilstöcker). It continued until December (GL44864/14) and was stopped for lack of funding. There are scanty published preliminary reports (*Alon* **1** (1949): 2–3; **2** (1950) 24). Unfortunately Guy died in 1952, so details of the excavation remain unpublished.

15 MYTHS AND CONCLUSIONS

It is good to learn from the archaeologists the
humility *of Historical Perspective*
Minister M. Ben-Tov, speech to the IES 5th
Annual Conference (*BIES* **15** (1948/49): 48)

In the preceding chapters we have traced the history of early Israeli archaeology (for this term see Rosen, in press) and its many failures and successes. I wish to review its growth here and touch briefly on its role in the framework of nation building. Documents from the state archive naturally stress the IDAM, so conclusions regarding other bodies are limited.

We have seen how plans for a general survey failed completely for lack of budget (Ch. 2). Only some limited surveys were carried out, such as by Anati and Glueck in the Negev (Yeivin 1955b: 17–18) (Fig. 34), Aharoni in the Galilee (*Alon* **5–6** (1957): 45–9; *BIES* **19** (1954/55): 136–7; Aharoni 1956; Yeivin 1960: 47–9) and in Nahal Hever. The Judean Desert survey of 1960–61 was mainly aimed at finding scrolls (Bar-Adon 1980; Yadin 1963). The 1950s also saw the start of small-scale surveys before development (e.g. GL44883/12, 4.12.58).

We have noted the shortage of professional archaeologists (see pp. 126, 249, 303; *Alon* **2** (1950): 3; **5–6** (1957): 2; Mazar 1952: 18). The IDAM started with 11 workers (Yeivin 1955b: 3, 1960: 1; *Alon* **1** (1949): 24). By 1951 there were 39 (*Alon* **3** (1951): 64), and from 1952 about 50–55 regular workers (including guards; Yeivin 1960: 1; GL44868/7 no. 7652). By 1973 there were 86 regular workers. Academic positions remained very few, with seven teaching positions in archaeology at the Hebrew University in 1955 (Yeivin 1960: 2). In July 1955 archaeologists in Israel were recognized as a professional group and in December 1958 they joined the workers' organization (*Histadrut*) (an association of workers' unions). At that time they numbered 37 archaeologists (GL44889/2, 12.12.58, 21.12.58; *Davar* 19.12.1956).

Figure 34. Negev survey luncheon. (Photograph by Anati, IAA 12,429)

In the area of inspection and conservation we have seen many problems and failures to protect sites, and severe lack of funding for conservation (Yeivin 1960: 2, 54; GL44833/11, report 1956; GL44883/9, 13.5.53). After 1958 the GTC took over the major sites and their "development".

The budget of the IDAM shows considerable growth (Table 6). The budget for activities amounted to about 60 percent of the entire budget. Data on the Ministry of Education have been added for comparison. Data for the IES were published in *BIES* until 1956 and data related to the university are not available at present.

The IDAM started from scratch in 1948 and managed to build a significant library and archive. In 1948 it had a hundred or so books on one shelf in the Schocken Library. Yeivin understood that "no scientific action is possible without a rich and professional library" (GL44883/8, 29.11.48). He allowed each supervisor three or four days a month for library and archive work. In 1950 the library of the IDAM included about 2,000 volumes and received 46 periodicals; in 1958 it had about 7,000 volumes and 136 periodicals (GL44883/12) and by 1967 it had about 14,000 books (GL44889/5, 9.73; *Alon* **2** (1950): 7; **3** (1951): 5–6; Cassuto-Saltzmann 1965: 25–7). In 1958, the archive had 1,820 files of sites, 2,650 maps and about 35,000 negatives (GL44883/12).

The IDAM organized a temporary exhibition in July 1949 and permanent exhibitions soon after (*Alon* **3** (1951): 56–7; **4** (1953): 11–15; **5–6** (1957): 3; Yeivin 1960: 54–5; IAA 1965: 20–21). During the first decade, 36,000 people saw these exhibitions, of which about half were of school age. The IDAM was also involved with exhibitions abroad. The first was "From the Land of the Bible" in 1953–55; it travelled to New York, Washington, London, The Hague, Stockholm and Oslo. Yeivin said that it made real the Biblical times and was a "successful

Table 6. IDAM budget (Lira) (GL files 1430/14, 44883/8, 44883/9, 44883/10, 44883/11, 44883/12, 44883/13, 44884/4, 44884/9; *BIES* **15–22**; Israel Government Yearbook and Statistical Abstract of Israel).

Year	IDAM general budget	IDAM proposed general budget	IDAM activities budget	IDAM proposed activities budget	Ministry of Education budget	IES total budget	IDAM total expenses (budget used)	Notes
1948/49	8,405	5,190–17,520	4,500*	–	583,000	979		Budget of IDAM for the period after June
1949/50	38,815	55,413	19,820	–	2,260,000	2,736	24,938	
1950/51	72,700	73,380	44,900	46,950	4,678,000	7,993		Excavations used 14,300
1951/52	92,300	102,920	58,250	57,925	8,353,000	7,744		
1952/53	113,320	132,131	83,340	71,385	16,004,000	10,170	118,651	Ministry used 15,179,000
1953/54	169,400	171,500	88,440	88,800	28,782,000	27,053	173,813	
1954/55	228,400	317,940	117,180	145,810	36,165,000	43,010	213,331	
1955/56	277,000	271,000	146,200	140,200	40,337,000	52,604		
1956/57	296,400	407,414	145,850	218,355	62,643,000		282,051	
1957/58	310,000	380,167	147,000	179,198	73,302,000			
1958/59	343,000	340,000	158,000	158,000	82,100,000			
1959/60	370,000	370,000	176,500	176,500	95,200,000			
1960/61		421,500		183,700	112,900,000			
1962/63	473,500		407,300		162,400,000			
1963/64		564,150		469,600	203,000,000			
1964/65	746,000		477,500		255,200,000		843,997	
1965/66	845,400		521,400		321,000,000			
1966/67		999,400		699,100	456,000,000			

* indicates estimation. In the first years, the budget was not separated between activities and other items, and reserves from former years could be used in the following year. In 1948, the IDAM was under the Ministry of Labour, whose budget for the half year of 1948 was 553,000 Lira. Budgets for the Ministry of Education are rounded, usually including development budgets. The IES budget was calculated from October to September (following the Hebrew calendar). For example, IES budget year 1948/49 means October 1948 to September 1949. Until 1958, the IDAM kept to its budget limits (Yeivin, report 4.12.58, GL44883/12).

means of presenting the State of Israel and its cultural mission" (1955b: 20–21; 1960: 56; this exhibition deserves a separate study).

The IDAM encouraged regional/municipal museums. By 1955 there were 7 municipal museums and 29 local ones (Yeivin 1955b: 21). By the end of the 1950s they numbered 58 museums and collections; Jerusalem was leading with 9 museums (*IEJ* 1: 121–3, *Alon* 3 (1951): 4–5, 56; 4: 14; Yeivin 1960: 55–61). The Hebrew University developed its own museum (Mazar 1952: 24). The period saw the Dead Sea Scrolls attract a lot of attention, with the building of the "Shrine of the Book" (Roitman 2003; Landau & Zalmona 1998).

In the field of publication the situation was not pleasing. The "strenuous work" did not leave much time (Yeivin 1960: 56; IAA 1962: Introduction). Until 1955 the IDAM only had the small *Alon* (six volumes over 1949–57, with a long delay from 1954 to 1957; *Alon* 5–6 (1957): 1). It is a valuable source for the period, but not a professional publication. There were also a few popular small site guides (Yeivin 1955b: 21; 1960: 57). The journal *'Atiqot* appeared in December 1955. It was the IDAM's first professional publication. True to its tradition, even today it includes many scientific reports and very few anecdotes. In December 1961 *Hadashot Archaeologyot* [*Excavations and Surveys in Israel*] was added by the IDAM, continuing the concept of *Alon*. In the Hebrew University, the short-lived *Bulletin of the L.M. Rabinowitz Fund for the Exploration of Ancient Synagogues* ceased to exist, and *Qedem* was halted until 1975 (Mazar 1952: 24; Yeivin 1960: 57). The one exception to the decline in publications was the IES, which expanded its publications considerably: the bulletin (*BIES*) continued; the series *Eretz Israel* started in 1951, the first large-format book series of Israeli archaeology; the English *Israel Exploration Journal* was launched in 1950. The IES also published annual conference proceedings and other studies.

THE END OF EARLY ISRAELI ARCHAEOLOGY

Although a few of the chapters of this volume ventured into later years, the 1967 War marked the end of early Israeli archaeology. The change happened gradually between 1962 and 1967. The end is marked, for better or for worse, by the following developments:

- the renewal of the archaeological council in 1962;
- the creation of an association for survey (ha-Agudah le-Seker);
- the beginning of underwater archaeology, about 1964;
- the founding of additional universities, first in Tel Aviv, then later Beer-sheba, Bar Ilan and Haifa, which meant more students and professional archaeologists;

- growing professionalization and a demand for academic degrees;
- the end of relief work;
- the beginning of the "interdisciplinary approach" (Dever 1985: 39–42) and later "new archaeology";
- the creation of the Nature and Parks Authority in 1963;
- a significant increase in foreign expeditions and in numbers of excavations;
- the founding of the Israel Museum in 1965;
- registration (licensing) of all excavations from 1963;
- the 1967 War and the occupation of the territories.

EARLY ISRAELI ARCHAEOLOGY AND NATIONALITY

Archaeology is entangled with many fields of human interest. It is crucial to discuss structures and politics, no less than sites, strata and finds. Still, one hesitates before venturing into the minefield of archaeology and nationalism. I think we can reach better conclusions by asking first what we would do "in their place". Then, we should try not to defend the past nor conceal its dark side; nor abuse it for a modern political aim.

The common view is that early Israeli archaeology in the 1950s was overtly nationalistic, a willing tool in the hands of the regime. This finds some corroboration in the following story. The "Jewish Palestine Exploration Society" decided to change its name in 1951. This was prompted by a letter from Prime Minister Ben-Gurion, that was read at its conference:

> Allow me to wonder at the translation of the society's name in English …
> I wonder about the name Palestine that you still use. A land of this name
> does not exist (and in my view never existed). The origin of this name is
> not pure: it was given by Greeks who hated Israel. It related to an ancient
> tribe of which no remains are left. It defines no area. It is meaningless. In
> place of it, one must simply say Land of Israel, if for any reason one does
> not want to say just Israel … If you use this name you do not need to use
> the words "Hebrew" or "Jewish".   (*BIES* **16** (1951/52): 74–5)

Many took part in the discussion that followed, so apparently there was disagreement; but the publication failed to note voices of dissent. The society decided to drop the offending word from its English name and became the Israel Exploration Society.

Archaeology and "knowledge of the country" (*yedi'at ha-aretz*) were the *bon ton* of the regime. President Ben-Zvi was symbolically leading the IES and was a member of the managing committee; meetings of IES bodies were often held in his house. The first time the President did not attend the annual IES conference was in 1959 and he apologized for that (*BIES* **24** (1959/60):149). Annual conferences attracted the Prime Minister and other senior ministers. The Chief of Staff, managers of the JNF and the Jewish Agency, city mayors and other dignitaries made their annual pilgrimages to the conferences. Their speeches and blessings were published in *BIES*, forming an important source about the way archaeology was grasped and used by the leaders. In the 1960s, archaeological substance replaced the speeches and blessings, so the last were barely mentioned any more in the publications.

The first to notice the use of archaeology by the state in Israel was Elon (1971), followed by many (Shay 1989; Zerubabel 1991; 1995; Ben-Yehuda 1995; 2002; Abu el-Haj 2001; cf. Kempinski 1994; Elon 1997; Hallote & Joffe 2002; Joffe 2003). Albright (1970: 60–61) had already written that "archaeology helped to produce, among Israelis, a sense of belonging", but he was in favour of myths, not their deconstruction (cf. also Broshi 1986; Shavit 1997; for foundation myths in the pre-state period see Sterenhall 1998). I do not intend to defend early Israeli archaeology by negating its nationalism because it would not be true, but the "myth busters" are becoming trivial (e.g. Geva 1994; Ben-Yehuda 1995, 2002) by overlooking the core of the issue. If readers are surprised that after exposing the secrets of Israeli archaeology I now want to defend it, I ask for their patience in order to clarify my position.

The documents studied in this book show that the conceived picture of a nationalistic archaeology is too simplistic. It is true that most Israeli archaeologists of the 1950s ignored late, especially Moslem, periods (even Yeivin 1960: 3–47, reaching only the Byzantine period). Ignorance of late periods (mainly Medieval to Ottoman) was typical of Near-Eastern archaeology in general at the time. Even in Turkey, Ottoman remains are still not considered "old" by the public and are facing destruction as a result (Özdoğan 1998: 119), although this observation is made in the context of defence from accusations about destruction of "Greek remains". Israeli archaeologists did stress "Jewish" themes, for example, synagogues, but this was typical of the Mandatory period as well, and people are often particularly interested in their own culture.

Most Israeli archaeologists in the 1950s were honest. They were the product of their time, as we all are. They did not abuse archaeology on purpose (as poignantly concluded already by Elon (1997: 38–9); cf. Rosen (in press)). They served the regime, but also harnessed it to their needs, in the form of help from the army, funding for projects, and so on. One should remember that the "regime" and the senior archaeologists were not separate in the 1950s: the latter were part and parcel of the elite. Not all the interest expressed by the elite in archaeology was faked. For example, President Ben-Zvi was a keen scholar; Dayan's obsession with antiquities was sincere (but in opposition to academic interest).

315

The IDAM was probably the least nationalistic of the three academic bodies (despite being part of the state apparatus), which was very much thanks to its professional origin (the Mandatory Department, and hence British tradition) and to its leadership under Yeivin. Compare what Yeivin said in a 1951 lecture to development bodies (i.e. the elite), and later published in *Alon*:

> Most of the late monuments are not Jewish. But if we demand that foreigners respect the remains of our past, we must respect theirs. It is one of the Ten Commandments: thou shall not kill … also applies to murder of cultural remains and spiritual possessions. I have seen it fit to stress this matter because from my experience in recent years I have learned that among many circles of serious people there is a complete contempt [*zilzul*] for foreign remains in our land; especially when Arab remains are concerned.
>
> (*Alon* **4** (1953): 7)

Yeivin even criticized the developers for building "rectangular boxes of white houses" for the immigrants at Ramla, instead of drawing "some inspiration from the old architecture of Ramla" (*ibid.*: 8). Personal integrity varied, and there were archaeologists who used the past to enhance their position by selling to the regime, or to the public, what they expected to hear. Yadin developed and used the myth of Masada following his excavations there in 1963–65 (Ben-Yehuda 1995, 2002; but see Avni 2003: 1254). However, Yadin did not invent this myth; it existed before. He was also part of the regime as Chief of Staff and later a party leader. After 1967 he mocked the worship of national and religious relics (Elon 1997: 41). Abuse of archaeology came mainly from its "consumers" among leaders and politicians (cf. Elon 1997: 39; Feige 1998).

It is crucial not to isolate Israel from other nations in similar stages of nation-building (cf. Baram & Rowan 2004; Joffe, in press; Rosen, in press). The elite of Israel, Yadin included, did not invent anything new in using the "Masada myth" or archaeology in general. It was no different from countless other examples of the use of archaeology by nationalistic movements. Ideas about a direct continuation of Biblical Joshua, or the Hasmonaeans, or the "rebels" of Masada, were only typical (cf. Kohl & Fawcett 1995; Silberman 1989; 2001; Hallote & Joffe 2002: 64–6). Only the details and the degree of success vary. The Baath party in Iraq conducted an educational campaign about the significance and "historical relevance" of the Mesopotamian past, in order to create an Iraqi nation separated from other Arab groups. Saddam Hussein portrayed himself as direct heir to Hammurabi (Baram 1994). Compare Iran (Abdi 2001). In Turkey of Ataturk, creating a nation was made by an opposite "fervent desire" to break off from the recent past, for example, by adopting a new capital and a new script (Kadioğlu 1996; Özdoğan 1998). In Lebanon, the "Phoenician movement" failed. Naccache (1998) mourns the destruction of archaeological remains in Beirut mainly because it prevented their use for nation-building. For example, he mourned the loss of context of an ostracon inscribed "Abdo", because in his view both Moslems and Christians could identify with this name. This loss "denied the Lebanese an opportunity to acquire a common ancestor, i.e. to have a common history" (*ibid.*: 150). He writes: "the proper archaeological study of Beirut would have been a first step towards the writing of the much sought-after 'Unified Lebanese' history book" (*ibid.*: 148).

In Egypt, the sculptor Mahmud Mukhtar made a huge granite statue called "The Awakening of Egypt", completed in 1928. Now standing in the avenue leading to the University of Cairo, this monumental statue symbolized Egypt's renewed interest in the pharaonic past and the efforts to detach Egypt from Arab and African backgrounds. When it was revealed, the Prime Minister spoke about the bond uniting different phases of Egyptian history and declared: "civilization and wisdom spread from here to the Greeks, to Rome, to the radiant Arab state and to Europe" (Baram 1994: 187; Hassan 1998: 206). The reopening of the tomb of Tut-Ankh-Amun in 1924 became a political rally (Wood 1998: 183). After the Second World War, in the 1950s, Egyptian President Abdel-Nasser denied the "pharaonic past" in favour of "Arab nationalism" (Hassan 1998: 207–9). And President Sadat's term in office marked a partial return to the Egyptian past; for example, he insisted that the mummy of Ramses II, when taken to Paris for restoration, should be greeted at Charles de Gaulle airport with a 21-gun salute, as if a head of state were coming (Wood 1998: 186). Compare how bones from Judean Desert caves found in 1960 were re-buried with much fanfare by the Begin government in 1982 as remains of heroes from the Jewish revolt against Rome (Aronoff 1991: 181–2; Elon 1997: 41). Incidentally, Hassan (1998: 212) rightly describes the architectonic "pastiche" of Cairo (it fits many other cities in the region, Jerusalem included), but he forgets to mention Cairo's (former) Jewish community and synagogues. Palestinians in the past decade seem to be in a stage of nation-building that demands archaeology in much the same way as Israel in the 1950s (Elon 1997: 46).

These reinterpretations of the past are not limited to Middle Eastern nations. After the Second World War France chose to ignore Vichy, and Italy looked with embarrassment towards Imperial Rome because of Mussolini's appropriation of its symbols; suddenly the Etruscans were "in" (Wood 1998: 193). Eurocentrism was fuelled by the idea that ancient Greece (and Rome) was the cradle of Europe, with the exclusion of the "barbarian" nations (chiefly the Ottoman countries, although other countries could conveniently fill this role).

> The nationalistic myth that has both inspired and burdened modern Greeks ever since they won their independence was inspired by a European fantasy of classical Greece that had nothing to do with modern Greece and little to do with the ancient. (Holst-Warhaft 1997: 284–5)

Is it any wonder, then, that there is ongoing conflict over (the Former Yugoslav Republic of) Macedonia's right to use the name "Macedonia"? And what are we to make of the French adoration of the Gauls (Dietler 1994)? We can be amused by these practices of nations, but we should realize their importance for nation-building. They are no more "faked" than other human social customs. Such practices appear in many nations during nation-building.

This is also true for other related features, used by "myth busters" as weapons against Israeli archaeology: for example, Jewification of site names (e.g. Abu el-Haj 2002: 53–4). Abu el-Haj has not discovered something new; the use of names to create a "Hebrew map" has been pointed out by Israelis since the 1990s (Jacoby 2000: 121–30, with references). We touched on this practice briefly in the debate following the interdepartmental committee (Ch. 2). Why pick up on Hebrew archaeologists of the 1930s or Israeli archaeologists of the 1950s? Show me a long-term (historically known) conqueror of Palestine/Israel in the past 20 centuries that did not leave site names behind. The loss of old site names is a pity and a shame, but who is responsible for it? Those who lost the names also bear responsibility. Hebrew site names are often older than those whose loss is mourned by Abu el-Haj; they are also a small remnant from the past. There is nothing wrong with using names such as Gezer or Megiddo when the identification is secure.

It also seems that some "myth busters" treat national myths only in negative terms, as forgery or as deceit. Anderson (1983), Smith (1991) and others showed that the nation is an "invented community". A nation is almost by necessity structured out of the fabric of myths: myths about history, myths about origins. The elites (because such myths are almost always the product of the elites) "invent" the myths; but this invention is a powerful feature of the world of nations in which we live. Myths are there not just to deceive, but also to create, and it is a powerful creation. While the world of nations is far from an ideal world, only prophets know alternatives. To see just the negative sides of nationalism would be similar to seeing just the negative sides of, say, the institution of the family.

Deconstruction of national myths or, better phrased, discussion of myths, with separation of fact from legend, is a sign of maturity of a society (Elon 1997: 45). It happens when the nation is secure, so that its foundation myths are no longer so sacrosanct. Israel has only recently started this process, and needs to address mainly the "myth of the empty land". It was the decision not to let the 1948 refugees return and the occupation or demolition of their houses that created the empty land. The debate between historians and "new historians" is not so much about facts, but about consequences (cf. Lochery 2001; vs. Karsh 1997). Palestinians would also have to address their myths, mainly the "myth of return" (e.g. Karmi & Cotran 1999: part II), not because there is any irreversible act in history, for it is all a matter of circumstance; nor on account of the practical reasons against return, although they are formidable (Benvenisti 2000: 315–19), but because the past is beyond reach. Even if Palestinians would one day have the power to force return, they would never find their past, only reverse the wheel of guilt. Such forced return might mean vast human misery, on a scale much larger than the 1948 *nakba*.

Early Israeli archaeology has something to be ashamed of and much to be proud of. It was not inherently different, in the nationalistic sense, from all other archaeologies of nations and states in the making: "We all turn history into myth and ritual and into symbols that give meaning to life" (Elon 1997: 44). It was a quite naive nationalism, full of hopes and dreams, many too ideological to become possible. The issue can be summarized by Ben-Gurion: "we have no alternative but to cut ourselves off from recent past" (1953: 27). He meant the Arab periods, the refugees, and the entire time in exile and Diaspora from 587 BCE to 1948 CE (cf. the amnesia defined by Elon 1997: 43). This was the heavy price of nation-building; but now Israel must regain its past. Israelis must lose their "national" innocence in order to do so. To paraphrase Yeivin, a nation cannot mark time, it either develops or dies; Israelis have to pass the phase of myth-breaking and forge, at the same time, new myths or, better, common ground.

Finally, early Israeli archaeology stands in sharp contrast, in my view, with the situation after 1967. To paraphrase Yeivin again, after 1948 excuses could be made of lack of experience and hard circumstances; this will not fit the period after 1967.

CONCLUSION

In the remaining space I wish to move to more modest, but pressing, observations. The first years of Israel as a state were decisive for the establishment and creation of Israeli archaeology. It was in many respects created from scratch, materially speaking, but it had many achievements and it would be wrong to forget them. They include: the antiquities guards; the preservation efforts; the battle for salvage excavations and the old cities; the wide public interest; the archives and museums; the Hazor excavation (and many other excavations that could not be covered in the limited space available in this book); the Friends of Antiquities; and the return of foreign expeditions to Israel.

For several years until 1955, development of Israeli archaeology followed a model of a strong state archaeology headed by a central department of antiquities, based on the British Mandatory period model. Other academic institutions were mainly involved in research and teaching. However, in the few short years of 1955–59, as a result of conflict with the GTC and the Hebrew University/IES, the IDAM lost this position. The state decided to choose the Hebrew University and the IES as its centres for Israeli archaelogy. From being an equal and even central partner the IDAM became a marginal body. It lost the museum, the restoration and guarding of major sites, the authority over excavation licences and the responsibility for formulating new legislation. Not all of this was tragic, and some of the losses resulted in worthwhile creations (such as the Israel Museum); one should not confuse the goal and the means. The most tragic loss, strange as this seems, was the loss of the IDAM's scientific aspiration to be an equal partner in Israeli archaeological research. The degradation of the IDAM in this respect was tragic for salvage archaeology. Despite a short period of significant recovery in the 1990s, under Amir Drori, the IDAM never regained this loss. Years of salvage archaeology being despised and considered secondary resulted in the fact that its place is secured neither by legislation nor by the ethics of the archaeological community in Israel.

The "allure of the archive" is deep (Freshwater 2003: 737), but still, in reading thousands of IDAM documents, I was much impressed by Yeivin's letters. They show his deep understanding, commitment and affection for archaeology, and his clarity of grasp and vision. He fought, under very difficult circumstances, for the "old" cities, for preservation of sites and for their professional maintenance regardless of their cultural affiliation or period. He had the first dreams and made the first plans for a central antiquities museum in Jerusalem. He maintained his integrity and his loyalty to the state despite the bitter experiences he endured. I trust that the publication of this study will do justice to this figure, which was for so long neglected.

In writing *Just Past?* I often wondered how many current debates were already ongoing in the 1950s: is anything new under the sun? I repeat these Biblical words on purpose, for many archaeologists currently prefer to treat the Bible with ignorance, as if it were written on some other planet. Being secular and sceptical is not a licence for ignorance. Thus, I would like to end this book by quoting the last verses of Ecclesiastes, where he speaks of death, but the music of the words is the music of life; although there is no life without death, death is always preceded by life:

> ... because man goeth to his long home, and the mourners go about the streets: Or ever the silver cord be loosed, or the golden bowl be broken, or the pitcher broken at the fountain; or the wheel broken at the cistern. Then shall the dust return to the earth as it was: and the spirit shall return unto God who gave it.
> (Ecclesiastes 12:5–7)

Appendix

OTHER DOCUMENTS FROM
THE IDAM FILES

A "DINOSAUR" IN TEL AVIV?

The following memorandum was headed "Finding a bone of a large mammal":

> Following a verbal notice given by Mrs Yeivin about a huge bone, maybe
> of a prehistoric animal, lying in the Tel Aviv–Jaffa road; and a verbal
> communication from Mr Handler about the same matter, we visited the
> place on Friday noon (members Handler, Yeivin, [Pinkas] Linder [then
> head of the Department of Public Works], Pinkerfeld). Military policeman
> R. informed us that he had collected the bone from a heap of rubbish in
> the middle of the street (near house no. 11, south of the entrance to the
> German Colony in Jaffa). After investigation of a nearby shop owner, it
> was discovered that the bone was found in this shop when it was given to
> her by the Committee for Refugee Housing in Jaffa. One has to clarify to
> whom the shop belonged earlier; maybe the Unit of Agriculture?
> [Addition] 24.8.48. On Tuesday morning (9:30) the bone was brought to
> the Measuring House [the office of the IDAM at that time] to storage no. 4
> (with objects that belong to the Post Office unit).
> [signed] S. Yeivin   (GL44880/18 no. 1)

There was similar news in Tel Aviv in 2005:

> "We have found a dinosaur!" , cried an IAA archaeologist from one of the
> pits of the excavation … The excavator, Dr Edwin van den-Brink hastened
> to correct [that declaration] with sorrow [saying] that it was the bones of
> a hippopotamus from 6000 years ago.   (Bar-Yosef 2005: 16–17)

TWICE 3,000 YEARS OF JERUSALEM

A company called Binyaney ha-'Umah [Buildings of the Nation] was building a large conference centre in Jerusalem. It planned a celebration, but Yeivin begged to disagree:

> My Dear Sir
>
> I saw in the press lately announcements about a conference that the Binyaney ha-'Umah Company is arranging on the occasion of 3,000 years since the declaration of Jerusalem as the capital of Israel, but knowing how the press works, and their often limited accuracy, I paid little attention to this notice. On the night of 7 July I was present at a party of the journalists' journal [*iton ha-itona'im*], held in the Orion cinema and dedicated to the matter of the Binyaney ha-'Umah. There I heard from you that, indeed, the company contemplates arranging a national conference in the spring of 1952 symbolizing the anniversary of 3,000 years of the declaration of Jerusalem as Israel's capital by King David. Naturally, you will understand that I do not wish, nor am I permitted, to interfere with conferences and ceremonies … but when they touch on areas that are in the IDAM's interest, I see it as my duty not just to send you my notes, but to request you to act accordingly.
>
> In recent years I myself have dealt extensively with the question of the chronology of the kings of the early Israelite Kingdom (Saul, David and Solomon) and reached the final conclusion that the reign of David must be set as 1006–966 BCE. Since David occupied Jerusalem in his seventh year, this event must be placed at 1000/999 BCE. Therefore, the 3,000 years of this event happen in 1000/2000 [mistake for 1999/2000], that is, approximately fifty years from now. Indeed, some scholars have fixed on slightly different dates for the reign of David; many set his rise to power in 1010 BCE, but as far as I know, no one as yet set his crowning to a date prior to 1020 BCE. In any case, one simply cannot date the occupation of Jerusalem by David to 1048 BCE … It is an historical absurdity that on no account can be harmonized with the Biblical or foreign sources known to us at present.
>
> I do not intend to cancel the conference that you are designing to hold in the spring, and I also have no objection to you connecting it to the fact that Jerusalem is the eternal capital of Israel; but in no way can I agree that you celebrate 3,000 years of the conquest of Jerusalem by David. Perhaps it is necessary to celebrate with a large international "fanfare" in Jerusalem, but we must not make ourselves a laughing stock in the eyes of the whole world, especially in the eyes of the scientific world, by such a distortion of the historical viewpoint. Of course, I do not want to publicize my position in public before having expressed it to your company. I hope that you will

fix this distortion [*'ivut*], which, no doubt, happened unknowingly ...
I should be very grateful, if you could inform me as soon as possible what you intend to do about this matter, in order to make right from wrong.
(GL44868/3 no. 3283-1, 18.7.50)

Despite his "politeness", Yeivin sent copies to everybody. In due course in 1996, the 3,000 years of Jerusalem were celebrated with much pomposity, despite rumours that King David had never existed.

THE BOY O WRITES TO THE IDAM

In May 1961 a young boy wrote to "The Hebrew University–the IDAM, Jerusalem":

> I am a boy who learns in grade V. I am interested in antiquities and the history of the people of Israel. I have been at many excavations and was very impressed by the work of the excavators. Once I found an ancient vessel. I knew that this was the property of the government and I left it in its place. I thought: maybe the vessel will help the excavators, so I left it there. I was right: one day the excavators came. The vessel was already with them. I saw that it is worth leaving property so that it will reach [the hands] of the expedition. If you could give me some ancient vessel, I would be very pleased and would thank you. This vessel will stand in a respectable place in my room.
> Yours, O   (GL44873/12)

The main concern of the letter was the vessel as property. By not taking the one he found, O "gave" it to the excavators, so he believed he had the right to receive another vessel instead. Rahmani answered, perhaps not so pedagogically mentioning a skeleton in a tomb:

> To: the Boy O, Tel Aviv
> My dear O,
> Thank you for your beautiful letter about ancient vessels. You did the right thing in leaving a vessel inside its ditch until the excavators–scholars could come and find it in its layer. Truly that vessel belongs to our state and people (not to the government, which only keeps these vessels and antiquities as a servant of the public). Furthermore, only within its layer can such a vessel help reveal the culture of its period. For example: suppose an ancient tomb is discovered and in the right hand of the skeleton is found an ancient oil

lamp – there is meaning here. Perhaps the buriers believed that he lived on in the tomb, and needed the lamp to light his way in the netherworld. But if a skeleton were found with the lamp at its feet the explanation may be different: perhaps the buriers thought about light as only symbolic for the dead. So every detail in an excavation – the situation of vessels, their quantity, the way they stand and more – is important. All those who take an ancient vessel from the ground, by necessity they ruin part of the general picture, and that [picture] is the main thing.

Now regarding your request for an ancient vessel for your room. First let me tell you a secret. I have been dealing with antiquities for about 25 years and do not have at home even one ancient vessel. If I want to see ancient vessels I go to the museum. There one can see not just single vessels but the whole story in entirety: the tools, weapons, inscriptions and statues. Together they start to whisper and tell their stories, not just to me, but to every visitor.

At home? At home I have books and pictures and new vessels, from our time, and they are nice, very nice. If someone tells you that in our days no nice vessels are made, and a long time ago it was all better, do not believe him, O. It simply is not true. Most things are made much better now than in former times, and also not less beautifully, just differently. The beauty and interest lie, indeed, in the differences.

Since you are really an enthusiast, here is what I can send to wise boys like you as an object: a booklet [meaning the IDAM's *Alon*] about what is happening in archaeology by your faithful servant, the IDAM.
Yours [signed] L. Y. Rahmani   (GL44873/12)

It is as if O's letter predicted future events, for he was to become quite a famous collector of antiquities (or perhaps faked antiquities!).

EPITAPH OF Z

The following letter was written by Yeivin to Ory, inspector of the southern district, on 16 October 1956:

In reply to your letter … I am to notify you that generally it is forbidden to grant use of any ancient remains for making tombstones of any kind or type. In the present case of the late Dr Z, I am ready to take into account the many services of the late Dr Z to the matters of antiquities research in our land in the environs of Ashkelon, and ask the honourable Minister of Education and Culture to allow use of a fragment of a column from the ruins of Ashkelon for erection of the tombstone on the deceased grave.

When I have the minister's approval, and only he can legally give it, I will notify you. In any case, if the minister does approve it, you will have to go to Ashkelon and choose a fragment of a column for that [purpose]. Let it be clear that you will not damage [anything while] taking out the column and that it would not form part of a possible building there.

With blessings [signed] S. Yeivin   (GL44880/12 no. 2565)

Dr Z was Yehezkel Zonband (*BIES* **19** (1954/55): 113), the manager of the Afridar Company, who built parts of the new city of Ashkelon. He was the first mayor after the unification of Ashkelon into a local council in 1953. He died suddenly in the same year. This was not the first case of antiquities being used for modern memorials. According to Rony Reich (pers. comm. 2004), when Eliezer Ben-Yehuda, the modernizer of the Hebrew language, died in December 1923, the mourners had received permission from the Mandatory Department of Antiquities to place a pillar from Bet She'arim on his tomb. Finally, the grave of Havah-Rachel Rickelmann (one of the first Zionist settlers of Zichron Ya'acov in 1882, and grandmother of the famous Aharonson family) had an ancient sarcophagus as a tombstone. It is now displayed in the courtyard of the Aharonson House Museum in Zichron Ya'acov.

JOB OPENING IN THE IDAM, 1953

In 1953 Yeivin was looking to fill a "scientific secretary" position: a sort of right-hand man. He wrote the following letter on 29 December 1953:

Subject: Appointment of a new worker in the position of Scientific Secretary
In answer to the internal advertisement [*hakhraza pnimit* – the word *mikhraz* used today had not yet been coined] on substituting the position of Mr M. Avi-Yonah who resigned, the IDAM received an application from Mr Yohanan Aharoni, currently Supervisor of Antiquities in the northern district. This candidate is fit to receive the position in terms of his scientific education and personal abilities; yet his knowledge both in English and in Hebrew leaves room for pursuing a greater perfection. Therefore, I would wish that this position be publicly advertised, as there might be found as a result a candidate whose knowledge of these two languages outdoes that of Mr Aharoni. Indeed, as far as I know there are no obvious suitable candidates on the horizon, yet one should not be distracted from the possibility that someone suitable might be found.

325

I attach Mr Aharoni's request; if among the applications that may arrive in response to the open advertisement that I here request no better candidate is found for the said position, I will heartily recommend the acceptance of Mr Aharoni. Of course, in that case it will be necessary to publish an advertisement regarding the position of Supervisor of Antiquities in the northern district.

[signed] Y. Yeivin, Director   (GL44880/13 no. 2737a)

Aharoni spoke fluent German, but so did Yeivin and many of the scholars of that time in Israel. It was not enough. One wonders what would have happened if Aharoni had received this more central position in the IDAM. As it was, he resigned later (1955), much to Yeivin's regret. The two met again at Tel Aviv University in the 1960s when Aharoni became the head of the Institute of Archaeology. Human destinies: who is the scientific secretary who registers them?

THE WONDERFUL STONE OF REVEREND P

On 20 November 1960, Yisrael Zuriel, the GTC supervisor for the promotion of tourism, wrote to the IDAM:

> We attach sections of a letter that our office in London received from a priest (*komer*) named Rev. P, which speaks for itself. The said priest visits Israel as head of pilgrim groups at least once a year, if I am not mistaken, and he has continued this blessed operation for 30 years already. Therefore, and since he is a friend of Israel, we must give some answer even if the problem that he raises is not to your liking.
>
> We ask you to check especially whether there is any scientific basis to the priest's assumption that the stone mentioned in the attached letter is not [made] of glass, but of a wonderful other material which "has no similarity on earth".
>
> I am awaiting your fast reply ...
>
> [signed] Y. Zuriel   (GL44882/9 no. 421)

The section of Rev. P's letter, dated 15 November 1960, reads as follows:

> *Extract of Letter from Reverend P of Brighton, England*
> ... Lately I have found much more interest taken in prophecy, and this is where Israel can show much which is of interest.
>
> One of the most important sites is almost forgotten. This is the Elijah's

place of Sacrifice, near the summit of the inland end of Mount Carmel. Coaches cannot go the whole way along the top and drivers of touring cars are reluctant. Even this time, the driver told me that the last part of the way is in very bad condition. I know the Roman Catholics tell their people that all took place near the Stella Maris, that the water was brought up from the sea, that Elijah triumphed by the grace given of the virgin Mary, that the cloud which came over the sea was like Mary's foot, etc. It is all wrong, very, very, wrong. I want Israel to triumph in displaying the facts, and with the help of the Hebrew version, it can be done.

Alas, when I saw the well the side had fallen in. I contacted several centres to get repairs done, but I don't know if they have been done. Right down the ages that well has been called Elijah's well, the water never fails and the shell life in it bears witness of this. Surely, it is remarkable that there should be this unfailing supply of water, 1600 feet above sea level, and close to the steep slope.

One of my greatest treasures is a small piece of rock, permeated by a glass condition and I found it in the very centre of the Arena. Two of our best scientists have examined this stone, and both previously denied that the glass substance was glass. Verdict I. "We have never seen anything like it, we have nothing like it. Go and tell your story for nothing else can account for it. This is a creation by some fire or heat which never originated on earth." It is indeed a very hard glass substance, and I believe it must be a fragment of Elijah's altar. Verdict No. 2. "P remember, you are holding London's greatest treasure, never let it out of your hands."

Rahmani answered on 22 November 1960:

Subject: The Wonderful Rock of Priest P
Thank you for your letter no. 421 of 20 November 1960, which gave us great pleasure. As for our opinion about the nature of the rock, which the said priest says is "the greatest treasure of the city of London", unfortunately we cannot help, because we do not have the rock. Even if we did, the examination would have to be performed by a geological institution. As for the mystical qualities of this rock, it seems that only qualified religious institutions have the authority to state an opinion on it.

(GL.44882/9 no. 6777)

However, Rahmani did not resist the temptation to explain the rock:

In continuation to my letter ... I wish to draw your attention to a note that appeared in the *Observer* of 18 December 1960, page 9, according to which an American scientist explains the appearance of tactites on Earth as particles of the "seas" of the moon, blown at one time by meteorites into space, some reaching our Earth. Tactites or moldawites are small pieces of a glass-like material, discovered at Bohemia, Australia and various parts of America and Sweden. Their extra-terrestrial origin is undoubted. I am not the person to decide to what extent these details can help the religious questions in relation to this material ...

(GL44882/9 no. 6967, 22.12.60)

ROYAL VISITS

Tourists were rare in the 1950s, but the trickle became a flood in the 1960s. Biran served as a diplomat in the US and had many connections to nurture. One visitor from New York was offered a tempting cultural package:

Thank you for your letter of 3 March and the good news of your arrival in Israel. The museum will be open and we will be glad to guide you through the exhibition halls ...

Independence Day is on 25 April and perhaps you will want to go to Haifa to see the parade or attend the Jerusalem Tattoo on the evening of the 24th. If your agent hasn't gotten any tickets, please let me know and I'll see what can be done..."

Yours sincerely, A. Biran   (GL44875/6 no. 10827, 11.3.66)

The following answer arrived on 18 March 1966:

Thank you for your kind note of 11 March. Frankly, we are so sick of the military that any display of arms even in beloved Israel is something we could do without. However, if we don't have the choice of sitting on Ted Kollek's living room floor with our head on Marlene Dietrich's legs, then we will be happy to join you at the Jerusalem Tattoo on the evening of 24 April ...   (GL44875/6 no. 11999)

Another letter of 14 February 1963 recommended two visitors:

Dear Avraham [Biran],

A good friend of mine, R, whose purchase [of Israel Bonds] on 31 December 1962 of $5,000 put us over the million dollar mark, will be in Israel as follows [details of dates and hotels]. I have given him your address at the IDAM and he may contact you. If so, he is a terrific young boy ... You will have great pleasure meeting him if you have the chance and time to spend with him.

Also you may get a phone call from Dr M, who purchases Israel bonds in exact inverse proportion to his income. He will be in Israel for a couple of days and is an amateur archaeologist, if there is such a category of human being.

Sitting in front of me is a box of cigars and a bottle of Chivas Regal. Thinking of you fondly and maintaining the nail in the box of cigars and the seal on the bottle of liquor, I am

Yours devotedly, [signed] S.

Biran answered on 5 April 1963:

Sitting in my office and smoking one of your excellent cigars brings back wonderful memories of San Francisco, but especially of yourself ... Your friend R never called our office. My secretary was all set to give him the royal treatment, but he wasn't around. Next trip – maybe. However, Dr M was well taken care of and he wrote to us to say so.

Happy Pesach (and Easter) and "lomir zad zein".

With fondest regards, [signed] A. Biran

YEIVIN AND HEBREW

Yeivin's deep knowledge and affection for Hebrew was famous. He took puritanical steps to promote its correct use and published extensively in *Leshonenu*, a Hebrew linguistic journal. On 2 November 1956, Yeivin wrote to Ory, inspector of the southern district, concerning damage to antiquities at Nirim. He added "a technical matter":

The forms "from ... to" are intended to be used only for interdepartmental correspondence and should in no case be used for letters to members of the general public who are not civil servants. It is not the question of form only, but the question of the outside style of the letter and the accepted etiquette of writing such letters. Letters to the public should open in the usual formula of politeness: Sir, My Honourable Sir, Dear Sir, Dear Mr So and So; and end also in one of the commonly accepted forms: With feelings of honour and blessing, Sincerely yours, etc. To the letter one must add at the beginning or end the address of the person to whom the letter is addressed. Only in interdepartmental letters was an order given to omit the polite etiquette of opening and signature, in order to save time and space. (GL44880/12 no. 2752)

In April 1950 Yeivin drove on the Jerusalem–Tel Aviv road, and was blocked on his way by a lorry working for the Jerusalem water pipeline project. The drivers were quarrelling with other drivers. Yeivin:

> approached the lorry driver and asked very politely for the cause of the blockade of the road, but he answered extremely rudely: if you have complaints go to the police. I asked with utmost politeness how long the dispute would take, but he continued to answer me rudely with much impoliteness, until my patience expired, and I called him "donkey" [*hamor*, also a widely used curse]. Then both he and the other driver, with whom I had not talked at all, opened up with such disgraceful curses that they cannot be placed on paper … (GL44880/17 no. 2577, 19.4.50)

For an early draft from 1949 for a new Antiquities Law, Yeivin used the reverse of a page of a manuscript entitled "The Sarcophagus Inscription of a Jewish Sage" by Professor Moshe Schwabe of the Hebrew University. Schwabe wanted to dedicate the paper to "A. Reifenberg, AMICO QUINQUAGENARIO DEDICATUM". Yeivin, who edited it, remarked: "To Professor Schwabe: I ask that you write the dedication in Hebrew! What reason can there be for having such a Latin dedication in a Hebrew periodical?" Yeivin suggested a Hebrew translation of the dedication: "Dedicated to my friend A. Reifenberg, for his Jubilee" (GL1342/22). The paper was published with the Latin motto in 1950 (Schwabe 1950).

Sometimes Yeivin was flexible. Someone complained that invitations to an exhibition in 1952 had been printed in both Hebrew and English. Yeivin explained that to save paper they had printed the invitations in two languages on the same sheets. They should have been cut in the middle, and the English versions sent to foreign scholars, but someone forgot. Nevertheless:

> I see no harm … Surely we all respect our language and work on its development and progress. The past of the employees of the IDAM and their battle for the rights of the Hebrew language during the days of the Mandatory government are a trustworthy indication of their attitude. But I think that being over-meticulous, in that some are erasing any Latin letter from the official documents of the state, does not show cultural maturity, but has something of an undesired cultural chauvinism [*shuviniyut*].
> (GL44874/3 no. 8696, 25.5.50)

CRUCIFIXION MATTERS

When a crucified man was found by the IES at Givʻat ha-Mivtar, Jerusalem (Haas 1970: 49–58), many people wrote to the IDAM seeking information. The ossuary with the crucified remains carried the name "Yehohanan", so a file under this name was opened for the letters. Some thought that the bones were related, if not actually belonged, to Jesus Christ:

> Dear Doctor Biran,
> The English newspapers carry the story of your find of the skeleton of the crucified Jew found in Israel. I am a student of Judaism of Israel as [of] Sindonology – the science of the Shroud – [which] leads us to a greater understanding of Judaism and of course to a deeper affection and respect of the race of Jesus Christ. I would be so grateful if you would let me have whatever information you have … Do please help. I only know one word of Hebrew but an important one viz. Shalom.
> (GL44881/9 no. 8531, 4.1.71)

The IDAM answered such letters under reference IEJ 20, noting that crucifixion was a common Roman method of execution. It convinced one writer:

> From the desk of Evangelist JR … USA
> Dr Avraham Biran,
> You were right; it is a mere fantasy to say that the skeleton found there recently with the nail through its ankle would be that of Jesus Christ. He will be back in Body with scars. Not just because of the name YEHOHANAN, but because JESUS CHRIST ascended into Heaven according to the Bible, and True Christian Reality. It was mentioned by my wife, that it could be that of one of the Malefactors Crucified at the side of Christ, and I'll go along with this. I welcome your reply,
> May God Bless You, [signed] JR   (GL44881/9, 5.1.71)

It is always wise to agree with one's wife! Rather more unusual was the following letter:

> Dear Dr Biran
> I have done extensive studies on the medical and scientific aspects of crucifixion and would be extremely grateful if you could supply me with additional information concerning your discovery of the crucified individual named Yehohanan and a photograph, if possible. I am also interested in having a photograph of the nails and a rough sketch of a nail with measurements...

Thanking you in advance, I am sincerely yours,
[signed] Chief Medical Examiner, Office of the Medical Examiner, County
of Rockland   (GL44881/9, 8.1.71)

I hope that the interest was purely academic and not related to the practical work of the examiner. Another writer knew the identity of the deceased and the reason for his death:

Honourable Avraham Biran
Tonight at midnight I heard to my great joy your name on VOA [Voice of America radio station] about the "crucified Man", which I also read later in today's *Ma'ariv* newspaper. The crucified [man] was surely a rebel, a hero who fought the cruel Roman rule; and even if he was not a "rebel" in public, nevertheless it is certain that the depressing conditions of life pushed him to actions, [so] that the Romans sentenced him to crucifixion without justice and without mercy. In my view, one ought to build a mausoleum for the tomb of our brother, this crucified [man], may his memory be blessed.
With great honour, [signed] PN   (GL44881/9, 4.1.71)

I am not certain if rebels to the rule of Rome would appreciate burial in a structure so typical of the culture of the empire. It seems that Israeli archaeology is forever doomed to suffer follies, and they will be around to entertain us for as long as archaeology is.

BIBLIOGRAPHY

Abbasi, M. 2003. Safed in the War of Independence: A New Look. *Cathedra* **107**: 115–48 [Hebrew].

Abdi, K. 2001. Nationalism, Politics and the Development of Archaeology in Iran. *American Journal of Archaeology* **105**: 51–76.

Abu el-Haj, N. 2001. *The Facts on the Ground: Archaeological Practice and Territorial Self-Fashioning in Israeli Society.* Chicago, IL. University of Chicago Press.

Abu el-Haj, N. 2002. Producing Artifacts: Archaeology and Power during the British Mandate of Palestine. *Israel Studies* **7**(2): 33–61.

Adams, D. 1980. *The Restaurant at the End of the Universe.* New York: Pocket.

Adler, A. 1987. A Psychoanalytical Biography: Yes or No? *Israeli Quarterly of Psychology* **5**: 31–40 [Hebrew].

Aharoni, M. C. 1998. *Yohanan Aharoni: His Life.* Tel Aviv [Hebrew].

Aharoni, Y. 1955. Ramat Rahel: Notes and News. *Israel Exploration Journal* **5**: 127.

Aharoni, Y. 1956. Galilean Survey: Israelite Settlements and their Pottery. *Eretz Israel* **4**: 56–63.

Aharoni, Y. (ed.) 1973a. *Excavations and Studies: Essays in Honour of Shemuel Yeivin*, Tel Aviv University Monographs 1. Tel Aviv: Institute of Archaeology.

Aharoni, Y. 1973b. Remarks on the "Israeli" Method of Excavation. *Eretz Israel* **11**: 48–53 [Hebrew].

Aharoni, Y. 1978. *The Archaeology of the Land of Israel,* rev. edn 1982, A. F. Rainey (ed.). Philadelphia: Westminster Press.

Aharoni, Y. 1986. *The Land of the Bible: A Historical Geography,* 2nd edn, A. F. Rainey (ed.). London: Burns and Oates.

Albright, W. F. 1949. *Archaeology of Palestine.* Harmondsworth: Pelican.

Albright, W. F. 1970. The Phenomenon of Israeli Archaeology. In *Near Eastern Archaeology in the Twentieth Century: Essays in Honor of Nelson Glueck*, J. A. Sanders (ed.), 57–63. New York: Doubleday.

Amikam, B. 1983. Robbery of Antiquities in Israel. *Archaeologya: Bulletin of the Israel Association of Archaeologists* **2**: 83–4 [Hebrew].

Amir, Y. 1955. Youth – the Enemy of Antiquities. *Ma'ariv* (10 April) [Hebrew].

Amitai, M. 1998. The Story of a Sabre: Review of *Courage* by E. Ben-Ezer. *Ha'aretz Literary Supplement* (14 April): 8 [Hebrew].

Anderson, B. 1983. *Imagined Communities.* London: Verso.

Aranne, Z. 1957. Speech at the Annual IES Conference. *BIES* **22**: 100 [Hebrew].

Ariel, Y. 1968. A Complaint about a Digging made by M. Dayan in a Historical Site. *Ha'aretz* (17 November) [Hebrew].

Ariel, Y. 1986. The Antiquity Robbery and Dayan's Collection. *Ha'aretz* (13 April): 9 [Hebrew].

Ariel, Y. 1987. The Struggle to Prevent Antiquity Robbing. *Ha'aretz* (29 November): 12 [Hebrew].

Aronoff, M. J. 1991. Myths, Symbols and Rituals of the Emerging State. In *New Perspectives on Israeli History: The Early Years of the State*, L. J. Silberstein (ed.), 175–92. New York: New York University.

Avigad, N. 1989. Yigael Yadin – A Portrait. *Eretz Israel* **20** (Yadin volume): x.

Aviram, Y. (ed.) 1965. *Western Galilee and the Coast of Galilee. The Nineteenth Archaeological Convention, October 1963*. Jerusalem: Israel Exploration Society [Hebrew].

Avi-Yonah, M. *et al.* 1957. *Masada: Survey and Excavations 1955–1956*. Jerusalem: Israel Exploration Society.

Avni, G. 2003. Review of Ben-Yehudah, "Sacrificing Truth". *American Historical Review* (October): 1254.

Avramski, S. (ed.) 1970. *Yeivin Festschrift (Sefer Shemuel Yeivin)*. Jerusalem: Society for the Study of the Bible in Israel [Hebrew].

Avrech, Y. 1976. *Pirkei Yotam: A Selection of Essays*. Tel Aviv: Am Oved Publishing [Hebrew].

Avrech, Y. 1990. *Statures. Essays*. 3 vols. Tel Aviv: Dvir Publishing [Hebrew]. [*Volume II: The Courage to be Generous; Volume III: The Flag and the Staff*].

Avrech, Y. 1991. *In the Margins*. Tel Aviv: Dvir Publishing [Hebrew].

Bachi, R. 1957. Demography. In *Encyclopaedia Hebraica Vol. VI: Eretz Israel*, B. Netanyahu & A. Pel'i (eds), 665–707. Jerusalem: Hevrah Le-Hoza'at Encyclopaedia [Hebrew].

Bar-Adon, P. 1980. *The Cave of the Treasure: The Finds from the Cave in Nahal Mishmar*, I. Pommerantz (trans.). Jerusalem: IES.

Baram, A. 1994. A Case of Imported Identity: the Modernizing Secular Ruling Elites of Iraq and the Concept of Mesopotamian Inspired Territorial Nationalism. *Poetics Today* **15**(2): 279–319.

Baram, U. & Rowan, Y. 2004. *Marketing Heritage: Archaeology and the Consumption of the Past*. Walnut Creek, CA: Altamira.

Barkay, G. 1992. The Excavation Methods of Kathleen Kenyon. *Archeologya* **3**: 41–58 [Hebrew].

Bar-On, M. 1991. *Challenge and Quarrel: The Road to Sinai, 1956*. Beersheba: Ben Gurion University [Hebrew].

Bar-On, M. 1994. *The Gates of Gaza: Israel's Road to Suez and Back, 1955–1957*. New York: St Martin's Press.

Bar-Yosef, O. & Mazar, A. 1982. Israeli Archaeology. *World Archaeology* **13**: 310–25.

Bar-Yosef, Y. 2005. Ancient Man in the Ayalon. *Yediot Akhronot* (30 June), "24 hours supplement": 16–17 [Hebrew].

Bazin, A. 1978. *Orson Welles: A Critical View*. New York: Harper & Row.

Ben-Amotz, D. 1974. *Reflections in Time [Kri'ah Tamah]*. Tel Aviv: Bitan [Hebrew].

Ben-Arieh, Y. 1999a. Non-Jewish Institutions and the Research of Palestine during the British Mandate Period, Part 1. *Cathedra* **92**: 135–72 [Hebrew].

Ben-Arieh, Y. 1999b. Non-Jewish Institutions and the Research of Palestine during the British Mandate Period, Part 2. *Cathedra* **93**: 111–42 [Hebrew].

Ben-Arieh, Y. 2000. The Ottoman Law of Archaeological Excavations in Palestine – 1884. In *Landscape of Israel: Azaria's Alon Jubilee Volume*, Ariel 100–101, G. Barkay & E. Schiller (eds), 272–82. Jerusalem: Ariel Press [Hebrew].

Ben-Arieh, Y. 2001. Developments in the Study of Yediat Ha'aretz in Modern Times, up to the Establishment of the State of Israel. *Cathedra* **100**: 306–38 [Hebrew].

Ben-Ezer, E. 1997. *Courage: The Story of Moshe Dayan*. Tel Aviv: Ministry of Defence [Hebrew].

Ben-Gurion, D. 1952. Israel Among the Nations. *State of Israel Governmental Yearbook* **5713**: 1–47 [Hebrew].

Ben-Gurion, D. 1953. Jewish Survival. *State of Israel Governmental Yearbook* **5714**: 1–50 [Hebrew].

Ben-Horin, N. 2002. Relations between Israel and the Vatican. In *Ministry for Foreign Affairs: The First 50 Years*, M. Yegar, Y. Govrin & A. Oded (eds), 993–1032. Jerusalem: Keter Press [Hebrew].

Ben-Tor, N. 1989. Yigael Yadin: The Archaeologist. *Eretz Israel* **20** (Yadin volume): xii–xiii.

Ben-Tor, A. & Bonfil, R. (eds) 1997. *Hazor V. The James de-Rothschild Excavation to Hazor. An Account of the Fifth Season of Excavation, 1968*. Jerusalem: Israel Exploration Society.

Benvenisti, M. 2000. *Sacred Landscape: The Buried History of the Holy Land since 1948*. Berkeley, CA: University of California.

Ben-Yehuda, N. 1995. *The Masada Myth: Collective Memory and Mythmaking in Israel*. Madison, WI: University of Wisconsin.

Ben-Yehuda, N. 2002. *Sacrificing Truth: Archaeology and the Myth of Masada*. Amherst, NY: Humanity Books.

Ben-Zvi, Y. 1955. *Eretz Israel under Ottoman Rule*. Jerusalem: Bialik Institute [Hebrew].

Bialer, U. 1985. Jerusalem 1949: Transition to Capital City Status. *Cathedra* **35**: 163–91 [Hebrew].

Biran, A. 1962. The Israel Department of Antiquities and Museums (Annual Summary). In *Israel Government Yearbook* [Shnaton Memshelet Yisrael], 174–75 [Hebrew].

Bisheh, G. 2001. One Damn Illicit Excavation after Another: The Destruction of Archaeological Heritage of Jordan. In *Trade in Illicit Antiquities: The Destruction of the World's Archaeological Heritage*, N. Brodie, J. Doole & C. Renfrew (eds), 115–18. Cambridge: MacDonald Institute.

Blakely, J. A. 1993. Frederick Jones Bliss: Father of Palestinian Archaeology. *Biblical Archaeologist* **56**(3): 110–15.

Bligh, A. 1998. Israel and the Refugee Problem: From Exodus to Resettlement. *Middle Eastern Studies* **34**(1): 123–42.

Blunden, E. 1930. *Collected Poems*. London: Cobden-Sanderson.

Borges, J. L. 1970. *Labyrinths: Selected Stories and other Writings*, D. A. Yates & J. E. Irby (eds). Harmondsworth: Penguin.

Borodkin, L. 1995. The Economics of Antiquities Looting and a Proposed Legal Alternative. *Columbia Law Review* **95**: 377–417.

Bowman, J. & Isserlin, B. 1955. The University of Leeds, Department of Semitics. Archaeological Expedition to Jaffa. *Proceedings of the Leeds Philosophical Society* **7**(4): 231–50.

Braun, E. 1992. Objectivity and Salvage Excavation Policy in Mandate Palestine and the State of Israel: An Appraisal of its Effects on Understanding the Archaeological Record. In *The Limitations of Archaeological Knowledge*, T. Shay & J. Clottes (eds), 29–37. Liège: Université de Liège.

Broshi, M. 1986. Religion, Ideology and Politics and their Impact on Palestinian Archaeology. *Israel Museum Journal* **6**: 17–32.

Broshi, M. 1991. *The Shrine of the Book*. Israel Museum Catalogue No. 317. Jerusalem: Israel Museum.

Buttita, T. 1982. *Uncle Sam Presents: A Memoir of the Federal Theater 1935–1936*. Philadelphia, PA: University of Pennsylvania Press.

Cassuto-Saltzmann, M. 1965. The Library. *Hadashot Archaeologiyot* [*Excavations and Surveys in Israel*] **16**: 25–7 [Hebrew].

Churchill, W. S. 1949. *The Second World War. Vol. II: Their Finest Hour*. London: Cassell.

Cohen, A. 1991. And We Loved to See Him as the Bad Guy. *Al Ha-Mishmar* (27 September): 16–17 [Hebrew].

Cohen, Sh. 1959. The Antiquities Department. *Jerusalem Post* (10 July).

Conan-Doyle, A. 1891. *The Boscombe Valley Mystery*. Reprinted in *Sherlock Holmes: The Strand Stories, Illustrated by Sydney Paget* (Ware: Wordsworth, 1996).

Curtis, J. A. E. 1992. *Mikhail Bulgakov: Manuscripts Don't Burn. A Life in Diaries and Letters*. London: Harvill.

Damati, I. 2002. Sites and Places in Safad. *Ariel* **157–8**: 141–70.

Davies, H. A. 2001. Facing the Crisis of Looting in the United States. In *Archaeology and Society in the 21st Century: The Dead Sea Scrolls and Other Case Studies*, N. E. Silberman & E. S. Frerichs (eds), 155–9. Jerusalem: Israel Exploration Society.

Dayan, M. 1976. *Story of My Life*. London: Weidenfeld and Nicholson.

Dayan, M. 1978. *Living with the Bible*. Jerusalem: Edanim [Hebrew] and London: Weidenfeld and Nicholson [English].

Dayan, R. and Dudman, H. 1973. *Or Did I Dream a Dream?: The Story of Ruth Dayan*. Jerusalem: Weidenfeld and Nicholson [Hebrew].

Dayan, Y. 1985. *My Father, His Daughter*. London: Weidenfeld and Nicholson.

Dayan, Y. 1986. Inheritance and Legacy in Dayan's Collection. *Davar* (16 May): 15–17 [Hebrew].

de Hart, J. S. 1967. *The Federal Theater, 1935–1939: Plays, Relief and Politics.* Princeton, NJ: Princeton University Press.

Deutsch, R. 2001. *Ancient Coins and Antiquities.* Auction no. 26 (4 October). Tel Aviv: Archaeological Center.

Dever, W. G. 1973. Two Approaches to Archaeological Method: The Architectural and the Stratigraphic. *Eretz Israel* **11**: 1–8.

Dever, W. G. 1980. Archaeological Method in Israel: A Continous Revolution. *Biblical Archaeologist* **43**: 40–48.

Dever, W. G. 1985. Palestinian Archaeology 1945–1979: Portrait of an Emerging Discipline. In *The Hebrew Bible and its Modern Interpreters*, D. A. Knight & G. Tucker (eds), 31–74. Philadelphia, PA: Fortress.

Dever, W. G. 1989. Yigael Yadin: Prototypical Biblical Archaeologist. *Eretz Israel* **20**: 44*–51*.

Dietler, M. 1994. Our Ancestors the Gauls: Archaeology, Ethnic Nationalism and the Manipulation of Celtic Identity in Modern Europe. *American Anthropologist* **96**: 584–605.

Dissentchick, I. 1981. We Are all Guilty – Except Dayan. *Ma'ariv Weekend* (29 May): 12–13.

Drawer, M. 1985. *Flinders Petrie – A Life in Archaeology.* London: V. Gollancz.

Drawer, M. 2004. *Letters from the Desert: The Correspondence of Flinders and Hilda Petrie.* London: Arris and Phillips.

Eliav, M. 1978. *Eretz-Israel and its Yishuv in the Nineteenth Century.* Jerusalem: Keter Press [Hebrew].

Elon, A. 1971. *The Israelis: Founders and Sons.* London: Weidenfeld and Nicholson.

Elon, A. 1997. Politics and Archaeology. In *Archaeology and Society in the 21st Century: The Dead Sea Scrolls and other Case Studies,* N. E. Silberman & E. S. Frerichs (eds), 34–47. Jerusalem: Israel Exploration Society.

Ephrat, E. 1997. The Development Towns. In *The First Decade: 1948–1958*, Z. Zameret & H. Yablonka (eds), 103–12. Jerusalem: Yad Izhak Ben-Zvi [Hebrew].

Eytan, W. 1958. *The First Ten Years: A Diplomatic History of Israel.* New York: Simon & Schuster.

Falk, A. 1985. *Moshe Dayan, The Man and the Myth: A Psychoanalytic Biography.* Jerusalem: Cana Publishing.

Feig, N. 2002. Salvage Excavations at Meiron. *'Atiqot* **43**: 87–107.

Feige, M. 1998. Archaeology, Anthropology and the Development Town: Constructing the Israeli Place. *Zion* **63**(4): 441–59 [Hebrew].

Fierman, F. S. 1986. Rabbi Nelson Glueck: An Archaeologist's Secret Life in the Service of the OSS. *Biblical Archaeological Review* **12**(5): 18–22.

Fischbach, M. R. 2003. *Records of Dispossesion. Palestinian Refugee Property and the Arab–Israeli Conflict.* New York: Columbia University Press.

Fishbain, E. 1999. The Plan of the Employment Service – Relief Works. *Ha'aretz* (26 November), B.6 [Hebrew].

Flanagan, H. 1940. *Arena: The History of the Federal Theater.* New York: Benjamin Bloom.

Freshwater, H. 2003. The Allure of the Archive. *Poetics Today* **24**(3–4): 729–57.

Gal, Z. 1996. Ecological Aspects of Archaeology in Israel. *Qadmoniyot* **112**: 120–22 [Hebrew].

Ganor, A. 2002. Antiquities Robbery in Israel. *Excavations and Surveys in Israel* **115**: 68*–70*.

Garstang, J. 1922a. Second Annual Report. *Bulletin of the British School of Archaeology in Jerusalem* **1**: 4.

Garstang, J. 1922b. Eighteen Months' Work of the Department of Antiquities for Palestine, July 1920–December 1921. *Palestine Exploration Fund, Quarterly Statement* **55**: 57–62.

Garstang, J. 1923. Third Annual Report. *Bulletin of the British School of Archaeology in Jerusalem* **2**: 4.

Gelber, Y. 2004. *Independence and Nakba: Israel, the Palestinians and the Arab Countries, 1948.* Tel Aviv: Dvir [Hebrew].

Geva, Sh. 1994. Israeli Biblical Archaeology: The First Years. *Zemanim* **42**: 93–102 [Hebrew].

Gibson, S. 1999. British Archaeological Institutions in Mandatory Palestine, 1917–1948. *Palestine Exploration Quarterly* **118**: 115–43.

Gill, G. E. 1988. *White Grease Paint on Black Performers: A Study of the Federal Theater, 1935–1939.* New York: Peter Lang (American University Studies IX/40).

Golan, A. 2001. *Wartime Spatial Changes: Former Arab Territories Within the State of Israel, 1948–1950.* Beersheba, the Ben Gurion Research Center: Ben Gurion University Press.

Golan, A. 2003. Lydda and Ramle: from Palestinian-Arab to Israeli Towns, 1948–1967. *Middle Eastern Studies* **39**(4): 121–39.

Golani, M. 1998. *Israel in Search of a War: The Sinai Campaign 1955–1956.* Guildford: Sussex Academic Press.

Government of Palestine 1929. Government of Palestine: Antiquities Ordinance. *Laws of Palestine* vol. 1 (31 December): 24 [Hebrew], 28 [English].

Greenberg, O. 1989. *A Development Town Visited.* Tel Aviv: Hakkibutz Hameuchad [Hebrew].

Grunfeld, F. 1988. *Prophets without Honour*, A. Amir (trans.). Tel Aviv: Am Oved Publishing [Hebrew].

Guy, P. L. O. 1957. Ayyelet ha-Shahar. *Alon Mahleket Ha'atiqot: Bulletin of the Department of Antiquities of the State of Israel* **5–6**: 19–20 [Hebrew].

Ha'aretz 1948. First Licence to Excavation of Antiquities. *Ha'aretz* (2 November): 2 [Hebrew].

Haas, N. 1970. Anthropological Observations on the Skeletal Remains from Giv'at ha-Mivtar. *Israel Exploration Journal* **20**(1–2): 38–59.

Hacohen, D. 1994. *Olim Be-Se'arah.* Jerusalem: Yad Yizhak Ben Zvi [Hebrew].

Hacohen, D. 1996. The Veteran Yishuv and the Immigrants: Local Authorities versus Transit Camps. In *Israel and the Great Wave of Immigration 1948–1953*, D. Ofer (ed.), 98–116. Jerusalem: Yad Izhak Ben Zvi.

Hallote, R. S. & Joffe, A. H. 2002. The Politics of Israeli Archaeology: 'Nationalism' and 'Science' in the Second Republic. *Israel Studies* **7**(3): 84–116.

Harrison, A. St B. 1935. The Palestine Archaeological Museum, Jerusalem. *The Architects and Buildings News* **143**: 263–4, 278–82.

Hassan, F. A. 1998. Memorabilia: Archaeological Materiality and National Identity in Egypt. In *Archaeology Under Fire*, L. Meskell (ed.), 200–216. London: Routledge.

Herscher, E. 2001. Destroying the Past in Order to "Save" it: Collecting Antiquities from Cyprus. In *Archaeology and Society in the 21st Century: The Dead Sea Scrolls and Other Case Studies*, N. E. Silberman & E. S. Frerichs (eds), 138–54. Jerusalem: Israel Exploration Society.

Hirschberg, H. Z. 1961. In Memoriam M. Narkiss. *Eretz Israel* **VI**: 1–2.

Holst-Warhaft, G. 1997. Great Expectations: The Burden of Philhellenism and Myths of Greek Nationalism. In *Greeks and Barbarians: Essays on the Interaction between Greeks and Non-Greeks in Antiquity and the Consequences for Eurocentrism*, J. E. Coleman & C. A. Waltz (eds), 273–89. Bethesda, MD: CDL Press.

Holtzman, A. 1996. Between Newcomers and Veterans in the Mirror of Israeli Literature. In *Israel in the Great Wave of Immigration, 1948–1953*, D. Ofer (ed.), 312–21. Jerusalem. Yad Ben-Zvi [Hebrew].

Ilan, Z. 1986. Dayan's Collection as an Example of Continuing "Mehdal". *Davar*: 7 [Hebrew].

Illife, J. H. 1938. The Palestine Archaeological Museum, Jerusalem. *The Museums Journal* **38**: 1–22.

Illife, J. H. 1949. *A Short Guide to the Exhibition Illustrating the Stone and Bronze Ages in Palestine.* Palestine Archaeological Museum Guides 1. Jerusalem: Palestine Archaeological Museum.

Ish-Shalom, M. 1989. *Besod Hozevim u-Bonim.* Jerusalem: Graph-Hen [Hebrew].

Israel Antiquities Authority (IAA) 1962. "Introduction". *Excavations and Surveys in Israel [Hadashot Archaeologiyot]* **2** [Hebrew].

Israel Antiquities Authority (IAA) 1965. *Excavations and Surveys in Israel [Hadashot Archaeologiyot]* **13** [Hebrew].

Israel Exploration Journal 1955. Notes and News. *IEJ* **5**: 268–76.

Israel Exploration Journal 1956. Notes and News. *IEJ* **6**(2): 126–32.

Israel Exploration Journal 1995. In Memoriam: Professor Benjamin Mazar, 1905–1995. *IEJ* **45**: 209–11.

Israel Exploration Journal 1957. Personal News. *IEJ* **7**: 129.

Israel Government 1959. *Book of Regulations [Qovetz Takanot]* **886** (27 March). Jerusalem: Government Press.

Israel Government Yearbook 1962. *Israel Government Yearbook* (5723). Jerusalem: Central Office of Information, Prime Minister's Office.

Jackier, E. & Dagan, S. (eds) 1995. *Shimon Avidan. The Man who Became a Brigade.* Daliya: Ma'arechet.

Jacoby, D. (ed.) 2000. *Nation Building.* Jerusalem: Magnes Press [Hebrew].

Jewish National Fund (JNF) 1950. *Newsletter* (17 July).

Joffe, A. H. 2003. Review of R. Deutsch, "Messages from the Past" and R. Deutsch and A. Lemaire, "'Biblical Period Personal Seals in the Shlomo Moussaieff Collection". *Journal for Near-Eastern Studies* **62**: 119–24.

Joffe, A. H. in press. Review of Abu el-Haj, N., 2001, "Facts on the Ground". *Journal for Near-Eastern Studies.*

Junkaala, E. 1998. *From the Ancient Sites of Israel: Essays on the Archaeology, History and Theology in Memory of Aepeli Saarisalo.* Helsinki: Theological Institute of Finland.

Kadioğlu, A. 1996. The Paradox of Turkish Nationalism and the Construction of Official Identity. *Middle Eastern Studies* **32**(2): 177–93.

Kafka, F. 1974 [1925]. *The Trial*, I. Parry (trans.). London: Penguin.

Kafka, F. 1935. *Parables and Paradoxes.* New York: Schocken.

Kanterovitch, A. 1997. *The Status of the Jewish Agency from the Creation of the State of Israel to the Enactment of the Status Law (1948–1952).* MA thesis, Department of Jewish History. Tel Aviv University [Hebrew].

Kark, R. 1990. *Jaffa: A City in Evolution 1799–1917.* Jerusalem: Yad Izhak Ben-Zvi [Hebrew].

Karmi, G. & Cotran, E. (eds) 1999. *The Palestinian Exodus, 1948–1998.* Reading: Ithaca Press.

Karsh, E. 1997. *Fabricating Israeli History: The "New Historians".* London: Frank Cass.

Karsh, E. 2001. Naqbat Haifa: Collapse and Dispersion of a Major Palestinian Community. *Middle Eastern Studies* **37**(4): 25–70.

Katz, S. & Heyd, M. 1997. *The History of the Hebrew University of Jerusalem.* Jerusalem: Magnes Press.

Katz, Y. 2002. *"And the Land shall not be Sold in Perpetuity": The Legacy and Principles of Keren Kayemet Leisrael (Jewish National Fund) in the Israeli Legislation.* Jerusalem: Institute for the History of the Jewish National Fund [Hebrew].

Katz, Y. 2004. *To Stop the Bulldozer: Establishing Institutions for the Preservation of Nature and the Historical Heritage of Israel.* Ramat Gan: Bar Ilan University [Hebrew].

Kelso, J. L. 1950. The Palestine Archaeological Museum. *Archaeology* **3**(2): 66–9.

Kempinski, A. 1994. The Influence of Archaeology on Israeli Culture and Society. In *Landscape of Israel: Azaria's Alon Jubilee Volume*, Ariel 100–101, G. Barkay & E. Schiller (eds), 179–90. Jerusalem: Ariel Press.

Kenyon, K. M. 1952. *Beginnings in Archaeology.* London: J. M. Dent (2nd edn 1961).

Khalidi, W. (ed.) 1992. *All that Remains.* Washington, DC: Institute for Palestine Studies.

Kimmerling, B. 2004. *Immigrants, Settlers, Natives: The Israeli State and Society between Cultural Pluralism and Cultural Wars.* Tel Aviv: Am Oved [Hebrew].

Kletter, R. 2003. A Very General Archaeologist. Moshe Dayan and Israeli Archaeology. *Journal of Hebrew Scriptures* **4**: Article 5 (www.purl.org.jhs).

Kletter, R. & de Groot, A. 2001. Excavating to Excess? Implications of the Last Decade of Archaeology in Israel. *Mediterranean Journal of Archaeology* **14**: 76–85, 103–15.

Kletter, R. & Kersel, M. forthcoming. Heritage for Sale of the State of Israel?

Kletter, R. & Zwickel, W. forthcoming. The Assyrian Building of Ayyelet Ha-Shahar: After 50 Years.

Kochavi, M. 1981. Y. Aharoni: in Memorium. *Eretz Israel* **20**: ix–xi [Hebrew].

Kohl, P. & Fawcett, C. (eds) 1995. *Nationalism, Politics and the Practice of Archaeology.* Cambridge. Cambridge University Press.

Kollek, T. & Goldstein, D. 1994. *Teddy's Jerusalem.* Tel Aviv: Ma'ariv [Hebrew].

Kroyanker, D. 1991. *Jerusalem Architecture: Periods and Styles (V). Modern Architecture outside the Old City Walls, 1948–1990.* Jerusalem: Maxwell-Macmillan-Keter [Hebrew].

Kroyanker, D. 1999. *The Terra Santa Compound, Jerusalem.* Jerusalem: The Hebrew University [Hebrew].

Kroyanker, D. 2002. *The Edmund J. Safra Campus, Givat Ram: Planning and Architecture 1953–2002.* Jerusalem: The Hebrew University.

Landau, G. 1967. The Site of Tiberias. In *All the Land of Naphtali: The 24th Archaeological Convention, October 1966*, Y. Aviram (ed.), 170–79. Jerusalem: Israel Exploration Society.

Landau, S. & Zalmona, Y. (eds) 1998. *Hekhal ha-Sefer (Jerusalem, Israel): Exhibitions*. Israel Museum Catalogue No. 408. Jerusalem: Israel Museum.

Lavie, Z. 1956. Aesthetic Crimes and Criminals in Israel. *Bamahane* (IDF journal) (August) [Hebrew].

Leaming, B. 1985. *Orson Welles: A Biography*. London: Weidenfeld and Nicholson.

Lehm, W. 1988. *The Jewish National Fund*. London: Kegan Paul.

Levi, Sh. 1960. The Synagogue at Maon (Nirim). *Eretz Israel* **6**: 77–93 [Hebrew].

Lochery, N. 2001. Scholarship or Propaganda: Works on Israel and the Arab–Israeli Conflict, 2001. Review Article. *Middle Eastern Studies* **37**(4): 219–36.

Marquez, G. G. 1967. *One Hundred Years of Solitude* (G. Rabassa, trans., 1970). London: Penguin.

Masalha, N. 1999. The 1967 Palestinian Exodus. In *The Palestinian Exodus 1948–1998*, G. Karmi & E. Cotran (eds), 63–109. Reading: Ithaca Press.

Mazar, A. 1990. *Archaeology of the Land of the Bible: 10,000–586 BCE*. New York: Doubleday.

Mazar (Maisler), B. 1936. *Toldot Ha-Mehkar Ha-archeology be-Erets Israel [History of Archaeological Research in the Land of Israel]*. Tel Aviv: Bialik Institute [Hebrew].

Mazar, B. 1951. The Excavations at Tell Qasile. *Eretz Israel* **1**: 45–80.

Mazar, B. 1952. Archaeology in the State of Israel. *Biblical Archaeologist* **15**(1): 18–24.

Mazar (Maisler) B. 1973. *Beth She'arim I: Report on the Excavations during 1936–1940*. Jerusalem: Israel Exploration Society.

Merom, Sh. 1997. *The Social Policy of Israel in the 1950s and 1960s and the Creation of the "Poor Strata"*. MA thesis, Department of History, The Hebrew University, Jerusalem [Hebrew].

Merom, Sh. 2003. From Socialism to a Socialist Welfare State. *Ha'aretz* (12 September): section B8 [Hebrew].

Miberg, R. 1991. The Man who Came to Take. *Hadashot Supplement* (17 September): 20–21 [Hebrew].

Ministry of Labour 1951. *Annual of Labour [Yarkhon ha-Avodah]* **26**(11) (November).

Ministry of Labour 1958. *Labour and National Insurance [Avoda u-Bitu'akh Le'umi]*, monthly review. Jerusalem: Ministry of Labour.

Momigliano, N. 1995. Duncan Mackenzie: A Cautious Canny Highlander. In *Essays in Honour of J. N. Coldstream*, BICS Supplements 63. C. Morris (ed.), 139–70. London: Klados.

Moorey, P. R. S. 1979. Kathleen Kenyon and Palestinian Archaeology. *Palestine Exploration Quarterly* **111**: 3–10.

Moorey, P. R. S. 1992. British Women in Near Eastern Archaeology: Kathleen Kenyon and the Pioneers. *Palestine Exploration Quarterly* **124**: 109–23.

Morris, B. 1987. *Birth of the Palestinian Refugee Problem, 1947–1949*. Cambridge: Cambridge University Press.

Morris, B. 1993. *Israel's Border Wars, 1949–1956: Arab Infiltration, Israeli Retaliation and the Countdown to the Suez War*. Oxford: Clarendon Press.

Morris, B. 1994. *1948 and After: Israel and the Palestinians*. Oxford: Clarendon Press.

Morris, J. 1978. *The Oxford Book of Oxford*, 6th edn. Oxford: Oxford University Press.

Naccache, A. F. H. 1998. Beirut's Memorycide: Hear No Evil, See No Evil. In *Archaeology Under Fire*, L. Meskell (ed.), 140–58. London: Routledge.

Naipaul, V. S. 1969. *A House for Mr Biswas*. Harmondsworth: Penguin.

Naor, M. (ed.) 1986. *Olim and Ma'abarot 1948–1952*. Jerusalem: Yad Izhak Ben-Zvi [Hebrew].

Naor, M. (ed.) 1988. *Jerusalem in 1948*. Jerusalem: Yad Izhak Ben-Zvi [Hebrew].

Ornan, T. 1986. *Man and His Land: Highlights from the Moshe Dayan Collection*, Exhibition Catalogue No. 270. Jerusalem: Israel Museum [Hebrew and English].

Özdoğan, M. 1998. Ideology and Archaeology in Turkey. In *Archaeology Under Fire*, L. Meskell (ed.), 111–23. London: Routledge.

Palestine Official Gazette 1920. "Antiquities Ordinance". *Official Gazette of the Government of Palestine*, no. 29 (15 October).

Palestine Official Gazette 1985. "Antiquities Enclosures Ordinance, Government of Palestine". *Official Gazette of the Government of Palestine*, no. 530, appendix 1 (15 August): 144 [Hebrew], 147 [English].

Palestine Official Gazette 1948. "Palestine Order-in Council, 1948". *Official Gazette of the Government of Palestine* 1663, supp. 2 (22 April): 615–19.

Pappe, I. 1988. *Britain and the Arab–Israeli Conflict 1948–51*. New York: St Martin's Press.

Paz, Y. 1998. Conservation of the Architectural Heritage of Abandoned Urban Neighborhoods Following the War of Independence. *Cathedra* **88**: 95–134 [Hebrew].

Pedersen, J. 1928. *Inscriptiones Semiticae Collectionis Ustinowianae*. Oslo: Symbolae Osloenses Fasc. Supplement II. A. W. Brøgger(s).

Perrot, J. & Ladiray, D. 1980. *Tombes à Ossuaires de la région côtière palestinienne au Ive millénaire avant l'ere chrétienne*. Paris. Association Paléorient.

Phytian-Adams, W. J. 1924. *Guide Book to the Palestine Museum of Antiquities*. Jerusalem: Government of Palestine.

Pilowsky, V. (ed.) 1988. *Transmission from "Yishuv" to State 1947–1949: Continuity and Change*. Haifa. University of Haifa, Herzl Institute for Research in Zionism.

Pinkerfeld, G. 1955. Two Fragments of a Marble Door from Jaffa. *'Atiqot* [English series] **1**: 89–94.

Porath, Y. 2004. Home Thoughts from Abroad (Review of Gelber, Y. 2004). *Ha'aretz* (30 July): section B8.

Prag, K. 1992. Kathleen Kenyon and Archaeology in the Holy Land. *Palestine Exploration Quarterly*: 109–23.

Qadmoniyot 2005. In Memoriam Hannah Katzenstein. *Qadmoniyot* **129**: 64 [Hebrew].

Rahmani, L. Y. 1964. The Tomb of Yason. *'Atiqot* **4**: 1–38 [Hebrew].

Reich, R. 1975. The Persian Building at Ayelet Ha Shahar: the Assyrian Palace of Hazor? *Israel Exploration Journal* **25**: 233–6.

Reich, R. 1978. Archaeological Sites within the City of Natanya. In *The Book of Natanya*, A. Shemueli & M. Brawer (eds), 101–14. Tel Aviv: Am Oved [Hebrew].

Reich, R. 1987. On the History of the Rockefeller Museum, Jerusalem. In *Zeev Villnai Book* II, E. Shiller (ed.), 83–92. Jerusalem: Ariel [Hebrew].

Reich, R. 1992a. Major Trends in the Development of the Archaeological Method in Palestine, 1890–1920. *Archeologya* **3**: 9–16 [Hebrew].

Reich, R. 1992b. The Hebrew Episode in the Typography of Eric Gill. *Gutenberg Jahrbuch* (1922): 305–8.

Reich, R. 1995. *Invitation to Archaeology*. Tel Aviv: Dvir [Hebrew].

Reich, R. 2001. The Rockefeller Museum in Jerusalem and the "Monkey War". *Mitekufat Haeven* **31**: 219–26.

Reich, R. & Sussman, A. 1993. The Rockefeller Museum Building. *Israel Magazine* **49**: 8–18 [Hebrew].

Riemer, S. 1957. Economy. In *Encyclopaedia Hebraica. Vol. VI: Eretz Israel*, B. Netanyahu & A. Pel'i (eds), 729–807. Jerusalem: publisher [Hebrew].

Roitman, A. 2003. *Envisioning the Temple: Scrolls, Stones and Symbols*. Israel Museum catalogue no. 483. Jerusalem: Israel Museum.

Ron-Feder, G. 1986. *Rhymes for Liki and Jonathan*. Jerusalem: Domino Press [Hebrew].

Rosen, S. in press. Coming of Age: The Decline of Archaeology in Israeli Identity. *BGU Review*.

Rosenberg, I. 1949. *The Collected Poems of Isaac Rosenberg*, G. Bottomley & D. Harding (eds). London: Chatto and Windus.

Rosin, O. 2002. *From "We" to "I": Individualism in Israeli Society in the early 1950s*. PhD thesis, The Chaim Rosenberg School of Jewish Studies, Tel Aviv University [Hebrew].

Sahar, Y. 1992. *My Life*. Tel Aviv. Ministry of Defense [Hebrew].

Sandberg, H. 2002. Ownership of State Lands: History and Reality (Review of Katz 2002). *Cathedra* **112**: 169–74 [Hebrew].

Sandburg, C. 1918. *Cornhuskers*. New York: Henry Holt and Co. [reprinted in *Collected Poems* (New York: Harcourt, Brace and Co., 1950)].

Sarid, D. 1983. The Distress of the Yishuv and the Mission's Activity in Tiberias in 1884–1914. In *Mituv Tiberias 2*, M. Hildesheimer (ed.), 21–32. Jerusalem.

Schwabe, M. 1950. The Sarcophagus Inscription of a Jewish Sage. *BIES* **14**: 109–10 [Hebrew].

Seale, P. 1966. Row over Old City Archaeological Collection is "Settled": Jordan takes over Famous Museum. *Jerusalem Post* (5 November).

Segev, T. 1984. *1949: The First Israelis*. Tel Aviv: Domino Press [Hebrew].

Segev, T. 1986. Man and His Land. *Archaeologya* **1:** 61–2 [Hebrew].

Shai, A. 2002. The Fate of Abandoned Arab Villages in Israel on the Eve of the Six-Days War and its Immediate Aftermath. *Cathedra* **105:** 41–81[Hebrew].

Shavit, Y. 1989. Truth Shall Spring from the Earth: the Development of Jewish Popular Interest in Archaeology in Eretz-Israel. *Cathedra* **44:** 27–54 [Hebrew].

Shavit, Y. 1997. Archaeology, Political Culture and Culture in Israel. *The Archaeology of Israel. Constructing the Past, Interpreting the Future*, JSOT Supplement Series 237, N. E. Silberman & D. Small (eds), 48–61. Sheffield: Sheffield Academic Press.

Shay, T. 1989. Israeli Archaeology: Ideology and Practice. *Antiquity* **63**: 768–72.

Shelli-Newman, E. 1996. The Nocturnal Travel: Encounters between Newcomers and their New Place. In *Israel in the Great Wave of Immigration, 1948–1953*, D. Ofer (ed.), 285–98. Jerusalem. Yad Izhak Ben Zvi [Hebrew].

Shenhav, Y. (ed.) 2003. *Space, Land, Home*. Tel Aviv: Hakkibutz Hameuchad [Hebrew].

Sheri, M. 1998. The Archaeological Turnover. *Haʾaretz* (27 November): B6 [Hebrew].

Shulewitz, M. H. (ed.) 1999. *The Forgotten Millions: The Modern Jewish Exodus from Arab Lands*. New York: Cassell.

Silberman, N. A. 1982. *Digging for God and Country*. New York: Doubleday.

Silberman, N. A. 1989. *Between Past and Present: Archaeology, Ideology and Nationalism in the Modern Middle East*. New York: Henry Holt and Company.

Silberman, N. A. 1993. *A Prophet from Amongst You. The Life of Yigael Yadin: Soldier, Scholar, Mythmaker of Modern Israel*. Reading, MA: Addison-Wesley.

Silberman, N. A. 2001. If I Forget Thee, O Jerusalem: Archaeology, Religious Commemoration and Nationalism in a Disputed City, 1801–2001. *Nations and Nationalism* 7: 487–504.

Silberstein, L. J. (ed.) 1991. *New Perspectives on Israeli History: The Early Years of the State*. New York: New York University Press.

Sivan, E. 1991. *The 1948 Generation: Myth, Profile and Memory*. Tel Aviv. Ministry of Defence [Hebrew].

Skupinska-Løvset, I. 1976. *The Ustinov Collection: The Palestinian Pottery*. Oslo: Universitets-vorlaget.

Slater, R. 1991. *Warrior Statesman:. The Life of Moshe Dayan*. New York: St Martin's Press.

Smith, R. H. 1981. *OSS: The Secret History of America's First Central Intelligence Agency*, 2nd edn. Berkeley, CA: University of California Press.

Smith, A. D. 1991. *National Identity*. Harmondsworth: Penguin.

Sorely, C. H. 1916. *Marlborough and Other Poems*. Cambridge: Cambridge University Press.

Statistical Yearbook of Israel 1971. *Statistical Yearbook of Israel* [*Shnaton Statisti*], vol. 22. Jerusalem: Central Bureau of Statistics.

Statistical Yearbook of Israel 2001. *Statistical Yearbook of Israel* [*Shnaton Statisti*], vol. 52. Jerusalem: Central Bureau of Statistics.

Sterenhall, Z. 1998. *The Foundation Myths of Israel: Nationalism, Socialism and the Making of the Jewish State*. Princeton, NJ: Princeton University Press.

Stern, E. (ed.) 1993. *New Encyclopedia of Archaeological Excavations in the Holy Land*, 4 vols. Jerusalem: Israel Exploration Society.

Stern, E. 2001. *Archaeology of the Land of the Bible, Vol. II: The Assyrian, Babylonian and Persian Periods (732–332 BCE)*. New York: Doubleday.

Sterne, L. 2004 [1760]. *The Life and Opinions of Tristram Shandy, Gentleman*. New York: Random House.

Stock, E. 1988. *Chosen Instrument: The Jewish Agency in the first Decade of the State of Israel*. New York: Herzl Press.

Sukenik, E. L. 1952. Twenty-Five Years of Archaeology. In *Hebrew University Garland. Silver Jubilee Symposium*, N. Bentwich (ed.), 43–57. London: Constellation Books.

Sussman, V. & Reich, R. 1987. The History of the Rockefeller Museum. In *Zeev Vilnay Jubilee Volume*, E. Schiller (ed.), 83–92. Jerusalem: Ariel Press [Hebrew].

Szymborska, V. 1997. *Poems New and Collected*, S. Baranczak (trans.). New York: Harcourt, Brace and Co.

Tamir, T. 1990. The Israel Museum: From Dream to Fulfilment. *Israel Museum Journal* **9**: 7–16.

Taslitt, I. I. 1969. *Soldier of Israel: The Story of General Moshe Dayan*. New York: Funk and Wagnalls.

Teveth, S. 1969. *The Cursed Blessing: The Story of Israel's Occupation of the West Bank*. London: Weidenfeld and Nicholson

Teveth, S. 1972. *Moshe Dayan*. London: Weidenfeld and Nicholson.

Tovi, J. 2002. *Israel's Policy towards the Palestinian Refugees Problem, 1949–1956*. PhD thesis, Department of Land of Israel Studies, Haifa University (Hebrew).

Troen, I. 1996. New Beginnings in Zionist Planning during the Great 'Aliya: The Idea of Development Towns in the First Decade of the State. In *Israel in the Great Wave of Immigration 1948–1953*, D. Ofer (ed.), 125–40. Jerusalem: Yad Izhak Ben-Zvi [Hebrew].

Ussishkin, D. 1982. Where is Israeli Archaeology Going? *Biblical Archaeologist* **45**: 93–5.

Ustinov, P. 1977. *Dear Me*. London: Penguin.

Vitelli, K. D. (ed.) 1996. *Archaeological Ethics*. Walnut Creek, CA: Altamira.

Wood, M. 1998. The Use of the Pharaonic Past in Modern Egyptian Nationalism. *Journal of the American Research Center in Egypt* **35**: 179–96.

Wright, G. E. 1969. Archaeological Method in Palestine: An American Interpretation. *Eretz Israel* **9**: 120–33.

Wright, G. E. 1970. The Phenomenon of American Archaeology in the Near East. In *Near Eastern Archaeology in the Twentieth Century: Essays in Honor of Nelson Glueck*, J. A. Sanders (ed.), 3–40. New York: Doubleday.

Wright, G. R. H. 1966. A Method of Excavation Common in Palestine. *Zeitschrift des Deutschen Palästina Vereins* **82**: 113–24.

Yadin, Y. 1956. Excavations at Hazor 1955. Preliminary Communiqué. *Israel Exploration Journal* **6**(2): 120–25.

Yadin, Y. 1957. Excavations at Hazor 1956. Preliminary Communiqué. *Israel Exploration Journal* **7**: 118–23.

Yadin, Y. 1963. *The Finds from the Bar-Kochva Period in the Cave of Letters*. Jerusalem: Israel Exploration Society.

Yadin, Y. 1972. *Hazor. The Schweich Lectures*. Oxford: Oxford University Press [on behalf of the British Academy].

Yadin, Y. *et al.* (eds) 1959, 1960, 1961. *Hazor*, vols 1, 2, 3–4. The James A. de-Rothchild Expedition at Hazor. Jerusalem: Israel Exploration Society.

Yannai, N. 1988. The Transition to the State of Israel without Constitution. In *Transition from "Yishuv" to State 1947–1949: Continuity and Change*, V. Pilowsky (ed.), 23–35. Haifa: Herzl Institute, University of Haifa [Hebrew].

Yarom, U. 2001. *Jolly Wings*. Tel Aviv: Ministry of Defense [Hebrew].

Yeivin, Sh. 1955a. Archaeology in Israel (November 1951–January 1953). *American Journal of Archaeology* **59**: 163–7.

Yeivin, Sh. 1955b. *Archaeological Activities in Israel (1948–1955)*. Jerusalem: Ministry of Education and Culture, Department of Antiquities.

Yeivin, Sh. 1955c. Introduction. '*Atiqot* **1**: Preface [Hebrew].

Yeivin, Sh. 1957. *Studies in the History of Israel and its Country*. Tel Aviv: 'Asor Press.

Yeivin, Sh. 1960. *A Decade of Archaeology in Israel: 1948–1958*. Istanbul: Publications de l'Institut historique-Archeologique Neerlandais de Stamboul 8.

Yerofeev, V. 1970. Moscow Stations [*Moscow-Petushki*], S. Mulrine (trans., 1997). London: Faber and Faber.

Yizrael, R. 1996. The Sepharadi Ari Synagogue in Safad. *Ariel* **120**: 159–66 [Hebrew].

Yurman, P. (ed.) 1968. *Moshe Dayan: Portrait*. Tel Aviv: Massada Press [Hebrew, without page nos].

Zameret, Z. 1999. Ben-Zion Dinur between Statism and Voluntarism in Education. In *The Challenge of Independence: Ideologies and Cultural Aspects of Israel's First Decade*, M. Bar-On (ed.), 45–61. Jerusalem: Yad Izhak Ben-Zvi [Hebrew].

Zemer, A. (ed.) 1991. *Amendment to the Law Forbidding Trade in Antiquities and its Effects on Museums in Israel*. Haifa: ICOM Israel [Hebrew].

Zerubabel, Y. 1991. New Beginning, Old Past: The Collective Memory of Pioneering in Israeli Culture. In *New Perspectives on Israeli History: The Early Years of the State*, L. J. Silberstein (ed.), 193–215. New York: New York University Press.

Zerubabel, Y. 1995. *Recovered Roots: Collective Memory and the Making of Israeli National Tradition.* Chicago, IL: University of Chicago Press.

Zissu, B. 1996. Prevention of Antiquities Robbery. *Excavations and Surveys in Israel* **18**: 108–9.

Zur, Y. 1997. Immigration from the Islamic Countries. In *The First Decade: 1948–1958*, Z. Zameret & H. Yablonka (eds), 57–82. Jerusalem: Yad Izhak Ben Zvi [Hebrew].

AUTHOR INDEX

INDEX

Bold numbers indicate tables. Italics indicate illustrations. Asterisks indicate uncertain translations or names that could be transliterated differently